THE EARLY MUSLIM TRADITION OF DREAM INTERPRETATION

D1572346

SUNY series in Islam
Seyyed Hossein Nasr, editor

THE EARLY MUSLIM TRADITION OF DREAM INTERPRETATION

John C. Lamoreaux

STATE UNIVERSITY OF NEW YORK PRESS

Published by
State University of New York Press, Albany

© 2002 State University of New York

All rights reserved

Printed in the United States of America

No part of this book may be used or reproduced
in any manner whatsoever without written permission.
No part of this book may be stored in a retrieval system
or transmitted in any form or by any means including
electronic, electrostatic, magnetic tape, mechanical,
photocopying, recording, or otherwise without the prior
permission in writing of the publisher.

For information, address State University of New York Press,
90 State Street, Suite 700, Albany, NY 12207

Production by Cathleen Collins
Marketing by Fran Keneston

Cover photo by Benno Freidman

Library of Congress Cataloging in Publication Data

Lamoreaux, John C.
The early Muslim tradition of dream interpretation / John C. Lamoreaux.
p. cm. — (SUNY series in Islam.)
Includes bibliographical references and index.
ISBN 0-7914-5373-1 (alk. paper) — ISBN 0-7914-5374-X (pbk. : alk. paper)
1. Dreams—Religious aspects—Islam. I. Title. II. Series.

BP190.5.D73 L36 2002
297.5'7—dc21

2001049017

10 9 8 7 6 5 4 3 2 1

CONTENTS

ACKNOWLEDGMENTS

For helping fund this research, I wish to thank the Joint Committee on the Near and Middle East of the Social Science Research Council and the American Council of Learned Societies (with funds provided by the U.S. Information Agency). For additional funding, I am grateful to Duke University and Southern Methodist University. For help in obtaining permits, I am thankful to the Commission for Educational Exchange between the United States and Turkey. For aiding me in the process of obtaining yet other permits, I wish to thank Dr. Antony Greenwood of the American Research Institute in Turkey. To him I am also grateful for a hospitable place to live while in Turkey and for access to the excellent facilities of the institute. Among the many libraries that granted access to their manuscript collections, I wish especially to thank the Dil ve Tarih-Coğrafya Fakültesi Ktp. of the University of Ankara, the Biblioteca Apostolica Vaticana, the Bibliothèque nationale, the British Library, the Chester Beatty Library, the Ḥasanīyah Library, the İstanbul Üniversitesi Ktp., the Library of the Hebrew University of Jerusalem, the Köprülü Ktp., the Princeton University Library, the Süleymaniye Ktp., and the Topkapı Saray Müzesi Ktp. For their help in providing other materials, I owe thanks to Dr. Angelica Neuwirth and Ms. Ayşe Gül Manaf. Finally, many thanks are due to the members of my dissertation committee at Duke University, in particular Professors Elizabeth Clark, Vincent Cornell, and Bruce Lawrence, both for their help during the writing of an earlier version of this study and for their support over the years.

INTRODUCTION

Wishing to learn spoken Syriac, I once spent the summer in a Syrian Orthodox monastery in the Middle East. While language instruction consumed the daylight hours, the long summer evenings were free. These were spent on a veranda of the monastery, drinking tea and working through volume after dusty volume of medieval Arabic poetry under the tutelage of a Syrian friend, by profession a professor of Arabic literature. One evening as we were reading some remarkably bad poetry on the glories of Aleppo, my friend opined that of the whole corpus of medieval Muslim literature perhaps a third has been published, while another third remains to be published, while yet another third does not deserve to be published. Whether, in fact, a full third of medieval Muslim literature does not deserve publication is perhaps a matter for contention—and certainly the poetry we were then reading would be a strong contender for that dubious honor. It is the other two-thirds that are here of interest. I suspect that my friend's estimates were right when it comes to Koranic commentary, collections of prophetic traditions, historical treatises, and the like—subjects long of interest to researchers. He was far too optimistic in other instances. A case in point: the many forms of medieval Muslim literature on divination.

Whether by way of physiognomy, geomancy, palmistry, dream interpretation, or any of a dozen other methods, medieval Muslims evinced a lively interest in the arts of divination. The manuscript collections of the Muslim world are replete with hundreds of thousands of texts on these subjects. Despite their ubiquity, few have had the good fortune to attract the attention of researchers. Illustrative in this regard is Fuat Sezgin's magisterial, multivolume history of Arabic literature, the standard manual of reference for early Arabic literature. Notwithstanding the extent of Sezgin's labors, what he delivers belies his title. His is not a history of early Arabic literature, but of select moments in its history. One may note, in particular, his near total disregard of divinatory literature. How could Sezgin devote not a single volume nor even a single section of his projected fourteen volumes to the Muslim literature on divination?[1] Whatever Sezgin's reasons, future authors of general histories of Arabic literature might do well to structure their works according to the contours of the extant remains. And as for those contours, they have been best characterized by the orientalist Helmut Ritter—with, it should be noted, the approbation of Sezgin—in a programmatic statement on how to catalog Muslim manuscript collections by subject.[2] Among the twenty-three genres that Ritter distinguished: divinatory literature, a genre subdivided into twenty or so types of divinatory literature. Whether all of these forms of divination occupied the same cultural site in medieval Islam, whether some were more orthodox than others, whether all were equally popular—these are issues for another time. The merit of Ritter's classificatory scheme lies in its accurate reflection of the contours of the extant remains. Like it or not, the manuscript collections of the Muslim world contain a wide variety of works, including a great many on divination.

Given Ritter's characterization of the Muslim manuscript collections, one might think that divinatory literature would receive recognition in the catalogues of manuscript libraries. And sometimes it does—but not always. If those in charge of the libraries that preserve such texts cannot ignore their existence, they can cause them to fade from view, especially through the careful cataloging of them by subject. A single example: in the justly famous collection of manuscripts in the library of Istanbul University, there are no less than twenty-five texts on dream divination, including the only known copy of the Arabic translation of the dream manual of Artemidorus (the most famous dream manual of Hellenic antiquity), what may be the earliest dream manual in Persian, as well as a good number of other rare and unique works. Under what subject are these texts cataloged? Not under *ᶜilm taᶜbīr al-ruʾyā* (the discipline of dream interpretation), not under *ᶜilm al-firāsah* (physiognomy, sometimes used to mean divination in general), not under Sufism, philosophy, or medicine (execrable practices utilized in many of the cataloges of manuscripts in Turkish libraries), not even under a nice presentist category like psychology. Rather, the university's dream manuals—and them alone—are listed in the catalog under *Cabala*. While I don't know who was responsible for cataloging the manuscripts of Istanbul University, I am fairly certain that it was not Ritter, its one-time director. Leaving aside the fact that there is no Muslim Cabala, one might just as well have cataloged these dream manuals under *Mummery* or *Jugglery*—the effect would have been the same. Perhaps it is no wonder that the precious copy of Artemidorus' dream manual lay hidden so long, its existence being revealed only in the late fifties through a fortuitous encounter between its future editor and the index cards of a young Turkish researcher named Fuat Sezgin,[3] index cards that the latter was unfortunately unable to incorporate into his future history of Arabic literature.

DREAM INTERPRETATION AND DIVINATION

The present study is concerned with just one type of divination, dream interpretation. Researchers can study how medieval Muslims interpreted dreams through the manuals that they composed on the subject. Some of these works are short, roughly the length of, say, the Gospel of Matthew. Others are enormous, in some cases, up to fifty times that work's length. In terms of format, they are best likened to dictionaries. They consist generally of two parts: an introduction, usually rather brief, offering an overview of the author's methodology, and then a list of dream symbols and their meanings. In most cases these lists are organized by subject—dreams of fish, weapons, flowers, occupations, and so on. As for the meanings of the dreams, these are generally stated under the form of a condition: "If one dreams of a yellow rose, this will happen. If one dreams of a red rose, that will happen. If one dreams of a petunia, this other thing will happen." Thus the authors proceed, listing the three hundred and ninety-two types of flowers, only then to turn their attention to another, equally elaborate and detailed class of dream symbols.

The number of dream manuals written by medieval Muslims is nothing short of staggering. Over thirty years ago, Toufic Fahd undertook to compile a general survey of medieval Muslim divinatory literature.[4] As part of his survey, Fahd prepared a preliminary bibliography of works on dream interpretation.[5] One cannot overemphasize the significance of Fahd's labors. For the first time, researchers could glimpse something of the importance of this tradition to medieval Muslims and something of the scope of the extant remains.[6] Although Fahd confessed that his was only "a first step toward a massive study,"[7] he was able to call attention to 158 different dream manuals in Arabic, as well as another 23 in Persian and Turkish—all but a few accessible only in manuscript form.[8]

The majority of the works identified by Fahd stem from the later Middle Ages. From the earliest period of the Muslim oneirocritic tradition, up to the early fifth century A.H., Fahd could find only three extant works, the earliest of which was written in 399/1008. My own research has uncovered further works, more than trebling the corpus of early dream manuals. Among these texts, whether newly discovered or for the first time accurately identified: a dream manual written by the last Ṣaffārid amir of Sijistān, the earliest example of a dream manual in verse, and a corpus of four dream manuals composed by a single North African jurist. In sum, around a dozen dream manuals are now known to be extant from the earliest period of the tradition—enough, in fact, that one can now analyze its earliest history in some detail.

While the aforementioned works have survived, other early dream manuals have not. Indeed, far more have disappeared than have been preserved. Even so, it is sometimes possible to uncover information about these lost works. Fragments are at times preserved in later texts: late medieval oneirocritic compilations can occasionally shed important light on lost dream manuals. In other cases, the medieval Muslim biographical and bibliographic tradition has preserved knowledge of lost works. A systematic survey of these fragments and testimonies adds approximately fifty other, early dream manuals to the number discovered so far.

The large number of early dream manuals should not be lightly passed over. It offers a superficial if telling indication of the importance of dream interpretation to Muslims of the early Middle Ages. Indeed, to judge from number alone, one would have to conclude that the interpretation of dreams was as important to these Muslims as the interpretation of the Koran. Some sixty dream manuals were composed during the first four and a half centuries of the Muslim era. During that same period, very nearly exactly the same number of Koranic commentaries were composed.[9] In short, early Muslims composed as many commentaries on their dreams as they did on their Koran. Whatever else it was, dream interpretation was popular. As such it merits the attention of researchers, if only that we might understand why it was so widely cultivated and why it attracted the attention of such famous figures as the litterateur Ibn Qutaybah, the historian Ṭabarī, and the philosopher Ibn Sīnā.

It should be emphasized that Muslim dream interpretation is quite different from the forms of dream interpretation practiced in modern psychoanalysis. Muslim oneirocrits were not concerned with dreams for the light they might shed on the workings of the unconscious. They studied dreams because they believed that by properly interpreting them it was possible to discover things about the world outside the dreamer, things that could not otherwise be known. Dream interpretation offered Muslims a royal road that led not inward but outward, providing insight not into the dreamer's psyche but into the hidden affairs of the world. In short, the aim of dream interpretation was not diagnosis, but divination.

Unlike the ever humble and unpresuming advocates of psychoanalytic techniques of dream interpretation, Muslim oneirocrits claimed to offer nothing less than access to divine prophecy. On the day before his death, they said, the prophet Muḥammad announced in the mosque of Medina that "when I am gone there shall remain naught of the glad tidings of prophecy, except for true dreams." While the prophet's death would signal the end of Koranic revelation, God would continue to reveal himself to the Muslim community through dreams. Muslim oneirocrits never tired of citing this tradition. It contained key elements that in conjunction with others helped them to develop a theology of dreams. In this theology, the true dream was understood to be a form of divine revelation and a chronological successor to the Koran. In it, each good Muslim could expect guidance from God in dreams. At the same time, it presented dreams as no less than the bearers of "revelation" (*waḥy*) and "prophecy" (*nubūwah*), two highly significant terms also used to describe the Koran—lofty claims, to be sure, especially to the extent that dream interpretation offered a form of access to God that was unmediated, thus circumventing the vaunted institutions of Koran and Sunnah.

It has not always been acknowledged that Muslim dream interpretation is a form of divination. At times, modern Muslims have treated it as a precursor crying in the wilderness, seeking to make straight the way for Sigmund Freud. Such a strategy is evident, for instance, in the work of one author who sought to find confirmation in the Muslim dream manuals of the existence of a "universal oneiric language," the contents of which presciently foreshadowed the discoveries of Freud.[10] Other Muslims have also sought to elide the differences between the techniques of medieval and modern oneirocrits. This can be seen, for instance, in the popular editions of late medieval dream manuals, to this day widely circulated in the Middle East and elsewhere. Almost invariably their introductions link Muslim dream interpretation to psychoanalysis. Sometimes this is done in a subtle fashion: by providing lists of "the great and marvelous interpreters of dreams," lists that begin with the more important medieval Muslim oneirocrits and invariably end with Freud.[11] Usually, it is left to readers to infer that the whole edifice of psychoanalysis was thus really discovered by the scholars of medieval Islam. At other times, more explicit claims are made. One might note, for instance, a recent English adaptation of a series of medieval dream manuals—adaptation rather than translation, in that the text has been updated for modern Muslims, including now clues for interpreting dreams of missile launchers, supermarkets, oil refineries, and the like.[12] To lend the work an air of authority, its translator solicited a forward from a famous Muslim scholar, who sought to legitimize this sort of literature by suggesting that it shows ever so clearly that the findings of modern psychoanalysis were long ago discovered "by the sages and prophets of traditional cultures and religions"—most notably, it seems, by those of Muslim persuasion.

While such interpretive strategies are, I think, indefensible, they are not distinctly Muslim. There has been a similar tradition of western scholarship on the dream manual of Artemidorus. This tradition's foibles and crotchets, its "ethnocentric and Whiggish tendencies," have been laid bare in inestimable fashion by S. R. F. Price.[13] Nor for that matter need these strategies proceed in just one chronological direction. By eliding the differences between his own form of dream interpretation and the techniques of the ancients, Freud himself had sought to provide psychoanalytic dream interpretation with a venerable pedigree.[14] Notwithstanding the long history of these interpretive strategies, I would submit that it is simply untenable to turn a blind eye to the radical differences that distinguish ancient forms of dream interpretation from the various uses to which dreams have been put by modern psychoanalysts.

CONTEXT, HISTORY, AND DISCIPLINARY BOUNDARIES

It has been said that "the good historian is like the ogre of the fairy tale: he knows that wherever he catches the scent of human flesh, there his quarry lies."[15] Because dream manuals are basically long lists, often rather tediously long lists, it might well be imagined that they do not readily exude the scent of human flesh. The soporific state they induce on reading is not the least of the difficulties confronting the researcher. Much more serious: these texts are authorless. I mean this not in the sense that they lacked authors. They obviously did not, and usually we know who their authors were. These texts are authorless in the sense that their authors seldom spoke with their own voices. They expressed themselves, rather, through the compilation and crafting of earlier materials. In short, they did not write their own dream manuals, but pillaged earlier texts and skillfully mounted the spoils in their own works. As for the authors, they are seldom heard, except occasionally at the interstices, as they linked together materials appropriated from earlier works, making arguments and refuting opponents largely without ever speaking in their own voices.

With authors who fade all too easily from view behind the seeming anonymity of compilation, dream manuals present a forbidding facade to researchers. One of the primary aims of this study will be to breech this facade of anonymity behind which the authors sought to conceal themselves, to see whether it is not after all possible to detect in these works the scent of human flesh. While there are many ways that such texts might be approached with this end in view, here I am primarily concerned with understanding the circumstances surrounding the composition and circulation of the early dream manuals. I shall attempt, in short, to understand the early Muslim oneirocritic tradition in its social and cultural contexts. In this regard, my first goal in this study will be to answer three distinct but interrelated questions, all of which contribute to an understanding of this tradition's social and cultural contexts.

First, just who among the early Muslims were writing and reading dream manuals? To answer this question fully, it is not enough simply to discover their names and a little bit about who they were—although such information is obviously indispensable, especially as this study seeks to offer the first general account of this tradition's early development. A full answer to this question demands that broader patterns be sought. This is now possible. A great deal of information about both the writers and the readers of this literature has survived, enough that one can step back from the details and investigate the social and cultural contexts in which these texts were produced and consumed. In this regard, I am especially concerned to determine whether the religious scholars or ulema were implicated in the writing and reading of dream manuals. It was the ulema who were the self-proclaimed arbiters of orthodoxy and orthopraxy; it was they who defined the contours of what came in time to be considered normative or sharᶜī Islam. To determine their role in the production and consumption of this literature is thus partly to determine whether dream interpretation itself should be considered an aspect of sharᶜī Islam.

Second, was there a single oneirocritic tradition? We are dealing with a corpus of texts written over a period of several hundred years, with authors hailing from one end of the Muslim world to the other. Do these texts exhibit a single tradition of dream interpretation? or multiple traditions? The diversity of the early oneirocritic tradition might be evident in any number of ways. Most obviously, it might be displayed in the interpretations being offered for individual dream symbols. Did a yellow rose mean the same thing to the oneirocrits of fifth-century A.H. North Africa as it did to those of second-century Iran? The diversity of the tradition might, however, be evident in other, less obvious ways as well. Of particular concern is the epistemic foundations of the dream manuals: how their authors determined what counts as knowledge, the types of sources to which they appealed, and how they constructed arguments on the basis of those sources. Factors such as these must also be taken into account in any attempt to investigate the diversity of the early oneirocritic tradition. That said, in the final analysis an examination of the diversity of this tradition is interesting primarily for the light it can shed on the social and cultural contexts of dream interpretation, especially if the corpus of early texts evinces a diversity that can be correlated with different stages in the development of the tradition, different classes of the Muslim intellectual elite, or perhaps even different regions of the Muslim world.

As suggested above, the authors of the dream manuals made some lofty claims as to what they could deliver. My third question is simply this: Did anyone other than the authors of the dream manuals and their readers give credence to these claims? In particular, did the ulema as a whole subscribe to this theology of dreams? There are a number of ways that one might answer this question. I focus on the authoritative sources to which Muslim oneirocrits appealed to defend the legitimacy of dream interpretation. The authors of the dream manuals could, albeit with some difficulty, call on the Koran to justify their interest in dreams. They could find there expressions that, if properly interpreted, could be taken to suggest that Muslims ought to take an interest in their dreams. They could also cite sayings ascribed to Muḥammad, sayings that seemed to legitimize their interest in dreams. Did the ulema understand these sources to bear the same meaning? Did they read the Koran as legitimizing dream interpretation? Did they know the same prophetic traditions, consider them authentic, and interpret them in the same way? How these questions are answered has important implications for how the social and cultural contexts of dream interpretation are understood. In particular, they help to specify further whether dream interpretation should be considered an aspect of sharᶜī Islam.

Too often the cultural discourses of early Islam have been studied as if they existed in a vacuum, being treated as if they were unrelated to pre-Islamic discourses and qualitatively distinct from the discourses of non-Muslims. They have, in short, too often been assumed to lack both a history and a context. In this study, I hope to suggest that such an approach to the cultural discourses of early Islam is neither profitable nor justified and that much light can be shed on the Muslim oneirocritic tradition if an attempt is made to historicize it and contextualize it, to examine whether it was related to pre-Islamic traditions of dream interpretation and to investigate whether Muslims and non-Muslims may have shared and contested a common tradition of dream interpretation. It is this attempt to historicize and contextualize the early oneirocritic tradition that forms the second goal of this study.

Muslims were not the first in the Near East to interpret dreams. This type of divination had a long history, and Muslims were not ignorant of that history.

Further, the understanding of dreams forged in Muslim circles exercised an irresistible appeal to those outside the fold of the faithful. Muslim oneirocrits stood, thus, at the center of two metaphorical streams. One welled up in the past and flowed toward the Muslims. The other sprang up among Muslims and flowed outward. This metaphor is imperfect if it is understood to suggest that influence operates only in one direction, from source to recipient. This is not the case: influence is sterile without a desire to appropriate, a desire that takes hold the resources of the past and molds them in ways relevant to the needs of the present. It is in this sense alone that Muslims can be said to have been influenced by earlier techniques of dream interpretation and in turn to have influenced others. A full examination of the history and context of the early Muslim oneirocritic tradition is an immense topic, one beyond the scope of the present study. I limit myself to just three of its trajectories, ones that can be traced in some detail given the surviving evidence.

First, as a result of the near total darkness that overshadows the first hundred years of Muslim cultural history, any inquiry into the origins of the Muslim oneirocritic tradition can only be speculative. As yet, one cannot know whether the interpretation of dreams was something indigenous to the Arab conquerors of the Near East or something they learned from their subjects and converts. By the second century A.H., when at last we have access to written sources, a tradition of dream interpretation is both well in place and distinctively Muslim. While a search for origins may be impossible, one can analyze what happens over the next two or three centuries as this seemingly indigenous, Muslim tradition confronted earlier, non-Muslim forms of dream interpretation. Of particular interest is the reception given by Muslims to the dream manual of Artemidorus. This work, the most famous dream manual of Hellenic antiquity, was translated into Arabic in the third century A.H. by the Christian physician Ḥunayn b. Isḥāq.[16] While many of the Muslim dream manuals examined here made use of Artemidorus' dream manual, each took a different stance toward it: Artemidorus meant different things to different people. And as will be argued, to understand the varied reception of his work is to understand, in part, how and why the Muslim oneirocritic tradition developed as it did.

Second, no Muslim ever read the dream manual of Artemidorus. What they read was Ḥunayn's version of that text, which was not so much a translation as an adaptation. There were many things about Artemidorus that would have been offensive or unintelligible to readers in the early Islamic period, whether Muslim or Christian. Most important, Artemidorus was a pagan, and accordingly his dream manual was replete with references to pagan deities and pagan religious rites. To make matters worse, Artemidorus lived and wrote in a distant age. Much had changed since the second century A.D. Many of the civic institutions that Artemidorus mentioned (the gymnasium, for instance, or city councils) were no longer features of the society of his later readers. When Ḥunayn set himself to translate Artemidorus' dream manual, he was thus faced with the daunting task of creating a version that was intelligible to his contemporaries. To understand how Ḥunayn accomplished this task is key to understanding the Muslim reception of Artemidorus, and thus ultimately, how and why the Muslim tradition of dream interpretation developed as it did.

Third, it was a Christian who mediated the work of Artemidorus to Muslims. There were also Christians who, in or around the fourth century A.H., began to take an interest in Muslim techniques of dream interpretation. Two Christian dream manuals survive from this period: one is in Greek and is of Byzantine provenance; the other is in Arabic and was written by a Nestorian in Baghdad. These works are the first Christian dream manuals ever written, and both, I argue, made direct use of Muslim sources. While it is now possible to analyze the identity of their sources, the interest of these Christian dream manuals does not end there. These two works were written in different cultural contexts and their authors were confronted with different problems as they sought to appropriate and engage the Muslim oneirocritic tradition. These different problems, in turn, entailed different strategies of appropriation and engagement. To understand these strategies is, in part, to understand the extent to which Christians and Muslims in the early medieval Near East may have shared and contested a common oneirocritic tradition.

To trace the above-mentioned trajectories is to go part of the way toward historicizing and contextualizing the Muslim tradition of dream interpretation. Even so, a full investigation of this tradition's history and context would require additional research. It was not only Greeks who taught Muslims about the interpretation of dreams. Echoes of the voices of Persian and Indian sages are also encountered. So also, these two Christians were not the only non-Muslims to appropriate and engage the Muslim tradition of dream interpretation. There were further Christians who did the same, as well as Jews and others. These are issues that this study does not take up in detail: although I often allude to the fuller history and context of the Muslim oneirocritic tradition, I do not attempt to investigate it in depth. And yet, while I am content to trace just a few trajectories, it is my hope that enough is elucidated to show that the cultural discourses of early Islam were not *sui generis* and that it is only by historicizing and contextualizing them that one can begin to understand them.

This study, then, has two major goals. The first is to discern the contours of the Muslim oneirocritic tradition: in short, to write an internal history of the tradition, with a particular eye to the social and cultural contexts in which works on this subject were produced and consumed. The second is to historicize and contextualize this tradition: in short, to place it against a broader historical backdrop and to situate it within a broader framework. Uniting these goals is a methodological experiment, an attempt to break down some of the disciplinary boundaries that characterize the study of the cultural history of the early medieval Near East.

Muslim cultural discourses have too often been treated as if they were capable of being studied apart from their history and context. At the same time, Byzantinists and scholars of oriental Christianity have too often been content to study their respective cultural spheres without reference to the world of Islam, except perhaps as some developmental terminus or intractable other. What I hope to suggest here is that these disciplinary boundaries can with profit be blurred. Much light can be shed on the cultural discourses of early Islam if attention is paid to how they were related to pre-Islamic discourses. Insight into these same Muslim discourses can be gained if one is open to the possibility that non-Muslims may have played a role in their articulation, not only as mediators of pre-Islamic materials, but also as integral participants in the discourses themselves. At the same time, the cultural discourses of Byzantium and of the various oriental Christian communities can be better understood if an attempt is made to interpret them against the backdrop of a broader canvas, one that includes the discourses of Islamic civilization. In short, what is needed is an interdisciplinary approach to the cultural history of the early medieval Near East. Such an approach is not entirely novel. Even so, its validity and usefulness need to be emphasized, now more than ever.

The changing contours of the discipline of Islamic studies since World War II have meant that fewer students are coming to the study of early Islam from backgrounds in Classics or Semitics. Linguistic versatility in the study of early Islam now usually means that—in addition to Arabic—an Islamicist studies Persian or Turkish, but not Greek, Syriac, or Hebrew, let alone Armenian, Georgian, or Coptic. Today, a comparative study of slavery in early Islam means that one will compare Muslim institutions of slavery in North Africa, Syria, and Persia, while ignoring potentially fruitful comparisons with similar institutions in the empires of late antiquity. A study of early Muslim jurisprudence now too often means the study of Muslim jurisprudence alone, with little or no attention to the possibility that Muslims may have drawn on the legal resources of non-Muslims, whether late Romans, Persians, or Jews. Similarly, an examination of the early history of Arabic theology is too often focused solely on Muslim works, while ignoring some of the earliest theological texts in Arabic, simply because they were written not by Muslims but by Christians and Jews. To the extent that these observations reflect the present state of the discipline, the study of the cultural history of early Islam risks becoming insular. Now more than ever, it is simply too easy to treat early Muslim cultural discourses as if they lacked a history whose roots were struck deep into the past of the Near East and as if they lacked a context broader than themselves.

SCRIBES AND SELECTIVE MEDIATION

Other questions might be asked of the early Muslim oneirocritic tradition. How, for instance, were the forms of dream interpretation enshrined in texts related to nonliterary forms? Might there not have been competing forms of dream interpretation—scholarly, bookish forms and regionally diverse popular forms? What about the social roles played by dream interpreters? Might not dream interpreters have competed with other religious specialists (saints, for instance, or jurists) for recognition as mediators between this world and the next, between the God who sends revelation and the humans who receive it? And what of those oneirocrits who did not happen to be male? Might there not have been female interpreters of dreams and perhaps even distinctively female modes of dream interpretation? Such questions are easier to ask than answer. The sources, or at least those known to me, shed little light on such issues.

The types of information preserved in the extant sources effectively limit the questions that can be asked of the early Muslim oneirocritic tradition. This is clear. The nature of the extant sources limits researchers in another, more grievous way as well. For a medieval book to be preserved, it was necessary that it be copied: it was necessary that there be later scribes and patrons who took an active interest in its preservation. Not all early materials were of equal interest to these later scribes and patrons, and the choices they made as to what should be copied have largely determined the contours of the extant remains. The interests and concerns of these later Muslims have, in effect, acted as a filter, selecting some materials for preservation and letting others pass into oblivion through neglect. This type of scribal filtering is important. It is no less important than other, more dramatic instances of selective transmission—the compiler, for instance, who has access to three sources but chooses to cite only one. In both cases, later tradition selectively mediates earlier tradition.

Ibn Qutaybah's (d. 276/889) is the earliest extant Muslim dream manual. While this work was once very popular, today it is preserved in full in just a single manuscript. Other texts utilized in this study have also just barely survived, in just one or a handful of manuscripts. Yet other texts here studied were more fortunate, existing today in thirty or forty copies. And there were yet other dream manuals, from the later Middle Ages, that were truly classics, surviving today in hundreds of copies. Later tradition clearly exercised a form of selective transmission: some works were widely copied; others were not. It was also this later tradition that was responsible for letting the majority of early dream manuals disappear. Why were these texts not transmitted? Were their contents at odds with later consensus? Were they supplanted by later, more systematic and thus more useful syntheses? While answers to these questions can only be speculative, one can conjecture that the surviving works were preserved precisely because they contained nothing offensive to the sensibilities of later Muslims.

Although this is ostensibly a study of the early Muslim tradition of dream interpretation, it is more accurately a study of that tradition after it has been vetted by later Muslims. What is at issue is not the early tradition itself but what later Muslims chose to bequeath of it. There may well have been a dozen competing versions of dream interpretation in the early centuries of the Muslim era; and if so, as shall be seen, all but one have largely disappeared. As for the version that has survived, it enjoyed its good fortune only insofar as it complemented the views of later Muslims. I do not wish to suggest that it is therefore impossible to discover anything useful about the early Muslim tradition of dream interpretation. I only wish to caution the reader, suggesting in advance that much of the seeming homogeneity discovered in the course of this study may be illusory, a result of the selectivity of later tradition.

Later tradition gave the gift of life to some works; others it let pass into oblivion. It also seems to have filtered out nearly all hints of dissent occasioned by the interpretation of dreams. I simply cannot believe that early Muslims were in total agreement as to the nature of dream interpretation and as to the role it should play in the good Muslim's life. Nevertheless, such is very nearly the picture that emerges from the extant sources. It is only on the rarest of occasions that one can detect the distant echoes of the controversies once occasioned by dream interpretation, echoes now quite faint and well-nigh unintelligible. The famous jurist Shāfiᶜī (d. 204/819) once proclaimed:

> I have left behind in Iraq something that the Manicheans concocted, calling it dream interpretation. It is with it rather than the Koran that they occupy themselves.[17]

By chance, Shāfiᶜī's saying has been preserved in a later compilation. What it meant when first uttered, if indeed it is authentic, what its original context was, what debates it played a role in—these are matters that cannot now be known. Two things alone are certain. First, the *extant* sources do not support Shāfiᶜī's version of the origins of Muslim dream interpretation. Second, the arguments of the advocates of dream interpretation carried the day—and it was those advocates and their descendants who tried to filter out dissenting voices.

These cautionary remarks must be kept in mind throughout the course of this study. Researchers cannot but deal with oneirocritic texts that have received the imprimatur and nihil obstat of later tradition, ferreting out where possible polemical subtexts and using them to reconstruct now silent debates. As a whole, however, we, the modern voyeurs, can view the early Muslim oneirocritic tradition only with the help of Muslims of a later age. As yet there is no cache of desert documents to help us, no Nag Hammadi corpus or Dead Sea scrolls, no means of gaining an unmediated access to the oneirocritic traditions of an earlier age.

THE STRUCTURE OF THIS STUDY

I begin in chapters 1 and 2 by constructing a history of the early development of the Muslim tradition of dream interpretation. Among the many issues treated in these first two chapters, the most important for the overall thematic of this study are how an indigenous form of dream interpretation arose among Muslims already by the second century A.H. and how this tradition evolved over the course of the next three centuries, eventually fracturing into a number of competing legacies, in part through the varied reception of Ḥunayn's expurgated version of Artemidorus. Chapter 3 seeks to determine whether there was a single Muslim tradition of dream interpretation. Chapter 4 examines the social contexts in which early Muslim dream manuals were produced and consumed, and the extent to which the ulema were involved in this process. Chapter 5 turns to the afterlife of the Muslim oneirocritic tradition in two Christian contexts—among those living under Muslim rule and among those of Byzantium—and the various strategies that Christian oneirocrits had to employ to appropriate and engage Muslim techniques of dream interpretation. I conclude with some reflections on how early Muslim cultural discourses might best be studied, especially to the extent that they are enmeshed in a context that predates the rise of Islam and are capable of diffusion beyond the borders of Islamic civilization. An appendix contains what I hope is a fairly exhaustive account of the sixty or so Muslim dream manuals composed in the first five centuries of the Muslim era.

It should be emphasized that this study is concerned with the early Muslim tradition of dream interpretation, from its inception in the second century A.H. to the early fifth century. This early tradition I divide into two parts: its "formative period" (early second century to mid-fourth century) and what I characterize as the period in which it fractured (late fourth and early fifth centuries). How these periods differ is explained in chapters 1 and 2. But why follow the history of this tradition only to the early fifth century? Was there something special about the dream manuals written after this date, something that marked them off from earlier texts? Judging from the hundreds of later Arabic, Persian, and Turkish dream manuals that I have examined—the short answer is no. Most later texts work within lines that had already been laid down in the earlier tradition. Later texts do not innovate wholly new types of dream interpretation as much as they probe the potential resources of earlier types. This is not to say that some of these later works are not interesting. Some are, especially those that toy with the boundaries of dream interpretation and other disciplines: Sufi self-examination, for instance, or philosophic reflection on the physiology of dreams and the nature of prophecy. But these are stories for another time. Here I am content to trace the history of Muslim dream interpretation from its birth in the second century A.H. to its maturation in the early fifth, leaving for another time the study of its senescence. By coincidence, and it really is a coincidence, the early fifth century also marks the end point of Sezgin's masterful history of early Arabic literature. Let this study be considered, then, as a supplement to Sezgin's project of making known the riches of the early Arabic literary tradition, in all its diversity.

CHAPTER ONE

From Anecdote to Formalism

This chapter treats of the formative period of the Muslim tradition of dream interpretation. My goal is not to ascribe specific aspects of the earliest examples of works in this tradition to specific Persian, Hellenic, or Indian influences. To trace such lines of influence, whatever its intrinsic interest, is here impossible. The origins of the Muslim tradition of dream interpretation are lost in the near total darkness that overshadows the first hundred years of Muslim intellectual history. We know not whether Muḥammad himself evinced an interest in dream interpretation, as hundreds of prophetic traditions would have us believe. We know not whether a concern for dream interpretation was something native to the Muslim conquerors of the Near East or something learned from those they conquered, or perhaps even something imported by converts. Answers to these questions can only be speculative. When our evidence begins to shed light on the formative period of the tradition already one hundred years have passed since the conquest. Already by this time dream interpretation is understood to impart a type of prophetic knowledge. Already by this time the tradition is well established, and for the next couple of centuries we can look on as it begins to blossom. It is the contours of the tradition in this period between the late first and the mid-fourth centuries of the Muslim era that are the focus of the present chapter. In examining these contours there are three principal questions that the analysis seeks to answer.

The first is simply this: When did written texts on this subject first appear? And how, if at all, did these texts change over the course of the next couple of centuries? Any answer to this question is immediately confronted by the limitations of the evidence. In terms of the extant remains, however, a clear pattern is evident. As will be argued, the earliest texts on this subject, written toward the end of the second Islamic century, consisted of collections of autonomous, anecdotal narratives recounting the interpretation of specific dreams by specific persons, most often by those imbued with religious authority. Although written texts are first encountered only at the end of the second century, there are sound reasons for believing that such anecdotal narratives began circulating far earlier, in some cases perhaps as many as one hundred years earlier. Regardless, by the third century we begin to encounter texts that in part maintained this anecdotal format while at the same time offering more formalized modes of presentation. This transition from anecdote to formalism continued, such that by the mid-fourth century a strict formalism had all but displaced the anecdote as the primary mode of expression in Muslim dream manuals.

The second principal question of this chapter concerns the social locus for the composition of these texts. Which class or classes of Muslim intellectuals were responsible for the composition and circulation of dream manuals in the formative period? Given the limitations of the evidence, an answer to this question can only be tentative. Nonetheless, with regard to the extant remains, a clear pattern is evident: an interest in dream interpretation was intensively cultivated by that same class of scholars responsible for the collection and circulation of prophetic traditions—first by the muḥaddiths or transmitters of prophetic traditions and then by the ulema or religious scholars. In this respect, the tradition's social locus was to be found at the center rather than the periphery of early Muslim intellectual concerns. Those same scholars responsible for formulating the contours of a sharᶜī or orthodox Islam were also responsible for cultivating the interpretation of dreams in the formative period.

The third principle question to be investigated in this chapter concerns how the dream manuals of the formative period sought to ground their authority. Did they look back to the diverse cultures of the pre-Islamic past, appealing to the tradition of dream interpretation as it had been cultivated by the Hellenes, Persians, or Indians? Or did they ground the tradition in the figures of prophetic monotheism, whether that of pre-Islamic sacred history or that specific to the Muslims? Once again we are hindered by the limitations of the evidence at our disposal. With regard to the extant remains, however, a single strategy is evident: from the beginning to the end of the formative period, the tradition of dream interpretation sought to ground itself in the major figures of prophetic monotheism. Sometimes the prophecy at issue was that of a pre-Islamic sacred history—including the major prophetic figures of Judaism such as Abraham, Daniel, and Joseph. At other times the interpretation of dreams was grounded in the specific moment in this prophetic history characterized by the career of Muḥammad and his closest followers.

Allusions to the limitations of the extant remains have already been made. As will be seen, many sources from the formative period have been lost. The medieval Muslim bibliographic and biographical tradition knows of over thirty dream manuals composed during this period. Most have vanished without a trace, although it must be remembered that far too little is at present known about far too many important Muslim manuscript collections. Many collections remain uncataloged or only partially cataloged. Moreover, many of the available cataloges are insufficiently detailed to allow for an accurate identification of the texts they purport to describe. These difficulties are exacerbated by a constant tendency for Muslim dream manuals to drift toward pseudonymity—most often coming to be ascribed to the eponymous founder of the Muslim tradition of dream interpretation, a figure named Ibn Sīrīn, and coming to receive generic titles like *Kitāb taᶜbīr al-ruʾyā* (The Book of the Interpretation of Dreams) or *Kitāb tafsīr al-manāmāt* (The Book of the Exegesis of Dreams).

As for the majority of the lost dream manuals mentioned in the medieval Muslim bibliographic and biographical tradition, often the only things we know are their titles and the names of their authors, and sometimes not even that. Put bluntly, we know next to nothing about most of these texts, their sources, and their format. Perhaps more detrimentally, we are unable to determine the relative significance of any of these works over against the works of their contemporaries. The popular works of, say, the third century A.H. may not be the same works with which we are now familiar from that century. Given this state of affairs, it is impossible at present to give a full account of the tradition in its formative period. And yet, even if a history of the tradition as a whole cannot yet be written, it is possible to investigate some key stages in its development as they were understood by a Muslim who lived toward the close of its formative period.

KHALLĀL AND THE HISTORY OF DREAM INTERPRETATION

Sometime in the fourth century of the Muslim era, a certain al-Ḥasan b. al-Ḥusayn al-Khallāl composed a massive biographical dictionary in which he described no less than 7,500 people renowned for their skills as interpreters of dreams.[1] This work he entitled *Ṭabaqāt al-muᶜabbirīn* (The Classes of the Dream Interpreters). Khallāl's voluminous opus is no longer extant. At some point, however, he epitomized the work, selecting six hundred of the most important of these dream interpreters. This epitome he included in a dream manual he was then writing. This text, as well, is no longer extant. Toward the end of the fourth century, however, Khallāl's dream manual was read by Abū Saᶜīd Naṣr b. Yaᶜqūb al-Dīnawarī who was then in the process of compiling an enormous work of his own on the interpretation of dreams.[2] Dīnawarī found Khallāl's epitome interesting and included a summary of it in the introduction to his own dream manual, a work that *is* extant.

In his summary, Dīnawarī explicitly restricts himself to the most famous of the interpreters mentioned by Khallāl. At the same time, he states that he will pass over in silence all of Khallāl's data on the dream interpreters of India, and this, because they were foreigners and because their names were difficult to read. Dīnawarī singles out for mention exactly one hundred interpreters. These he divides into fifteen classes, which he organizes in accordance with their religious authority. Thus, at the head of his list stand those prophets known to have been skilled in the interpretation of dreams. Of these, the most recent is none other than Muḥammad himself. Following the prophets, Dīnawarī treats of companions, successors, jurists, and ascetics. He then moves on to more suspect individuals: philosophers, doctors, Jews, Christians, Magians, pagan Arabs, diviners, magicians, and physiognomists.

It is no longer entirely clear why Khallāl mentioned certain of the figures in his biographical dictionary. Was Aristotle listed because Khallāl knew that he had written on dream interpretation—which he did, but only to reject it? or because he was so famous that it would be unthinkable not to have him in the discipline's pedigree? what of Plato and the "philosopher" Ptolemy? or Galen and Hippocrates? On the other hand, one can often understand why other figures were deemed worthy of mention by Khallāl. The prophets Daniel and Joseph, for instance, were both noted in scriptural accounts for their abilities to interpret dreams. Of the companions and successors, some were transmitters of prophetic traditions on dreams, whereas others were thought to have been personally concerned with the interpretation of dreams. As for the pre-Islamic pagan Arabs mentioned by Khallāl, many were depicted as interpreters of dreams in the biographies of Muḥammad. Other figures, particularly those from Khallāl's latter classes, take us well into the realm of folklore. Such is the case, for instance, with the diviner Saṭīḥ, a curious being whose body had no bones, excepting his head, which was, however, attached to the middle of his chest—an unfortunate handicap that necessitated that whenever he was lying on his bed and needed to be moved, he had first to be rolled up like a rug.[3]

For our purposes, the most relevant part of the summary of Khallāl's epitome is its sixth class, a list of those "who wrote books on the subject of dream interpretation." Aside from Khallāl himself, six individuals come in for a mention. One of these figures, a certain Muḥammad b. Ḥammād al-Rāzī al-Khabbāz, is apparently otherwise unknown.[4] Last in the list is "Artemidorus the Greek." It will be recalled that the work of this famous Hellenic interpreter of dreams was translated into Arabic in the third century A.H. by the Christian physician Ḥunayn b. Isḥāq.[5] The remaining four are Muḥammad b. Sīrīn (d. 110/728), Ibrāhīm b. ᶜAbd Allāh al-Kirmānī (fl. late 2nd/8th century), ᶜAbd Allāh b. Muslim al-Qutaybī, that is, Ibn Qutaybah (d. 276/889), and Abū Aḥmad Khalaf b. Aḥmad (d. 399/1008).

Inasmuch as these were not the only Muslims to write dream manuals in the tradition's formative period, Khallāl must be seen as offering an account either of those texts that alone were known to him or of those that alone he considered important. Khallāl's list presents, nonetheless, a remarkably concise account of those figures from the tradition's formative period about whom we happen at present to be most well informed. Whereas other dream manuals have largely disappeared, works by these authors were read and copied by later Muslims. Two of them are still extant in manuscript form—the dream manuals of Ibn Qutaybah and Khalaf b. Aḥmad. As for the work of Kirmānī, although no longer extant, it is possible to learn something about it from discussions of it in other, later Muslim works on the interpretation of dreams. The case of Ibn Sīrīn is special. While this person, the eponymous founder of the Muslim tradition of dream interpretation, probably never wrote a dream manual, evidence preserved largely in manuscript form provides sound reasons for thinking him to have been responsible for putting into circulation much oral lore on the interpretation of dreams. It is to this evidence that we now turn.

THE LEGACY OF IBN SĪRĪN

Ibn Sīrīn was born in 34/654 toward the end of the reign of the caliph ᶜUthmān.[6] His father is said to have been taken prisoner in Iraq during the early stages of the Muslim conquests.[7] Initially a slave, his father was later set free by the caliph ᶜUmar. As for his mother, she was a slave of the caliph Abū Bakr. Ibn Sīrīn himself was by profession a merchant of cloth, apparently rather an unsuccessful one—judging from his constant struggles with debt. He is said to have had no less than thirty children by a single wife, only one of whom survived. Although deaf, he became famous for his integrity as a muḥaddith or transmitter of prophetic traditions. He was equally renowned for his deep piety. He died in 110/728. Is there any compelling reason for thinking that Ibn Sīrīn was the author of a dream manual?

Certainly not one of the dozen or so published dream manuals ascribed to Ibn Sīrīn is authentic: all bear marks that betray later dates of composition. Likewise, I have examined around one hundred manuscripts containing dream manuals ascribed to Ibn Sīrīn. In all but a few cases it was readily apparent that these works were composed at later dates. Often it was possible to determine that the works were in fact written by other, named individuals. Indeed, it was not uncommon to find texts ascribed on their title pages to Ibn Sīrīn, while their introductions specified the names of their real authors. Even when it was not possible to discover the identity of the authors of these dream manuals, it could frequently be established that they were of later provenance, usually because they cited sources stemming from after Ibn Sīrīn's death.

No dream manual written by Ibn Sīrīn is at present known to be extant. It is also highly unlikely that Ibn Sīrīn ever wrote such a text. On the one hand, he flourished at a time when the use of writing to transmit religious knowledge was only beginning to be employed by Muslims. On the other hand, the earliest biographical notices on Ibn Sīrīn make almost no mention of his abilities as an interpreter of dreams, much less of his having written a book on the subject. So also, there seem to be no references to such a work in literature of the second and third centuries A.H., or even in the first half of the fourth century.[8] In particular, no early dream manual seems to have drawn on a written work by Ibn Sīrīn.[9] In this regard, the testimony of Kirmānī's dream manual is key. This text, discussed further below, was written in the later second century A.H. Kirmānī specified that he used materials from Ibn Sīrīn. The way he described his use of those materials suggests, however, that he was drawing not on a written source, but rather on anecdotal accounts of dreams that Ibn Sīrīn had interpreted, accounts transmitted to him in an oral fashion.

While Ibn Sīrīn is unlikely to have written a work on the interpretation of dreams, it is clear that with the passage of time he was transformed into the eponymous founder of the Muslim tradition of dream interpretation—"the most adept of the forebears in the science of interpreting dreams" and "the leader of his age in this discipline."[10] About him the renowned historian Ibn Khaldūn (d. 808/1406) could write: "Muḥammad b. Sīrīn was one of the most famous scholars of this subject. By him were written various guides that have been transmitted even unto the present day."[11] Authors of later biographical dictionaries were likewise quick to point out his precedence in this field. "He had great power in the interpretation of dreams."[12] "Many marvelous interpretations of dreams were carried out by Ibn Sīrīn. . . . In this field he had divine support."[13] Adding to his reputation, in time hundreds of dream manuals came to be ascribed to him, texts written not only in Arabic, but also in Persian, Turkish, and Malay, and even quite recently in English. How did Ibn Sīrīn come to merit this exalted reputation? Did the Ibn Sīrīn of history actually display an interest in dream interpretation? There are two arguments that can be mustered to support a positive answer to this question.

First, consider the most famous prophetic tradition on dream interpretation.

> According to Abū Hurayrah, the prophet said: In the end times, the dream of the Muslim will scarcely be able to be false. Those of them who have the truest dreams are likewise those who speak most truly. There are three types of dreams: the good dream that is "a glad tiding from God" (Q 10:64), the dream in which a man's own soul speaks, and the dream that Satan sends to make him sad. If one of you sees a dream that he dislikes, let him not talk to anyone about it; instead, let him stand up and spit. To see neck-irons in a dream signifies resoluteness in religion, whereas to see leg-irons is worse than that.

This tradition is widely transmitted. It is found in nearly all of the canonical collections of prophetic traditions, in many of the noncanonical ones, and in other places as well.[14]

G. H. A. Juynboll has developed a tentative method for dating when and by whom prophetic traditions were first put into circulation.[15] What Juynboll proposes is that one systematically compare the chains of authorities or isnāds of a tradition as they are preserved in diverse texts to find their "common link"—the common link of a tradition being that transmitter up to whose time the text of the tradition is transmitted through a single line of transmission, but after whose time the lines of transmission branch out. Juynboll has argued at great length that "the [common link] can on the whole be held responsible not only for the strand back to the prophet but also for the proliferation of the text (*matn*) of the report or tradition, or in any case for the transmission of that *matn*'s most ancient wording."[16] Put another way, it is the common link who is responsible for first putting the tradition into circulation.

If we perform a common-link analysis on the tradition cited above, we discover that the tradition is invariably prophetic: that is, it is traced back to the prophet rather than to one of his companions. Abū Hurayrah is the only one to transmit it from the prophet. So also, Ibn Sīrīn is the only one to transmit it from Abū Hurayrah. Beginning with Ibn Sīrīn, however, the chains of authority begin to blossom. No less than nine individuals transmit the tradition from Ibn Sīrīn, and each was in turn responsible for transmitting it to yet other individuals, sometimes to more than one. At issue here is a classic case of the common-link phenomenon. From this it can be concluded that Ibn Sīrīn was himself responsible for first putting this tradition into circulation. Whether he himself derived it from oral tradition or in fact forged it—this is a question that cannot be answered. Regardless, a common-link analysis of this tradition offers solid grounds for believing that Ibn Sīrīn must in fact have taken an interest in dream interpretation.

The second argument supporting the conclusion that the Ibn Sīrīn of history took an interest in dream interpretation is based on the date we first encounter dream lore ascribed to him. Toufic Fahd has argued that Ibn Sīrīn did not attain his exalted reputation as an interpreter of dreams until the second half of the third century A.H.[17] His arguments in this regard rest largely on the silence of the early biographical tradition as to Ibn Sīrīn's abilities as an interpreter of dreams and on the near total lack of traditions relating to his interpretations prior to those found in the works of Jāḥiẓ (d. 255/869) and Ibn Qutaybah (d. 276/889). My own research vitiates such a late date for the beginnings of Ibn Sīrīn's reputation as an interpreter of dreams, suggesting instead that already within a single generation of his death a great deal of lore about his feats of interpretation was being widely circulated. In this regard, particularly important is one of the unedited dream manuals of Qayrawānī, a figure who flourished in the early fifth century.[18]

Qayrawānī recounts in his dream manual hundreds of traditions about dreams interpreted by Ibn Sīrīn. He had access to these traditions through a number of sources written in the late second and early third centuries A.H. Most of these sources are otherwise unknown. Four are especially important. Almost every page of Qayrawānī's massive dream manual bears one or two traditions from the dream manual of Misᶜadah, who probably flourished in the late second century. From this text Qayrawānī took anecdotal accounts of Ibn Sīrīn's interpretations of dreams. These accounts are usually transmitted at one remove, most often by a certain Sulaymān Abū Muḥammad, less frequently by Ibn Sīrīn's own son, ᶜAbd Allāh b. Muḥammad. From a work on dream interpretation written by Nuᶜaym b. Ḥammād (d. 228/844), Qayrawānī likewise received numerous traditions about Ibn Sīrīn. These Ibn Ḥammād equips with full chains of authorities, usually containing one or two intermediary transmitters. A dream manual by the Mālikī jurist Ibn Ḥabīb (d. 238/852) also supplied Qayrawānī with many traditions about Ibn Sīrīn's feats of interpretation. These traditions are usually transmitted without chains of authority. Finally, Qayrawānī made use of a work on dream interpretation written in the early third century A.H. by Ibn al-Mughīrah. From this text he took mostly traditions about Ibn Sīrīn transmitted at one remove.

The import of these new discoveries is clear: already within a generation of Ibn Sīrīn's death there was a massive body of lore in circulation concerning his interpretations of dreams. This lore was formally transmitted by students of Ibn Sīrīn and even by his son and as early as the end of the second century A.H. had come to be written down. Qayrawānī chose to transmit from these four works by and large only traditions about Ibn Sīrīn. This does not mean that these works must have been made up only of such materials. Such works, however, may very well have been in circulation already by the late second and early third centuries, for another source used by Qayrawānī was a work on dreams written by ᶜĪsā b. Dīnār (d. 212/827) entitled *Kitāb Ibn Sīrīn* (The Book of Ibn Sīrīn). So also, Madāᵓinī (d. 225/839) is said to have compiled a work entitled *Kitāb akhbār Ibn Sīrīn* (The Book of Ibn Sīrīn's Anecdotes).[19] While nothing is known of this latter work's contents, nor even whether it was a dream manual, its title is suggestive.

If it must be concluded that the Ibn Sīrīn of history took a lively interest in dream interpretation and that he was responsible for putting into circulation a great deal of dream lore, it is more difficult to determine why Ibn Sīrīn may have taken such an interest in dreams and what sort of sources he may have had at his disposal. Our only clues are found in three traditions. The first is said to stem from Ibn Qutaybah (d. 276/889):

> [Ibn Sīrīn] said: In a dream I saw Joseph the prophet over our prophet. To him I said: "Teach me the interpretation of dreams." He replied: "Open your mouth." This I did. He then spat into it. When morning dawned—behold, I was an interpreter of dreams.[20]

A similar oneiric encounter between Ibn Sīrīn and Joseph is narrated in another tradition:

> Ibn Sīrīn said: I dreamt that I entered the Friday mosque. With me were three older men and one handsome young fellow. I said to the young fellow: "Who are you?" He replied: "I'm Joseph." I said: "And who are these older men?" He answered: "My fathers, Abraham, Isaac, and Jacob." I said: "Teach me what God has taught you." Ibn Sīrīn continued: He then opened his mouth and said: "What do you see?" I replied: "Your tongue." He opened his mouth further and said: "Look now! What do you see?" I said: "Your uvula." He opened his mouth still further and said: "Look now! What do you see?" I said: "Your heart."

He then said: "Interpret and conceal nothing." Ibn Sīrīn continued: When morning came, whenever anyone told me about a dream it was as if I could see it in the palm of my hand.[21]

This special connection between Ibn Sīrīn's knowledge of dream interpretation and the prophet Joseph is evident in a final tradition.

It is said on the authority of Yaḥyā b. ᶜAbd Allāh: I heard al-Layth b. Saᶜd say that Ibn Sīrīn said: I learned from Saᶜīd b. al-Musayyib six hundred chapters of *The Interpretation of Joseph the Prophet*. al-Layth said: I know not whence Saᶜīd b. al-Musayyib got them.[22]

This third tradition is interesting not only for its linkage of Ibn Sīrīn and Joseph and its reference to this unknown "work" by Joseph, but also for the connection it draws between Ibn Sīrīn and Ibn al-Musayyib. The latter died ca. 94/712.[23] He was a famous Medinese muḥaddith who stood at the close of the period of the successors and is said to have transmitted prophetic traditions from such notables as Abū Hurayrah, Ibn ᶜAbbās, and others. There is a strong and relatively early tradition attributing to him great abilities as an interpreter of dreams. In particular, Ibn Saᶜd (d. 230/844) transmits from Wāqidī (d. 207/822) the following:

Saᶜīd b. al-Musayyib was among the best of dream interpreters. He received his knowledge in this field from Asmāᵓ, the daughter of Abū Bakr. She in turn received it from her father, Abū Bakr.[24]

Ibn Saᶜd also includes in his work a collection of twelve traditions on dreams and their interpretation, all ascribed to Ibn al-Musayyib, all collected by Wāqidī.[25] Judging from the chains of authorities of these traditions, Wāqidī had not collected them from a single prior source. Rather, he had gathered them from no less than seven of his teachers. A short excerpt should help illustrate the character of this collection.

[Ibn Saᶜd] said: Muḥammad b. ᶜUmar [al-Wāqidī] said: I was told by al-Ḥakam b. al-Qāsim, who received it from Ismāᶜīl b. Abī Ḥakīm, who said: A certain man said: I saw in a dream as if ᶜAbd al-Malik b. Marwān urinated four times in the prayer niche of the mosque of the prophet. I mentioned this to Saᶜīd b. al-Musayyib. He said in response: "If your dream is true, four caliphs arising from his loins will stand in [that mosque]."

[Ibn Saᶜd] said: Muḥammad b. ᶜUmar [al-Wāqidī] said: I was told by ᶜAbd al-Salām b. Ḥafṣ, who received it from Sharīk b. Abī Namir, who said: I said to Ibn al-Musayyib that I saw in sleep as if my teeth had fallen out into my hand and that I then buried them. He said in response: "If your dream is true, you will bury the people of your family."

> [Ibn Saᶜd] said: Muḥammad b. ᶜUmar [al-Wāqidī] said: I was told by Ibn Abī Dhaᵓb, who received it from Muslim al-Khayyāṭ, who said: A man said to Ibn al-Musayyib: "I saw myself urinating into my hand." He replied: "Fear God, for you have contracted an illicit marriage." He investigated the matter and found that he and one of his wives were related through having nursed together.—Another man came to him and said: "Abū Muḥammad [Ibn al-Musayyib], I dreamt that I urinated onto the stem of an olive tree." He replied: "Take a look at those with whom you have contracted a marriage—one of them is illicit." He investigated the matter and found that it was not permissible for him to have married one of his wives.

> [Ibn Saᶜd] said: Muḥammad b. ᶜUmar [al-Wāqidī] said: I was told by Ṣāliḥ b. Khawwāt, who heard it from Ibn al-Musayyib, who said: The end of the dream is forty years, that is, in interpretation.

This last tradition probably means that events predicted by a dream can take up to forty years to come to pass. An interesting aspect of these and the other traditions collected by Wāqidī is the way that Ibn al-Musayyib is presented as grounding the authority of his interpretations. He does not cite earlier sources such as the Koran or prophetic traditions to justify his interpretations. He does not attempt to explicate in any way the linkage between the dream symbol and its meaning, although sometimes it is possible to discern what those links might have been. In the first dream, the act of urination is apparently being likened to the act of engendering a child, the emission of urine being symbolically like the emission of semen, while in the second tradition the interpretation apparently turns on a metaphorical use of the word "tooth" to mean "life." (Even as one can say in Arabic: "I have surpassed the teeth of the people of my house," meaning "I have outlived them.") As for the third tradition, the act of urinating on oneself is like emitting semen on a relative and thus intimates an incestuous marriage. In general, the validity of Ibn al-Musayyib's interpretations turns not on his having justified them, whether by an appeal to an earlier authority or by an appeal to the underlying symbolic link between the dream symbol and its meaning. The validity of his interpretations rests on the fact of his own authority, a personal authority derived from his standing in a prophetic lineage that linked him to Asmāᵓ and thus to Abū Bakr and thus ultimately to Muḥammad, whose companion Abū Bakr was. The act of interpreting a dream was a charismatic act. It was itself an instance of prophecy.

While there are few reasons for thinking that Ibn Sīrīn wrote a dream manual, there is every reason to believe that Ibn Sīrīn had taken a lively interest in the subject of dream interpretation. He put into circulation one of the most famous prophetic traditions on dreams. Moreover, a great many traditions about dreams he interpreted were transmitted by his students and even by his son, until eventually by the end of the second century A.H. they came to be written down. While the authenticity of the dream manual of Ibn Sīrīn such as it might have been known to Khallāl is doubtful, we stand on firmer ground when we turn to the work of Kirmānī.

KIRMĀNĪ AND THE BEGINNINGS OF A WRITTEN TRADITION OF DREAM INTERPRETATION

Kirmānī's dream manual is no longer extant.[26] We can, however, infer some things about it from the comments of medieval authors who were familiar with it. The title of Kirmānī's work seems to have been *al-Dustūr fī al-ta^cbīr* (The Book of Rules on the Interpretation of Dreams), although it did circulate under other, more generic titles.[27] We know little about the author of this text. Often he is referred to as Kirmānī; sometimes as Ibrāhīm al-Kirmānī; sometimes as Abū Isḥāq al-Kirmānī.[28] That he was the son of ᶜAbd Allāh is attested by a number of different sources.[29] We can thus surmise that he bore the name Abū Isḥāq Ibrāhīm b. ᶜAbd Allāh al-Kirmānī. Regardless, this person seems to have left no mark on the biographical tradition.[30] Two separate considerations converge to suggest, however, that he flourished in the latter half of the second century of the Muslim era.

First, a number of anecdotes were in circulation in the Middle Ages that show Kirmānī acting as dream interpreter for two late second-century Abbasid caliphs. One records that the caliph Mahdī (r. 158–169/775–785) had a dream in which he saw his face turn black.[31] Alarmed, he consulted several interpreters, but was unable to divine the meaning of the dream. Finally he turned to Kirmānī, who opined that the dream foretold the birth of a daughter to the caliph. For his services Kirmānī was given one thousand dirhems. That same day, when in fact a daughter was born to the caliph, Kirmānī was given another ten thousand dirhems. The second anecdote records that the caliph Hārūn al-Rashīd (r. 170–193/786–809) saw in a dream that he was in the sacred precinct (*ḥaram*) of the Kaᶜbah suckling on the teats of a gazelle.[32] When Kirmānī was consulted, he responded that the act of suckling after weaning means imprisonment, but that insofar as people of the caliph's station cannot be cast into prison, the dream must mean that he will be imprisoned by love for a slave girl who is forbidden (*ḥarumat*) to him. The provenance of these anecdotes is unknown. It is not impossible, however, that Kirmānī had included them in his dream manual.[33] There are, secondly, three extant riwāyahs for the dream manual of Kirmānī,[34] all of which trace the first stage of its transmission through the famous muḥaddith Isḥāq b. ᶜĪsā, a scholar who flourished toward the end of the second century, dying ca. 214/829.[35] One of these is found in a work dating from the later sixth century A.H. It states that Ibn ᶜĪsā went to Kirmān where he met personally with Kirmānī and presumably at this time copied his dream manual.[36] Two further riwāyahs can be found in a later dream manual, the author of which had access to the "Book of Kirmānī" in two different versions, both of which identified the same Isḥāq b. ᶜĪsā as having been responsible for transmitting the work from its author.[37]

It is said that Kirmānī claimed to have learned the interpretation of dreams from no less exalted a disciplinary forebear than the prophet Joseph.

> Ibrāhīm b. ᶜAbd Allāh al-Kirmānī saw in a dream that Joseph was speaking to him. [Kirmānī] said to him: "Teach me of that which God has taught you." He replied: "Arise!" He then took off his mantle and clothed him with it. [Kirmānī] said: "I tarried and then awoke with a complete knowledge of interpretation. If I had not tarried, my knowledge would not have spread to the horizons."[38]

For Kirmānī, the interpretation of dreams was something prophetic. It was something passed on to him by that prophet best known for his abilities to interpret dreams. As for the mantle he received, this symbolized Kirmānī's reception of Joseph's prophetic authority. This same tradition continues by noting that Kirmānī did not include in his work anything that he himself had not tested one hundred times. As to Kirmānī's own sources, a tradition preserved by Ḥājjī Khalīfah and others offers our only clue.[39] It records that Kirmānī's sources included a number of pages (*ṣuḥuf*) ascribed to the prophet Abraham, "books" (*kutub*) of the prophet Daniel, as well as traditions "from Saᶜīd b. al-Musayyib and Ibn Sīrīn."[40] There is nothing in this report to suggest that Kirmānī drew on written sources from the latter two figures. Note again the ascription to Kirmānī of a scholarly lineage that linked him to the figures of a prophetic past.

Kirmānī's dream manual was hugely popular as a source for later Muslim dream manuals. Among later authors to make use of it: Ibn Qutaybah (d. 276/889), Maᶜāfirī (fl. fourth century A.H.), Qayrawānī (fl. early fifth century A.H.), Tiflīsī (d. 629/1231), Sālimī (d. 800/1397), and Ibn Shāhīn (d. 872/1468).[41] Kirmānī even received Ibn Khaldūn's nod of approval: his is one of the few dream manuals that the famous jurist mentioned by name in his survey of world history.[42] Furthermore, Kirmānī's text was one of only a few dream manuals to be subject to commentary in the Middle Ages.[43] One such commentary was made by Abū ᶜAbd Allāh Muḥammad b. Yaḥyā b. al-Ḥadhdhāᵓ (d. 416/1025), his *Bushrā fī ᶜibārat al-ruᵓyā* (Glad Tidings in the Interpretation of Dreams), an exposition (*sharḥ*) of the "Book of Kirmānī in fifteen parts."[44] This must have been a massive work, for it is recorded that it consisted of no less than ten volumes.[45] Another was written about a generation later by the famous jurist Ibn al-Bannāᵓ (d. 471/1078), his *Sharḥ kitāb al-Kirmānī fī al-taᶜbīr* (An Exposition of the Book of Kirmānī on the Interpretation of Dreams).[46] Neither commentary is known to be extant, although there is every reason to hope that as more manuscript collections are cataloged a copy of Kirmānī's dream manual or one of its commentaries may turn up. Although no copies of Kirmānī's text are at present known to be extant, his work was extensively used by the next work to be considered, the dream manual of Ibn Qutaybah, the earliest extant Muslim text on dream interpretation.

THE DREAM MANUAL OF IBN QUTAYBAH

Born in 213/828 at Kūfah, Ibn Qutaybah spent the first half of his adult life engaged in a number of government posts, first as a judge at Dīnawar, later as a hearer of complaints (*maẓālim*) at Baṣrah.[47] After 257/871 he settled in Baghdad to teach. There he died in 276/889. The subjects to which Ibn Qutaybah devoted himself were diverse. They included poetry and literature. Such secular pursuits, however, do not represent the sum of Ibn Qutaybah's interests, for he was also "profoundly *ḥadīth*-minded in his religious views."[48] Among his works on religious subjects can be counted texts on most of the subjects of concern to the ulema of the day: theological treatises, discussions of legal matters, commentary on prophetic traditions, Koranic studies. Also extant is a dream manual. This work is preserved in two manuscripts. The first is in the library of the Hebrew University of Jerusalem;[49] the second, a partial copy only, in the library of the Language, History, and Geography Faculty of Ankara University.[50] Unfortunately, both manuscripts have suffered much in transmission.[51]

Some doubts have been expressed as to the authenticity of Ibn Qutaybah's dream manual. Even before the manuscripts of the work were discovered, it was known from the medieval biographical and bibliographic tradition that there had once been in circulation a work on dream interpretation ascribed to Ibn Qutaybah.[52] G. Lecomte summarized the state of the question before the discovery of the manuscripts when he declared that the attribution of this work to Ibn Qutaybah was "at present doubtful," although less problematic than some of the other pseudepigraphic works attributed to Ibn Qutaybah.[53] Even after a manuscript of the text was discovered, however, doubts as to its authenticity continued. Most important, Toufic Fahd, himself responsible for discovering the first copy of the text, largely withheld judgment on the question, stating that "a long, comparative study would be required to establish this work's authenticity."[54]

That Ibn Qutaybah did write a dream manual is clear beyond doubt, for he mentions just such a text in the introduction to another of his works.[55] There is, moreover, much evidence to suggest that already by the fourth century A.H. there was in circulation a work on dreams attributed to Ibn Qutaybah.[56] These facts do not, however, establish the authenticity of the dream manual ascribed to Ibn Qutaybah and preserved in the Jerusalem and Ankara manuscripts. For this purpose one must appeal to other criteria, the cumulative weight of which strongly supports the authenticity of the text. First, the traditions cited in the preserved dream manual are almost all derived from men we otherwise know to have been among the more important teachers of Ibn Qutaybah.[57] Second, the Jerusalem version of the dream manual is provided with a full riwāyah, which traces its transmission to Aḥmad b. Marwān (d. 333/944).[58] This person is well known from other contexts as a conveyor of Ibn Qutaybah's works.[59] He is also specifically recorded elsewhere as having transmitted Ibn Qutaybah's dream manual.[60] There is, it must be concluded, little reason to doubt that the dream manual preserved in the Jerusalem and Ankara manuscripts is an authentic work of Ibn Qutaybah.

The Methods of Dream Interpretation

Ibn Qutaybah's dream manual is divided into two sections. The first, its introduction, encompasses a little less than half its total length.[61] Ibn Qutaybah opens with an artfully constructed prologue in praise of the marvels of God's creation.[62] Among the wonders whereby God's generosity and power are made manifest are dreams. In them we perceive things while our senses and minds are inactive. In them we travel to distant lands "with bodies reclining and feet unmoved." Ibn Qutaybah continues by noting that in both Islam and in the time before Islam there was near universal assent to the truth of dream interpretation. It was denied only by certain atheistic fatalists and by certain ancient physicians. As for the pious physicians, they both affirmed and denied dreams, but inconsistently, he claims. They affirmed them because of their religion—in particular, the stories of Joseph and other prophets who interpreted dreams. They denied them because of what they received from the ancient physicians, who used to say that dreamers see only what has been conditioned by the four humors. Ibn Qutaybah grants that there are some dreams that result from the influence of the humors, but these are nothing more than confused dreams (*aḍghāth*), a category of dreams also spoken of by the prophet Muḥammad. As for true dreams, these an angel brings from "the tablet of the mother of the book." This angel creates "likenesses and images" in dreams, to give tidings about something good that will happen, or at other times, to warn about disobedience or something unpleasant shortly to happen.

Ibn Qutaybah states in no uncertain terms why he wrote his work:

> Among the types of knowledge and the varieties of wisdom with which humans occupy themselves, there is none more obscure, none more refined, exalted, and noble, none more difficult . . . than the dream, for it is one of the parts of revelation (*waḥy*) and one of the modes of prophecy (*nubūwah*).[63]

Moreover, the interpretation of dreams is a discipline of far greater complexity than most, inasmuch as the methodology one must employ to interpret any individual dream varies in accordance with the circumstances of the dreamer (his religion, for example, or occupation), the time of the year in which the dream is seen, and other such considerations. At the same time, sometimes dreams bear the opposite of their apparent meaning; while at other times the meaning of the dream is not applicable to the dreamer, but to someone else; while at yet other times they lack all meaning and thus ought not be interpreted.

Because of the difficulties inherent in the study of dreams, Ibn Qutaybah argues, the properly trained interpreter must be possessed of many intellectual virtues—far more than are required for the study of other disciplines.

> It is incumbent on him to be learned in the Book of God and in the traditions of the prophet . . . in the proverbs of the Bedouin and in well-known verses of poetry, and in etymological and dialectical studies. He must moreover be refined in his character, a quick study, equipped with a thorough practical understanding of men and their characters, knowledgeable in the use of analogy and able to memorize lots of material.[64]

Such accomplishments of the intellect, however, are of no value if not accompanied by an earnest piety. In particular, the interpreter of dreams must not eat food forbidden to Muslims, must not have committed any grave sins, and must not be in a state of grave bodily impurity.[65] Having introduced his work and hinted at the complexities of dream interpretation, Ibn Qutaybah enters on a discussion of nine different methods for the interpretation of dreams.[66] As will be seen, these methods will in time become an important element in the developing Muslim oneirocritic tradition.

The first method (*taʾwīl al-asmāʾ*) focuses on the etymology of the dreamer's name or the name of the object appearing in the dream.[67] Thus, a dream seen by someone named Rāshid can mean "guidance" (*irshād*), while one seen by someone named al-Faḍl implies "the conferring of benefit" (*ifḍāl*). On the other hand, a dream in which one sees a lily of the valley (*sūsan*) hints that something evil (*sūʾ*) will happen to the dreamer, whereas dreams of quince (*safarjal*) indicate a journey (*safar*). This latter interpretation is confirmed by the verses of an anonymous poet:

> She gave him a quince and he saw an evil omen
>   in this, and spent the day in contemplation.
> He was afraid to leave, for the beginning of the word is "journey."
>   He was right to draw an evil omen.[68]

Closely related to this method is another that Ibn Qutaybah calls "interpretation via meaning" (*taʾwīl bi-l-maʿnā*).[69] This involves taking a characteristic associated with the object of one's dream and using this as the basis for one's interpretation. For example, a woman saw in a dream that her husband gave her a narcissus while he gave to another of his wives a myrtle. The dream interpreter said: "You he will divorce, while her he will keep, for the poet says: 'The narcissus doesn't last for long; myrtle does.'"

The next three methods identified by Ibn Qutaybah concern the authoritative sources that can provide the clues needed to interpret one's dreams. These methods create symbolic links between the objects mentioned in those sources and the objects seen in one's dreams. The Koran is the first such source (*taʾwīl bi-l-Qurʾān*).[70] Thus, for example, dreams in which eggs appear have something to do with women, for eggs and women are linked at Koran 37.49, where chaste women who restrain their eyes are likened to "well-guarded eggs." The prophetic traditions are another such source (*taʾwīl bi-l-ḥadīth*).[71] Muḥammad, for example, was wont to call ravens and mice "corrupt."[72] For this reason, dreams of ravens and mice signify corruption. Prophets other than Muḥammad can likewise supply the needed symbolic link. To dream of a physician, for instance, signifies a specialist in Islamic law, for the prophet Jesus said that "the physician comes only to the sick"—"likening thereby the physician to the scholar and the sick person to one with many sins." In much the same way, well-known proverbs can provide the needed clues (*taʾwīl bi-l-mathal al-sāʾir*).[73] To dream of washing your hands with potash, for example, signifies despair of obtaining something, for there is a proverb that states of one who despairs of something that "he has washed his hand of it with potash." Similarly, snot in a dream has something to do with your child. It is, after all, commonly said of a child who resembles his father that he is "his father's snot"—a drip off the old snout, if you will—while tomcats are often called the "snot of lions."

The next method is what Ibn Qutaybah calls "interpretation through opposition and inversion" (*taʾwīl bi-l-ḍidd wa-l-maqlūb*).[74] This method usually entails interpreting a dream symbol to mean the opposite of its apparent meaning. Weeping means joy, while laughing means sadness. At other times, however, it involves interpreting what was seen in the dream in terms of a common euphemism or metaphor. Thus, for example, dreams of war may imply a plague, while dreams of a plague may signify a war, even as dreams of a flood can signify an enemy, while an enemy in a dream means that there will be a flood. Closely connected with this technique is another called "interpretation through increase and decrease" (*taʾwīl bi-l-ziyādah wa-l-naqṣ*).[75] In this regard, Ibn Qutaybah suggests that one and the same dream symbol may have opposite meanings, depending on certain quantitative factors. To dream of weeping means joy, but if one is both weeping and screaming, it means the opposite, some sort of impending calamity. Fish in a dream, if they can be counted, signify women; if they cannot be counted, money or booty.

The last two methods are presented rather briefly. The meaning of a dream can vary with the time of the day or year in which it occurs (*taʿbīr al-ruʾyā bi-l-waqt*).[76] To dream at night of riding an elephant signifies a weighty matter, but to have that same dream during the day means that one will divorce one's wife or that evil will befall one by reason of her. In general, the most truthful dreams are seen either just before dawn or during one's midday nap, especially during the time of the year when flowers blossom and fruit ripens and is harvested, whereas the most deceitful dreams are had in the winter. As a whole, moreover, dreams seen during the day are stronger than those seen at night. As to the last of his nine methods for interpreting dreams, Ibn Qutaybah argues that the interpretation given to a dream can vary in accordance with the state of the dreamer.[77] In this regard, such factors as the dreamer's occupation or religion are key. Ibn Qutaybah's discussion of this last topic is so brief as to be almost unintelligible.

Ibn Qutaybah next provides a collection of roughly one-hundred anecdotes that relate the interpretation of particular dreams, usually at the hands of Ibn Sīrīn.[78] In length they range from five or six lines to well over a page. Most are provided with full chains of authorities. Judging from these, it is clear that Ibn Qutaybah is gathering these anecdotes from a host of different sources and that he is not drawing them or even a large portion of them from a prior written compilation. The anecdotes are not organized in any discernible way. As Ibn Qutaybah states at the end of this collection, he included them so that the reader might know how to organize an inquiry when asked to interpret a dream and how to transfer a dream "from aspect to aspect while interpreting"—meaning, most likely, how to apply the nine methods he had just outlined. It is more likely that Ibn Qutaybah simply could find no suitable place in his work to incorporate some of the notes he had taken on this subject.

Two of Ibn Qutaybah's anecdotes are especially interesting as they are autobiographical.[79] The first records that Ibn Qutaybah was once asked by a friend about the meaning of the word *janahī* (a form of Indian cane or a delicate branch). He had no idea and confessed his ignorance. One night as he slept, there appeared in a dream a certain man who told him that the word was synonymous with *khayzurān* or bamboo. Ibn Qutaybah asked for a proof text and received one. Desiring further confirmation, he waited and soon heard someone recite some verses. These were already familiar to Ibn Qutaybah. The first line, however, he knew in a different version, one that substituted *khayzurān* for *janahī*. He could thus confidently conclude that *janahī* and *khayzurān* were synonyms. The second records that when Ibn Qutaybah was a young man he dreamt of many books containing rare words and examples of their usage. He was able to memorize some of them, but soon forgot all but one. At the time he did not know the meaning of one of the words in this verse. Later, however, he found out that it was synonymous with another word, one of which he did know the meaning. Dreams of a true scholar!

Ibn Qutaybah concludes his introduction with a discussion of the proper behavior of dream interpreters and dreamers.[80] The good interpreters of dreams will never be hasty, but always careful. They will not be afraid to admit that there are some dreams they cannot interpret. They will listen carefully to the description of the dreams and proceed in an orderly fashion to analyze them according to established principles, all the while invoking God's aid. When they find that a dream can be interpreted in different ways, they will apply specific rules to determine which is the proper interpretation. Ibn Qutaybah continues by noting that sometimes interpreters will be able to avert inauspicious outcomes by giving dreams good interpretations. They must be careful, however, never to give an honest interpretation to dreams that predict that the dreamer will engage in a grave sin, for this can incite the dreamer to the performance of the sin—it is better to err on the side of caution, he states, for it is always possible that the interpreter is wrong, especially insofar as interpretations are never more than educated guesses.

As for dreamers, they must always be scrupulously honest about what was seen in the dream. In particular, they must never introduce extraneous elements when they recount it, for such amounts to lying and is subject to religious sanction. If dreamers see something in a dream that scares them or makes them sad, on waking they should recite the Throne Verse and spit over their left shoulder three times and then recite the following prayer:

> I take refuge with the Lord of Moses, the Lord of Jesus the son of Mary, the Lord of Abraham, the Lord who can redeem a dream from evil lest it harm me in matters spiritual or material—may his glory and fame be exalted and may it be recognized that there is no deity other than he.[81]

According to Ibn Qutaybah, such wicked dreams are said by the prophet to come from Satan. There are, however, limits to the damage Satan can do in dreams. In particular, he suggests, Satan can appear to the dreamer neither as God or the Koran, nor as the sun, moon, heavens, earth, or clouds, nor in particular as Muḥammad, for the prophet said: "Whosoever sees me in a dream has seen me in a waking state, for Satan cannot imitate me."

Dreams and Their Interpretation

The second part of Ibn Qutaybah's dream manual consists of a highly formalized presentation of the meanings of the various objects appearing in one's dreams.[82] His materials are arranged by subject and divided into forty-six chapters of unequal length. The early chapters deal with dreams of a religious character: dreams of God, the resurrection, paradise, angels, prophets, the Koran, prayer leaders, and so on. These are followed by a chapter on dreams of the sun, moon, and stars; several chapters on objects related to human beings; and a few chapters on geographical features and natural phenomena. Most of the remaining portions of the text are concerned with dreams of animals, wild and domestic, and of birds, fish, and reptiles. The penultimate chapter treats dreams of occupations. The final, rather lengthy chapter treats of "oddities." In this chapter, Ibn Qutaybah has apparently included interpretations of all sorts of objects and actions for which he could not find a place in the earlier chapters.

For all the space devoted in the introduction to the different methods needed for interpreting dreams, such considerations do not figure prominently in the second part of the text. Ibn Qutaybah's manner of presentation is more laconic than one might have expected. For the most part he simply sets up analogical relations or symbolic links between dream symbols and their meanings. These are sometimes in the form of a conditional sentence ("whoever sees this, that will happen," or "if he does this, that will happen"). "Whoever sees the sun going into eclipse, there will be an eclipse of the king's power."[83] Occasionally such conditions are qualified further. "Whoever sees himself become the sun, he will become a king with power in proportion to the sun's rays—if, that is, he is worthy of such a station."[84] Equally common are simple sets of equivalencies ("this is that").

> The moon is the king's wazir. Venus is the king's wife. Mercury is the king's scribe. Mars is his minister of war. Jupiter is his finance minister. Saturn is his minister of justice. The rest of the stars are his nobles.[85]

Ibn Qutaybah occasionally supports his interpretations with a verse from the Koran, a saying of the prophet, or a line of poetry. Such supporting texts are, however, the exception rather than the rule. More often Ibn Qutaybah leaves it to the reader to determine the analogical relation or symbolic link between the dream symbol and its meaning.

What sources did Ibn Qutaybah use in his dream manual? Most of the introduction consists of materials that Ibn Qutaybah compiled from other authorities. His sources were freestanding anecdotes or verses of poetry transmitted to him by his teachers. Such materials were then strung together by Ibn Qutaybah with brief commentary and transitional sentences. Only very rarely does he offer extended comments of his own. Far more often, he crafts and arranges transmitted materials, bringing together dispersed anecdotes and weaving them together in a coherent fashion. As for the second half of the text, Ibn Qutaybah himself states his sources:

> To give an account of the principles [of dream interpretation] we have made a summary of the science of Ibrāhīm b. ᶜAbd Allāh al-Kirmānī and others and of a selection of anecdotes . . . adding what was neglected and not mentioned by the ancients.[86]

This probably means that Ibn Qutaybah compiled the second part of his text from the dream manual of Kirmānī, as well as from other unspecified texts and anecdotes, although the fact that Kirmānī alone is mentioned by name suggests that this was Ibn Qutaybah's major source. What is most important, in this regard, is that here also he is following prior sources and is thus best seen as a compiler rather than an original author.

Ibn Qutaybah's dream manual exercised a considerable influence on the developing Muslim tradition of dream interpretation. Dārī (wr. between ca. 400/1009 and 635/1237) and Qayrawānī (fl. early fifth century A.H.), for example, made direct use of Ibn Qutaybah's introduction, including large portions of it verbatim or nearly so in their own dream manuals.[87] Their citations are so extensive that any future edition of Ibn Qutaybah's text would have to give their testimony great weight. So also, in the fourth century A.H., Bar Bahlūl, a Nestorian Christian, made use of Ibn Qutaybah's text—indeed, the majority of his own dream manual was a summary of Ibn Qutaybah's, which he follows so closely that his work as well would be an important witness for any future edition of Ibn Qutaybah's text.[88] Another fourth-century dream manual, this time in verse, also had access to Ibn Qutaybah's text.[89] And finally, once again in the fourth century, Ibn Qutaybah's work, especially his discussion of the various methods for interpreting dreams, was extensively used by Sijistānī, the subject of the next section.

THE DREAM MANUAL OF SIJISTĀNĪ

Khallāl's Abū Aḥmad Khalaf b. Aḥmad is none other than the last and indeed the most famous Ṣaffārid amir of Sijistān.[90] Born in 326/937, he ascended the throne of Sijistān in 352/963, when his father was murdered. Initially Sijistānī was dependent on the authority of Abū al-Ḥusayn Ṭāhir b. Muḥammad, whom he officially associated with his rule. Leaving Ṭāhir in charge of Sijistān, Sijistānī went on pilgrimage in 353/964 to fulfill a vow he had made at the time of his father's murder. On returning (354/965), Sijistānī became embroiled in a long civil war, first with Ṭāhir and later with Ṭāhir's son. This war lasted for close on twenty years, coming to an end only in 373/983. With the rise of Maḥmūd of Ghazna, already by 390/1000 Sijistānī was beginning to feel pressures, for he was then forced to pay tribute to Maḥmūd, place his name in the Friday sermon, and acknowledge his suzerainty on coinage. Within a few years Maḥmūd had invaded Sijistān, besieging Sijistānī and forcing him to abdicate in 393/1003. Sijistānī spent his remaining years in exile, dying in 399/1008.

Sijistānī pursued a course of study not unlike that of ulema of the time, probably before his accession.[91] He is depicted as receiving and transmitting prophetic traditions in many parts of the eastern Islamic world. There is extant, in fact, a selection of a work of his on prophetic traditions, as yet unpublished.[92] As to his legal school, Sijistānī was a follower of Shāfiᶜī, even though the region over which he ruled was largely Ḥanafī in orientation.[93] Sijistānī was also a patron of literature. Among the most famous of those to seek his patronage were the poet Abū al-Fatḥ al-Bustī (d. ca. 400/1009) and the celebrated stylist Badīᶜ al-Zamān al-Hamadhānī (d. 398/1007).[94] Sijistānī is best remembered, however, for a massive Koranic commentary he commissioned, a work that is said to have consisted of no less than one hundred and twenty volumes.[95] Sijistānī's work on dream interpretation is extant in a number of manuscripts. Some of these maintain the ascription to Sijistānī.[96] Others transmit it anonymously or under the name of Ibn Sīrīn.[97] It is also likely that a Persian translation of Sijistānī's dream manual is extant.[98] The original title of his dream manual was probably *Tuḥfat al-mulūk* (The Precious Possession of the Kings).[99]

Sijistānī's is a remarkably concise dream manual.[100] Not a word is wasted in conveying the knowledge necessary for the interpreter of dreams. It is, in fact, for the sake of such concision that Sijistānī wrote the text. This he explains in his introduction.[101] He wanted those interested in dream interpretation to be free of the need for many books. For this reason, he gathered together the works of previous interpreters and epitomized them to the greatest extent possible, while at the same time avoiding trivial accounts, vulgar diction, and erroneous materials. Furthermore, as he explains, to make his work "user friendly," he devised a novel system of indexing. He numbered the pages of his work with the letters of the Arabic alphabet in accordance with their numerical values and provided it with a table of contents that noted for each chapter the page on which it began.[102] Sijistānī seems to have envisaged that the users of his work would not be reading it from cover to cover, but using it as a reference book, an encyclopedia of dream symbols.

Following his short introduction and the promised table of contents, Sijistānī turns to the substance of his dream manual. He begins with a chapter on theoretical matters.[103] In this he treats of "the generic and specific principles of dream visions" and how one can distinguish true and false dreams. He provides, first, a sixfold division of dreams. There are three types of true dreams: dreams of warning, dreams of glad tidings, and dreams of revelation. All these are delivered by an angel. This angel disposes of such dreams only insofar as it is permitted by God to look down on the Preserved Tablet and read therein the good and evil that are destined for the sons of Adam. Likewise, there are three types of deceitful dreams: anxiety dreams, dreams arising from sickness, and Satanic dreams. The first two originate in the self: the first from a constant preoccupation with the affairs of the world, the second from illness of one sort or another. The third category of deceitful dreams is broader. It includes any dreams that result in emissions necessitating ablutions and any dreams that present fantastic situations that cannot exist in reality. All such dreams come from Satan. True dreams, Sijistānī concludes, are subject to interpretation, whereas deceitful dreams lack divinatory meaning.

Displaying a marked penchant for lists, Sijistānī next proceeds to detail the fourteen grades of dreamers,[104] ranking them in accordance with the general truth or falsity of their dreams: a Muslim's dreams are more truthful than a non-Muslim's; veiled women have truer dreams than those who do not wear the veil; the rich have more truthful dreams than the poor; and so on. This list is followed by an account of the four humors and how they affect a person's dreams when they are out of balance.[105] Sijistānī next treats of the proper behavior of both the dreamer and the dream interpreter.[106] Dreamers are instructed as to the proper preparation for sleep, how to sleep, what to say on waking if a bad dream has been seen, and the necessary demeanor with which to consult the interpreter. As for dream interpreters, Sijistānī argues that they must be of a pious disposition and that they must be learned in all the relevant branches of knowledge: the Koran, traditions of the prophet, Arabic, poetry, proverbs, anecdotes, and so on. In general, the interpreter must have mastered the traditional fields of knowledge of concern to the ulema. Here Sijistānī is dependent on Ibn Qutaybah's dream manual.

Sijistānī then turns his attention to the "aspects of interpretation"[107] It is this subject that will hold his attention throughout the duration of his introductory chapter. In this regard, he signals no less than thirty-five different "aspects." Sijistānī is here actually concerned with two quite distinct sorts of phenomena. Among the aspects of interpretation, he counts the different methods that might be applied to the interpretation of dreams. Any number of techniques might be used: the key to a dream's meaning might be a Koranic verse, a well-known proverb, a verse of poetry, the meaning of the first letter of the most prominent symbol in the dream, or perhaps even an etymological consideration. Such considerations had largely been laid down by Ibn Qutaybah, who is here being followed. Sijistānī is quite unique, however, in that he also utilizes the techniques of other sorts of divination to interpret dreams. Drawing on the lore of divination via the flight of birds, for example, one of the aspects of interpretation that he signals is that "according to the method of birds." Just as it is considered auspicious for a bird to fly from behind a person and pass on to that person's front, so also in a dream any object that comes from behind and goes to the front will have an auspicious interpretation. Sijistānī also includes in his discussion of the aspects of interpretation a treatment of how the meaning of a dream is dependent on the status of the dreamer or the external circumstances that accompany the dream. A dream's meaning, for example, can vary in accordance with the time of the year or the day of the week. It can mean one thing for a Muslim and another for a Jew or Christian. Similarly, the meaning of a dream can vary with a person's country of origin or the customs of the inhabitants of that country. Like Ibn Qutaybah before him, however, although Sijistānī spends a great deal of time discussing the aspects of interpretation, such concerns play only a small part in his dream manual.

Sijistānī organizes his dream manual proper according to subject.[108] He divides the work into fifty-seven chapters, each treating of a broad category of dream symbols. When Sijistānī turns to the individual symbols, he organizes his work in an extremely concise manner, one that I have not seen in any other Muslim dream manual. He begins with a statement of equivalence: any particular dream symbol equals a discrete number of objects, persons, or actions in reality. Take, for example, his discussion of dreams of the sun. He writes:

> The sun is interpreted in nine ways: a prayer leader, a king, a leader, a scholar, a manifest matter, justice, a father, a husband, and a woman.[109]

Sijistānī then goes on to provide a number of more specific examples, this time using a more traditional manner of presentation: "if someone see x, y will happen":

> Examples: if someone sees the sun prostrating itself to him, the sultan will incline himself to him and act humbly towards him—or one of the other [nine] that we have named; or justice will be found in that place, spreading from one of those [nine] that we have mentioned. If he sees that its rays are beautiful, the state of the one to whom it pertains will be beautiful; if the opposite, the same and all goodness and wickedness will cease in it, as a result of the one to whom it pertains.[110]

Sijistānī maintains this rigorously concise manner of presentation—first giving the aspects and then the examples—throughout the first part of his dream manual. Eventually, by the time he reaches his fourteenth chapter, he ceases to provide the initial summary and contents himself with giving the examples. Unlike Ibn Qutaybah, Sijistānī does not employ anecdotes in his presentation.[111] Only very occasionally does he attempt to ground his interpretations in the authority of earlier figures or with the sorts of interpretive techniques discussed in his introduction.[112] More commonly, he simply states how a dream symbol is to be interpreted and then moves on to the next symbol. The concision that characterizes Sijistānī's dream manual accords well with his own stated objectives in the introduction as well as with its character as a work of reference that was not to be read from cover to cover, but only consulted as need arose.

CONCLUSIONS

The dream manuals discussed above were not the only ones written in the formative period. It is these about which we happen at present to be most well informed. There were yet other dream manuals written during the formative period, however—many others. These works are known from a variety of sources. The medieval biographical tradition often ascribes dream manuals to its subjects. Similarly, bibliographic texts frequently mention such works. So also, some later dream manuals provide lists of prior works on the subject—primitive bibliographies, if you will. Taken together, such sources make reference to some thirty other dream manuals composed during the formative period. (These are discussed in the Appendix.) Our knowledge of these texts is usually meager, however, usually restricted to the name of the work—and sometimes not even that—and the name of its author—and sometimes not even that. Moreover, most of these texts have disappeared without leaving significant traces, not even citations in later works—with one exception. The only other dream manual extant from the formative period is a didactic poem by Maᶜāfirī. This work, as yet unpublished, is at the same time the earliest known dream manual in verse.[113]

Maᶜāfirī's dream manual is entitled *Urjūzah fī taᶜbīr al-ruʾyā ᶜalā ṣifat khalq al-insān* (A Poem in the *Rajaz* Meter on the Interpretation of Dreams according to the Attributes of the Creation of Human Beings). While the author of this work is seemingly unknown to the biographical tradition, there is solid evidence to conclude that he flourished in the mid-fourth century A.H.[114] Maᶜāfirī's work opens with a short introduction:

> Praise be to God for his providence
> since he has graced man in creating him!
> You who ask about manifold dreams
> and what people see in their sleep
> Of the form of man and his construction,
> member upon member—if it comes
> From God and the prophet it's to be followed;
> if from another, it's innovation.[115]

As might be inferred from the title and introduction of his work, Maᶜāfirī is interested only in dreams of the body and its various members and activities. He begins with the head and its "members" (eyebrows, eyes, ears, lips, and so on) and then slowly passes down the body until at last, after some four hundred lines, he reaches the feet and the toenails. Following this, he appends some thirty lines on what in general it means to dream of men and women, as well as of youths, and concludes with a statement of his own name and of the sources on which he drew.[116] Of these there were three: Ibn Sīrīn, Kirmānī, and Ibn Qutaybah.

Maᶜāfirī's manner of presentation in the body of his dream manual is quite laconic. He simply states the nature of the dream symbol and offers its interpretation:

> A beard that is black when interpreted
> fame and wealth to him shall come.[117]
> If he sees hair grow on his tongue
> that is the business of one busy with something.[118]
> If he sees shaved the scalp of his head
> that is death, quick and painless.[119]
> Loins and hips in interpretation
> life and money for such a one.[120]

Such brevity, which must in part stem from the constraints of the poetic form, lends Maᶜāfirī's work an oracular quality reminiscent of the omen texts of the ancient Near East.

Of the thirty some other dream manuals said to have been composed during the formative period, a few are almost certainly pseudepigraphic. They are first mentioned in works from the later Middle Ages and are ascribed to authors about whom there clustered large collections of pseudepigraphic works. Unless exemplars of these texts happen one day to show up in the manuscript collections, exemplars with strong claims to authenticity, it is prudent for now to withhold judgment on their genuineness.[121] Yet other of these dream manuals were probably not originally independent works on the interpretation of dreams, but chapters in larger treatments of either philosophic or theological issues.[122] It is even possible that some of these texts may not be concerned with dream divination per se. If all we have is a title, it is often difficult to be entirely sure of the contents of a work. Works such as these may be concerned with the philosophic or theological aspects of dreams but may not focus on their use for divinatory purposes.[123]

There are, nonetheless, some lost works about which it is possible to determine something as to their contents and format. Our knowledge of these texts is almost wholly dependent on fragments preserved in later dream manuals. Some of the more important of these lost texts were treated above, in discussing the legacy of Ibn Sīrīn—the dream manuals of Misᶜadah, Nuᶜaym b. Ḥammād, Ibn Ḥabīb, Ibn al-Mughīrah, and so on. Aside from these works and those discussed elsewhere in this chapter, most of the other dream manuals of the formative period are now, largely, nothing more than names.[124] How dearly would we like to find a copy of the dream manual of the renowned historian Abū Jaᶜfar al-Ṭabarī (d. 310/923), his *Kitāb fī ᶜibārat al-ruᵓyā* (Book on the Interpretation of Dreams)? or that of the famous poet, Abū Ṭālib al-Maᵓmūnī (d. ca. 383/993), his *Kitāb kanz al-ruᵓyā* (Book of the Treasury of Dreams)? There is every reason to hope that as more and more manuscript collections are catalogued further light will be shed on texts such as these.

Clearly, much has been lost from the formative period, nor are such losses likely to have been entirely fortuitous. As suggested in the introduction to this study, later tradition needed to take an active interest in earlier works for them to survive. In this respect, later tradition exercised a form of *ijmāᵓ* or communal consensus, choosing from the earlier tradition what it considered valuable, while letting pass into oblivion that with which it was not concerned. In terms of the extant remains, in short, what was preserved was that deemed worthy by the consensus of later tradition. Even so, Khallāl's list of written works on the interpretation of dreams offered a remarkably accurate account of those figures from the formative period about whom we are at present most well informed. Whereas other texts have disappeared, works by these authors were read and copied. For this reason, it is not improbable that Khallāl's account represents what was a developing communal consensus as to which texts and authors from the formative period were most significant. Granted these limitations of our evidence, that we are constrained to study the formative period of the Muslim tradition of dream interpretation in the contours bequeathed by later communal consensus, let us return to the questions with which this chapter opened.

Continuity and Change in the Formative Period

When did written dream manuals first appear? And how, if at all, did they change over the course of the formative period? While Ibn Qutaybah's is the earliest extant Muslim dream manual, we must not treat it as the fount of a developing tradition. We do not find in his work the beginnings of the Muslim tradition of dream interpretation. Such beginnings are rather to be found in the nexus of personal relations that characterized the transmission of knowledge in the late first and early second centuries A.H., the passing of anecdotes on dreams from teacher to disciple. Dream lore was in this earliest period transmitted in much the same fashion as other types of knowledge, whether Koranic commentary, traditions on the spiritual life, or information concerning the life of Muḥammad and the formative period of Islamic history. The persons to whom such traditions were ascribed varied. Muḥammad and his companions were prominent. By the beginning of the second century, however, dream lore began to be associated particularly with Ibn Sīrīn.

It was not until the end of the second century that anecdotes on dreams came to be written down. Many questions surround the format of these earliest dream manuals. Were they organized by topic? In this case they may have consisted of collections of anecdotes organized by the types of dream symbols. Or were they perhaps arranged by interpreter? We might then imagine that there were separate chapters on dreams interpreted by Muḥammad, Abū Bakr, Ibn Sīrīn, and so on. Certainty escapes us. We can only surmise that such texts may have been not dissimilar to the "dream manual" of Ibn al-Musayyib, as preserved by Ibn Saᶜd—although surely of greater length. What is clear is that the majority of these late second-century compilations must have still largely maintained an anecdotal format. This was the case, for example, with the works of Misᶜadah, Nuᶜaym b. Ḥammād, Ibn Ḥabīb, and Ibn al-Mughīrah. One at least of these late second-century dream manuals, however, that of Kirmānī, had probably already begun to shift from the use of anecdotes to a more formalized manner of presentation, offering not stories, but a list of dream symbols and their meanings. As Kirmānī's work is not extant, any opinion formed of it depends, largely, on the use made of it by Ibn Qutaybah. While certainty lacks in the case of Kirmānī, the work of Ibn Qutaybah definitely does present the beginnings of this shift from anecdote to formalism.

Ibn Qutaybah's dream manual stood in the midst of a tradition that was already well established, and it allows us to understand how that tradition had been developing since the end of the second century A.H. In it we see, for the first time, the beginnings of a systematic presentation of methods for interpreting dreams. At the same time, Ibn Qutaybah's dream manual also evinces our earliest extant, formal presentation of the meaning of dream symbols. The collection of autonomous anecdotes had begun to give way to the dictionary or encyclopedia. A work such as Ibn Qutaybah's could be consulted as need arose. The various dream symbols could be found with ease and their meaning could be readily discerned. Although Ibn Qutaybah's dream manual varies in these significant ways from its predecessors, it still partakes of its anecdotal past. Over half the text is still a collection of autonomous anecdotes strung together with slight transitional comments.

By the fourth century A.H. formalism had all but replaced the anecdote as the primary mode of expression in Muslim dream manuals. Indeed, it is hard to imagine a dream manual more formal than that of Sijistānī. His was a work of reference, and to facilitate such a use Sijistānī provided his work with a novel system of indexing. With the work of Sijistānī and the ascendancy of formalism over anecdote we encounter for the first time in the Muslim tradition a dream manual with a format that resembles the dream manuals of an earlier, pre-Islamic past, whether that of the Hellenic tradition (Artemidorus), or those of an even more ancient past, such as the fragmentary dream manuals extant in Demotic and Akkadian. When in the next chapter we turn to the great compilations of the late fourth and early fifth centuries, we shall find that all maintain this formalistic mode of presentation. Anecdotes have not entirely disappeared, but they are now used only to illustrate the basic data being presented in a formalized manner.

The Social Locus of the Tradition

Which class of Muslim intellectuals was responsible for the composition and circulation of dream manuals in the formative period? In terms of the extant remains, a clear pattern is evident. Dream interpretation in the formative period was not being pursued by marginal figures, but by those very same folk who came to be considered with the passage of time as having defined the contours of a normative Islam. The tradition's social locus was thus to be found at the center rather than the periphery of early Muslim intellectual concerns. There is no justification for thinking dream interpretation to have been an pursuit cultivated by those on the fringe. It was, instead, an object of concern to the same people who were compiling collections of prophetic traditions, commentaries on the Koran, accounts of Muḥammad's life, legal treatises, and the like.

When toward the end of the first century A.H. it is finally possible to have access to the Muslim tradition of dream interpretation, it appears to have been of interest primarily to the muḥaddiths, the early transmitters of prophetic traditions—figures like Ibn Sīrīn and Ibn al-Musayyib. Over the course of the second century an interest in the tradition passed from the muḥaddiths to their heirs, the early ulema—men such as Misᶜadah, Nuᶜaym b. Ḥammād, Ibn Ḥabīb, and Ibn al-Mughīrah. The same pattern hold in the third and fourth centuries: Ibn Qutaybah and Sijistānī, it will be recalled, were both closely connected to the ulema. As for Ibn Qutaybah, he was "profoundly *ḥadīth*-minded in his religious views"[125] and wrote extensively on many of the traditional subjects of concern to the ulema. Sijistānī, too, pursued a course of study like that of the ulema. Not only did he receive and transmit prophetic traditions, he was also himself the author of a work on this subject. So also, all of those scholars whose names are found in the riwāyahs of the texts discussed in this chapter were themselves members of this same class. There is, moreover, yet another reason to associate the formative period of the Muslim tradition of dream interpretation with the muḥaddiths and the ulema—the manner in which dream lore was transmitted.

To guarantee the authenticity of traditions, the muḥaddiths devised the institution of the isnād. Affixed to the head of a tradition, an isnād was a chain of authorities that listed the various persons responsible for having transmitted the tradition in question: "I heard it from x, who heard it from y, who head it from z, who heard it from so-and-so, that the prophet once said. . . ." At a time when most knowledge was transmitted in an oral fashion, with much distrust of the vagaries of textual transmission, this practice was oriented toward ensuring that the traditions would be properly passed from teacher to pupil. Like the other traditions transmitted by the muḥaddiths, the earliest dream lore, too, was provided with these distinctive chains of authorities. Even after oral anecdotes came to be written down, moreover, the early ulema continued to supply these traditions with chains of authorities, a pattern that recurs in the first written dream manuals. Similarly, written works could also be supplied with metachains of authorities, riwāyahs, a practice developed by the early ulema to ensure the accurate transmission of written works from authorized teacher to authorized pupil. Not surprisingly, such riwāyahs are also to be found in the majority of the dream manuals considered in this chapter. The dream manuals of Kirmānī and Ibn Qutaybah had them, as did the oneirocritic poem of Maᶜāfirī, as did many of the dream manuals that are no longer extant.[126] In sum, the manner in which the dream lore of the formative period was transmitted closely parallels the distinctive manner in which the muḥaddiths and early ulema transmitted other forms of knowledge.

Authority and Dream Interpretation

How did the dream manuals of the formative period seek to ground their authority? If we consider the first part of the formative period we find a number of strategies at work. Sometimes appeal was made to a pre-Islamic prophetic legacy. Ibn Sīrīn received his knowledge of dream interpretation from no less exalted a forebear than the prophet Joseph. This knowledge was transmitted to him not only through a dream encounter, but also through the study of a "work" on dreams by Joseph. Kirmānī, too, drew on a pre-Islamic prophetic legacy. He received Joseph's prophetic mantle in a dream, while at the same time studying "works" on dreams attributed to the prophets Abraham and Daniel. At issue here is an attempt to reach outside the Muslim tradition proper to ground dream interpretation in the figures of a pre-Islamic prophetic past. There was another, parallel method of grounding dream interpretation in the formative period, however. It involved an appeal to authorities within the prophetic movement initiated by Muḥammad. Ibn Sīrīn did not receive the work of Joseph directly. He studied it under the tutelage of Ibn al-Musayyib, who in turn had learned dream interpretation from the daughter of Abū Bakr, who for her part had received it from her father, one of the closest companions of Muḥammad. Kirmānī, too, drew on dream lore derived from the prominent early Muslims Ibn Sīrīn and Ibn al-Musayyib, who themselves stood in this prophetic lineage.

The transition from anecdote to formalism entailed a shift in the way the authority of dream interpretation was grounded. Anecdotal interpretations of dreams by their very nature derive their authority from the authority of the people responsible for the interpretations. Only seldom were justifications offered for the seemingly arbitrary linkages between dream symbols and their meanings. With the dream manual of Ibn Qutaybah we begin to see the formulation of a series of different methods that could be applied to the interpretation of dreams, irrespective of the identity of the interpreter. Interpreters needed still to be of a pious disposition. They did not, however, need to be prophets or companions of prophets or even in some way or other heirs to an earlier prophetic tradition. Interpretation was now a methodical and systematic process rather than a charismatic act. At the same time, a work like Ibn Qutaybah's had at its disposal a whole series of sources stemming from an earlier period of Muslim history. The antiquity of those sources and in particular their association with prominent figures from early Muslim history lent them an authority of their own. In this regard, even in works from the latter part of the formative period, there was still an attempt to ground the authority of dream interpretation in the legacy of prophetic monotheism. The authors of these later works did not themselves need to be direct participants in that prophetic legacy. It was enough that their authorities were "ancient" representatives of Muḥammadan prophetic monotheism, those who had stood close spiritually and temporally to the revelation vouchsafed to Muḥammad.

We should note what is *absent* from the dream manuals of the formative period. Notwithstanding the industry of Khallāl and the scope of his biographical dictionary, the extant texts do not appeal to the authoritative dream interpreters of Greece, Persia, or India. Not one of the extant sources contained a single such appeal, nor is there evidence to suggests that any of the lost works from this period contained such appeals. Authority in the formative period of the tradition was solely prophetic—whether that prophecy be pre-Islamic or Islamic. The legacies of Greece, Persia, and India may be absent from the formative period of the Muslim oneirocritic tradition. They have not, however, been forgotten. Toward the end of the fourth century A.H., nonprophetic sources will become part of the reservoir of oneirocritic authorities, and the unified tradition of dream interpretation discerned in this chapter will lose its unity. It will be transformed into four distinct but overlapping traditions, each grounding itself on a different epistemic foundation, each connected with a different class of Muslim intellectuals. It is these transformations and the four traditions of dream interpretation that resulted that are the subject of the next chapter.

CHAPTER TWO

The Fracturing of the Tradition

There was continuous development in the Muslim tradition of dream interpretation in its formative period: in particular, a transition from anecdote to formalism. In other respects, the tradition was homogeneous. The dream manuals of the formative period were all composed by the muḥaddiths (the early transmitters of prophetic traditions) and their successors, the early ulema. Moreover, dream interpretation was roundly imagined to be something transmitted to the Muslims by prophets: sometimes pre-Islamic prophets like Abraham, Joseph, and Daniel; sometimes, Muḥammad. In this chapter I argue that the homogeneity of the Muslim tradition of dream interpretation ceased by the end of the fourth century A.H., that it fractured into a number of competing legacies, each seeking to ground dream interpretation on distinct epistemic foundations, each associated with a distinct cultural orientation. Two factors facilitated the fracturing of the tradition: the appearance of new sources and the rise of rival cultural orientations within the Muslim community.

In the dream manuals of the formative period, other cultures were thought to have contributed nothing to the Muslims' understanding of dreams. In the texts considered in this chapter, we encounter for the first time appeals to nonprophetic authorities. Sometimes these were members of other religious communities, Christians, Jews, or Hindus. Sometimes they stemmed from a remoter past, the sages of Zoroastrian Persia, for example. The most important new source was Hellenic, however—the Arabic version of Artemidorus. This work's influence can be discerned in many of the dream manuals here considered, although each appropriates it in a distinct fashion. It is, thus, partly through the assimilation of new sources that the Muslim oneirocritic tradition fractured.

Some sources may have been new, only now for the first time available to Muslims. Or it may well be that these sources had long been available. While Artemidorus, for example, had already been translated into Arabic by the end of the third century A.H., at roughly the same time that Ibn Qutaybah was composing his dream manual, there is no evidence that this Hellenic work was used in the formative period. Such non-Muslim sources might have been accessible and yet made no appearance because there was no desire to use them. In addition to new sources being available, for the Muslim oneirocritic tradition to fracture it was necessary that there be new conceptual horizons that deemed it appropriate to use these new sources. Such there were—and these new conceptual horizons come to the fore in other aspects of Muslim culture as well. In this regard, Marshall G. S. Hodgson has discerned in the High Caliphal period the emergence of four "rival cultural orientations,"[1] each associated with a particular class of Muslim intellectual.

The first of Hodgson's rival cultural orientations is "the sharīᶜah-minded programme."[2] This orientation was centered on the developing tradition of Islamic law and closely associated with the religious scholars or ulema. While these religious scholars were responsible for laying the foundations of Muslim legal discourse, their cultural purview was not restricted to law. They also participated in some fields of history, as well as in the development of the grammatical sciences and literary criticism, largely to explicate the Koran. Although the religious scholars were responsible for much public religious discourse, there were many aspects of High Caliphal culture that "escaped their zealous supervision."[3] Among these was the emerging tradition of Sufism, the second of Hodgson's rival cultural orientations.[4] While the Sufis' spirituality was not unrelated to earlier trends, these Muslims cultivated a novel, intensely personal vision of Islam, one that was concerned more with the "love of God, and hence tenderness to all His creatures," than with "reverence for God and justice to all His creatures . . . the heart of the Sharīᶜah."[5] Also outside the purview of the ulema was a third cultural orientation, that of adab, the worldly culture of the polite classes.[6] Characteristic of Muslim courtiers, administrators, and landowners, adab was heavily influenced by the Sasanian imperial tradition and was closely connected with the patronage of the eastern Muslim courts. The fourth cultural orientation signaled by Hodgson was philosophic speculation.[7] Building on foundations already laid in the Hellenic milieu, Muslim philosophers sought to develop a comprehensive view of the world that was largely independent of prophetic monotheism, and hence of the sharīᶜah.

These four rival cultural orientations were not self-contained, as Hodgson himself recognized. At times the boundaries separating them were not well demarcated. There were sharīᶜah-minded Sufis and litterateurs. There were philosophically oriented Sufis and litterateurs. There were mystically inclined philosophers. When Hodgson's typology does breaks down, it is usually because he tended to define each orientation in terms of its most partisan advocates. For Hodgson, for example, Bisṭāmī and the "drunken" Sufis were paradigmatic for Sufism, not Sulamī, Qushayrī, or Sarrāj. Similarly, Hodgson made courtly adab represent adab as a whole, while the adab cultivated by the ulema fades into the background.[8] Or again, only the most Hellenic philosophers were taken as paradigmatic, while the forms of philosophic discourse cultivated by litterateurs makes no appearance.[9]

Hodgson's typology is just that, a useful schema for classifying the diverse interests of Muslim intellectuals in the High Caliphal period. Notwithstanding these reservations, Hodgson's schema does fit well the materials considered in this chapter: each of the four oneirocrits treated here belonged to one of Hodgson's four cultural orientations.

Representing the sharīᶜah-minded program is a corpus of four dream manuals by the North African Mālikī jurist, Qayrawānī. Adab forms the cultural background of the dream manual of Dīnawarī. Associated with Sufism is the work of Kharkūshī. Representing the culture of philosophy is a dream manual written by none other than the most famous of Muslim philosophers, Ibn Sīnā. These four authors are contemporaries of one another: all lived and wrote toward the end of the fourth century A.H. Biographical information allows us to assign them to one of Hodgson's four rival cultural orientations. So also, their respective cultural orientations are mirrored in the epistemic foundations of their dream manuals: how they determined what counts as knowledge, the types of sources to which they considered it legitimate to appeal, and how they constructed authoritative arguments on the basis of these sources. Before turning to the fracturing of the Muslim oneirocritic tradition, it is necessary to understand, first, how Muslim interpreters of dreams came to have access to the most important of their new sources, the dream manual of Artemidorus, a work translated by the Christian Ḥunayn b. Isḥāq. Only by understanding how Ḥunayn mediated this work can one understand the Muslim reception of Artemidorus, and thus ultimately, how and why the Muslim tradition of dream interpretation developed as it did.

ḤUNAYN B. ISḤĀQ AND THE ARABIC VERSION OF ARTEMIDORUS

The most important new source for the developing Muslim oneirocritic tradition was the dream manual of Artemidorus. Composed in Asia Minor in the second century A.D., this work is the only Hellenic dream manual to survive in its entirety into the present day.[10] It is also the only Hellenic work on dreams to have been translated into Arabic. For this translation we must thank the Nestorian Christian physician Ḥunayn b. Isḥāq.[11] Born in the late second century A.H. in the city of al-Ḥīrah, Ḥunayn studied medicine in his youth, travelling widely in Muslim lands for this purpose. While the reports are not wholly reliable, it is said that after a falling out with one of his teachers, he went to Byzantium for a number of years, and that there he learned Greek. Regardless, it is the case that Ḥunayn disappeared for a few years and that upon his reappearance he was appointed chief physician at the Abbasid court, a post he held until his death in 264/877, apart from a brief period of imprisonment as a result of the machinations of his fellow Nestorians.

Ḥunayn is remembered today primarily for his labors as a translator. He and others like him, mostly Christians, were responsible for transmitting the philosophic and scientific heritage of Hellenic antiquity to the Muslims. As for Ḥunayn himself, medieval biographers credit him with an enormous number of translations, some of which were almost certainly undertaken by his students. Most of these translations were of medical texts—but not all. Ḥunayn also concerned himself with philosophy and science, as well as with magic and divination. In addition to his translations, Ḥunayn composed a number of original works. While in subject matter they ranged from theology to meteorology, medical subjects predominated.

Among Ḥunayn's translations is a version of Artemidorus' dream manual.[12] This work survives today in a single manuscript, one that is lamentably incomplete: the final two of Artemidorus' original five books are lacking. In 1959 Toufic Fahd discovered and prepared an edition of this important work.[13] Because it reflects an exemplar that predates all known Greek manuscripts of Artemidorus' dream manual, Ḥunayn's translation has excited a great deal of interest among researchers seeking to establish the Greek version of Artemidorus.[14] Ḥunayn's translation of Artemidorus is useful to these scholars because it is quite literal, marked by a close adherence to its exemplar. Although his was a literal translation, Ḥunayn was not always content to let Artemidorus speak in his own voice. As the latter was an unrepentant polytheist, there was much about his work that was offensive to its translator and medieval readers.

Ḥunayn once described his approach to the Hellenic classics as follows:

> If the reader finds a remark in classical works beginning with the words "Galen (or Plato, Aristotle, etc.) says," and it turns out to be a strictly scientific discussion of the subject under investigation, he should study it carefully and try to understand it. If, on the other hand, it concerns questions of belief and opinion, he must take no further notice of it, since such remarks were made only to win people over to the ideas expressed in them or because they concern old, deeply rooted views.[15]

In other words, the rational traditions of the Greeks are to be given the utmost respect, while their religious views are to be dismissed as superstition. This same willingness to distinguish Hellenic science and religion governs Ḥunayn's techniques as a translator of Artemidorus. As already suggested, most of Ḥunayn's translation faithfully renders its exemplar. When it comes to Artemidorus' all too frequent expressions of religious sentiment, however, Ḥunayn is unwilling to let such scurrilous references past his censorious pen. He is compelled to rewrite his source, in nearly every instance seeking to make Artemidorus' religion more nearly monotheistic.[16] While Ḥunayn does not go so far as to make Artemidorus into a Christian, he does convert him into what might be termed a generic monotheist, one whose views would be intelligible and acceptable to most of Ḥunayn's potential readers, whether Muslim, Christian, or Jewish.

Faced with Artemidorus' references to the Hellenic gods, Ḥunayn consistently rewrites his exemplar. Sometimes Artemidorus' "many gods" become the one "God" (*Allāh*),[17] while on other occasions they become "the Lord" (*al-Rabb*).[18] More commonly, instead of changing the many gods into one, Ḥunayn substitutes in their stead "angels."[19] At times he even converts Artemidorus' gods into "God and the angels" (*Allāh wa-l-malāʾik*).[20] It is thus that Artemidorus' reference to the "Olympian gods" becomes in Ḥunayn's version "the angels of heaven," while chthonic Hecate becomes "the angel of the earth."[21] As for Apollo, he gets demoted to a hitherto unknown angel by that name.[22] There being a singular lack of female angels, sometimes the goddesses must undergo a little gender-bending. Athena, for instance, becomes "a [male] angel named Athīnā" (*al-malak alladhī yuqāl lahu Athīnā*).[23] On other occasions, the gods suffer worse demotion. Artemidorus opined: "Someone seemed [in a dream] to be eating with Chronos, and when dawn came he was thrown into prison."[24] This Ḥunayn translates: "Someone dreamt that he was eating with *a man*. When dawn came, he was seized and thrown into prison."[25]

Sometimes it is not enough for Ḥunayn simply to convert Artemidorus' gods into angels. Occasionally, to bring his source into closer conformity with the dictates of monotheism, he has to introduce more substantive changes. Once, discussing dreams in which the goddess Selene is seen, Artemidorus opined:

> For, in general, all the gods [in a dream] bear a certain resemblance to rulers. The male ones [signify] male rulers; the female ones, female rulers. The ancient saying correctly states: "To rule has the power of a god."[26]

In this case, Ḥunayn cannot simply change the gods into angels: the meaning of this type of dream turns on the relation between male and female deities, and as we have seen, Ḥunayn is chary of female angels. Ḥunayn gets out of the impasse by translating as follows:

> All the angels resemble rulers. Those with names in the masculine gender (*al-mudhakkar al-asmāʾ*) signify men. Those with names in the feminine gender (*al-muʾannath al-asmāʾ*) signify women. What was said of old is compelling: "The strength of the angels resembles the strength of the ruler."[27]

Ḥunayn's adaptation is subtle but effective: it is no longer a case of male and female gods, but of angelic names in the masculine and feminine gender.

If angels have no gender, they cannot be related to one another as mother and father, brother and sister, and so on. This poses a special problem for Ḥunayn, for Artemidorus often referred to the genealogies by which the gods and goddesses were related to one another. For instance, when Artemidorus mentioned "she who is called the Mother of the gods" (Cybele),[28] Ḥunayn needs to find a way to do away with the genealogical reference. He thus translates the phrase: "The angel who is called D.n.dūmī, who is considered to be the greatest of the angels" (*al-malak alladhī yuqāl lahu d.n.dūmī alladhī yuẓann bihi annahu akbar al-malāʾik*).[29] In effect, Ḥunayn changes Cybele into a male angel and makes of her not a mother but some sort of archangel. As for the epithet *D.n.dūmī*, this probably represents Δινδυμήνη, an adjective derived from Cybele's cultic home, the Phrygian mountain of Δίνδυμον. Although this epithet does not appear in the Greek text of Artemidorus as presently preserved, it has been suggested that it may be a marginal gloss that has worked its way into Ḥunayn's exemplar.[30]

Another problem for Ḥunayn are Artemidorus' many references to the various religious actions that humans do with respect to the gods. If the gods are no longer gods, but angels, it is no longer appropriate to do those actions. For instance, Artemidorus once mentioned in passing the worship of Asclepius:

> [To dream of] Asclepius seated in a temple and standing on a pedestal, all the while being gazed upon and worshipped (ὁρώμενος καὶ προσκυνούμενος)—this is good for all [dreamers].[31]

As Ḥunayn thinks worship appropriate only to God, he cannot simply change the reference to Asclepius into a reference to an angel by that name; he has to introduce more substantive changes.

> As for the angel called Asclepius, when someone saw him as if he was in a temple or standing on a pedestal, *howsoever he saw him* (*kayf mā raʾāhu*)—this is a good sign in all things and all actions.[32]

Or again, according to Artemidorus, to dream of cleaning the image of a god signifies that the dreamer has committed a sin against that god. Indeed, Artemidorus records that he once knew a man who had exactly such a dream. This man had, in fact, broken an oath to a god, and his dream thus signified that "it is necessary to propitiate that god" (δεῖν ἱκετεύειν τὸν θεόν). As it is quite improper to propitiate an angel, Ḥunayn translates the offending phrase as follows:

> And I know a man who saw a dream like this . . . that dream signified that it was necessary for him to venerate (*yakarrim*) that angel.

If it is improper to propitiate the angels, there is nothing amiss in venerating them.

An alternative strategy for Ḥunayn is to find for the pagan rituals analogous rituals in his own social-historical context. In this regard, he occasionally transmutes Artemidorus' references to animal sacrifices into references to the Muslims' ritual slaughtering of animals during the Feast of Immolation (*ʿīd al-aḍḥā*). Thus, for instance, Artemidorus' reference to "feasts and sacrifices" (ἑορταῖς καὶ θυσίαις) becomes in Ḥunayn's translation a reference to "wedding feasts or festivals" or "the days of the immolations" (*ayyām al-aḍāḥī*).[33] Similarly, Artemidorus' reference to "the offering of customary sacrifices to the gods" (θύειν θεοῖς τὰ νενομισμένα) takes on an equally Muslim tenor, becoming in Ḥunayn's version: "the offering of immolations according to the Sunnah" (*yuḍaḥḥī ka-l-sunnah*).[34]

The above examples should suffice to give a sense of Ḥunayn's approach to the dream manual of Artemidorus. They suggest that we should look on Ḥunayn's version not so much as a translation as an adaptation. On leaving Ḥunayn's hands, Artemidorus had not only been Arabicized. He had also been baptized, if not into the Christian faith, at least into the community of monotheists. When Ḥunayn finished with him, Artemidorus had come to speak the language of generic monotheism, a language intelligible to all of the monotheists of the early medieval Near East, whether Christians, Muslims, or Jews.

The character of Ḥunayn's version corresponds well with the context in which it was produced. Ḥunayn worked in the midst of the Greco-Arabic renaissance, a "movement closer in spirit and character to the European renaissance than any of the movements to which it has been the fashion to apply the term 'renaissance' during recent decades."[35] Coinciding with the mid-third through mid-fifth centuries A.H., this renaissance saw the wholesale transmission of Hellenic philosophy and science to the lettered elite of the Arab world. How massive was this transmission? As one of its foremost modern scholars has argued, the Greco-Arabic renaissance saw the transmission of nearly the whole of the Hellenic philosophic, medical, and scientific traditions to the Muslims, to the extent that those traditions had survived into the late antique period. It is thus that this same scholar could conclude, with no exaggeration, that "our knowledge of Greek works in these fields does not substantially differ from that of the Arabs."[36]

What united the participants of the Greco-Arabic renaissance was not a shared religion: some were Muslims, while others were Christians, Jews, or pagans. In part they were united by a shared language, the Arabic koine. More important even than language, however, was a shared interest in the Hellenic rational tradition. In fact, it was as such that the participants in this renaissance formed a distinct class of intellectuals, marked off from other classes of intellectuals, especially the more strictly religious. As I argue in this chapter, Muslim oneirocrits were divided as to whether and how to appropriate the products of the Greco-Arabic renaissance. Some eschewed any attempt to appropriate the legacy of Artemidorus. Others sought in varying degrees to synthesize the Muslim discourse on dreams with the Hellenic tradition represented by Artemidorus. Yet others cast their lot with Artemidorus, rejecting the whole of the Muslim oneirocritic tradition and substituting in its stead a version derived from Artemidorus. It is to the variegated reception of Artemidorus' dream manual that I now turn.

QAYRAWĀNĪ: A SHARĪᶜAH-MINDED INTERPRETER OF DREAMS

Toward the end of the Middle Ages, describing some of the dream manuals with which he was familiar, the famous historian and jurist Ibn Khaldūn stated: "Also in circulation among the people of North Africa at present are the books of Ibn Abī Ṭālib al-Qayrawānī, one of the religious scholars of Qayrawān: for example, his *al-Mumatti*ᶜ and other books."[37] A copy of Qayrawānī's *Mumatti*ᶜ has now come to light in manuscript form. It is also now possible to reconstruct a corpus of three additional, shorter dream manuals by this author, all extant only in manuscript form. Notwithstanding the extent of his oneirocritic labors, this Qayrawānī seems to have escaped the notice of the medieval biographical tradition, including that specifically devoted to the religious scholars of Qayrawān.[38] Modern researchers, as well, have been able to determine little about him.[39] Sufficient evidence is now available, however, to determine that the author of these dream manuals was a Mālikī jurist who flourished in the early fifth century A.H.

In the introduction to his *Mumatti*ᶜ, Qayrawānī supplied a list of the major sources on which he relied. Each of these sources was provided with a full riwāyah. The last links in these riwāyahs were Qayrawānī's teachers and can thus provide an approximate date for his own work. Among those with whom he studied, two of the most important were Abū ᶜImrān al-Fāsī (d. 430/1038) and Abū ᶜAbd Allāh al-Anṣārī (d. 428/1036).[40] Moreover, the *Mumatti*ᶜ must have been written after 420/1029: this is clear from a passage where Qayrawānī dates his reception of a certain prophetic tradition to that year.[41] Qayrawānī's full name was Abū al-Ḥasan ᶜAlī b. Saᶜīd al-Khawlānī commonly known as Ibn al-Qaṣṣār al-Qayrawānī, although he was also called Abū al-Ḥasan ᶜAlī b. Abī Ṭālib.[42] That he was a member of the Mālikī school of law is clear. It is suggested by his association with Abū ᶜImrān al-Fāsī, a prominent North African Mālikī jurist of reformist bent. As just noted, from him Qayrawānī received a number of his sources. In his *Mumatti*ᶜ, Qayrawānī also often cited traditions in his name and even called him "our shaykh."[43] Moreover, it was to Abū ᶜImrān al-Fāsī that Qayrawānī dedicated one of his shorter dream manuals.[44] His juridical affiliation is also indicated by his links to the well-known Mālikī jurist Abū Dharr al-Harawī (d. 434/1042).[45] Also suggestive is a later tradition stating that a certain Abū al-Ḥasan b. Abī Ṭālib "the dream interpreter" wrote a work entitled *Muwaṭṭa*ᵓ *al-muwaṭṭa*ᵓ, apparently an abridgment of Mālik's *Muwaṭṭa*ᵓ.[46] This much and little else is known of Qayrawānī. The only other information on him that I have been able to discover is a short tradition recounting a dream consultation between him and a certain North African ruler.[47]

Qayrawānī's Shorter Dream Manuals

As noted above, Ibn Khaldūn ascribed to Qayrawānī not only the *Mumatti*ᶜ, but also "other books" on the interpretation of dreams.[48] Three such works have come to light in manuscript form. The first of these shorter dream manuals is preserved in five manuscripts: two in Istanbul,[49] and one each in Paris,[50] Rabat,[51] and Milan.[52] This work is arranged by subject and divided into thirty chapters, the order of which follows closely his *Mumatti*ᶜ. In a short preface, Qayrawānī states that by the providence of God a certain person had asked him to compose an abbreviated work on the interpretation of dreams, one that accords with the opinions of earlier writers on the subject. The person requesting the work insisted further that it be provided with Koranic proof texts, so that it might be easier to memorize, and that it be small enough to carry around with ease. Qayrawānī obliged and compiled the present work. A cursory introduction seeks to show that true dreams are "glad tidings sent by God for the community of Muḥammad following the cessation of revelation."[53] This section consists largely of prophetic traditions in which Muḥammad declared dreams to be a form of prophetic knowledge or that show Muḥammad and his companions to have themselves been interpreters of dreams. Almost all of these traditions are also found in his *Mumattiᶜ*. A few are provided with abbreviated isnāds specifying that Qayrawānī derived them from ᶜAbd al-Malik b. Ḥabīb.[54] Qayrawānī himself aptly sums up the import of these traditions: "Thus, learned folk agree that the prophet of God interpreted dreams; not him alone, for the companions and successors, as well as those who came later, were also keen on this subject."[55]

The second of Qayrawānī's shorter dream manuals is extant in a Vatican manuscript[56] and perhaps also in a manuscript in Cairo.[57] It, too, is arranged according to subject. Qayrawānī divides the work into fifty-eight chapters, the order of which diverges sharply from that found in his *Mumattiᶜ*, and following the latter, the first of his shorter dream manuals. Apart from a rather generic offering of praise to God, the work has no preface. Qayrawānī begins immediately with his introduction, the themes of which and even at times its exact wording parallel closely the first of his shorter dream manuals.

The third of Qayrawānī's shorter dream manuals is extant in a single Moroccan manuscript.[58] Qayrawānī indicates in his preface that he wrote it for Abū ᶜImrān al-Fāsī (d. 430/1038), whom he expressly identifies as "our shaykh." He further states that this was the second work on dreams that Abū ᶜImrān had asked him to write. The earlier work had apparently fallen short of the needs of its readers. In particular, because it was difficult to memorize, students "were going astray in their attempts to interpret dreams and were unable to get a handle on the science." Qayrawānī responded by reorganizing the earlier work. Instead of structuring it by dream symbols, he would group in each of its thirty chapters all dreams that bear the same meaning, a format unique among Muslim dream manuals. The following is typical:

> Chapter Five: *On Signs Indicating the Proper Conduct of Scholars and Rulers or the Just Action of Administrators, Judges, and Those in Power*: Such signs are manifold. Example—if a holy book or scale or measure descends from the heavens into a city with which you are familiar, justice and truth will descend on that land, from the king, from its judge, from one of its scholars, or from one who resembles these. Example—if you see that the resurrection has taken place and

> that God . . . is judging between men, there will be justice in that place, those who are oppressed will be victorious, while those who oppress will be subject to vengeance, even as takes place in the world to come. Example—if rain falls everywhere and the ground becomes verdant, justice will appear in the land because of the action of the sultan, though occasionally it means forbearance and mercy; sometimes also it is a righteous prayer leader who will bring justice and blessings and restore the land from death and corruption.[59]

Continuing thus, Qayrawānī lists the other dreams indicating the same outcome, while in the next chapter he lays out those dreams that indicate the opposite. He follows this procedure for the whole of the work, dividing it into fifteen parts, presenting first an auspicious meaning and then its opposite. It is Qayrawānī's hope that this manner of organization would facilitate memorization. Indeed, he declares himself confident that each of its thirty chapters would take no more than "one day and a night" to memorize in its entirety.

Qayrawānī's Mumatti^c^

Qarawānī's *Mumatti^c^* is extant in just a single manuscript, preserved in the Süleymaniye.[60] This manuscript has, lamentably, suffered much in the course of its transmission and contains a number of lacunae.[61] It is thus fortunate that there are two anonymous dream manuals that made wide use of Qayrawānī's work, so much so that any future edition of the *Mumatti^c^* would have to make extensive use of their testimony. Both are extant in apparently unique copies in the Süleymaniye.[62] Qayrawānī's *Mumatti^c^* is immense. It is by far the largest compilation extant from the late fourth and early fifth centuries A.H. It is divided into two parts. The first is an introduction.[63] The second is the dream manual proper. The latter Qayrawānī organizes by subject, dividing it into thirty-two chapters, each of which is subdivided a great many times. The numerous lacunae in the text make it impossible to determine the original number of subdivisions: the text as it now stands has about four hundred and fifty.

Like earlier works, in his dream manual proper Qayrawānī begins with dreams of God, angels, prophets, paradise, and the rituals of Islam, before taking up more mundane dream symbols. On the whole, Qayrawānī presents his data in a formalistic manner. "If someone see something, such and such will happen." This general pattern is only occasionally varied. Sometimes he includes an anecdote about dreams interpreted by Muḥammad or one of the companions. Sometimes he attempts to justify the interpretations by appealing to proof texts from the Koran or the words of anonymous poets. Such variations are rare, however. The majority of his dream manual follows a strictly formalistic manner of presentation.

Qayrawānī does not explain in detail why he composed his *Mumatti*ᶜ. In a short preface, he simply states that a certain person had requested it and that this was a result of God's providence. While Qayrawānī does not identify this person, his language suggests that the recipient of the work was a jurist.[64] As for his introduction, in it Qayrawānī seldom speaks with his own voice: most of it consists of traditions stemming from an earlier age. These Qayrawānī dutifully copies out verbatim, grouping them into related categories, weaving them together to make of them a more or less coherent whole. His own voice appears only occasionally: sometimes to introduce the general topic of a series of traditions; very occasionally to comment on those traditions.

Qayrawānī's *Mumatti*ᶜ is almost unique among Muslim dream manuals for its tendency to cite books rather than people as its authorities. Because of this, it offers valuable information—usually without parallel—on the earliest period of the Muslim tradition of dream interpretation. It will be recalled from the previous chapter how important Qayrawānī's testimony was for determining the contours of Ibn Sīrīn's legacy. Some of the sources to which Qayrawānī has access are well known: the *Kitāb al-manāmāt* (Book of Dreams) of Ibn Abī Dunyā and the dream manuals of Kirmānī and Ibn Qutaybah,[65] or collections of prophetic traditions by Bukhārī, Ibn ᶜUyaynah, Nasāʾī, and Ibn Wahb. Others are less well known.

Qayrawānī makes extensive use of a book on dreams by a certain Ibn al-Mughīrah. He provides a riwāyah for this work in his introduction[66] and gives a fuller version of the author's name—ᶜAbd al-Raḥmān b. al-Mughīrah al-Ḥizāmī. I have been unable to identify this person.[67] Regardless, his *floruit* can be firmly placed in the beginning of the third Islamic century, for, according to its riwāyah, Ibn al-Mughīrah's work was first transmitted by Hārūn b. Mūsā al-Farwī (d. 253/867).[68] Judging from the numerous citations found in the *Mumatti*ᶜ, Ibn al-Mughīrah's dream manual consisted largely of anecdotes attributed to Ibn Sīrīn. Most of these Ibn al-Mughīrah transmitted at one remove. There are a great many citations from Ibn al-Mughīrah's text in the *Mumatti*ᶜ. They average about one per page.

Qayrawānī also makes extensive use of a number of works by the Mālikī jurist Abū Marwān ᶜAbd al-Malik b. Ḥabīb al-Sulamī (d. 238/852).[69] Qayrawānī mentions by name an otherwise unknown work of his on the creation of the world.[70] He also occasionally cites Ibn Ḥabīb's collection of prophetic traditions.[71] More intriguing, however, are the numerous references to a certain "book of Ibn Ḥabīb." From it Qayrawānī takes anecdotal accounts of Ibn Sīrīn's interpretation of dreams, usually without providing any isnāds. Citations from this text can be found on nearly every page of the *Mumatti*ᶜ.

Qayrawānī also frequently cites a work on dream interpretation by the famous traditionist Nuᶜaym b. Ḥammād (d. 228/844),[72] a text known from other sources.[73] Like the dream manuals of Ibn al-Mughīrah and Ibn Ḥabīb, Nuᶜaym's work appears to have consisted largely of anecdotal narratives. Of the numerous citations found in the dream manual of Qayrawānī, most are anecdotes concerning Ibn Sīrīn and his interpretations of dreams. Most are transmitted at one remove, though some rely on two intermediate transmitters. I would estimate that there are about one hundred citations of Nu^{c}aym's text in the *Mumatti^{c}*.

Qayrawānī also has frequent recourse to the dream manual of a certain Mis^{c}adah b. Yasa^{c}. While the medieval biographical tradition knew little about this person, he is said to have transmitted prophetic traditions from the last of the successors.[74] Qayrawānī supplies a riwāyah for his dream manual.[75] Based on this, Mis^{c}adah's *floruit* can be placed in the beginning of the third Islamic century. Qayrawānī transmits from Mis^{c}adah traditions about Ibn Sīrīn's feats of interpretation—usually at one remove. The most frequent intermediary was a certain Sulaymān Abū Muḥammad. Some traditions, however, are transmitted by the son of Ibn Sīrīn.[76] Mis^{c}adah's is the text most frequently cited in the *Mumatti^{c}*, once or twice on almost every page.[77]

Other works are utilized less frequently. In his introductory chapter,[78] Qayrawānī cites a well-known prophetic tradition to the effect that dreams are from God, whereas nightmares are from Satan, and that should a nightmare be seen, the dreamer should spit thrice to his left and take refuge with God. His source for this was a work entitled *Kitāb Ibn Sīrīn* (The Book of Ibn Sīrīn) by ^{c}Īsā b. Dīnār (d. 212/827).[79] Elsewhere Qayrawānī appeals to an anonymous book on the interpretation of dreams.[80] From this he takes a number of traditions, mostly prophetic, touching on dreams. Qayrawānī makes occasional use of an otherwise unattested dream manual by Abū Ja^{c}far Muḥammad b. ^{c}Amr b. Mūsā b. Ḥammād al-^{c}Uqaylī (d. 322/933).[81] He also employs a work on the interpretation of dreams by a certain Abū Bakr al-Mawṣilī.[82] Also intriguing are the occasional references to a work by a certain Abū Ṭalḥah "in the riwāyah of Hishām,"[83] a work that is also at times referred to simply as the book of Hishām[84] or as the book of Abū Ṭalḥah.[85] This text supplies Qayrawānī with anecdotes about Ibn Sīrīn.

Qayrawānī's *Mumatti^{c}* is distinguished from other, contemporary dream manuals not only by its propensity to cite books rather than people, but also by its tendency to ground dream interpretation solely in an archetypal, Islamic prophetic past. Qayrawānī seeks to explicate the principles governing dream interpretation, and even at times defend its legitimacy, by absorbing into his own work the authoritative testimony of Muḥammad and his closest followers. While he places primary emphasis on the Koran and the example of Muḥammad, also significant are those who were intimately linked to Muḥammad, whether companions or successors. It is from such authorities that he compiles his introduction, and beyond their testimony he seldom traverses. Three examples may serve to illustrate Qayrawānī's overall methodological orientation.

The first is Qayrawānī's discussion of the nature of dreams, at the very beginning of his introduction.[86] Following his short preface, Qayrawānī turns immediately to a discussion of "the dream and its power," by which he means the nature of dreams and their exalted status. He begins by citing a Koranic verse generally taken to apply to God's granting of prophetic dreams: "Those who believe and are pious have glad tidings (*al-bushrā*) in this world and the next" (Q 10.63–64). Next, in quick succession, he provides an overview of the major prophetic traditions justifying the legitimacy of dream interpretation, of which he notes six: good dreams are a part of prophecy; Muḥammad's revelation came through true dreams; following Muḥammad's death, only dreams remain; with the death of Muḥammad, the sending of divine messages and prophecy itself are cut off, while dreams remain; Abū Bakr used to ask Muḥammad about the interpretation of dreams. In this first section of his introduction, Qayrawānī's own voice intrudes into the discussion only once—to gloss the word *al-bushrā* in the Koranic citation: "It is said that *al-bushrā* is a true dream that a good man sees or that is seen for him." In fact, his gloss is itself a paraphrase of a prophetic tradition.[87] Qayrawānī's procedure in this section is typical. He restricts himself to topics already present in materials stemming from the age of the prophet, especially the Koran and the example of Muḥammad. He constructs his arguments through appeals to these materials, and beyond them he is unwilling to go.

The second example comes from the end of his introduction, where Qayrawānī treats of a number of puzzling prophetic traditions.[88] His job here is that of exegete and harmonizer. He tries to provide interpretations of these traditions that harmonize with the meaning of other, more manifest traditions. One such puzzling tradition reads: "A dream has its surnames (*kunan*) and its given names (*asmāʾ*), so call them by their surnames and interpret them by their given names."[89] A strange tradition, but not as strange as it might at first seem. Following an earlier authority, Qayrawānī explains that the "names" by which one is enjoined to interpret dreams are actually the names of the persons who have such dreams. Thus, for example, someone named Saʿīd ("happy") will have dreams relating to happiness, and so on for other names with auspicious etymologies. Such explanations are insufficient, however. Qayrawānī must also find a prophetic example to justify this interpretation. One lies close at hand, which he cites at length:

> The prophet said: I saw in a dream that I was in the house of ʿUqbah b. Rāfiʿ and that I was brought some fresh dates from the supply of Ibn Ṭāb. I interpreted this as follows: We shall have elevation (*rifʿah*) in this world and a reward (*ʿāqibah*) in the next world. Moreover, our religion has come to fruition (*ṭāb*).

In this anecdote, the meaning of the dream turns on the etymology of the names in it. Accordingly, Qayrawānī can conclude that Muḥammad himself had appealed to etymology to interpret dreams. An explicit prophetic tradition thus provides Qayrawānī with the key to unlock the meaning of an otherwise obscure prophetic tradition.

Third, for Qayrawānī, the sole foundation on which a dream manual could be constructed is that of an archetypal, Islamic prophetic past. This past provides Qayrawānī not only with the raw materials out of which to construct an account of dreams and the proper methods for interpreting them. It also provides him with a model for proper human conduct, a model to be followed by both dreamer and dream interpreter. For example, making use solely of materials drawn from prophetic tradition, Qayrawānī finely scripts the act of a dreamer's coming to a dream interpreter, reporting a dream, and receiving its interpretation.[90] Even the very words one uses during the consultation are laid down by prophetic example. When the dream is narrated, the interpreter must say, following the prophet: "By God, if your dream is auspicious, may it apply to you; if inauspicious, to your enemies." When beginning to interpret the dream, following the example of Muḥammad's close followers, one must preface one's interpretation with the words: "If your dream speaks truth. . . ." Only then is it permitted to offer an interpretation.

All three examples point up how thoroughly Qayrawānī relies on prophetic traditions as his primary authorities and how he attempts to ground dream interpretation in this aspect of knowledge alone. This is not to say that Qayrawānī is ignorant of other, later Muslim oneirocritic works. While he uses such works, it is only because they had cited earlier, prophetic authorities. Indeed, throughout his dream manual Qayrawānī is always careful when using these later works to reproduce fully their own chains of authority. In general, these later works are significant for him only insofar as they offer access to an earlier, prophetic past.

One may also note what is absent from Qayrawānī's dream manual. He makes no use of authorities stemming from a pre-Islamic past. Although he explicitly recognizes that the pre-Islamic prophets had all been experts in the interpretation of dreams, he does not appeal to them. There is no hint of the authorities of the formative period—Daniel, Joseph, or Abraham. Equally absent from his dream manual are appeals to non-Muslim authorities. Other contemporary Muslim dream manuals make extensive use of dream lore stemming, so they believed, from the Zoroastrians or Indians, or from the other religious communities of the Near East, or even from Greece and Rome. Qayrawānī wholly eschews such sources. To my knowledge, not once in his massive work does he cite such authorities, or even betray a knowledge of their existence.

Qayrawānī shows, further, a marked tendency to avoid speculating about topics not explicitly treated in the prophetic traditions. He prefers a pious ignorance to an impious prying into questions not treated in his sources. Consider, for example, his treatment of how dreams are able to convey knowledge of future events.[91] The spirit (*rūḥ*) or soul (*nafs*) ascends in sleep and come into the presence of the throne of God. There the angel of dreams, Ṣidūq (vocalization uncertain), shows them information found on the "well-preserved tablet." A number of prophetic traditions are cited to this effect, most derived from the earlier discussion of Ibn Qutaybah. Qayrawānī admits that his discussion of this subject does not provide all that one might like to know. Other authors, indeed, had offered more thorough discussions of these subjects. He, however, will not treat such matters. He is content to know that the existence of spirit and soul are confirmed by prophetic traditions. And in the end, he takes refuge in our inability to know the precise significance of spirit and soul, being justified in this by the humbling Koranic verse: "They will ask you about the spirit. Say: The spirit is of the command of my Lord. You have been granted of knowledge nothing but a little" (Q 17.85).

Qayrawānī's tendency to avoid speculation appears to be linked to an apologetic subtext running through his work. He seems to be trying to answer the objections of certain opponents who did not approve of dream interpretation. He wants to suggest that those who reject dream interpretation also reject the prophet, whose example justifies, indeed mandates an interest in the subject. One may note, for instance, his appeal to the testimony of an unnamed scholar, one of the very rare nonprophetic authorities cited, who was "well-versed in the science of dreams," and who argued that "those who reject and scorn the science of dream interpretation and induce other people to avoid it, such as these have belittled what the prophet has exalted."[92] In other words, to reject dream interpretation is to reject the prophet and his commands. Through his assembly of prophetic testimony, Qayrawānī argues, in effect, that it is incumbent on good Muslims to attend to their dreams and their prophetic significance, and that the interpretation of dreams is a sharᶜī or normative discipline, a practice justified by the example of Muḥammad and his early followers.

In effect, Qayrawānī limits the scope of his dream manual by limiting the types of sources to which appeal is permitted. This means that his work evinces no interest in speculative matters. In this regard, his dream manual differs markedly from other contemporaneous texts, in particular those of Dīnawarī and Ibn Sīnā. Both authors can ask questions of a speculative nature—What is sleep? How does prophecy occur in dreams? and so on—because they are willing to use different sources, in particular those of Hellenic derivation. Qayrawānī, by contrast, avoids such questions, structuring his work around a thematic bequeathed to him in prophetic materials.

THE DREAM MANUAL OF THE LITTERATEUR DĪNAWARĪ

In the month of Ramaḍān 399/1008, Abū Saᶜd Naṣr b. Yaᶜqūb al-Dīnawarī finished compiling a massive work on the interpretation of dreams. This text he dedicates to the Abbasid caliph al-Qādir Billāh (r. 381/991–422/1031). Seemingly playing on the name of his patron, he entitled it *al-Qādirī fī ᶜilm al-taᶜbīr* (Qādir's Work on Dream Interpretation, or The Powerful Work on Dream Interpretation). Dīnawarī's compilation was enormous—the copy used here consists of almost four hundred and fifty folios with approximately twenty lines per page. Notwithstanding its size, it enjoyed a wide circulation among later readers. I know of more than forty copies in manuscript form.[93] It was an important source for a number of subsequent Muslim dream manuals.[94] It was also translated into Persian in the Middle Ages.[95]

While the medieval Muslim biographical tradition has preserved little information about Dīnawarī, enough is known to associate him with the adab culture of the court. The only independent biographical notice on Dīnawarī seems to be that written by his contemporary Thaᶜālibī.[96] As to profession, Dīnawarī was apparently a government functionary or clerk. Writing in 403/1012, Thaᶜālibī records that Dīnawarī was at that time a resident of Nishapur and that there he was charged with overseeing and distributing military pensions.[97] Dīnawarī was also linked to the rising star of Maḥmūd of Ghazna. So impressed was the latter with Dīnawarī's abilities as a stylist that he often employed his services when in need of a gracious letter to send the caliph al-Qādir Billāh.[98] Also intriguing is an obscure passage in Thaᶜālibī that may suggest that Dīnawarī had been at one time a courtier in the circle of the amir and oneirocrit Sijistānī.[99] Dīnawarī was a master of Arabic verse. Fragments of his poems have been preserved.[100] He was best known, however, for his compositions in rhymed Arabic prose. Thaᶜālibī opined that Dīnawarī's works were splendid examples of this genre and in proof of this opinion included in his biographical notice a large sample of his work.[101]

In addition to a dream manual, Dīnawarī wrote a number of other works. Two treated literary themes. The first seems to have concerned metaphors used to describe Persians, while the second seems to have treated innovative metaphors in general.[102] Neither text is extant. Also no longer extant is a work entitled *Kitāb al-adᶜiyah* (The Book of Invocations), which apparently consisted of a collection of anecdotes concerning pious invocations.[103] Another work by Dīnawarī concerned stones and their virtues.[104] Although this work is no longer extant, one of Dīnawarī's contemporaries, Bīrūnī (d. 440/1048), made use of it and incorporated enough citations to allow one to grasp something of its character.[105] Judging from these, Dīnawarī's concern for stones was not natural science for its own sake. Rather, he was interested in the telling anecdote and in accounts of oddities and marvels. Dīnawarī wrote the text in Persian. This should not be surprising: the cultivation of literary Persian began only in the fourth century A.H., largely by litterateurs, as an alternative to the ulema's monopoly on Arabic.

Dīnawarī opens his dream manual with an artfully constructed prologue.[106] He praises God for his providential care, especially for his having taught Muḥammad the interpretation of dreams. God taught this science not only to the prophet of Islam, but also to earlier ones such as Abraham, Jacob, and Joseph. In addition to the prophets, God taught others about the interpretation of dreams: "the rightly guided caliphs, the companions, the emigrants and the helpers, the successors, jurists, saints and ascetics." At this point in his preface, Dīnawarī "protects" his work, mentioning first his own name and then the title of his text. He then specifies that the work was composed for al-Qādir Billāh, whom he praises in ebullient fashion. He continues by suggesting the wide range of sources on which he drew in the compilation of his work: reliable interpreters of dreams, Koranic commentators, saints, philosophers, doctors, poets, pre-Islamic diviners, physiognomists, magicians, bishops, monks, and scholars of the Koran, Gospel, Pentateuch, and traditions of the prophet. He then disclaims any originality, confessing himself only a compiler who faithfully transmits the materials of earlier experts. He concludes by noting the date on which he finished compiling the work (Ramaḍān 399/1008).

Following his preface and a table of contents, Dīnawarī turns to theoretical matters of interest to the interpreter of dreams.[107] He divides this, his introduction, into fifteen sections:

1. The nature of sleep.
2. How the dreamer should behave to have true dreams.
3. How dreams are able to predict the future.
4. Ṣidīqūn (vocalization uncertain), the angel of dreams.
5. The definition of dreams and their relation to prophecy.
6. On the various types of true dreams.
7. On the various types of false dreams.
8. When in the day dreams are most true.
9. When in the year they are most true.
10. The nature of dream interpretation.
11. The proper behavior of the dreamer.
12. The proper behavior of the dream interpreter.
13. How to use omens to interpret dreams.
14. How the day in which a dream is seen affects its meaning.
15. Summary of Khallāl's *Ṭabaqāt al-muᶜabbirīn*.

Many of the topics treated in Dīnawarī's introduction are paralleled in other Muslim dream manuals. The last three sections alone are unique. Sections thirteen and fourteen concern how omens can provide clues for interpreting dreams. The former describes how to interpret dreams based on the names of people one encounters at random in the street or the cries of animals, while the latter treats the auspiciousness of each of the days of the week. The final section contains a summary of Khallāl's biographical dictionary of interpreters of dreams. If many of the topics in Dīnawarī's introduction are not new, some of his sources are. Alongside common traditions from the prophet or his companions, we also find extensive appeals to non-Muslim authors.

Sometimes Dīnawarī refers to Hellenic sages. Aristotle provides him with definitions of sleep and dreams.[108] From Artemidorus Dīnawarī takes his typology of dreams: there are two types of true dreams, those that are manifest and thus do not need interpretation, and those that are symbolic and demand interpretation.[109] From Artemidorus he likewise takes his discussion of false dreams.[110]

In addition, Dīnawarī appeals to the authority of a mysterious Greek called Afrīṭis (vocalization uncertain).[111] He also cites the opinions of contemporary Byzantine Christians.[112] At issue is a series of distinctions concerning the relative truth and falsity of dreams: the earlier in the night that the dream appears, the less true it is; the later in the night, the more quickly it comes true; dreams had while lying on one's right side arise from gluttony, while those had while on the left are true; those had while lying on one's back arise from desire, unless one is a sage, priest, or monk, whereas those that take place when one sleeps on one's stomach arise from lust. And finally, Dīnawarī makes extensive use of traditions ascribed to the prophet Daniel.[113] Much of his discussion of omens in sections thirteen and fourteen is based on his authority, as is his analysis of how dreams are able to convey knowledge of the future and his provision of the dimensions of the angel Ṣidīqūn, a being so massive that a journey from his earlobes to his shoulders requires a journey of seven-hundred years.

For all its apparent erudition, Dīnawarī's introduction does not rise above being a relatively undigested compilation of disparate materials. The diverse traditions and opinions that he cites are seldom linked together by the author's own narration; instead, they stand next to one another in relative isolation. It is left to the reader to draw out their implications or resolve their contradictions. As an example of this phenomenon, consider the third section of Dīnawarī's introduction, the ostensible purpose of which is to explain "the how of dreams" (*kayfīyat al-ruʾyā*).[114] The author opens with a quotation from "Daniel the prophet," in which it is explained that, in dreams, spirits are taken to the seventh heaven into the presence of the Lord, where they are urged to prostrate themselves, those pure doing so beneath the throne of the Lord, those impure doing so farther off. The moral of this story is then explicitly stated: "Hence the need for a man to sleep only after ablutions." The narrative has, however, been transferred from its original context and cited here for its account of the ascent of spirits in their dreams. Dīnawarī next cites the opinions of certain unnamed "Muslim interpreters of dreams." These opined that it is the spirit that sees the dream and the mind that understands it. Spirit resides in the blood of the heart, whereas mind dwells in the fat of the brain. Spirit is further said to be dependent on soul. When sleep occurs, spirit goes forth like a lamp. By its light and the light of God it sees what the angel of the dream wishes to show it. When one awakes, the spirit remembers what it saw and represents it to the soul in such a way that it becomes like something seen by the eyes. Then follows an obscure and unrelated quote from Aristotle: "Spiritual sense signifies what really is, that is, the dream; animal [sense] signifies what exists, that is, in waking." This is followed by an even more obscure statement of Afrīṭis the Sage, to the effect that soul goes from the body to heaven, roams about in the kingdom and the two earths, sees what God wills, and returns to the body, whereas spirit ascends to heaven in a dream and goes forth from the soul and sees what it could not see while awake. Thus ends the section. Other than in the title of the section, there is no place where the authorial voice of Dīnawarī intrudes. He cites the four traditions, but makes no attempt to synthesize or otherwise reconcile their diverse or contradictory contents.

Dīnawarī organizes his dream manual proper by subject. As with other Muslim dream manuals, he begins with dreams of God, the angels, prophets, and the companions. Following such matters, he turns his attention to more mundane dream symbols. Dreams of other religious subjects, such as the Koran or the various rites and institutions associated with Islam are interspersed among the later divisions of the text. Dīnawarī divides his work into thirty divisions. Each of these divisions is further subdivided into chapters, sometimes a great many. Division Six, for example, which treats of "Dreams of Man and His Members from Birth to Death," is subdivided into no less than 152 chapters. In total, the work contains 1,396 such chapters.

There is little novel about the way Dīnawarī presents his interpretations of the various dream symbols. On the whole he follows a formalistic methodology. He habitually avoids cluttering up his presentation by relegating any anecdotes or entertaining stories to separate chapters that immediately follow his initial presentation of the data on any particular dream symbol. These chapters are invariably entitled either *Fī ᶜilāwah min al-ruʾyah al-muᶜabbarah* (In Addition: From the Interpreted Dream) or *Fī ᶜilāwah min al-ruʾyah al-mujarrabah* (In Addition: From the Tested Dream). The subjects of these anecdotes have already been seen in other Muslim dream manuals: Muḥammad, various companions, Ibn Sīrīn or Ibn al-Musayyib, or occasionally literary and religious notables from the second or third centuries A.H. It should be emphasized, however: Dīnawarī is quite sparing in his inclusion of such stories. In much the same fashion, Dīnawarī seldom complicates his presentation with justifications of the interpretations that he offers. Aside from an occasional Koranic verse, the validity of an interpretation is either simply assumed or resides in the authority to whom it is ascribed.

While Dīnawarī's format is not terribly novel, the sources to which he appeals are. The various interpretations that he offers are often anonymous. Sometimes, however, he specifies his sources. Occasionally the Muslims are explicitly acknowledged as his authorities: "The Muslims say. . . ." More noteworthy are the numerous interpretations ascribed to the various religious or cultural communities of the Near East. Dīnawarī's purview is far reaching, both geographically and historically. Numerous dreams are interpreted by the legendary Zoroastrian sage, Jāmāsb. Other interpretations are ascribed to the Indians: including a number of anecdotes that present Brahmins as interpreting dreams. Yet other interpretations are ascribed to anonymous Greeks or even at times to certain Byzantines. The only Greek oneirocrit cited by name, however, is Artemidorus. Dīnawarī uses Ḥunayn's version of Artemidorus extensively: indeed, nearly all of it is included in direct citations in his text. Dīnawarī also has no problem using the testimony of certain anonymous Christians and Jews, who are constantly cited as authorities for the interpretation of dreams.

Dīnawarī's voice only appears occasionally in the course of his presentation, most often when he wants his readers to know that he has treated some particular topic elsewhere in the dream manual. If Dīnawarī's own voice is often silent, so also is any attempt to privilege the authority of the Muslim interpreters of dreams over any of the others whose opinions he cites. He is content to refer to the varying opinions of the diverse interpreters of dreams. It is in this sense that his dream manual can be called "cosmopolitan," that it can be associated with the litterateurs, and that it is most markedly distinguished from the dream manuals of his contemporaries and predecessors. Nevertheless, while Dīnawarī made extensive use of non-Muslim sources, in particular Artemidorus, the structure of his dream manual still follows that of the works of Qayrawānī. Dīnawarī has not subordinated the Muslim tradition of dream interpretation to the oneirocritic traditions of other cultures. In this regard, his work is not dissimilar to that of Kharkūshī.

KHARKŪSHĪ: SUFISM, DREAM INTERPRETATION, AND TRADITION

The author of the next dream manual to be considered was the Sufi Abū Saᶜd ᶜAbd al-Malik b. Abī ᶜUthmān al-Wāᵓiẓ al-Kharkūshī (d. ca. 406/1015).[115] Few details about Kharkūshī are preserved in the frequent but repetitive biographical notices on him.[116] We gather that he was born in Nishapur and that his place of residence in that city was the alley of Kharkūsh, whence his name. It is said that his father was ascetically inclined, a practice taken up by his son. It is further recorded that he made his living by making and selling the *qalansuwah*, a type of hat. He could hardly have been poor, however: almost all biographical notices take care to note his pious building projects, including mosques, cisterns, bridges, and roads, as well as a hospital and a school. Kharkūshī is said to have traveled widely in the pursuit of learning. Places where he studied included Iraq, the Hijaz, Egypt, and Syria. He made the pilgrimage at least twice. He died in 406/1015 or the following year and was buried in Nishapur in the alley of Kharkūsh.

Contemporaries and later generations remembered Kharkūshī for his piety, good works, and ascetic renunciation. He was also renowned as the author of a number of works—in addition to his dream manual. Some are extant. One is a manual of Sufism, a work dependent on a similar manual written by one of Kharkūshī's rather more famous Sufi contemporaries, Sarrāj.[117] Another is a biography of Muḥammad.[118] Also ascribed to him, but no longer extant, are a work on Koranic commentary, as well as a number of other works.[119] As for his dream manual, Kharkūshī entitled it *al-Bishārah wa-l-nidhārah fī taᶜbīr al-ruᵓyā* (Glad Tidings and Warnings: On the Interpretation of Dreams). The number of extant copies attests its popularity with medieval readers,[120] as does its wide use by authors of later dream manuals.[121]

Kharkūshī begins his dream manual with a short preface in rhyming prose.[122] He praises God for making the night a protective covering, and dreams a means of rest, while he reserved the day for activity. He continues by acclaiming God for his foreknowledge, power, and providential care for his creation, but most especially for his having chosen Muḥammad as a prophet. The themes of Kharkūshī's preface are rather generic. He does not explain the reasons why he wrote his dream manual, nor the sources on which he drew, nor the methodology that he employed.

As for Kharkūshī's introduction, it is a collection of traditions arranged by topic.[123] The author seldom intrudes his own voice into the presentation. When he does, it is usually to offer a heading for the traditions being presented or a short summary of the import of the traditions that have been presented. Most of the traditions he includes are well known from other contexts—either collections of prophetic traditions or other dream manuals. On the whole, Kharkūshī's manner of presentation lends his introduction a fragmentary character: it is a collection of self-contained traditions strung loosely together with topic statements and one-sentence summaries.

Kharkūshī begins his introduction with a discussion of the difference between prophets and messengers: the former receive revelation in dreams; the latter, from the tongue of an angel, while in a waking state.[124] He follows this with a collection of (largely) prophetic traditions that mention dreams. The import of this collection is explicitly stated to be that of showing that dreams can be true. He next turns to a series of narratives that depict various prophets as concerning themselves with dreams. He begins with Adam and ends with Muḥammad. At this point, Kharkūshī intrudes himself into his collection of traditions, saying that some sciences offer benefit for religion (*dīn*), while others offer benefit in worldly affairs (*dunyā*); yet others do both, an example of the latter being the science of dream interpretation. This distinction is followed by a lengthy discussion of how to ensure that one has true dreams.[125] Again, at issue is a collection of (largely) prophetic traditions: to have true dreams, be truthful in your speech; follow hygiene rules, in particular keep your fingernails short; sleep on your back or your right side; say certain prayers before bed. Two such prayers are mentioned. The first is ascribed to ᶜĀʾishah: "God, I beseech you to grant dreams that are true rather than false, beneficial rather than harmful, remembered rather than forgotten." The second's source is unspecified: "God, I take refuge with you from nightmares and their evil; may Satan not toy with me while I am either awake or asleep."

Kharkūshī next distinguishes two types of dreams, again relying mostly on prophetic traditions: those that are true and those that are false.[126] The former arise from balanced humors and right desire, nor can they be nullified by ritual impurity or menstruation, while the latter arise from the self, from excessive concern with worldly objectives or from desire. No false dreams can be interpreted. Indeed, prophetic traditions prescribe actions to be undertaken should they be seen: if the dream caused a nocturnal emission, ablutions should be performed; spit thrice over your left shoulder; take refuge with God; arise and pray; do not tell anyone about the dream. Yet other traditions, he continues, specify what times of the night give rise to the most auspicious dreams. Still others tell of the best person to ask about one's dreams, while at the same time advising against telling one's dreams to enemies, those who are ignorant, or women. Kharkūshī concludes his introductory chapter with yet another long series of prophetic traditions, mostly on the proper conduct of dream interpreters.[127]

Following his introduction, Kharkūshī offers in chapter two a collection of traditions on dreams interpreted by Muḥammad.[128] These traditions are seldom provided with chains of authorities or isnāds, usually being introduced with the formula "it is reported" (*ruwiya*). The following are typical:

> It is reported concerning the Messenger that a certain man came to him and said: "Messenger of God, I saw in a dream that I came across twenty-four dinars; I put all of them down, later I picked up only four of them." [The prophet] said: "You are a man who has forsaken the community by praying by yourself."

> ᶜAbd Allāh b. Sallām saw in a dream that he was hanging by a golden noose. He told this to the prophet, who said: "God willing, you will die a natural death."

> A woman came to the Messenger of God and said: "I saw in a dream that part of your body was in my hands." [The prophet] said: "Fāṭimah shall give birth to a child and you shall be his wet nurse." In the end, Fāṭimah gave birth to Ḥusayn and this woman was his wet nurse.

About thirty such dreams are mentioned, some had by Muḥammad, others by his companions. In all cases, however, it is Muḥammad who does the interpreting. Only after citing these traditions does Kharkūshī begin his dream manual proper.

Kharkūshī begins with chapters on dreams of God, the prophets, angels, and so on, before turning to dreams of the rites, institutions, and major objects of Muslim belief: for instance, the Throne, the Bridge, Paradise, and Hell. Having treated such exalted dreams, he then considers dreams of a more mundane nature. On the whole, Kharkūshī presents his interpretations of the individual dream symbols in a formalistic manner. Almost invariably, the interpretations he offers are not supported by evidence—but not always. He occasionally cites Koranic verses or anecdotes. These anecdotes are most often ascribed to Ibn Sīrīn, though occasionally to other early authorities, including Muḥammad.

Thus far, it may seem that Kharkūshī's dream manual differs little from Qayrawānī's. This initial impression is in part justified. Like Qayrawānī, Kharkūshī grounds his dream manual in the figures of an Islamic prophetic past. The only authorities to whom he appeals in his introduction are prophetic: the Koran and traditions of the prophet or his close companions. Moreover, like Qayrawānī, the questions that Kharkūshī investigates are dictated by the contours of the prophetic traditions: not once does he appeal to non-Muslim traditions or bring up philosophic questions. Thus far, the only major difference between the dream manuals of Kharkūshī and Qayrawānī is their methods of citing earlier authorities. Whereas Qayrawānī appeals to books rather than people, the opposite pattern in found in Kharkūshī's work. Nowhere does the latter mention earlier written works on the subject of dream interpretation, either to cite them or even to acknowledge their existence. It is only when one turns to Kharkūshī's dream manual proper that one can discern characteristics that mark it off from Qayrawānī's. Of these, there are two: first, Kharkūshī evinces a strong interest in the dreams of Sufis, and second, Kharkūshī is willing to make use of non-Muslim sources, albeit surreptitiously.

At the beginning of the individual chapters in his dream manual, Kharkūshī often introduces one or more anecdotes that recount dreams told to him by his teachers. Occasionally, these anecdotes treat dreams interpreted by the prophet. At other times, they record the dreams of famous Sufis. For instance, three times in his dream manual Kharkūshī records dreams transmitted to him in the city of ᶜAkkā by one of his teachers. All three anecdotes concern dreams had by Abū ᶜUbayd al-Busrī (d. 245/859), an important figure in the history of Sufism in Syria.[129] The anecdotes are as follows:

> Abū ᶜUbayd al-Busrī said: I saw in a dream that the resurrection had taken place and that I had arisen from my tomb. I was brought a mount and on it was taken to heaven. And behold, in it was a garden. I wanted to alight there, but a voice said to me: "This is not your residence." I was then taken to other heavens, in each of which there was a garden. Eventually, I reached the highest one. There I alighted. I wished to sit down, but a voice said to me: "Will you sit before you see your Lord?" I said: "No." I then stood there until I was led to a certain place where I saw God, in whose presence was Adam. When Adam saw me, he sat me down on his right in the manner of a petitioner. I said: "Lord, I ask your pardon for this old man." I then heard God say: "Arise, Adam; I have pardoned you."[130]

> Abū ᶜUbayd al-Busrī said: I dreamt that someone called me: "Abū ᶜUbayd (you on whom God showers mercy) get up and come to pray." But I stayed sound asleep. Yet again he called. This time I woke up and found that his hand was on my head and that he was saying: "Arise, my beloved, for God has had mercy on you."[131]

> Abū ᶜUbayd al-Busrī said: I saw in a dream that the resurrection took place and that the people were gathered together. Behold, the voice of

> one crying: "All those who fasted in the world, let them come and eat." One by one the people arose. The voice then said to me: "Abū ᶜUbayd, arise." I arose and tables were laid. I then said to myself: "Arriving on time is not easy for me."[132]

In other Muslim dream manuals, the use of anecdotes is not unusual. In those texts, however, anecdotes are cited to show the proper interpretation of dreams. Kharkūshī's anecdotes are cited for another purpose. In the above examples, all three anecdotes concern dreams had by Abū ᶜUbayd; they are not concerned with dreams interpreted by him. In the three examples, not one of Abū ᶜUbayd's dreams receives an interpretation, nor in fact needs one. Rather, all three show the advanced spiritual status attained by Abū ᶜUbayd. They are not meant to show his abilities as an interpreter of dreams; they are meant to establish his nearness to God.

As suggested above, Kharkūshī often appeals to the prophet and his companions. This pattern holds not only in his introduction, but also in the body of his dream manual. On numerous occasions, however, Kharkūshī does make vague references to a figure, the identity of whom is never specified. This authority he calls "a certain one of the ancients" (*baᶜḍ al-awāʾil*), an innocuous expression that need not imply that this person was other than Muslim.

> A certain one of the ancients said: A butcher in a dream signifies hardship (*shiddah*) in all circumstances except two—in the case of debt, for then it signifies release; in the case of fetters, for then it signifies his redemption, for [butchers] divide meats and separate between them.[133]

> A certain one of the ancients said: To dream of a cook in a house signifies joy and marriage for the rich and the poor—in the case of the sick, it signifies the hardship of the inflammation (*iltihāb*) of their sickness.[134]

> A certain one of the ancients said: Whosoever sees in a dream that he wishes to drink but does not, he shall not attain something he needs.[135]

In fact, Kharkūshī has disguised here his use of the dream manual of Artemidorus. In Ḥunayn's version, the respective passages read.

> Butchers . . . signify hardship (*shiddah*) and danger. . . . As for those who are in debt and bound up, in that case they signify taking care of the debt and freedom from bonds, for [butchers] partition and cut up meats.[136]

> To dream of a cook, if he is cooking in someone's house . . . is good for someone who wishes to marry . . . in the houses of the rich also. . . . In the case of the sick, they signify the violence of their sickness and its inflammation (*iltihāb*).[137]

> If a man sees that he wishes to drink but is not able to drink anything . . . that signifies that he will not acquire something he needs.[138]

As the above-cited examples show, sometimes Kharkūshī paraphrases, but on the whole he faithfully reproduces Ḥunayn's version of Artemidorus.

Kharkūshī never explains how he gained access to the dream manual of Artemidorus. This can be determined, however. As will be argued in chapter 3, Kharkūshī's major source throughout his own work is the dream manual of Dīnawarī. Kharkūshī adopts from Dīnawarī not only these materials from Artemidorus, but also a great deal of additional information. Indeed, so extensive are his borrowings that Kharkūshī's work must be viewed as an abridgment of Dīnawarī's dream manual. And yet, although Kharkūshī adopts much from Dīnawarī's dream manual, including many traditions ascribed to non-Muslim authorities, he never acknowledges his dependence, nor is he willing to let it be thought that such materials are of non-Muslim provenance. Materials from Artemidorus he sometimes ascribes to "a certain one of the ancients." More commonly, he simply adopts Dīnawarī's non-Muslim sources without ascription. While both Dīnawarī and Kharkūshī made use of non-Muslim sources, in particular Artemidorus, it should be noted that the structure of their dream manuals still follows that of more traditional works. Neither Dīnawarī nor Kharkūshī had subordinated the Muslim tradition of dream interpretation to the oneirocritic traditions of other cultures. In this regard, their works differ markedly from that of Ibn Sīnā.

IBN SĪNĀ: PHILOSOPHY, DREAM INTERPRETATION, AND THE LEGACY OF HELLENISM

Born in 370/980, Ibn Sīnā spent his early years in Bukhārā.[139] A child protégé, he quickly mastered the traditional subjects and then turned his attention to matters of medicine and philosophy. At a young age, his medical skills earned him the admiration and patronage of Nūḥ b. Manṣūr, the sultan of Bukhārā. After the death of his father, Ibn Sīnā entered on the life of a peripatetic scholar and received the patronage of many Iranian princes in rather quick succession. Eventually, around the age of forty-four, he was taken in at the court of the prince ᶜAlā al-Dawlah (d. 433/1041). There he spent his remaining years in relative tranquillity, dying in 428/1037. The corpus of Ibn Sīnā's compositions is immense, well in excess of two hundred works. Among these is a dream manual, a text extant in more than a dozen copies.[140] Of these, I have had access to four: one from Princeton University Library, another from the British Library, and two from Istanbul.[141] Other copies include: five preserved in India, four in Iran, and one in private possession.[142]

Ibn Sīnā opens his dream manual with an artful prologue in praise of his unnamed patron (perhaps ᶜAlā al-Dawlah).[143] Water flows to the sea not because the sea lacks water, but because it is natural that like merge with like and thus gather strength from unity. Similarly, Ibn Sīnā wrote this work to render the court service: not because the court lacks wisdom, but that whatever wisdom there is in his book might return to its source and thus participate in its proper unity. Many have written on dreams and their interpretation, he continues. Some were Greeks; others, Arabs. Because there are so many works on the subject, he decided to compile his own, in the hope that it would alleviate the need for those other works. He would, he claims, gather together all that should be known about dream interpretation, keeping only what is correct and casting away superfluous and superstitious materials. Ibn Sīnā is careful to add, however, that he is more than a compiler. Many topics were not treated in earlier works: What is sleep? What faculties are required for dreams? What are the different kinds of dreams and how are they interpreted? These topics, too, he will consider. This manner of treating the subject will, he hopes, cause "this book to be like the fruit of the many other works written on this subject."

True to his promises, Ibn Sīnā opens his introduction with a philosophic discussion of sleep and dreams.[144] Of key importance for understanding this subject is the role played in the soul by the faculty of imagination. This faculty is one of three that make up the faculty of intellect, the others being memory and discernment. The faculty of intellect, in turn, is one of three faculties that compose the ruling or sensible soul. This soul has its seat in the brain, where it is closely connected with the rational spirit. Though having its seat there, the ruling soul makes use of the rational spirit, which is diffused throughout the body by the nerves, to move the body, make use of the senses, and undertake various intellectual processes, in particular, those of imagination, discernment, and memory. It is not possible, however, for these processes to take place continuously.[145] The numerous parts of the soul grow tired through overuse. Sleep offers a period of rest and refreshment. When sleep comes, most higher faculties cease working. Sense perception, in particular, comes to a halt, for the faculty of common sense ceases to process its images. Only the faculty of imagination continues to function.[146] Indeed, this faculty is more active in a sleeping than a waking state, for it is no longer disturbed by sense images or by the constraints of the faculty of discernment. The images seen in such a state are dreams.

Not all dreams are significant, Ibn Sīnā continues. Sometimes the images seen are merely the remnants of objects that were observed during the day. At other times they are faint reflections left in the imagination by the faculty of choice, as, for example, when one continues in sleep to be haunted by a desire for something. Yet another type of dream lacking significance results from an imbalance of the humors of the rational spirit, which in some sense is a substratum for the imaginative faculty. The images presented to the imagination in this last case are not unique to the sleeping state—the mad and the feverish also see them. These three types of dreams give rise to dreams that are confused and disorderly. They lack significance and cannot be interpreted. There are other kinds of dreams, however.[147] These arise not from within, but from an outside cause. Human beings contribute nothing to them, except being prepared to see them and willing to receive them from an externally subsisting efficient cause. Such dreams are sent by this efficient cause through its ability to implant them in the imaginative faculty.

What is the efficient cause that gives rise to dreams? According to Ibn Sīnā, it is a Divine Force (*qūwah ilāhīyah*), "not in the sense that it is God or a part of God—may God be exalted above that—but in the sense that it is an action that proceeds from him."[148] That such a being exists is no new discovery, he claims.[149] There is no group of people endowed with reason that does not recognize it. The Sabians know it as the Nearest Ruler (*al-mudabbir al-aqrab*),[150] while the Greeks call it the Divine Emanation (*al-fayḍ al-ilāhī*) or the Divine Providence (*al-ᶜināyah al-ilāhīyah*). Syrians refer to it as the Word (*al-kalīmah*), the same being known in Arabic as the Indwelling (*al-sakīnah*) or as the Holy Spirit (*rūḥ al-qudus*). Even the Zoroastrians and Manicheans recognize it: the former, as the Amesha Spentas; the latter as the Good Spirits (*al-arwāḥ al-ṭayyibah*).[151] As for the Arabs, by which Ibn Sīnā means the Muslims, they refer to this being as angels (*malāʾikah*) and the Divine Strengthening (*al-taʾyīd al-ilāhī*).

The more pious one is, Ibn Sīnā continues, the closer one will be to the Divine Force. Indeed, "if there were someone and this power safeguarded his affairs and helped and taught him to the greatest extent possible, that person would be a prophet and would receive divine revelation."[152] In fact, the Divine Force has particular regard not for prophets but for kings and sages. From these two classes flows the greatest amount of benefit for the rest of humankind. Indeed, lacking them, the world and its inhabitants would quickly perish. Kings and sages also enjoy this special providence because in concert with it they aim at the good order of the world and because they more than any others are hated and envied by those whom they seek to guide.[153]

After discussing dreams influenced by the faculties of discernment and memory, which lack significance and cannot be interpreted,[154] Ibn Sīnā turns his attention to true dreams, which the Divine Force causes to be seen.[155] True dreams are of two types: those that are explicit and do not need interpretation and those that are allegorical and need interpretation. The former receive the greater measure of Ibn Sīnā's attention, for they are more indicative of the Divine Force's providential care for creation. They are especially frequent when a person stands in dire straits or on the verge of despair. There is a further distinction to be made, however.[156] Most people believe that dreams of glad tidings come true only after a time, while dreams of warning come true quickly. This assumption is partly true, he admits, but is based on an improper distinction. In reality, the Divine Force shows a person dreams of warning about an impending evil fate only when that fate is almost ready to take place. The Divine Force does this to minimize the anxiety such dreams might cause. Contrariwise, dreams of glad tidings are shown long before the events they foretell, to prolong the period of joy attendant on the expectation they excite.[157]

"Every science whose first principles are not laid down in a clear and orderly fashion—this science has not beauty in it, nor any reason for accepting it, neither is the soul able to find rest in it or be certain about it."[158] To lay down such first principles has been Ibn Sīnā's task thus far. This has been necessary, he claims, because of the inadequate manner in which his predecessors had treated the subject.[159] They did not realize the difficulty of dream interpretation, that it requires a knowledge of many different sciences and that it demands a subtle intellect. Ibn Sīnā wants his readers to be perfectly clear as to the nature of his own contribution in this regard: "Everything that I have discussed thus far, from the beginning of this work up to this point, is derived from me personally."[160] He further distinguishes what has preceded from what follows. The remaining portions of his introduction are derived from what has been written on dreams by the sages of Greece and by the Arabs. He will be careful to ascribe everything to its proper source, he adds. In this way, readers will know that only those materials that bear no ascription are his own.

Ibn Sīnā has given an accurate account of the remaining portions of his introduction. The first part of what remains is a synopsis of the theoretical portions of Ḥunayn's version of the dream manual of Artemidorus—though without mentioning him by name.

Ibn Sīnā secs. 18–25 = Artemidorus 1.1–8
Ibn Sīnā secs. 26–27 = Artemidorus 4.1–2 (including the preface)
Ibn Sīnā secs. 28 = Artemidorus 1.11–12

Ibn Sīnā's exposition is largely a summary of Artemidorus. He adapts his source, in the main, by excising its many examples. Only occasionally does he interject his own voice. Sometimes this is to bring his source into closer conformity with his own theory of the Divine Force. Sometimes it is to assure his readers that he himself can vouch for the accuracy of the views being presented: "All these materials I have found to be true by my own personal experience."[161] Sometimes it is to provide illustrations of the theoretical principles being presented.

The second part of the remaining portion of Ibn Sīnā's introduction offers a laconic summary of the topics treated in the introductions to more traditional Muslim dream manuals.[162] The following, by now familiar points are treated:

The four humors and their influence on dreams.
Dreams vary in accordance with the status of the dreamer.
The interpreter must be versed in many sciences.
The interpreter must be virtuous.
The use of etymology in interpretation.
The use of proverbs in interpretation.

The interpretation of dreams through opposites and inversion.
The interpretation of dreams through increase and decrease.
The proper behavior of interpreters of dreams.

Ibn Sīnā does not think much of these Muslim dream manuals, or as he calls them, these dream manuals of the Arabs. His presentation is at best perfunctory. Indeed, he summarizes to such an extent that these sections are at times almost unintelligible. Sometimes, in fact, he offers explicit objections to the opinions of the Arabs, as, for example, when treating the use of etymology in the interpretation of dreams: dreams of quince (*safarjal*) signify a journey (*safar*); a lily of the valley (*sūsan*) intimates an evil (*sūʾ*) manner of life (*sunnah*). To this Ibn Sīnā objects:

> The examples given here . . . are only valid for one who speaks Arabic and for one who lives in their country or who is one of them. If one sees a quince or a lily of the valley and is not an Arab or does not have Arabic as one's language, then the meaning of the dream is not the same as it is for the Arabs.[163]

Ibn Sīnā nowhere specifies the source or sources on which he draws in summarizing the views of the Arabs. Most of his materials are traditional. It is possible, however, that his main source was the dream manual of Ibn Qutaybah or a text that had made extensive use of Ibn Qutaybah.[164]

In the final section of his introduction, Ibn Sīnā discusses how he organizes his dream manual proper.[165] Greeks and Arabs do not agree on how dream manuals should be organized. Thus, he confesses that his presentation may seem unusual. The Arabs begin with exalted matters and pass to things less noble, while the Greeks begin with humans and first describe their circumstances. Indeed, the Greeks used to say:

> This science [of dream interpretation] is of particular benefit to humans and whatever benefit and harm it brings relate to them. Because they are the most noble of beings in the earth, the subject matter of dreams pertains on the whole to them and their circumstances. Although they sometimes see other things in dreams, the majority concern them. For this reason, it is necessary that humans be treated first and foremost—especially since their need of [dream interpretation] is greater and the benefit that they derive from it is more general and [as is said]: "The most important thing most certainly takes precedence."

Following his Greek predecessors, Ibn Sīnā also begins with humans and their circumstances, turning next to the things associated with them, and finally to things wholly unconnected with them. He explicitly acknowledges that his procedure is that of the Greeks. He further states that his treatment is almost wholly derived from them.

When Ibn Sīnā turns to his dream manual proper, he follows his source closely.[166] As he has already intimated, he takes the Greeks as his model. And in fact, nearly the whole of Ibn Sīnā's dream manual proper is derived from Artemidorus. In particular, he takes the first two books of the latter's work and from them derives the order of sections in his own. To illustrate this phenomenon, consider the opening sections of Ibn Sīnā's work:

Sec. 40: On Birth = Artem. 1.13–16
Sec. 41: On the Head = Artem. 1.17
Sec. 42: On the Hair of the Head = Artem. 1.18–22
Sec. 43: On the Forehead and Eyebrows = Artem. 1.23, 25
Sec. 44: On the Eyes and Sight = Artem. 1.26
Sec. 45: On the Ears and Hearing = Artem. 1.24
Sec. 46: On the Nose and Smelling = Artem. 1.27
Sec. 47: On a Man's Beard = Artem. 1.30
Sec. 48: On the Teeth = Artem. 1.31
Sec. 49: On the Head as a Whole and the Neck = Artem. 1.35–39
Sec. 50: On the Tongue = Artem. 1.32
Sec. 51: On the Back, Chest, and Breasts = Artem. 1.40–41

Only rarely does Ibn Sīnā break from this pattern, mostly by supplementing his presentation with materials drawn from the opinions of the Arabs. He is careful to mark out these chapters as deriving not from the Greeks, but "from the discourse of the Arabs." They make up only a small proportion of his dream manual proper.

Artemidorus not only provides Ibn Sīnā with the structure of his dream manual. The majority of the interpretations offered are also derived from him. The nature of Ibn Sīnā's borrowings is illustrated in Table 2.1, which compares the beginning of his dream manual proper with Ḥunayn's version of Artemidorus. It will be immediately obvious that all but one of Ibn Sīnā's interpretations is derived from Artemidorus. Similarly, only one of Artemidorus' interpretations is omitted, most likely because the Arabic version makes little sense. Ibn Sīnā does not copy his source slavishly, however. He consistently abbreviates, usually without dramatically changing the sense. At other times, particularly when the Arabic version of Artemidorus is not clear, he tinkers with or even reformulates his source. A good example is the last of the dreams cited. For a person in a foreign land to dream of being born means that that person will return to his homeland. Artemidorus had originally justified this interpretation by two analogies: because the child just born has come to its beginning or because the child, by coming into the world, has come to its proper homeland (for the world is the homeland of all human beings). The logic of the second explanation is obscured in the Arabic version. Ibn Sīnā thus supplies his own justification, which builds on the Arabic version but develops it in new ways. In general, it must be admitted that Ibn Sīnā's adaptation is clearer than the original.

TABLE 2.1
Ibn Sīnā's Use of Artemidorus

Ibn Sīnā, fols. 47b–48a	Artemidorus, *on.* 1.13
If a man sees that he's being born:	If a man sees in a dream that a woman is giving birth to him, his dream is interpreted as follows:
If he's poor, he'll find a patron to meet his needs, for a child has no need to earn a living.	If the dreamer is poor, it's a propitious dream, for it means that he'll find someone to nourish him and be his patron, just as a child has someone to do that.
If he's anxious about something, he'll be joyful and set free from anxiety, for the act of giving birth is a deliverance from dire straits into an expansive state.	
If he's occupied with his labors and good at them, he'll be kept from them and become weak, for when a child is first born it cannot work.	If the dreamer is a craftsman, it means the order of labor [?] and hindrances—that's because children are educated slowly.
If he's a ruler and answers to no one, he'll be conquered and come under the power of another, for a child is subject to the authority of others, whether or not it wishes to be.	If the dreamer is rich, it means that he'll not preserve his wealth and that another will be victorious over him from him to him [?]—that's because a child is subject to another who rules over it, without his wishing it.
	If the dreamer's wife isn't pregnant, it means that her bearing of children will cease and she'll bear no more—that's because children do not have sex with women.
If the dreamer is pregnant, he'll be blessed with a child, for the act of giving birth means a child.	If the dreamer has a pregnant wife, it means that a son like the dreamer will be born to her, just as he saw in his dream.
If he's the slave of another, he'll not be set free, for a child isn't in charge of its own affairs, but is subject to its parents.	If the dreamer is a slave, it means the love of his master for him, and that if he err, he will be forgiven, but not set free, even as children are not in charge of their own affairs, even if freeborn.
If he's brave, he'll grow weak, for a child is the weakest of creatures.	This dream is inauspicious for wrestlers—that's because children cannot walk or be present, nor are they able to go where they want, nor bear themselves.
If he's a foreigner, he'll return to his country, for the unborn child is like a foreigner in the womb of its mother, whereas the world is its place of residence to which it is coming.	As for a foreigner, this dream means that he'll return to his lands and go back to the place in which he was at first, even as he who is born is returning to the earth (i.e., its land), for the earth is the common land of all.

Ibn Sīnā's work contrasts markedly with other, contemporary dream manuals. First, as might be expected given Ibn Sīnā's cultural orientation, his dream manual contains by far the most sophisticated philosophic treatment of dreams. He conceptualized dreams and their prophetic ability wholly in terms of the Muslim neoplatonic tradition. Thus, for Ibn Sīnā the initial cause of dreams was not God (for "God is exalted above that")[167] nor even the angel of dreams, but the Agent Intellect. Nothing like this is found in any of the other dream manuals considered in this chapter. Second, Ibn Sīnā alone was willing to subordinate the Muslim tradition of dream interpretation to that of a pre-Islamic Hellenic past. While other oneirocrits had had access to Artemidorus' dream manual, they used it to garnish works that were otherwise thoroughly dependent on the Muslim oneirocritic tradition. Ibn Sīnā, by contrast, jettisoned that tradition and chose to construct his work solely on a Hellenic foundation, only occasionally and cursorily citing more traditional Muslim dream lore, often with explicit objections. Third, Ibn Sīnā's distinctive preference for a Hellenic approach to dream interpretation is further suggested by the silences of his work. Not once does he cite the Koran. Equally absent are prophetic traditions. Nowhere does he appeal to the angel of dreams or the Preserved Tablet. Even the mention of Muḥammad is lacking. Although Ibn Sīnā offhandedly suggests that the pious have greater access to the Divine Force and that someone "safeguarded in his affairs" by this force is a prophet, he carefully couches the suggestion in the form of a counterfactual condition. It is not prophets, but sages and kings on whom this force lavishes its attention. And perhaps no wonder, for Ibn Sīnā considered himself to be such a sage and wrote his text for such a king, who was also his patron.

CONCLUSIONS

The homogeneity of the Muslim oneirocritic tradition ceased by the end of the fourth century A.H. In its place arose a number of competing legacies, each grounding dream interpretation on a distinct epistemic foundation, each associated with one of Hodgson's four rival cultural orientations. Representing the sharīᶜah-minded are the dream manuals of Qayrawānī. He imagined the science of dreams to be grounded in an archetypal prophetic past. Not dissimilar to Qayrawānī's is the dream manual of Kharkūshī, a sharīᶜah-minded Sufi. Although Kharkūshī founded his work on this same prophetic past, even to the point of disguising his use of non-Muslim authorities like Artemidorus, his work differs from Qayrawānī's through its interest in the dreams of prominent early Sufis. While Kharkūshī avoided open reference to non-Muslim authorities, the litterateur Dīnawarī felt no such qualms. His cosmopolitan dream manual cast its net wide. Standing side-by-side in it were Jews, Christians, Hindus, and Zoroastrians, as well as, most prominently, Artemidorus. Without privileging Muslim sources over others, however, Dīnawarī maintained a largely traditional structure. The philosopher Ibn Sīnā, contrariwise, abandoned this traditional structure, in favor of one wholly dependent on his Hellenic forebear, Artemidorus. It is about this structure that he wove his own philosophic musings on dreams, as well as his cursory and even hostile presentation of traditional Muslim ("Arab") views. Ibn Sīnā sought, furthermore, to divorce prophetic dreams from prophetic monotheism, arguing instead that dreams are the special provenance of sages and kings.

Three of the legacies discerned in this chapter will continue to bear fruit for many centuries. In terms of their overall methodological perspectives, most later Muslim dream manuals will closely follow lines such as those laid down by Qayrawānī. There are many such sharīᶜah-minded dream manuals.[168] There are no later Muslim dream manuals precisely comparable to that of Kharkūshī, especially in terms of its attempt to fuse dream interpretation and Sufi dream narratives. The latter aspect of his work is paralleled in later Sufi circles, however, in texts recording the dreams of prominent mystics, in particular the founders of Sufi orders.[169] The culture of adab will also have its afterlife. Especially interesting are later Persian dream manuals that follow in the footsteps of Dīnawarī, although evincing an even stronger regard for the legacy of pre-Islamic Persia.[170] The dream manual of Ibn Sīnā alone seems to have lacked successors. I know of no later Muslim dream manuals that follow so closely the work of Artemidorus or attempt so thoroughly to divorce dream interpretation from prophetic monotheism.

There is much diversity in the dream manuals of the late fourth and early fifth centuries A.H. It is evident in the epistemic foundations of these texts. It is also to be seen in the meanings assigned to dream symbols: we can well imagine that Ibn Sīnā's interpretations, being almost wholly derived from Artemidorus, differ markedly from those of his contemporaries and predecessors. But what of the other texts—not only those considered in the present chapter, but also those discussed in chapter 1? When it comes to the meanings assigned to dreams, do these texts evince a unified system of dream interpretation? Or does each employ its own idiosyncratic system for interpreting dreams? And what of the respective theologies of these texts? Did the early Muslim tradition of dream interpretation know one or many such theologies? Put another way, is there a single, typically Muslim tradition of dream interpretation? An answer to this question is sought in the next chapter.

CHAPTER THREE

Homogeneity and Imitation

While most early Muslim dream manuals are now lost, a good number remain—enough are now known that researchers can at last trace the transformations of the Muslim oneirocritic tradition during the earliest stages of its development. This has been the task of chapters 1 and 2. There it was argued that the tradition was subject to a continual series of changes: the transition from oral to written modes of transmission; the rise of formalism and the displacement of anecdotes; the shift from its early grounding in prophetic monotheism to the more complex tendencies of the works of the late fourth and early fifth centuries A.H., works informed by a variety of rival cultural orientations and by concomitantly diverse strategies for appropriating earlier modes of dream interpretation. Based on the arguments of chapters 1 and 2, one might expect the early Muslim oneirocritic tradition to evince much diversity. After all, we are dealing with a continually changing tradition ensconced in a corpus of texts written over the course of some three centuries and stemming from one end of the Muslim world to the other. Surely we should expect these texts to exhibit much variety. Or should we? The arguments of chapters 1 and 2 might also lead us to expect the opposite. There is, after all, much textual interdependence evident in the extant works, enough to suggest if not perhaps a single tradition of dream interpretation, at the very least well-defined subtraditions. Is there, then, a single tradition of dream interpretation? This, briefly, is the question this chapter seeks to answer.

To determine whether there was a single Muslim oneirocritic tradition, it is necessary, first, to analyze the overall contours of the tradition. Two points are key. All Muslim dream manuals presuppose what might be called a "theology of dreams." This theology is concerned with a number of basic, yet essential questions. What are dreams? How do they convey prophetic knowledge? Who can have divine dreams? Very occasionally this theology is explicit; more often it is latent. Muslim dream manuals presuppose not only this theology of dreams, but also what might be called an "oneirocritic logic." How does one determine that this or that dream symbol bears this or that meaning? And why is this the case?

Like the theology of dreams, this oneirocritic logic is usually latent, presupposed but seldom exposited. By recognizing, analyzing, and comparing the theology of dreams and the oneirocritic logic found in the extant dream manuals one can go part of the way toward answering the principle question of this chapter.

To ascertain whether there was a single early Muslim tradition of dream interpretation, one must attend not only to its contours, but also to its contents. One must, in other words, adopt an approach that is more strictly textual, concerned not with the general theoretical underpinnings of the tradition but with the messy, concrete details of how individual dream symbols are interpreted. It is necessary to ascertain whether the oneirocrits of, say, the third century A.H. interpreted dreams in the same way as those of the early fifth century, whether North African oneirocrits assigned the same meanings to dreams as did those of Iran or Iraq, whether litterateurs, Sufis, philosophers, and religious scholars all interpreted dreams in the same ways. Given the extent of the surviving evidence, it is impractical to compare how the dream manuals interpret each and every dream symbol. One can, however, analyze a series of representative dream symbols. This has been the procedure adopted here. An analysis of these dream symbols offers, I think, an effective means for determining whether and to what extent the early Muslim dream manuals evince a single form of dream interpretation, and thus ultimately whether it is possible to posit a single tradition of dream interpretation.

THE CONTOURS OF THE EARLY MUSLIM ONEIROCRITIC TRADITION

All early Muslim dream manual were written with a single end in view. It did not matter whether they were collections of anecdotal narratives, didactic poems, or compilations informed by any of a number of cultural orientations. Whatever their format, each and every dream manual was first and foremost a work of divination. To borrow a definition from the ancient Stoic philosopher Chrysippus, these texts were written that their readers might be able to "see, understand, and interpret the signs given to human beings by the gods."[1] What do these signs signify? It might be tempting to suggest that they signify future events, and that the primary end of dream interpretation is thus the prediction of the future. Such a definition aptly characterizes much that is found in the early Muslim dream manuals. It is not, however, entirely adequate, for interpreted dreams often concern things and actions that do not lie in the future but in the present. A broader characterization is needed, one that focuses instead on what might be called "the occult" (*al-ghayb*).

The occult may be something that exists in the present time: sins committed unawares, the state of mind of a business partner, the location of buried treasure. Alternatively, it may be something that does not yet exist, a future occurrence. Regardless of their format, all early Muslim dream manuals were written that their readers might be able to obtain such occult knowledge. These texts are not concerned with dreams per se, but the occult knowledge that a proper understanding of dreams imparts. While early Muslim dream manuals were primarily works of divination, they could sometimes express an interest in dreams for other reasons. Kharkūshī, it will be recalled, included in his work accounts of dreams had by prominent early Sufis, accounts with no bearing on the use of dreams for divination. Or again, the introduction to Ibn Sīnā's dream manual encompassed a sophisticated, philosophic disquisition on dreams and their foundations in the various faculties of the soul. Such interests took second place to the primary purpose of the dream manuals, however—the pursuit of occult knowledge.

The Theology of Dreams

All of the dream manuals considered in this study share a common understanding of the goal of dream interpretation as divination. They also all share a similar theology of dreams. First and foremost, they are all resolutely theistic in their understanding of how one attains occult knowledge through the interpretation of dreams. There is a God who exercises a providential control over the events of the world. This same God, at times, uses dreams to inform human beings about those events. This is not to say that these texts posit all dreams as capable of providing occult knowledge. The dream manuals concur that many dreams are not in fact divine in their origin. Some result from Satan's machinations. Others arise from causes within the body or soul—anxiety, for example, or indigestion. Usually an appeal is made to prophetic traditions to support these distinctions. As one such tradition has it:

> There are three types of dreams: the good dream that is "a glad tiding from God" (Q 10:64), the dream in which our own souls speak, and the dream that Satan sends to make us sad.

Another common and oft-cited tradition sets up a twofold distinction between dreams that are from God (*ruʾyā*) and dreams that are from Satan (*ḥulm*). The latter are usually equated with the Koranic "confused dreams" (*aḍghāth al-aḥlām*).[2] Such dreams are also usually associated with dreams that occur as a result of an imbalance among the humors. The preponderance of one or another of these humors gives rise to dreams of diverse characteristics, a theme treated in nearly all dream manuals. As Ibn Qutaybah puts the matter:

> If black bile predominates, one sees corpses, tombs, black things, and frightful objects. If gall predominates, one sees fire, lamps, blood, and saffron colored objects. If blood predominates, one sees stringed instruments, drinking, wine, sprigs of basil, carousals, and songs. If phlegm predominates, one sees things that are white, water, dew, and waves.[3]

Such dreams stem not from God, but from the body. They cannot be interpreted. Those dreams capable of providing occult knowledge, contrariwise, are all understood to arise ultimately from God's providential interaction with his creation. Such dreams demand interpretation.

According to the authors of the dream manuals, the images that haunt the mind during sleep are intricately connected with what takes place in the world outside the mind. It is not a question here of a strict causal connection between the mind and the world. The reception of occult knowledge does not take place automatically. It is wholly dependent on God. There are times when God deems it necessary that intimations of external events be granted for the benefit of those they concern. As has been seen, the authors of our texts suggest some of the reasons why God chooses certain occasions for this to happen—generally, when the knowledge imparted will bear a special benefit for the dreamer, or when it will cause the dreamer to take care lest he or she fall into sin. Regardless, these intimations of the occult do not take place automatically, but are subject to the guiding hand of God. They are specific acts of his providential care.

In antiquity, a distinction was made between natural and technical divination.[4] The former was understood to be effective only because it was dependent on the gods. The latter was conceived as arising "without any influence, any impulse from the gods." The Muslim dream manuals are clearly an instance of natural divination. There is no question here of interwoven micro- and macrocosms as the source of dreams—a model of the world that alleviates the need for divine agency, other than as an amorphous initial cause. There is nothing here of, say, the Stoic view that "the world was designed in such a way that certain events would follow certain signs."[5] The God of the Muslim dream manuals imparts knowledge through dreams not after the image of the Stoics, but through discrete, ever-present acts of revelation. The interpreter of dreams does not read the signs of God that are ever and always available in nature. He functions rather after the fashion of an exegete, interpreting the signs that God has revealed through his direct, providential interaction with the world. In the end, dreams can convey knowledge only insofar as both the physical world and the world of dreams are ultimately dependent on the same divine source.

There is widespread consensus in the early Muslim dream manuals that God does not send dreams himself, but relies on an intermediary. As has been seen, this intermediary is usually identified as an angelic being named Ṣidīqūn, or some variant on that name. This angel does not have direct access to the plan of divine providence. He is required to gain his understanding of it from the celestial book, the Preserved Tablet. This point should be carefully noted, for implicit in it is an attempt to link the type of knowledge conveyed in dreams to the type of knowledge conveyed through the revelation of the Koran, for the latter originates from this same Preserved Tablet. Ibn Sīnā alone breaks with this general pattern. His understanding of how it is possible to have true dreams is theistic, but thoroughly integrated within an older, neoplatonic understanding of divine revelation and of the Agent Intellect's role in that process. Even his God, however, was required to make use of an intermediary to send dreams.

All Muslim dream manuals are in accord that there is no person who is not able to receive divinely sent dreams. It matters not whether one is a North African shoemaker, an Afghani holy warrior, or a menstruating woman. Various circumstances, however, can cause a person to be particularly receptive to divine influence, or contrariwise, particularly unreceptive. In this regard, the time of day, month, or year is important, as well as one's spiritual condition as reflected, for example, in one's bodily purity. All dream manuals presuppose such conditions on a person's receptivity. There are, too, certain people by nature more receptive to dreams. The most systematic treatment of this subject is found in the work of Sijistānī, who ranked dreamers as follows:

1. A Muslim's dreams are more truthful than a non-Muslim's.
2. Among Muslims, the dreams of prayer leaders, judges, jurists, and religious scholars are most truthful.
3. The dreams of freedmen are more truthful than those of slaves.
4. The dreams of a man are more truthful than those of a woman.
5. Among women, those who are veiled have truer dreams than those who are not.
6. The rich have more truthful dreams than the poor.
7. The elderly have more truthful dreams than the young.[6]

Generally, the higher one's status the more open one will be to true dreams. This is especially the case with Ibn Sīnā, who thought divine dreams the special preserve of kings and sages.

All Muslim dream manuals—even Ibn Sīnā's—concur that the knowledge gained in dreams is a form of prophecy (*nubūwah*) and revelation (*waḥy*), two highly charged terms also used to describe the nature of the Koran. As Ibn Qutaybah puts the matter: "The dream is one of the parts of revelation (*waḥy*) and one of the modes of prophecy (*nubūwah*)."[7] Such sweeping claims are occasionally qualified, usually by specifying that dreams provide only a fraction of prophecy—one forty-sixth or some variant on that figure. Invariably an appeal is made to prophetic tradition on this point: "The dream of the Muslim is one of the forty-six parts of prophecy (*nubūwah*)"—the standard against which they are measured being the Koran. There are, also, certain kinds of dreams particularly laden with prophetic significance. Usually these are identified as dreams in which Muḥammad appears.[8] The standard proof text for this is likewise a prophetic tradition: "Whosoever has seen me in a dream has seen me in truth, for Satan is not able to imitate me in a dream." Sometimes dreams of the Koran and other exalted objects are also included among these invariably true dreams. Ibn Qutaybah, for instance, suggests that Satan can appear to the dreamer neither as God or the Koran, nor as the sun, moon, heavens, earth, or clouds.[9]

Not only are dreams understood to be forms of prophecy and revelation, they are also usually considered to be nothing less than the chronological successors of Koranic revelation. Prophetic traditions to this effect abound and are widely cited in the dream manuals. Perhaps the most famous takes as its setting the penultimate day of Muḥammad's life. The prophet, now quite ill, is carried into the mosque on the shoulders of two companions. He tries to lead the prayer, but is too weak. He delegates his duties to Abū Bakr, and as he leaves, proclaims: "[When I am gone] there shall remain naught of the glad tidings of prophecy, except for true dreams. These the Muslim will see or they will be seen for him."[10] Dreams are, in short, the primary mode through which God will communicate with his community following Muḥammad's death and the cessation of Koranic revelation. They are, in short, the successors of Koranic revelation. Ibn Sīnā alone seems not to have shared this view, in large part as a result of his neoplatonic understanding of the function and character of prophecy.

The Logic of Dream Interpretation

As already suggested, the early Muslim dream manuals posit the interconnectedness of the dream world and the real world, under the divine aegis. Their task is not to discern why these worlds are interconnected. This is assumed. Muslim oneirocrits do occasionally attempt to understand how God sends dreams, in which case mention is usually made of the angel of dreams, the Tablet, and so on. Details of the process are seldom given, however. Of far greater interest to these oneirocrits is the understanding of the divine messages granted by God. This is, in fact, the main reason the dream manuals were written. They are code books that present the algorithms needed to unravel divine ciphers. That God would chose to send his messages as ciphers seems never to excite much interest. That he uses this opaque form of communication is simply presupposed. The task of the interpreter of dreams is not to understand why there is a code, but what the code means, what dream symbols intimate. Like geographers charting a distant land, Muslim oneirocrits sought to map the divine code that connected the objects of the night with the happenings of the world.

That which requires interpretation is normally called a *ruʾyā*, usually translated as "dream" or "vision," from a root meaning "to see."[11] This word is used to denote three very different sorts of experiences, ones that correspond closely to a series of distinctions first made in antiquity.[12] Some significant dreams (*somnium*) are "enigmatic": they conceal their true meaning and need interpretation. Other dreams (*visio*) are "visionary": they are literal, with contents identical to their meaning. Yet other dreams (*oraculum*) are "oracular": in these a person or god appears and reveals things to the dreamer in a fashion that does not require interpretation. These three types of dreams are denoted in Arabic by the single word *ruʾyā*. A dream can be considered oracular when, for example, God or an angel or Muḥammad appears to a believer and conveys some piece of information in a literal fashion. It is thus that Muḥammad, through the angel Gabriel, is said to have received his earliest revelations of the Koran.[13] A dream may be termed a vision when it conveys its occult knowledge in a literal fashion. The existence of such dreams is acknowledged in the dream manuals, but is otherwise of little concern: they do not, after all, require interpretation. The dream manuals are far more interested in the first class of dreams, those that are enigmatic and thus require interpretation if they are to yield their occult knowledge.

In its most general sense, the process of decoding a *ruʾyā* takes place by positing links between dream symbols and their meanings. The form in which the linkage is couched is of little importance. The linkage can be propositional: an interpreter posits a relation of equivalence between the symbol and its meaning, predicating the meaning of the symbol. "Venus is the king's wife."[14] It can also be conditional—"If he sees a frog speaking to him, he will obtain dominion."[15] (In a related fashion, an apodosis can be linked to an indefinite relative clause. "Whoever sees that the resurrection has happened in a place, justice will be spread in that place."[16]) Alternatively, it can be indicative: the dream symbol can be said to "indicate" (*dalla*) its meaning. "A turtle covered with mud indicates a woman who is perfumed and adorned, who presents herself lewdly to men."[17] Or finally, it can be anecdotal: a story can be told in which someone comes to a dream interpreter, narrates a dream, and receives its interpretation.

Regardless of the literary form in which the interpretation of the dream is presented, in each instance it is possible to discern two logical elements, a description of the dream symbol and a statement of its meaning. These two elements are related to one another under the logical form of a condition, whether expressed or not. The simple act of predication, for example, is really only a conveniently abbreviated mode of expression. Despite the actual words being used, the interpreter is not in fact suggesting that Venus is the king's wife, but rather that if one sees Venus in a dream, the dream has something to do with the king's wife. The statement of the dream symbol is the protasis of the condition. It is the omen that demands interpretation, the sign pointing to the signified. The statement of the meaning of the dream is the apodosis of the condition. It is the oracle to be derived from the omen, the signified to which the sign points. Muslim dream manuals are essentially long lists of these conditional sentences. The work of Ibn Qutaybah, for example, one of the shorter dream manuals considered in this study, contains approximately 1,600 of these conditional sentences. The protases of the conditions represent if not all possible dreams, at least those thought to be most common or most basic. It is presumably left to the interpreter to infer by analogy those not treated from those treated.

Within the protases a description of the various possible dreams are presented. Sometimes it is a question of actions; sometimes, of objects. In all cases, however, the presentation of the dreams is highly formalized. Muslim dream manuals are not in the least concerned with the narrative contents of the dreams they interpret. Through a process never described or explicitly acknowledged, before being interpreted dreams are subject to a process of selection that highlights certain parts of the dream and effaces others. In my own experience, people do not dream objects, but narratives. Dreams are more like motion pictures than still photographs. They offer a succession of events and objects, linked in some fashion, but often severely disjointed. Accordingly, when a dream of a frog is at issue in the dream manuals, we must assume that this symbol had originally been just one among many that occurred in the dream, and that through a process that is never explained it alone has been taken to be significant. Without positing this prior act of selection, we would have to suppose the dream world of medieval Muslims to have been qualitatively different from our own, consisting largely of single objects suspended against black backgrounds, floating before the dreamers' minds for the duration of their dreams.

In the dream manuals, the act through which one passes from the dream to its meaning is that of *taᶜbīr*, the verbal noun of *ᶜabbara*,[18] which is in turn the causative form of *ᶜabara*, meaning in its most basic sense "to pass over something from one side to another." According to medieval lexicographers,[19] the interpretation of dreams is called *taᶜbīr* because in reflecting on dreams one considers everything between their two ends, passing from the beginning of what is seen to its end. Alternatively, they suggest, the expression is an extension—not so much causative as intensive—of another usage in which one is said to *ᶜabara fī al-kitāb* ("consider, examine, study a book"). A more probable explanation of the word's usage would take it in its etymological sense. The act of *taᶜbīr* is the act of "making the dream pass" from one state to another. It entails the "transferring" of the dream from the symbol to its meaning, from the sign to the signified. We might even call this process an act of "translating" the dream, a usage paralleled in Syriac, where the causative form of the same root (*aᶜbar*) is used in expressions such as *aᶜbar men leshōnō ᶜebrōyō l-yawnōyō* ("he translated from Hebrew into Greek").

How is it possible to interpret a dream, to translate it from an unknown language into one that is known? The tool that makes this possible is the dream manual, a dictionary that juxtaposes the dream symbols with their semantic equivalents, the meanings of those dream symbols. What is it about the dream symbol and its meaning that allows the interpreter to understand them as semantic equivalents? The interpreter of dreams is able to pass from the dream symbol to its meaning because some sort of linkage between the two is perceived. There is something about the dream symbol that is inherently analogous or similar to the meaning it bears. Sometimes it is fairly easy to imagine of what this analogy or similarity consists. If one dreams of urinating into a vessel with a hole in the bottom, this means that the dreamer's wife is barren.[20] Linking the protasis with its apodosis, presumably, is the similarity between urine and semen, between the urine that leaks out of the vessel and the semen that "leaks out" of the dreamer's wife. To dream of urinating where another has already urinated signifies that the dreamer will marry a divorcée before the completion of her waiting period.[21] Urinating where another has already urinated is thus associated with the emission of semen where another has already emitted semen. Once again, urine and semen are equated. In much the same way, to urinate on a Koran indicates a child who will memorize the Koran;[22] to urinate blood, to have sex with a menstruating woman;[23] and to urinate excrement, to have anal sex with one's wife.[24] There need not be just a single association linked with each dream symbol. Muslim oneirocrits, for obvious reasons, also associated the act of urination with the experiencing of relief. Under this form, to deliver oneself of urine that has been held back signifies the cessation of anxiety or worry, while for one in debt it points to the settlement of the debt.[25] In each of the above instances, we can be fairly confident that we understand why the dream and its meaning are thought to be analogous or similar. Although separated by great cultural and temporal distance, it is still possible to discern the underlying oneirocritic logic that makes it possible to link the dream symbol and its meaning.

There are other times when the underlying link between protasis and apodosis is more opaque. We are simply unable to be sure what functioned to link the dream symbol and its meaning. If a man dreams that he is masturbating, this means that he will hold fast to the Sunnah.[26] The holding fast we can perhaps understand. But why the Sunnah? Or consider Ibn Qutaybah's treatment of dreams of snakes.[27] The basic meaning of this dream symbol has to do with an enemy, more specifically, an enemy who hides his anger. On the basis of this link between snake and enemy, Ibn Qutaybah puts forward some dozen or so permutations, all of which presuppose this basic meaning. (To fight a snake means you will fight your enemy. A dead snake is an enemy that God has requited for his evil. To fear a snake that you do not see is to be safe from your enemies. A snake coming out of your urethra indicates a child who will be an enemy. A snake in your house means that there is an enemy in your house. . . .) What is the underlying link between snake and enemy? We can only guess—perhaps because snakes are hostile to humans; perhaps because snakes "hide" their poison; perhaps because of the scriptural accounts of primeval history. Even so, why did Ibn Qutaybah think that a white snake signifies a weak enemy, while a black snake indicates one that is strong? It might be because white snakes were thought to be less poisonous than black snakes, or it might have something to do with the symbolic associations of the colors themselves, perhaps because black was the color of the

Abbasids. We can only guess: the underlying oneirocritic logic is inscribed in an ancient language, one that we are no longer fully able to understand.

The dream symbol and its meaning are linked because they are similar or analogous to one another. Or perhaps better, they are understood to resemble one another. The logical category of resemblance is notoriously malleable. As Charles Sanders Peirce many years ago argued, "any two things resemble one another just as strongly as any two others, if recondite resemblances are admitted."[28] Resemblance encompasses relations as diverse as the sharing of a common origin, the possession of identical qualities, homonymy, metonymy, antonomasia, and so on. There are, in fact, so many ways that one thing can resemble another that in principle, in the words of Umberto Eco, "Everything [can be connected] with everything else by a labyrinthine web of mutual referrals."[29] The flexible notion of resemblance in the dream manuals would be an instance of what Eco has further characterized as the interpretive habit of "unlimited semiosis," a form of thinking that sees everything as potentially linked together through similitude and resemblance, a form of thinking that he playfully suggests is characteristic of intellectual movements as diverse as Renaissance Hermeticism and certain forms of contemporary literary criticism.[30]

Does the notion of resemblance in Muslim dream manuals bear any relation to similar notions operative outside the textual world of the dream manuals? Qayrawānī once suggested that dreams of frogs signify pious persons.[31] He justified this interpretation through an appeal to a prophetic tradition in which the killing of frogs was forbidden on the grounds that they glorify God more than any other creatures, presumably through their croaking. Do frogs outside the dream world bear about themselves a halo of symbolic associations, one of which is piety? Does someone passing along a road at night and hearing their croaking call to mind the remembrance of God practiced by the Sufis? It is hard to be certain. At most we can say that there are many instances in the dream manuals where an attempt is made to link the logic of resemblance at work in the dream manuals with an identical logic at work in other contexts. This can be seen especially in those instances where the authors of the dream manuals attempt to justify their linking of dream symbols and their meanings through recourse to the value of the same symbols in other contexts—well-known proverbs, verses of poetry, sayings of Muḥammad, and so on. Whether such symbolic parallels exist anywhere but in the mind of the interpreters is another question.

The Boundaries of the Early Muslim Tradition of Dream Interpretation

Taken together, an analysis of the contours of the early Muslim dream manuals strongly supports the homogeneity of the early Muslim oneirocritic tradition. This homogeneity is evident in the common understanding of the purpose for which these texts were written, that of divination. It is also seen in the shared theological presuppositions of these texts: dreams are always understood within a theistic framework and are always presented as imparting a form of prophetic knowledge. Moreover, these texts all presuppose a similar oneirocritic logic, one governed by a notion of resemblance that justifies the linking of dreams and their interpretations. The notion of genre is sometimes rather slippery. Not here, however. These characteristics provide this corpus with a set of well-defined boundaries. At the same time that these characteristics mark off these texts as members of the same class, they also distinguish them from other types of early Muslim literature on dreams.

As researchers are now beginning to discover, medieval Muslims expressed an interest in dreams for a host of reasons. Accounts of dreams were collected and cited with a view to the probative value of their contents. They could be employed, for instance, to adjudicate between the merits of the legal schools,[32] to determine the correct reading of Koranic verses,[33] or to resolve theological questions.[34] Or again, the dream experience itself could become a matter for philosophic reflection.[35] Alternatively, accounts of dreams might be collected to establish the sanctity of the person who saw them.[36] One might note in particular the work of Zawawī (d. 882/1477), whose collection of dreams "could only confirm for his readers what Zawawī narcissistically believed, that he was the perfect man who stood at the head of all other *awliyā*ʾ" (saints).[37] In a similar fashion, dream narratives might be collected to testify to the learning of a particular person.[38] They might even function as "jacket blurbs." The work of Ibn Abī Jamrah (d. ca. 695/1296) is probably the most notable example of this phenomenon.[39] To his rather petty little abridgment of Bukhārī's famous collection of prophetic traditions, Ibn Abī Jamrah prefaced an account of sixty-nine dreams. These present Muḥammad or God testifying to the magnitude of Ibn Abī Jamrah's achievement—best book on prophetic traditions ever written, remarkably free of typos, belongs in every scholar's library, and so on.

Such nondivinatory literature of dreams needs to be distinguished from literature on dreams that is specifically divinatory. The point is important, for sometimes the distinction is glossed over. Toufic Fahd, in particular, in his foundational bibliography of "oneirocritic literature in Arabic,"[40] sometimes does not carefully distinguish between the different ends to which a concern for dreams might be put. Side by side in his survey of oneirocritic literature stand collections of Sufi dream narratives, philosophic works on dreams, and dream manuals proper. He makes no attempt to separate out literature that is specifically divinatory. In large part, however, he is being consistent, for he operates with a rather unusual definition of "oneirocriticism" as "literature concerned with dreams," while at the same time describing oneiromancy as "divination via dreams."[41] The point need not be belabored. It should at least be noted, though, that oneirocriticism and oneiromancy are usually considered to bear the same meaning and that in terms of their etymologies they are manifestly synonymous, both being traditionally used to denote the use of dreams for the purposes of divination. Perhaps one might rather denote divinatory literature as "oneirocritic" and "oneiromantic," reserving the adjective "oneiric" for this other, nondivinatory literature on dreams.

THE CONTENTS OF THE EARLY MUSLIM ONEIROCRITIC TRADITION

I turn now from the overall contours of the early Muslim oneirocritic tradition to its contents. The object here is to compare how the early Muslim dream manuals interpret dream symbols. Given the immensity of the surviving body of evidence, a comparison of each and every dream symbol as interpreted in each and every dream manual is obviously impossible. It is possible, however, to sample a number of different dream symbols. Dream manuals by the following authors will be taken into consideration: Kirmānī (where citations in later texts are available), Ibn Qutaybah, Sijistānī, Qayrawānī (his *Mumatti*ᶜ and the first two of his shorter dream manuals), Dīnawarī, Kharkūshī, and Ibn Sīnā. In the case of Ibn Sīnā's dream manual, I am concerned only with those sections in which "the interpretations of the Arabs" are presented: as argued in chapter 2, the other portions of his dream manual are wholly derived from Artemidorus. Given its stylistically problematic format, the third of Qayrawānī's shorter dream manuals has been excluded from consideration. So also, the poem of Maᶜāfirī is not taken into consideration: it is concerned only with dreams of the body and thus does not overlap with the symbols here analyzed.

Four sets of dream symbols are chosen for analysis—dreams of frogs, turtles, and crayfish; dreams of the resurrection; dreams of the five planets; and dreams of fullers, tailors, and carpenters. Why these four? They were chosen primarily because they offer relatively manageable amounts of information. Many dream symbols are associated with permutations, sometimes a great many, twenty, fifty, or even a hundred: dreams of the sun, the sun rising or setting, the sun in your pocket, hand, ear, nose, or bellybutton, the sun eclipsed by one, two, or three quarters, and so on. Each of the four clusters of dream symbols here analyzed presents just a few such permutations. In the end, however, it does not much matter which symbols are selected for analysis: as will be seen, in terms of content, the early Muslim tradition of dream interpretation evinces near total homogeneity. In short, all of the dream manuals interpret dreams the same way.

Dreams of Frogs, Turtles, and Crayfish

As for Ibn Qutaybah, he suggests that dreams of frogs can mean one of two things.[42] A single frog indicates a pious and earnest man (*rajūl ᶜābid wa-mujtahid*), who restrains (*kāff*) himself from causing injury to others. Alternatively, frogs that are multiplying signify that punishment will befall the place in which they multiply. These two dreams and the meanings that Ibn Qutaybah assigns to them are found in nearly all of the other early Muslim dream manuals. And as will be seen, the parallels are often quite specific: one may note in particular the frequent repetition of certain key words like *ᶜābid*, *kāff*, and *mujtahid*.

Sijistānī opines that a frog is a pious man (*ᶜābid*) of good repute, who is earnest (*mujtahid*) and restrains himself (*kāff*).[43] At the same time, frogs taking over a place signify the armies of God and a punishment that will befall the place. The parallels with Ibn Qutaybah are clear. Unlike Ibn Qutaybah, however, Sijistānī offers a proof text to justify the latter interpretation. The dream means this, he states, because God punished the children of Israel with frogs. It is surely a question here of Q 7.133 ("For we sent upon them the flood and the lice and the frogs and locusts . . ."), the only mention of frogs in the Koran.[44] The only other new information Sijistānī offers concerns dreams in which one pursues a frog. Such dreams indicate that the dreamer will pursue a man in the same way—a new permutation that is without parallel in the other early Muslim dream manuals.

Qayrawānī's treatment of frogs in his *Mumattiᶜ* is also similar to Ibn Qutaybah's.[45] A frog is a man who is pious (*ᶜābid*) and earnest (*mujtahid*) in his worship of God. Unlike both Ibn Qutaybah and Sijistānī, Qayrawānī offers a proof text—a tradition in which the prophet forbade killing frogs in that they glorify God more than any other creature. Expanding on this first basic interpretation, Qayrawānī adds that a group of frogs signifies a group of men who are well grounded in what is good. He then suggests that many frogs signify an army and that if they overcome a place through multiplying in it, this means that God will punish the people of that place. Qayrawānī, like Sijistānī, appeals to Q 7.133 as his proof text. Apart from a new proof text and some slight variants, Qayrawānī's treatment does not differ significantly from Ibn Qutaybah's. As for Qayrawānī's shorter dream manuals, these offer much the same. The first suggests, citing Q 7.133, that a single frog indicates a man who is "an ascetic and a worshipper" and that a group of frogs signifies a punishment that will befall a place.[46] The second follows similar lines.[47] A frog is a merciful man, while a group of frogs signifies either a group of worshipers or the army of God: to see them in a particular place, however, indicates specifically that they are the army of God.

Dīnawarī notes, first, that a frog is a man who is "pious (*ᶜābid*) and earnest (*mujtahid*) in his obedience to God."[48] While Qayrawānī had linked this interpretation to a prophetic tradition, Dīnawarī links it to an incident from patriarchal history—it was a frog that poured water on the fire of Nimrod. The remaining portions of Dīnawarī's treatment of frogs are attributed to non-Muslims:

> The Christians say: If someone sees that he is with a frog, his relationship with his relatives and neighbors will be good. If he sees that he is eating its meat, he will obtain benefit from them, at least a little.
>
> Artemidorus says: Frogs in a dream signify deceptive men and cheats. As for one who earns his living from the populace, it is a good sign.[49]
>
> Jāmāsb says: If you speak to a frog, you will obtain dominion.

Dīnawarī concludes by citing two anecdotes. The first concerns a Jew who saw frogs leave his land—the meaning of the dream being that punishment will be lifted from the land, as per the example of the plague of frogs sent upon Egypt.[50] Although basically a paraphrase of Exodus 8.8–13, in terms of content, this anecdote is equivalent to the more common equation of the multiplication of frogs with divine punishment. The second of Dīnawarī's anecdotes is derived from Artemidorus.[51] In general, Dīnawarī's treatment of dreams of frogs adds much that is novel. It should be emphasized, though, that he does not add anything new that is not explicitly attributed to a non-Muslim source.

Kharkūshī opens his treatment of dreams of frogs with the by-now predictable assertion that "a frog is a man who is pious (*ᶜābid*) and earnest (*mujtahid*) in his obedience to God."[52] Two other permutations on dreams of frogs are then offered:

> It is said that one who sees himself eating the meat of a frog will obtain a benefit from one of his companions.
>
> If he sees a frog speaking to him, he will obtain dominion.

It is clear that Kharkūshī is here dependent on Dīnawarī. While Dīnawarī had named his sources for these interpretations as the Christians and Jāmāsb, Kharkūshī cites them without attribution—a pattern that will recur in many of the other dream symbols here analyzed.

In sum, all seven dream manuals are unanimous that a frog signifies a man who is pious and earnest. There are, however, some occasional variations. Instead of pious and earnest, one sometimes finds ascetic or merciful, the meaning of which is more or less the same. These same dream manuals also differ as to their justification of this interpretation, offering in turn no proof text, a prophetic tradition, or a story about Nimrod. Six of the seven dream manuals also agree that a group of frogs, usually specified as multiplying or as being in a certain place, signifies the army of God or God's punishment that will befall the place in which the frogs are multiplying, an interpretation sometimes justified through an appeal to Q 7.133, on the plague of frogs that destroyed Egypt. Only Kharkūshī does not include this second interpretation. There is one unique tradition in Sijistānī's dream manual. Finally, Dīnawarī includes additional materials drawn from the Christians, Artemidorus, and Jāmāsb. Some of these same materials were adopted from him by Kharkūshī, although the latter did not include their non-Muslim attribution.

As for dreams of turtles, Ibn Qutaybah offers three interpretations.[53] A single turtle is a man who is ascetic, pious, and learned in the knowledge of old. Eating the meat of a turtle indicates that one will receive knowledge from such a pious and learned man. To see a turtle on a dunghill, contrariwise, means that there is a learned man who is neglected and unknown. At issue here is a single basic interpretation: a turtle is a pious and learned man. The other two interpretations are simply permutations on this basic theme. This same basic pattern will be found in nearly all of the other early Muslim dream manuals, very often also in the very same language.

According to Sijistānī, a turtle is "a man who is ascetic, pious, and learned in primeval knowledge, who is thoroughly versed in it."[54] Moreover, a turtle being honored means that knowledge is being honored. Thus far Sijistānī follows closely the lines laid down by Ibn Qutaybah. There is one difference, however. Instead of treating dreams of a turtle that is being disrespected, Sijistānī offers an interpretation of a turtle that is being honored. The underlying principle is nonetheless the same—how the turtle is treated indicates how knowledge is treated. And finally, Sijistānī offers a new permutation. "If someone sees that he takes a turtle and possesses it or that it enters his house, he will vanquish a man in the same way." This new permutation breaks with the general pattern established by Ibn Qutaybah. A turtle in this context seems not to have anything to do with a learned man. This new permutation, too, is without parallel in the other early Muslim dream manuals.

There is little new in Qayrawānī's treatment of dreams of turtles in his *Mumattiᶜ*.[55] A turtle is a man who is an ascetic, a jurist, and a worshiper, one grounded in ancient knowledge. To eat the meat of a turtle means that you will receive some of this learned man's knowledge and possessions in accordance with the amount you eat. A turtle stretched out on a road or a dunghill signifies neglect of knowledge in that place, while a turtle being honored signifies the opposite. The first of Qayrawānī's shorter dream manuals does not treat dreams of turtles. The second offers two interpretations: a turtle is a man who is ascetic and learned; to eat its meat means that one will receive this learned man's knowledge in proportion to the amount one eats.[56] There is nothing novel here.

Dīnawarī opens his treatment of turtles with a wholly new element. "A turtle covered with mud signifies a woman who is perfumed and adorned, who presents herself [lewdly] to men."[57] He then returns to more well-trodden paths: a turtle has to do with a judge or one who is pious. Dīnawarī is the first to attempt to justify this interpretation. Dreams of turtles mean this, he opines, in that they are "the wisest of the creatures of the sea and the most pious." Again following familiar lines, Dīnawarī continues by noting that a turtle being honored in a land or village indicates that the people of knowledge in that place will be honored. Dīnawarī next inserts a line the meaning of which is not entirely clear: "If he sees that, he will read the pages of Abraham the friend of God and the books of the rest of the prophets." Further, to dream of eating a turtle's meat signifies an increase in possessions or that the dreamer will acquire prophetic knowledge. Dīnawarī concludes by citing the opinion of the Christians on what it means to eat the meat of a turtle: "obtaining good and justice and benefit."

Kharkūshī's treatment of turtles offers little new.[58] "The turtle is the wisest of sea creatures. It signifies a judge. It is also said that it is a man who is worshipful and recites the Koran." A turtle covered with mud is a woman who is perfumed and adorned, "who presents herself [lewdly] to men." Thus far Kharkūshī is dependent on Dīnawarī. He continues by suggesting that the exaltation of a turtle is the exaltation of the people of knowledge, while a turtle on a dunghill is the neglect of the learned. And finally, to eat the meat of a turtle signifies that you will receive some good from a distant land.

In sum, six dream manuals agree that a turtle is a learned man of one sort or another. Excepting Sijistānī, all also agree that eating the meat of a turtle indicates the acquisition of knowledge or in some cases of possessions. In the same way, there is near unanimity that disrespect of a turtle implies disrespect of the learned, while treating one with respect indicates the opposite. Dīnawarī introduces a new tradition (a muddy turtle is a lewd woman) and is followed by Kharkūshī. There are only two unique traditions: one in Sijistānī and one in Dīnawarī, the latter being explicitly attributed to the Christians. From the third century A.H. to the early fifth there is, thus, near total agreement as to how dreams of turtles should be interpreted. Further, this same general pattern can also be discerned already in the work of Kirmānī.[59] He is said to have written that turtles mean three things: a man who is an ascetic, who is pious, who is learned in the ancient sciences; to acquire a turtle indicates that one will overcome another man in the same fashion; and a turtle in a place or on a road or on a dunghill signifies that a learned man is being harmed.

As for crayfish, Ibn Qutaybah suggests that they represent a man who is morally reprehensible, ambitious, stubborn, and unapproachable.[60] A similar interpretation is found in most later texts as well. Ibn Qutaybah goes on to note that if one sees that one is eating a crayfish this means that one will obtain money. This tradition will also be found in most of the later dream manuals. Ibn Qutaybah closes by citing a saying, the source of which is never specified: "It is said that the crayfish is the most exalted of animals in terms of the manner of its creation, after the snake."[61] Although this saying does not apparently have any bearing on the two interpretations, it too will nevertheless be found in many later dream manuals.

The dream manual of Sijistānī includes the same three traditions found in the work of Ibn Qutaybah.[62] The crayfish is a man who is morally reprehensible, ambitious in what concerns himself, not easily turned from what he is intent upon, a hard man when it comes to his work, exalted and unapproachable. To dream of eating the flesh of a crayfish means that you will obtain money and good from a far-off place. The crayfish is the most exalted of animals in terms of the manner of its creation, after the snake.[63] To these three traditions he add two others. The first is unique, being found in no other dream manual.[64] The second suggests, obscurely, that anything with which the crayfish comes into contact in the dream signifies something "interpreted of its owner and transferred to him." As will be seen, this tradition is found in only one other early Muslim dream manual.

Qayrawānī includes in his *Mumatti*ᶜ the same three traditions found in Ibn Qutaybah.[65] A crayfish is a man who is morally reprehensible, unapproachable, a hard man when it comes to his work and what he is seeking to obtain. To eat its flesh means that you will obtain something of that man's wealth or the wealth of another from a distant place. It is said: "The crayfish is the most exalted of animals in terms of the manner of its creation, after the snake." To these three traditions Qayrawānī adds another that is similar to one found in Sijistānī: "Similarly, everything into which the crayfish enters in the dream is interpreted of its owner and is transferred to the one seeking it." Only the second of Qayrawānī's shorter dream manuals offers an interpretation of crayfish, suggesting, unremarkably, that "to eat the flesh of a crayfish is to obtain wealth from a far-off place."[66]

Following earlier and by now familiar lines, Dīnawarī suggests that a crayfish is "a man full of guile—because of the multitude of its [the crayfish's] weapons—inspiring much dread, morally reprehensible, ambitious, not easily turned, a hard man on his companions."[67] To this he adds the predictable assertion that eating a crayfish indicates that one will obtain something good from a far-off land. Dīnawarī closes by citing the opinion of the Christians: crayfish in a dream signify forbidden wealth. Concerning dreams of crayfish, Kharkūshī suggests simply that they indicate forbidden wealth.[68] Once again he follows Dīnawarī, without reproducing the non-Muslim attribution of the tradition in question.

Again there is a remarkable degree of unity among the early dream manuals. Of the six texts that interpret dreams of crayfish, four agree that they signify a morally reprehensible person suffering from a series of prideful sins. Another five texts agree, with very little variation, even as touching the language used, that eating a crayfish signifies that wealth or something good will befall the dreamer. Three texts also cite the tradition on crayfish being among the most exalted of God's creatures. In addition to this general unanimity, there are two traditions that are each shared by two dream manuals. Only one tradition, found in Sijistānī's work, appears to be unique. Once again we are fortunate to have access to Kirmānī's interpretation of this dream symbol.[69] Not surprisingly, Kirmānī is said to have opined that a crayfish is a man who has an exalted opinion of himself, who is ambitious and endowed with a hard disposition.

In sum, it is necessary to highlight a number of the overall patterns that have emerged thus far. First, invariably the interpretations offered by Ibn Qutaybah are found in the later dream manuals. When later texts do not contain parallels, it is usually because the symbol in question is not being treated. (This is especially the case with the first of Qayrawānī's shorter dream manuals.) We need not suppose, however, that Ibn Qutaybah's work was the source behind the later dream manuals. It may well be that both Ibn Qutaybah and these later works made use of common sources. Twice, in fact, it has been possible to establish parallels with the dream manual of Kirmānī. Second, though following the common tradition, Sijistānī's work is notable for including additional interpretations not elsewhere paralleled. Third, Dīnawarī's departures from earlier tradition are usually attributed to non-Muslim sources. When Kharkūshī adopts Dīnawarī's materials, however, he drops their non-Muslim attribution. Regardless, both Dīnawarī and Kharkūshī usually include the more common materials found in earlier texts.

Dreams of the Resurrection

The homogeneity seen in the above instances is also evident in the treatment of other dream symbols. A case in point: dreams of the resurrection, a symbol treated in seven of the dream manuals here considered. Once again, by the time Ibn Qutaybah had completed his work, already the basic interpretation of this dream had been established. As the centuries pass, moreover, only minor variations will arise. According to Ibn Qutaybah:

> Whosoever sees the resurrection happen in a place, justice will be spread in that place for its people if they are being oppressed, and against them, if they are oppressors—for the day of the resurrection is the day of separation [of good from evil] and of retribution and judgment. For God said: "We shall place scales of justice for the day of the resurrection; not one soul will be treated unjustly" (Q 21.47).[70]

This same tradition is found in the other early Muslim dream manuals. Kharkūshī includes a version nearly identical to that of Ibn Qutaybah.[71] The same can be said of the version found in two of the works of Qayrawānī.[72] His *Mumattiᶜ*, for instance, reads:

> Whosoever sees the resurrection happen, justice will be spread in the place in which he sees that it happens; if in it there are those who are oppressed, they will be victorious; if they are oppressors, [God] will avenge himself on them and their affair will be separated. For God says: "The day of separation is the time appointed for them all" (Q 44.40).

Other dream manuals cite slightly periphrastic versions. Dīnawarī, for instance, suggests:

> [Resurrection in a dream means]: If the people of the place in which the resurrection happens are oppressors, [God] will take vengeance on them; or, [if they are] oppressed, they will be victorious, for the day of the resurrection is the day of justice.[73]

There are similar traditions in Sijistānī and one of Qayrawānī's shorter works.[74]

The above-cited interpretation is all that is offered by Ibn Qutaybah, Sijistānī, and the second of Qayrawānī's shorter dream manuals. The other four texts, however, all also agree that the accompanying portents of the resurrection mean pretty much the same, except that the good or bad predicted by the dream applies to the dreamer rather than to the land in which the resurrection is dreamed to occur. Kharkūshī, for example, states:

> Whosoever sees as if one of the portents of the Hour has appeared in a place, such as the rising of the sun from the west or the going forth of the Beast of the Earth[75] or the Impostor[76] or Gog and Magog—if [the dreamer] is one who is obedient to God, his dream is a glad tiding for him; if he is one who is disobedient to God or worried that he might be [disobedient], his dream is a warning for him.[77]

Similar materials are found in Qayrawānī's *Mumatti*ᶜ and the first of his shorter dream manuals,[78] as well as in the work of Dīnawarī.[79]

Also shared by three of the dream manuals is a tradition to the effect that dreams in which one is resurrected all by oneself foretell the death of the dreamer. In Kharkūshī's version, for instance, we read:

> If he sees that he alone has been resurrected, [the dream] signifies his death—in accordance with what is transmitted in the tradition: "Whoever has died, his resurrection has occurred."[80]

Similar interpretations are found in Qayrawānī's *Mumatti*ᶜ and in the dream manual of Dīnawarī.[81] Like Kharkūshī, both works also bring to bear proof texts to justify the interpretation. Dīnawarī cites the tradition known to Kharkūshī, explicitly ascribing it to Muḥammad. This same tradition is cited by Qayrawānī, although he attributes it to one of the companions. Qayrawānī further appeals to the verse of an anonymous poet: "There occurred the resurrection of him upon whom there descended the dove / The people and the child spent the night bewailing his death."

Thus far it is possible to discern a relatively large measure of homogeneity in how the dream manuals interpret dreams of the resurrection. As has been seen, seven works agree that a dream of the resurrection indicates justice for the oppressed and punishment for the oppressors. About half also concur that any of the portents of the resurrection indicate either glad tidings or warning, while half also agree that being resurrected all by oneself indicates that one will die. Around this basic core shared by the dream manuals, there are to be found in some texts a handful of unique or nearly unique traditions. At times these extra traditions are just permutations on more basic meanings of this dream symbol, at other times they present new elements. Dīnawarī, for instance, introduces an additional five interpretations that lack earlier parallels.[82] Not surprisingly, these were all borrowed, nearly verbatim, by Kharkūshī.[83] A single unique tradition is found in Qayrawānī's *Mumatti*ᶜ.[84] Another unique tradition is found in the dream manual of Dīnawarī,[85] while two further ones were cited by Kharkūshī.[86] Notwithstanding the presence of these unique or nearly unique traditions, it must be emphasized that the dream manuals agree as to the basic meaning of dreams of the resurrection.

Dreams of the Planets

As for dreams of the five planets, here the homogeneity of the early Muslim oneirocritic tradition is even more evident. Beginning already in the dream manual of Ibn Qutaybah we find the following propositions:

> Venus is the king's wife.
> Mercury is his scribe.
> Mars is his minister of war.
> Jupiter is his minister of finance.
> Saturn is his minister of justice.[87]

Nearly identical materials are found in the other dream manuals. Aside from transposing the dreams of Mercury and Mars, Sijistānī differs only by asserting that a dream of Jupiter can indicate not only a minister of finance, but also a judge or a minister of irrigation.

> Venus is the king's wife.
> Mars is his minister of war.
> Mercury is his scribe.
> Jupiter is his minister of finance and his judge.
> Saturn is his minister of justice.
> It is also said that Jupiter is the king's minister of irrigation.[88]

While the first of Qayrawānī's shorter dream manuals does not include a treatment of these dream symbols, his *Mumatti*ᶜ presents a version identical to Ibn Qutaybah's, as does the second of his shorter dream manuals. Even the order of presentation is the same.

> Venus is the king's wife.
> Mercury is his scribe.
> Mars is his minister of war.
> Jupiter is his minister of finance.
> Saturn is his minister of justice.[89]

> Venus is the king's wife.
> Mercury is his scribe.
> Mars is his minister of war.
> Jupiter is his minister of finance.
> Saturn is his minister of justice.[90]

Dīnawarī's version is likewise nearly identical, differing in just a few, minor ways.

> Saturn is the king's minister of justice.
> Jupiter is his minister of finances.

> Mars is his minister of war and his superintendent of prisons, though some say that he is [the chief] of police.
> Venus—and she is from Mars—is his wife; and whoever sees her will speak to a gorgeous woman with whom he is not related.
> Mercury is his scribe.[91]

Once again Kharkūshī is dependent on Dīnawarī. His version reads:

> Saturn is the sultan's minister of justice.
> Jupiter is his minister of finance.
> Mars is his minister of war; others say he is [the chief] of police.
> Venus is a wife.
> Mercury is his scribe.[92]

And finally, there happens this time to be a section in Ibn Sīnā's dream manual on "dreams of the planets according to the opinion of the Arabs."[93] There it is recorded that the Arabs believe:

> Venus is the king's wife.
> Mercury is his scribe.
> Mars is his minister of war.
> Jupiter is [his minister] of finance.
> Saturn is [his chief] of police and overseer of prisons or the one in charge of punishments.

Ibn Sīnā presents the five dreams in the same order as Ibn Qutaybah and differs only in his interpretation of dreams of Saturn. Otherwise their versions are nearly identical.

Dreams of Fullers, Tailors, and Carpenters

Nearly all Muslim dream manuals contain a chapter on the various occupations. Sometimes these chapters are brief, more often they are quite extensive—so much so that they have been able to provide researchers with a wealth of social-historical information.[94] Of the dream manuals considered in this study, only the first of Qayrawānī's shorter works lacks such a chapter. For the purposes of the present analysis, three occupations are of concern, dreams of fullers, tailors, and carpenters. A comparison of how these three dreams are interpreted points up, once again, the thorough homogeneity of the early Muslim oneirocritic tradition.

As for dreams of fullers, Ibn Qutaybah offers two interpretations.[95] Such dreams indicate either a man who causes alms to be given (*tajrī ᶜalā yadihi ṣadaqāt al-nās*) or a man who brings relief from anxiety. This he justifies by noting that "stains on clothing are sins and cares." Ibn Qutaybah was not the first to suggest this interpretation. Something similar was put forward already by Kirmānī, who is said to have believed:

> A fuller signifies a man who causes good deeds to be done and sins to be atoned for (*yajrī ʿalā yadayhi faʿl al-khayrāt wa-takfīr al-dhunūb*), a man famous for his kindness.[96]

Some dream manuals reproduce both of Ibn Qutaybah's interpretations, that fullers indicate either the giving of alms or the removal of anxiety. Qayrawānī's *Mumattiʿ*, for example, states:

> As for a fuller, he signifies someone who causes good deeds to be done and alms to be given (*yajrī ʿalā yadayhi al-khayr wa-l-ṣadaqāt*), or alternatively deliverance from worry, anxieties, and cares.[97]

The same is found in the work of Sijistānī.[98] Other dream manuals preserve only the first interpretation. Such is the case with the works of Dīnawarī[99] and Kharkūshī,[100] who is, once again, following Dīnawarī. Contrariwise, Ibn Sīnā's presentation of the views of the Arabs reproduces only the second interpretation.[101] Only the second of Qayrawānī's shorter dream manuals presents a significantly different interpretation, suggesting that fullers are interpreted as the angel of death.[102] Qayrawānī's variant interpretation is, however, very likely the result of scribal error: other dream manuals ascribe this interpretation not to dreams of a fuller (*qaṣṣār*) but those of a butcher (*qaṣṣāb*).[103] Whatever the case, it is clear that from Kirmānī to the works of the early fifth century A.H. there was substantial agreement as to the interpretation of dreams of fullers: of the eight dream manuals that treat this dream symbol, all agree that it indicates either atonement for sins or freedom from anxiety.

As for tailors, Ibn Qutaybah suggests that they indicate "a man at whose hands are brought together scattered affairs from among those of the world."[104] Once again we have a parallel from Kirmānī, one that is nearly verbatim: "A tailor is a man at whose hands are brought together scattered affairs."[105] Similar interpretations are found in all other early dream manuals. Sijistānī, for example, suggests: "A tailor is a man at whose hands are brought together scattered affairs."[106] So also, Ibn Sīnā cites the opinions of the Arabs to the same effect: "A tailor is a man who puts in order scattered affairs."[107] The only dream manual to offer a justification for this interpretation is Qayrawānī's *Mumattiʿ*, which suggests: "A tailor is one who fills the gaps in things that are torn. [For this reason, in a dream] he is a man at whose hands are brought together scattered affairs."[108] What this "bringing together of scattered affairs" may have meant seems to have been unclear to some oneirocrits. They thus endeavored to paraphrase the dictum in a more concrete fashion. The second of Qayrawānī's shorter dream manuals, for example, interprets it to mean a man who will "mediate between others in a marvelous fashion."[109] Similarly, Dīnawarī suggests that such dreams mean "a man who unites men, who ameliorates the affairs of the noble and the despised."[110] In this he is followed by Kharkūshī.[111] Dīnawarī, again followed by Kharkūshī, also notes, along the same lines, that if the sewing being done by the tailor is not good, then the attempt to unite these men will not be successful.[112] As seen a number of times already, Dīnawarī is often the source of additional permutations. Two such permutations are added by him in his consideration of dreams of tailors.[113] Both are appropriated by Kharkūshī.[114] In sum, all eight works agree that a tailor is a man who brings together what is scattered. Dīnawarī's work, though including this more common interpretation and a variant on it, also introduces two additional permutations, both of which were borrowed by Kharkūshī.

As for dreams of carpenters, Ibn Qutaybah states that they bear but a single meaning.[115] Invariably they point to "a man who corrects (*mu*ʾ*addib*) others and sets them straight (*muṣliḥ*) in what touches their worldly concerns." This interpretation he justifies by the analogy that subsists between the carpenter's shaping of wood, in particular his removing its blemishes, and the man whose sins are removed by one who corrects him and sets him straight.

> For wood is men in whose religion there is corruption (*fasād*), for he removes from that [corrupt religion] what the carpenter removes from the wood.[116]

Once again, Ibn Qutaybah was not the first to suggest this interpretation: Kirmānī had proposed something quite similar.[117]

> A carpenter is interpreted as a man who corrects and sets straight (*mu*ʾ*addib wa-muṣliḥ*), a man who possesses the ability to guide (*dhī tadbīr*) men in their religious concerns, a man who takes away the hypocrisy and corruption (*fasād*) from their religion.[118]

Other dream manuals offer closely parallel interpretations. Sijistānī's version, for example, reads:

> A carpenter is a man who corrects (*mu*ʾ*addib*) others, who vanquishes (*qāhir*) them, who guides (*mudabbir*) them in their worldly affairs, for wood is men in whose religion there is corruption (*faṣād*) and they are set straight (*yuṣlaḥūn*) from that in the same way that a carpenter sets straight the wood and straightens it out and carves it.[119]

Similarly, Dīnawarī's version reads:

> A carpenter is a man who corrects (*mu*ʾ*addib*) others, for a carpenter sets straight the wood and straightens it out and carves it; also, the man who corrects will vanquish (*yaqhar*) men in whose religion there is corruption (*fasād*), for he educates them and corrects (*yu*ʾ*addib*) them

> and teaches them what is right and proper, even as the tutor (*mu'addib*) of young people.[120]

Other dream manuals contain similar materials.

> A carpenter is a man who corrects (*mu'addib*) others.[121]

> A carpenter is a man who corrects (*mu'addib*) others.[122]

> A carpenter is a man who corrects (*mu'addib yu'addib*) others, who teaches them what is right, who vanquishes (*yaqhar*) the corrupt (*mufsidīn*); and the strengthening of the crooked found in religion.[123]

From the work of Kirmānī to the great syntheses of the early fifth century A.H., there is thus total agreement as to how dreams of carpenters should be interpreted.

To summarize, beginning with the work of Kirmānī in the late second century A.H. and ending with the compilations of the late fourth and early fifth centuries, interpretations of dreams of fullers, tailors, and carpenters were almost entirely consistent. Seven out of eight dream manuals agree that a dream of a fuller indicates either atonement for sins or freedom from anxiety. Only the second of Qayrawānī's shorter dream manuals offers a different interpretation, but this may in fact be the result of a scribal error. Seven out of seven dream manuals agree that a dream of a carpenter signifies a man who reforms the religion of others, while eight out of eight concur that a tailor represents a man who brings together what is scattered. Dīnawarī's work, while containing this latter interpretation and a variant on it, also introduces two additional permutations, which were also reproduced by Kharkūshī.

The Homogeneity of the Tradition

The following general patterns have emerged in the preceding analysis. The basic interpretations given to any particular dream in the work of Ibn Qutaybah are almost invariably found in later works. When we happen to have access to the dream manual of Kirmānī, through citations in later works, there are also strong parallels between it and the dream manual of Ibn Qutaybah. The basic interpretation given to a dream is only occasionally varied in later dream manuals. At times, when the interpretation contains a number of different parts, only some are found in the later works. At times, also, later works will omit altogether the treatment of a particular dream. What we do not find is equally important. Not one of the examples discussed above shows a later dream manual jettisoning the earlier tradition and starting from scratch, offering a fundamentally new interpretation of a dream symbol. This is not to say that there are not innovations in the later texts. Indeed, later works tend to be more expansive in their treatment of the individual dreams. Their expansiveness, however, stems not from the addition of fundamentally new interpretations, but usually from a willingness to add permutations to the basic data of the earlier tradition.

Sometimes later innovations are explicitly attributed to the Muslim community. At other times, especially in the work of Dīnawarī, they are ascribed to non-Muslims. Such foreign materials could, however, be assimilated to the explicitly Muslim tradition of dream interpretation. In particular, Kharkūshī often borrows Dīnawarī's non-Muslim traditions without their attribution. Kharkūshī's labors are eventually responsible for making such materials an integral part of the Muslim tradition of dream interpretation. But this is a tale for another time. Here it is sufficient to note that Kharkūshī's work was some centuries later epitomized by Abū ᶜAlī al-Dārī,[124] whose work was in turn one of the main sources of the dream manual of Nābulsī (d. 1143/1731). Both Dārī's and Nābulsī's texts circulated widely in manuscript form, especially the latter, one of the truly classic dream manuals. Moreover, by the latter half of the nineteenth century these same two texts had become the primary representatives of the Muslim tradition of dream interpretation, largely through their wide circulation in printed form.

The odd man out in this game is Ibn Sīnā, the avatar of an earlier age. Because his dream manual was so integrally linked to the work of Artemidorus, it is only with difficulty that one can consider it representative of the Muslim tradition of dream interpretation. Indeed, as suggested in chapter 2, Ibn Sīnā himself would probably have eschewed such an association. Regardless, when Ibn Sīnā does deign to consider the views of the "Arabs," when he turns from his Hellenic model to the works of his fellow Muslims, he is a faithful recorder of the same tradition of dream interpretation seen in other texts. Because Ibn Sīnā's work was so peculiar, so at odds with the general sense of the Muslim tradition of dream interpretation, it was to have almost no influence on later works in this genre. Although it enjoyed a fairly wide circulation in manuscript form, it seems to have had little impact on later texts: to my knowledge, it was never epitomized or used as a source by later Muslim dream manuals. Even the fact of its existence seems never to have been acknowledged in those later texts.

CONCLUSIONS

One might have expected that the Muslim tradition of dream interpretation would show greater diversity than it does. At issue here is a corpus of texts written over the course of approximately three centuries, texts that, geographically speaking, stemmed from one end of the Muslim world to the other, from the western regions of North Africa to the nether reaches of trans-Oxiana. Their authors, moreover, represented many of the diverse cultural orientations within the early Muslim community. Notwithstanding the heterogeneity of their provenance, diversity is hardly the most prominent feature of this corpus. As has been argued, the dream manuals considered in this study evince a remarkable degree of unity. They share a common understanding of the goal of dream interpretation, its theology, and its methods. Similarly, all interpret dreams in largely the same fashion. A frog meant the same thing in the second century A.H. as it did in the early fifth. It meant the same thing in North Africa as it did in Iran. In terms of its contours and contents, there is thus every reason to posit a single tradition of dream interpretation.

It must be remembered, however, that we are dealing with a relatively small portion of the early Muslim literature on dream interpretation. Many texts are no longer extant. As argued in the introduction, ancient and medieval literature needed to have bearers interested in its preservation for it to survive. In the case of the Muslim literature on dream interpretation, it is clear that its bearers preserved some parts of the early tradition while letting others die a silent death. It is possible that this process of selection did not operate in an entirely random fashion. Later tradition may have systematically appropriated only those works that were representative of the type of dream interpretation discerned in this chapter. In short, we cannot rule out the possibility that the homogeneity of the early Muslim tradition of dream interpretation is a result of the tacit censorship of the later bearers of the tradition.

Regardless, in the extant remains, whence the homogeneity of the tradition? Does it arise from textual interdependence? Or does it reflect an extratextual cause, such that parallels in the written works reflect a common derivation from a single, nonliterary tradition of dream interpretation? This latter possibility cannot be excluded. It may well be that the written texts are reflections of this primordial, nonliterary tradition. But if one is to judge strictly on the basis of the evidence of the texts themselves, it must be concluded that this nonliterary tradition was not primary: we are here dealing with texts that were, quite frankly, copying one another. This conclusion is supported by the nature of the parallels between the different texts, which are in most cases so specific that it is impossible to imagine them not to result from textual interdependence. It is also supported by the testimony of the authors themselves, most of whom showed no reticence about admitting their dependence on earlier sources.

It has been said of the late professor Tolkien's Hobbits that "they liked to have books filled with things that they already knew"—so also, the authors of the early Muslim dream manuals. These interpreters of dreams were first and foremost conservators of an inherited tradition. Once this tradition was in place, which must already have happened by the late second century A.H., the primary function of an author was that of transmitting the inherited tradition. As argued in chapters 1 and 2, the process of transmission did not function blindly. Each author made use of inherited materials, but crafted and arranged those materials in distinctive ways. Nevertheless, an author's creativity was expressed more through the manner of his compilation than through a manipulation of the contours and contents of the tradition. In an analysis of early Muslim poetry, Marshall G. S. Hodgson once suggested that such poetry could be effectively received only if it adhered to well-defined formal constraints and contained a “substance . . . familiar enough to allow each listener to concentrate on noting how well the thought had been put, without being distracted by considering overmuch the implications of the thought itself.”[125] Much the same dynamic is at work in the early Muslim dream manuals, in which creativity is expressed more through the manner of compilation than through the expression of unusual or unconventional ideas. In this sense, at least, it must be concluded that the old bugbear of *taqlīd* (“imitation”) characterized the Muslim tradition of dream interpretation from the very beginning.

CHAPTER FOUR

Dream Interpretation and Orthodoxy

In the preceding chapters, the development of the Muslim oneirocritic tradition has been treated largely as if it took place in a vacuum. It remains to be investigated how this tradition and its understanding of dreams relates to the understanding of dreams in other contemporary literary and cultural contexts. A full contextualization of the Muslim oneirocritic tradition would be an immense undertaking. Here I am content with a more modest goal—determining whether the ulema or religious scholars shared with the authors of the dream manuals a common understanding of the nature of dreams and their interpretation. How one answers this question is immensely important for understanding the social context of dream interpretation in early Muslim society. In particular, an answer to this question helps specify the extent to which dream interpretation was central to the concerns of those who formulated the contours of sharᶜī or orthodox Islam. Did the ulema consider dream interpretation one of the sharᶜī disciplines, an intellectual pursuit not just tolerated but approbated? Or was an interest in dreams regarded as an extracurricular pursuit, an avocation countenanced but not sanctioned, a religiously neutral discipline along the lines of, say, medicine or mathematics? Or were perhaps the ulema wary of dream interpretation, what with its seeming to offer a means of divine intercourse that bypassed the Koran and Sunnah?

If it can be shown that dream interpretation was central to the concerns of the ulema, there follow important implications for how one understands the cultural role of the discipline and the social locus for the composition and circulation of the early Muslim dream manuals. Most notably, dream interpretation will have to be classed with those disciplines more readily recognized as sharᶜī. It will have to be moved from the margin of Muslim intellectual concerns to the center. If dream interpretation is, in fact, a sharᶜī discipline, future discussions of the intellectual interests of the ulema will have to include dream interpretation alongside such topics as the Koran and its interpretation, prophetic traditions and their transmission, Arabic grammar, biography, and so on. In short, dream interpretation will have to be considered as one of the foundational, theological disciplines of sharᶜī Islam.

In what follows, I begin by examining the sources used in the dream manuals to justify an interest in dreams and their interpretation. I first investigate the Koranic proof texts utilized, those verses to which the authors of the dream manuals appealed to defend the legitimacy of dream interpretation. Did the ulema also find in those Koranic verses a validation of the prophetic character of dreams and of the need for interpreting them? I then explore the prophetic traditions cited in the dream manuals. As will be seen, it was with these traditions far more than the Koran that the authors of the dream manuals sought to justify their interest in dreams. Were the prophetic traditions cited in the dream manuals also found in the standard collections of prophetic traditions, and did the ulema find in those traditions the same justification of dream interpretation? Next, to understand better who among the early Muslims were reading dream manuals, I examine the social context within which such texts were circulating. This is accomplished through an analysis of the transmission-history of five dream manuals in an Andalusian context. And finally, I turn to one of the few sources offering insight into the concrete realities of dream interpretation among the ulema, the diary of a religious scholar of Baghdad, one who was also an interpreter of dreams.

FINDING A KORANIC FOUNDATION FOR DREAM INTERPRETATION

"An axial text is an end and a beginning, a *summa* and a programme for thought and action, a theory and its paradigms."[1] It is thus that Tarif Khalidi characterizes the impact of the Koran on the origin and development of historical thought in an Islamic context. The discipline of history as practiced by Muslims, he argues, simply cannot be understood apart from the Koran, its vision of history, its narratives of prophetic history, and its understanding of human nature. The Koran may have functioned as an axial text for the discipline of history. It did not function as such for the Muslim tradition of dream interpretation. As will be argued, while the Koran does contain narratives about dreams, it nowhere enjoins Muslims to interpret their dreams, nowhere suggests that God regularly communicates with Muslims through dreams, nowhere makes the interpretation of dreams one of the duties of Muslims. It is, thus, only with some difficulty that Muslim oneirocrits could find in the Koran a justification for their interest in dream interpretation, albeit one that was—quite frankly—slight. This section treats the *inventio* of this justification and seeks to determine whether the ulema shared with the authors of the dream manuals a common understanding of how the Koran might serve to justify an interest in dream interpretation.

The Koran on Dreams

The Koran does contain occasional references to dreams. Some speak in a general fashion about dreams. Others present the prophets as having divine dreams. Only once does it mention the interpretation of dreams. The Koran's one and only reference to dream interpretation occurs in its treatment of the prophet Joseph. To him and his oneirocritic abilities is devoted a whole sura (12), the very structure of which turns on the theme of dream interpretation. It opens with an account of one of Joseph's dreams, the meaning of which he knows not (12.4). There follows a prophecy from Jacob that God will teach Joseph the interpretation of dreams (12.6). Joseph is sold into slavery and eventually established in Egypt: again, the text specifies, that he might be taught the interpretation of dreams (12.21). In prison he interprets his first dreams. Eventually, he also interprets a dream of the Pharaoh. When at last his father and brothers are in Egypt, they fall in prostration before him—thus fulfilling his initial dream (12.100). The narrative closes with a prayer in which Joseph thanks God for teaching him the interpretation of dreams (12.101).

Joseph's oneirocritic abilities receive extensive treatment in the Koran. He is, in fact, the only prophet to be depicted as an interpreter of dreams. He is not, however, the only prophet to have had divine dreams. Abraham received such dreams. We are told that it was in a dream (*fī al-manām*) that God told him to sacrifice his son (37.102). And having made ready to fulfill the divine mandate, God called out to him, "O Abraham, you have fulfilled the dream" (*ru*ᵓ*yā*) (37.105). Muḥammad is also said to have received divine dreams. Two such dreams are mentioned. The first refers enigmatically to a dream (*ru*ᵓ*yā*) shown to Muḥammad as a trial for men (17.60). Medieval Muslim exegetes usually took this to be a reference to Muḥammad's heavenly ascent (*mi*ᶜ*rāj*).[2] The second is also rather allusive (48.27). It refers to a dream (*ru*ᵓ*yā*) shown to Muḥammad by God, a dream predicting that "You will enter the Sacred Mosque . . . with minds secure, heads shaved, hair cut short, and without fear." Medieval Muslim exegetes usually associated this verse with a dream seen by Muḥammad just prior to the Treaty of Ḥudaybīyah.[3]

The Koran, too, makes occasional references to dreams in general. Some of Muḥammad's critics seem to have referred to the Koran as being nothing more than "confused dreams" (*aḍghāth al-aḥlām*) (21.5, cf. 12.44), probably a metaphor for "ignorant imaginings." At the same time, those who criticize the Koran are said to do so because they are urged on by their dreams (*aḥlām*) (52.32), again presumably a metaphor for their ignorant imaginings. The remaining references to dreams in the Koran occur in lists of God's signs. "And among his [God's] signs is your dream (*manāmuka*) by day and by night" (30.23). So also, it is one of God's signs that "he takes souls at their death; while those who have not died [he takes] during their dream (*manāmihā*)" (39.42). The meaning of this last, rather obscure verse is probably best understood from the parallel at 6.60, where "the taking of a soul by night" is explicitly related to God's knowledge of what a person has done during the day.

If this is all that the Koran has to say about dreams, how did early Muslim oneirocrits justify their interest in the interpretation of dreams? What Koranic proof texts did they cite in their dream manuals? Ibn Qutaybah could find just one such proof text.[4] The Koran had promised "those who believe and fear [God]" that "they will have glad tidings (*al-bushrā*) in the life of this world and in the next" (10.64). This verse, in particular its *bushrā* or "glad tidings," Ibn Qutaybah takes as a reference to the true dreams that God sends Muslims. He supports this understanding of the verse through an appeal to two prophetic traditions. The first has the prophet say that "prophecy has passed, while the bearers of glad tidings (*al-mubashshirāt*) remain." Ibn Qutaybah thus links these "bearers of glad tidings," which he takes to be true dreams, with the Koranic "glad tidings." Ibn Qutaybah also appeals to an exegetical tradition ascribed to ᶜUrwah (d. 94/712). In this, the Koranic *bushrā* is said to be "the true dream that the good man sees or that is seen for him." Remarkably, this single verse identified by Ibn Qutaybah as providing a Koranic foundation for dream interpretation is also the only verse to which appeal is made in the other early Muslim dream manuals.

Qayrawānī's *Mumattiᶜ* notes, first, that "God said: 'Those who believe and fear [God] have glad tidings (*al-bushrā*) in this world and in the next.'"[5] And to this it adds: "It is said that the *bushrā* is the true dream that the good man sees or that is seen for him." Much the same is found in Qayrawānī's other works. In the first of his shorter dream manuals, to show that "the true dream is from God," Qayrawānī cites verse 10.64,[6] which he expounds through an appeal to the Mālikī jurist Ibn Ḥabīb (d. 238/852), who had suggested that it means that "in this world one has the true dream, while in the next world one has direct experience of God." The same holds for the second of his shorter dream manuals, in which Qayrawānī cites the same proof text and the same exegetical tradition.[7] The third of Qayrawānī's shorter dream manuals does not seek to justify dream interpretation. Its introduction is concerned solely with the circumstances that had led Qayrawānī to write yet another dream manual. Dīnawarī, too, appeals to verse 10.64, which he understands through the lens of the same tradition cited by Qayrawānī in his *Mumattiᶜ*.[8] He, however, cites neither the Koran nor the tradition directly, but weaves them together in his opening preface, concluding that "by means of the true dream, God gives glad tidings (*al-bushrā*) to those who believe and fear [God] in this world." As for Kharkūshī, his appeal to verse 10.64 occurs in the context of a tradition stemming from one of the companions, ᶜUbādah b. al-Ṣāmit (d. 34/654).[9] ᶜUbādah recorded that once he had asked the Messenger of God about verse 10.64 and that he responded: "You have asked me about something about which no one has ever asked before you. These [glad tidings] are the true dream that a man sees or that is seen for him."

Only Sijistānī and Ibn Sīnā do not appeal to verse 10.64. Sijistānī was content to justify the discipline of dream interpretation solely through prophetic traditions. And yet, while he does not explicitly cite verse 10.64, he does recall the prophetic tradition to the effect that "prophecy has passed, while the bearers of glad tidings (*mubashshirāt*) remain—that is, the true dream that the servant sees and that is seen for him."[10] As for Ibn Sīnā, he seems simply not to have been interested in such questions—perhaps not surprisingly, given the overall cultural orientation of his dream manual and his dependence on an earlier, Hellenic understanding of dreams.

The Koran, clearly, has little to say about either dreams or their interpretation—at least in an *explicit* fashion. There is Koranic justification for the belief that prophets can have significant dreams and even that they are able to interpret dreams. What one does not find in the Koran are passages that enjoin Muslims to interpret their dreams. There are, quite simply, no explicit proof texts that could be cited to justify an interest in dream interpretation. And yet, while explicit proof texts were lacking, the authors of the dream manuals were able to find at least one non-explicit one, verse 10.64. The witching rod to locate this passage was, however, extra-Koranic—traditions ascribed to Muḥammad or his companions. It was only through such traditions that Muslim oneirocrits could find a Koranic basis for their interest in dreams. On this point the early Muslim oneirocrits were agreed. Regardless, it should be noted that verse 10.64 does not on the surface lend itself to such an interpretation. From its context, it would appear that the "glad tidings" (*al-bushrā*) of which it speaks are the general blessings that God sends upon the pious. This is, in fact, one of the two main uses of the word *bushrā* in the Koran. Of this, there are numerous examples: the wind is a *bushrā* of God's mercy;[11] the good get *bushrā* on the day of the resurrection, while the wicked get the opposite;[12] God bestows his *bushrā* on the prophets.[13] The second, equally common usage of the word relates to the revelation of the Koran, which is said to be a *bushrā* from God;[14] similarly, the revelation of the Torah to Moses is said to be a *bushrā*.[15] In short, there is nothing to support the interpretation offered by the dream manuals. Granted this to be the case, how did other Muslims understand verse 10.64? Did they find in this verse a similar justification for the interpretation of dreams? In particular, is this how the ulema understood the verse?

Dreams and the Koran's Commentators

By far the most comprehensive treatment of verse 10.64 in early Koranic exegesis is that found in the commentary of Ṭabarī (d. 310/923),[16] a jurist and historian who was also the most famous of all early commentators on the Koran. After citing the verse in question and offering a paraphrase to explicate its grammar, he notes that exegetes of the Koran are at odds over the proper interpretation of the word *bushrā*. Some suggest, he notes, that the word means "the true dream that the Muslim sees or that is seen for him."[17] In support of this understanding of the verse, he cites no less than *forty* traditions, almost all stemming from Muḥammad. Among these traditions, there are two major classes. The first contains variants on the following:[18]

> ᶜUbādah b. al-Ṣāmit (d. 34/654) asked the Messenger of God about the verse "Those who believe and fear [God] have glad tidings in this world and the next." The Messenger of God answered: "You have asked me about something about which no one before you has asked. These [glad tidings] are the true dream that the good man sees or that are seen for him."[19]

The parallel versions differ little. Sometimes, it is "the believer" who sees the dream rather than the good man. At other times, it is "the servant," "the Muslim," or simply "the man." Whatever other differences there are do not affect the sense of the tradition. The second major class of traditions are variants on the following:[20]

> A certain man from Egypt asked Abū al-Dardāᵓ (d. 32/652) about the verse "They have glad tidings in this world and the next." He answered: "Apart from you, no one has asked me about this verse since I myself asked the Messenger of God about it—except for one man. I asked the Messenger of God about it and he said: 'Apart from you, no one has asked me about this verse since God revealed it—except for one man. It is a reference to the true dream that the Muslim sees or that is seen for him.'"[21]

There are no significant variants in the other versions of this tradition. Among the other relevant traditions cited by Ṭabarī, there is one in which Abū Hurayrah (d. ca. 57/676) records that Muḥammad said: "The good dream is a glad tiding (*bushrā*) from God. That is, they are bearers of glad tidings (*mubashshirāt*)."[22] Another has Ibn ᶜAmr (d. 69/688) transmit from the prophet that this verse is a reference to "the true dream with which God gives glad tidings to the servant—one of the forty-nine parts of prophecy."[23] Another is transmitted by Umm Kurz, who records that the prophet said: "While prophecy has ceased, bearers of glad tidings remain."[24] The remaining traditions are attributed to a number of different companions. Most state simply that the *bushrā* in verse 10.64 is "the true dream that the good man sees or that is seen for him."

As noted above, Ṭabarī suggests that there was a difference of opinion on the meaning of verse 10.64. To complete his presentation, he turns to the alternative interpretation. "There are others who say that it is the good tidings (*bishārah*) granted to believers, in this world, at the time of their death."[25] In support of this interpretation, he cites, not forty traditions, but *two*. Both suggest that God informs believers of their final state before their death. The first is transmitted by Zuhrī (d. ca. 124/741) and Qatādah (d. 118/736); the second, by Ḍaḥḥāk (105/723). Neither is prophetic. Not surprisingly, Ṭabarī casts his lot with the majority. The *bushrā* of verse 10.64, he concludes, is "the true dream that the Muslim sees or that is seen for him."[26]

Ṭabarī's understanding of verse 10.64 is identical to that of the early Muslim oneirocrits. Not only is the verse taken to mean the same thing, but also the extra-Koranic traditions cited are similar, and often even identical. It may be that Ṭabarī was not the most disinterested of exegetes, however, for he is said himself to have been the author of a dream manual. This work, entitled *Kitāb fī ᶜibārat al-ruᵓyā* (A Book on the Interpretation of Dreams), is said to have been based on prophetic traditions.[27] It is further recorded that it was left unfinished at the time of its author's death.[28] Whatever the case, Ṭabarī's own interest in dreams may have caused him to interpret this key verse accordingly. With this in mind, let me briefly compare Ṭabarī's understanding of verse 10.64 with a number of other commentaries by a diverse selection of ulema.

Consider, first, three commentaries predating Ṭabarī. The first is that of Muqātil b. Sulaymān (d. 150/767), a famous traditionist and exegete from Balkh who lived at the close of the Umayyad period. Verse 10.64 he interprets in a manner as laconic as it is definitive. He states, simply: the *bushrā* had by the pious in this world is "the true dream."[29] The next commentary is that of ᶜAbd al-Razzāq al-Ṣanᶜānī (d. 211/827), a traditionist and exegete from south Arabia. He records two traditions from his teacher Maᶜmar (d. 154/770) as to the meaning of the verse. The first cites the companions Qatādah and Zuhrī and states that the *bushrā* is the good tidings that occur at the time of a person's death. (These traditions were also known to Ṭabarī.) The second cites a tradition from Yaḥyā b. Abī Kathīr (d. 129/746), who transmits a prophetic tradition to the effect that the *bushrā* is "the true dream that the Muslim sees or that is seen for him."[30] The third commentary is that of Hūd b. Muḥakkam al-Huwwārī (fl. second half of the third century A.H.), an Ibāḍī traditionist and exegete.[31] He suggests that there are two ways to understand the verse.[32] The first is based on the tradition from Abū al-Dardāᵓ, cited above, which suggests that the *bushrā* in question is "the true dream that the Muslim sees or that is seen for him." The second draws on the use of the verb *bashshara* in Q 2.25, 10.2, and 33.47, where it is used with reference to God's proclamation of glad tidings for the Muslims with regard to their attaining of Paradise. The verse, he argues, may thus be a reference to the Koran's description of Paradise. In sum, in these commentaries there is some diversity of opinion as to the meaning of the verse. All agree, however, that verse 10.64 may be a reference to true dreams. This was the only option for Muqātil b. Sulaymān. For Ṣanᶜānī and Huwwārī, it was one of two possibilities. For both exegetes, however, it was an understanding of the verse supported by prophetic tradition.

Consider, next, three commentaries that postdate Ṭabarī. The first is that of the famous Shāfiᶜī jurist and exegete Baghawī (d. 516/1122). His commentary lists four possible interpretations of verse 10.64.[33] It may be a reference to true dreams. In this regard, two traditions are mentioned. The first is that of ᶜUbādah b. al-Ṣāmit, cited above. The second is from Abū Hurayrah. This states that he heard the prophet say: "There shall remain naught of prophecy [after my death] except for the bearers of glad tidings." Abū Hurayrah then asks Muḥammad what these glad tidings are. He replies: "The true dream." Another possibility has it that the verse is a reference to a Muslim's good reputation. Alternatively, based on the authority of Zuhrī and Qatādah, it is the descent of the angels "with good tidings from God at the time of death." Or finally, it may be a reference to the Koran itself, as well as to the prophet. While Baghawī does not attempt to adjudicate between these four possible understandings of the verse, the only interpretation supported with prophetic traditions is the first, that in which the verse is taken as a reference to true dreams.

The second commentary is that of Ibn al-Jawzī (d. 597/1200), the famous Ḥanbalī jurist, historian, and exegete. He gives three possible interpretations of the verse.[34] The first has it that it is a reference to "the true dream that the good man sees or that is seen for him." This is cited on the authority of ᶜUbādah, Abū Hurayrah, Abū al-Dardāᵓ, and Jābir b. ᶜAbd Allāh (d. 78/697), all of whom ascribe their interpretation to the prophet. Alternatively, he suggests, it may be a reference to the good tidings of the angels at the time of death. For this there are traditions from the companions, but none from the prophet. A final possibility would have it that the glad tidings are those verses found in the Koran that concern Paradise and its rewards. This last possibility is supported, Ibn al-Jawzī suggests, by parallels at Q 2.25, 41.30, and 9.21. It is also, he notes, the way the verse was read by two earlier exegetes, both of whom supported their interpretation by reference to the closing words of 10.64, which specify that "there is no change in the words of God." Ibn al-Jawzī himself thinks this third possibility "a good suggestion" (*qawl al-ḥasan*). He cannot, however, discount the testimony of the prophetic traditions. In the end, he refuses to come out strongly in favor of any one of the three possibilities.

While Ibn al-Jawzī made no attempt to reconcile the testimony of prophetic traditions with what seemed to be the more manifest meaning of verse 10.64, other exegetes felt compelled to find a way out of this impasse. Consider, for example, the commentary of Ibn ᶜAṭīyah (d. 546/1151), an Andalusian Mālikī jurist and judge renowned for his knowledge of prophetic traditions and Arabic grammar.[35] As for the glad tidings of this world, he suggests, there are numerous prophetic traditions that state that these are the true dreams that the Muslim sees or that are seen for him. There were many companions—four are cited by name—who asked the prophet about the meaning of this verse. In each instance the prophet answered that it was a reference to dreams. Moreover, he notes, in the collection of prophetic traditions compiled by Muslim (d. 261/874) there are traditions that link the passing of prophecy with the continuance of the "bearers of glad tidings." Ibn ᶜAṭīyah's problem is that this interpretation plays havoc with the sense of the verse when it is read in context. This context would suggest, he argues, that the *bushrā* in question is "the verses of the Koran that proclaim glad tidings." "The whole of this [second] interpretation, however, stands in contradiction to the words of the prophet—that it is a question here of dreams." Ibn ᶜAṭīyah is only able to resolve this seeming contradiction by supposing that when the prophet was interpreting the verse "he gave only one example of the glad tidings, one that was common to all people."

In these three commentaries postdating the work of Ṭabarī, we find some diversity of opinion as to the meaning of verse 10.64. Each commentary opens by suggesting that one possible interpretation of the verse is that it is a reference to true dreams. In support of this reading, all three commentaries cite prophetic traditions. Nonetheless, each of these commentaries also shows some hesitancy about accepting this reading of the verse, usually because it seems to contravene the manifest sense of the verse. None of these exegetes can, however, discount the testimony of the prophetic traditions, which would suggest that the *bushrā* of verse 10.64 is a reference to the true dreams that God shows to Muslims.

Dream Interpretation, the Ulema, and the Koran

There is in the Koran little to justify an interest in dreams and their interpretation. Although the Koran has some references to the prophets as having true dreams or even at times to their interpreting dreams, the authors of the dream manuals did not cite such texts to support their own interest in dreams. It was, quite simply, impossible to apply verses descriptive of the prophets to their own situation. There was, however, one verse (10.64) that could be interpreted as justifying an interest in dream interpretation. With the help of some very explicit prophetic traditions, this verse could be read as a reference to God's sending of dreams to Muslims—and nearly all of the dream manuals made this exegetic move. Early Muslim oneirocrits, perhaps not surprisingly, did not note that there were other ways of interpreting this key verse. In particular, they did not point out that this interpretation seemed to contravene the sense of the verse when taken in context.

The situation is somewhat more complicated in the Koranic commentaries of the ulema. All recognized that this verse had strong claims to be taken as referring to true dreams. For this interpretation there was plenty of explicit support in the prophetic traditions. There were, however, other possible readings. Prominent early Muslims had taken it to refer to the good tidings of the angels at the time of a person's death. More problematic, however, is the sense of the passage when read in context. This would suggest that the *bushrā* in question was either—in general—God's glad tidings to Muslims about the world to come or—more specifically—the Koran itself. Regardless, the testimony of the prophetic traditions could not be ignored. Sometimes commentators explicitly opted to interpret the verse in accord with the prophetic traditions. Sometimes they were content to cite the various possible interpretations, leaving it to the reader to chose between them. Only occasionally was an attempt made to reconcile the alternatives. It should be noted, however: not a single one of the exegetes did not think it possible or even likely that verse 10.64 was a reference to true dreams. Moreover, almost invariably this understanding of the verse was dependent on the testimony of the same prophetic traditions that had been cited by the authors of the dream manuals.

DREAM INTERPRETATION AND THE PROPHETIC TRADITIONS

There is, clearly, not much in the Koran to support an interest in dream interpretation. There is but a single verse that is called on to legitimize an interest in this subject. It is possible to read this verse as a proof text, however, only after it has been properly interpreted by means of prophetic traditions. It is, in fact, the traditions that generate the proof text. This is not the only function of prophetic traditions in the dream manuals. There is a whole series of traditions to which the dream manuals appeal. These traditions are largely shared by the early Muslim dream manuals. Most of them have already been mentioned in chapters 1, 2, and 3. They concern such things as the theoretical foundations of dream interpretation: that dreams are a part of prophecy, that they are the successors of Koranic revelation, and that a good Muslim can expect to receive from God messages in dreams. They also contain typologies of dreams. Two such typologies are especially prominent. One has it that there are two types of dreams: the dream that is from God and the nightmare that is from Satan. The other suggests, instead, that there are three types of dreams: glad tidings from God, dreams sent by Satan to make dreamers sad, and dreams that arise from the self. Also found in the dream manuals are traditions on the proper behavior of the dreamer: what to do if a bad dream has been seen, the need to report one's dreams in a truthful fashion, and when to remain silent about ominous dreams. And finally, there are in some dream manuals traditions on dreams interpreted by Muḥammad or his close companions. It is not the Koran, but traditions such as these that provided Muslim oneirocrits with their primary justification for an interest in dream interpretation.

Were such traditions also circulating in other contexts? In particular, were they also known to the ulema who compiled the collections of prophetic traditions? The short answer is that nearly all of the traditions cited in the dream manuals were also known to the compilers of the collections of prophetic traditions. Consider, first, the situation of the so-called canonical collections. Not one of these works does not devote a whole chapter to dream interpretation.

Bukhārī (d. 256/869), *Bāb al-taᶜbīr*, containing 60 traditions.[36]
Muslim (d. 261/874), *Kitāb al-ruʾyā*, containing 37 traditions.[37]
Ibn Mājah (d. 273/886), *Kitāb fī taᶜbīr al-ruʾyā*, containing 34 traditions.[38]
Abū Dāwūd (d. 275/888), *Bāb fī al-ruʾyā*, containing 9 traditions.[39]
Tirmidhī (d. 279/892), *Kitāb al-ruʾyā*, containing 23 traditions.[40]
Nasāᶜī (d. 303/915), *Kitāb al-taᶜbīr*, containing 38 traditions.[41]

Other, noncanonical collections of prophetic traditions likewise contained chapters on dream interpretation. To cite just a few examples:

ᶜAbd al-Razzāq al-Ṣanᶜānī (d. 211/826), *Bāb al-ruʾyā*, containing 15 traditions.[42]
Ibn Abī Shaybah (d. 235/849), *Kitāb al-Īmān wa-l-ruʾyā*, containing 85 traditions specifically concerned with dream interpretation.[43]
Dārimī (d. 255/868), *Kitāb al-ruʾyā*, containing 28 traditions.[44]

There are many other earlier and later compilations of prophetic traditions that contain similar collections of traditions on dream interpretation. Enough examples have been cited, however, to establish the centrality of this topic to the collections as a whole. What sorts of traditions are contained in these texts? The traditions found are largely shared from one work to the next. Bukhārī's collection is fairly typical. It is also considered one of the most authoritative collections of prophetic traditions. For these reasons, a brief analysis of its treatment of the subject can serve to introduce the contents of the other collections as well.

Bukhārī and Dream Interpretation

Bukhārī opens his chapter on dream interpretation by citing a long tradition that shows, he suggests, that "the first revelation received by the Messenger of God came through a true dream."[45] This tradition is the famous description by ᶜĀʾishah of Muḥammad's first encounter with the angel Gabriel, his taking refuge with Khadījah, and his consultation with Waraqah. This tradition was relevant to the discussion because ᶜĀʾishah had herself prefaced the description of these events with the words: "The Messenger of God's first experience of revelation (*waḥy*) occurred in a true dream that took place while he was asleep." Bukhārī next cites some prophetic traditions apparently intended to interpret the Koranic verse (48.27) about Muḥammad's dream concerning the Treaty of Ḥudaybīyah.[46]

> The good dream of a righteous man is one of the forty-six parts of prophecy.
>
> The dream is from God; the nightmare is from Satan.
>
> If anyone sees a dream that he likes, it is from God. He should praise God for it and report it to others. If he sees one that he does not like, it is from Satan. He should take refuge with God from its evil and not mention it to anyone, for [in this way] it will not cause him harm.

Bukhārī next cites a number of traditions that show that the true dream is one of the parts of prophecy. One tradition has it that good dreams are from God, while bad dreams are from Satan—the above-mentioned twofold typology—and that if a bad dream is seen one should take refuge with God and spit to the left.[47] This is followed by three traditions from Muḥammad that specify that the true dream is one of the forty-six parts of prophecy.[48] In his next section, Bukhārī cites just one tradition.[49] In it, Abū Hurayrah reports that Muḥammad identified the "bearers of glad tidings" (*mubashshirāt*) as the true dream.

Bukhārī's next section contains not prophetic traditions but citations from the Koran.[50] In it, he recapitulates the Koran's accounts of the dreams of Joseph and Abraham. This section is followed by another entitled "Section on the Agreement in regards to the Dream."[51] One tradition is cited. It concerns the dreams of certain unnamed contemporaries of Muḥammad. Some had been shown the Night of Power (*laylat al-qadr*) as taking place on the seventh day from the end of the month of Ramaḍān, while yet others had been shown it as taking place on the tenth day from the end of that same month. Muḥammad then tells his companions "to seek it out on the seventh night." It is a question here of Muḥammad choosing between two rival dreams, both of which claimed to have established the date of the enigmatic Night of Power mentioned in sura 97 (a topic on which there was much controversy).[52] Resuming his presentation of Koranic verses on dreams, Bukhārī entitles his next section: "A Section on Dreams of the People in Prison and on Wickedness and Associating [Partners with God]."[53] There follow extended citations of the Koran's account of Joseph's interpretation of the dreams of his companions in prison and of the Pharaoh. This section concludes with a prophetic tradition that comments on the verses in question. It has nothing to do with dreams, however.

Bukhārī next takes up the subject of dreams in which the prophet is seen.[54] Five very similar traditions are cited to support the contention that dreams of the prophet cannot be false. One transmitted from Muḥammad by Anas b. Mālik (d. ca. 91/709), for example, has Muḥammad say: "Whoever sees me in a dream, there is no doubt that he has seen me, for Satan cannot imitate my form." The next two sections concern dreams had during the night and during the day.[55] Under each heading Bukhārī introduces traditions that recount dreams had by the prophet. The time when the dreams were seen appears to be the only thing these dreams have in common. To illustrate the character of these traditions, consider the following:

> The Messenger of God used to visit Umm Ḥarām bt. Milḥān. . . . One day he visited her. She gave him food and began to check his head for lice. He fell asleep and then awoke with a laugh. She asked: "What makes you laugh, Messenger of God?" He replied: "I dreamt that people of my community were fighting in the way of God. They were sailing in the middle of this sea . . . like kings upon their thrones. . . ." Umm Ḥarām then asked: "Messenger of God, beseech God to make me one of them." This he did. He then lay his head down [to sleep]. He awoke with a laugh. Again she asked him why he was laughing. He responded as he had the first time. She then said: "Messenger of God,

> beseech God to make me one of them." He responded: "You are one of the foremost of them." [The transmitter of this tradition adds:] She sailed over the sea during the reign of Muᶜāwiyah b. Abī Sufyān. Coming ashore, she fell off the animal she was riding and perished.[56]

These sections are followed by another treating "the dreams of women."[57] Under this heading Bukhārī has just one tradition. In it, one of the close female companions of the prophet has a dream that confirms for her that a dead comrade's place is in Paradise. The following section treats of what should be done if a bad dream has been seen.[58] Just a single tradition is cited. In it, the prophet distinguishes the true dreams that are from God from the false dreams that are from Satan. He then counsels spitting to the left if a bad dream is seen.

The remaining portions of Bukhārī's chapter on dreams contain a series of traditions organized according to the objects seen in the dreams: dreams of silken cloth, milk, drawing water, circumambulating the Kaᶜbah, keys, flowing springs, and so on.[59] About thirty such topics are treated. Usually the dreams in question are had by close companions of Muḥammad. Usually, also, it is Muḥammad who is responsible for interpreting the dreams, for, as one tradition has it, "When the companions of the Messenger of God saw dreams while he was still alive, they would tell him about their dreams and he would interpret them as God willed."[60] Occasionally, theoretical matters are found in these sections. For example, Bukhārī includes the following, largely theoretical tradition under the heading "Dreams of Leg-irons":

> Muḥammad b. Sīrīn reported from Abū Hurayrah that the Messenger of God said: "In the end times, the dream of the Muslim will scarcely be able to be false. The dream of the Muslim is one of the forty-six parts of prophecy." Muḥammad [b. Sīrīn] said: "As for me, I say that he [also] said the following: 'It used to be said that there are three types of dreams: that in which a man's own soul speaks, that which Satan sends to make us sad, and that which is a "glad tiding" from God (Q 10.64). If one of you sees a dream that he dislikes, let him not talk to anyone about it; instead, let him stand up and pray.' He [also] said: 'Neck-irons in sleep are not liked, while people like to see leg-irons.'" It is also said: "Leg-irons [signify] resoluteness in religion."[61]

Bukhārī occasionally intersperses among these topical sections others devoted to theoretical issues. There are, for example, sections on sanctions against a dreamer's lying about what has been seen in a dream, the need to remain silent about bad dreams, and Muḥammad's habit of asking his companions after morning prayers whether any had seen dreams and if so interpreting them.[62]

There are very few differences between the traditions on dreams collected by Bukhārī and those found in the other canonical collections. Generally, those other works organize their materials similarly. They begin with traditions on theoretical matters: the relation of dreams to prophecy, dreams of Muḥammad, what to do if one sees a dream one dislikes, the various typologies of dreams. They then offer more or less extensive collections of traditions recounting dreams that Muḥammad interpreted. The differences between Bukhārī and these other works are relatively minor. First, Bukhārī's two long sections that cite *in extenso* the Koranic accounts of Joseph and Abraham are not found in the other collections. Second, the other collections tend to be more systematic in their organization of the materials they present, being careful to keep the theoretical traditions separated from the other materials.

As should now be evident, the traditions cited in the dream manuals are the same as those found in the collections of prophetic traditions. One finds, in both, identical traditions on the theoretical foundations of dream interpretation, the same typologies of dreams, shared materials on the proper behavior of dreamers, as well as a common set of traditions depicting Muḥammad as an interpreter of dreams. Often also, the structure of the chapters on dreams in the collections of prophetic traditions parallel the structure of the dream manuals: beginning with the theoretical foundations of dream interpretation, then turning to the different symbols that appear in dreams. As to the latter, it is not known whether the compilers of the collections of prophetic traditions thought that the meanings Muḥammad had assigned to these dreams were also the meanings they would have centuries later if seen by a Muslim. This was clearly the opinion of the authors of the dream manuals, however. Accounts of these dreams interpreted by Muḥammad are found in most of the early Muslim dream manuals. In sum, the collections of prophetic traditions offered just about all the raw materials needed by the authors of the dream manuals. Contained in them were the traditions needed to find a Koranic justification for dreams. They also encompassed a set of traditions that provided the theoretical foundations for the interpretation of dreams, as well as an image of Muḥammad as himself the quintessential interpreter of dreams.

From Commentary on Prophetic Traditions to Dream Manual

The chapters on dreams in the collections of prophetic traditions were not dream manuals. It was not too difficult to turn them into dream manuals, however. This phenomenon can be discerned in a number of commentaries on the prophetic traditions. To illustrate this process, consider Baghawī's (d. 516/1122) massive *Sharḥ al-sunnah* (Commentary on the Sunnah). There is in Baghawī's work a lengthy chapter in which he comments on the prophetic traditions on dreams.[63] Most of the traditions with which he deals are unremarkable, being found in just about all of the collections of prophetic traditions. Far more interesting are the materials he uses to comment on those traditions, most of which are taken from one or more dream manuals.

Among the materials that Baghawī takes from the dream manuals is his discussion of the various methods that can be utilized to interpret dreams. Commenting on a tradition that depicts Abū Bakr interpreting a dream under the supervision of Muḥammad,[64] Baghawī launch himself on a lengthy discussion of the methods utilized to interpret dreams. He identifies no less than seven such methods: Koran, prophetic traditions, well-known proverbs, names, meanings, opposition and inversion, as well as increase and decrease. It will be recalled from chapter 1 that these are the first seven of the nine methods that had been identified by Ibn Qutaybah. Similarly, Baghawī illustrates the use of these various methods by appealing to many of the same examples that Ibn Qutaybah had cited. For instance, to illustrate how to interpret dreams by means of prophetic traditions, Baghawī cites four examples: dreams of ravens, female mice, ribs, and long-necked bottles (in that order). In the same way, Ibn Qutaybah had illustrated his use of this method by citing a number of examples, the first three of which were ravens, female mice, and ribs (in that order). Similar parallels are found in Baghawī's discussion of the other methods.

Not only does Baghawī draw on the theoretical portions of the dream manuals. He also makes extensive use of their contents, how this or that symbol is to be interpreted. Consider, for example, his section on "Dreams of the Resurrection, Paradise, and Hell." Under this heading, he is able to cite just a single prophetic tradition. In it, one of the companions has two dreams that he tells to his sister. She, in turn, reports them to Muḥammad, who proffers their interpretation. Baghawī's commentary on this tradition is largely concerned with establishing its authenticity, which he does with ease. He then adds, in his own voice, a lengthy disquisition on other dreams falling under this heading.

> Whoever sees that the resurrection happens in a particular place, justice will spread there. If its inhabitants are being oppressed, they will be made victorious; if they are oppressors, vengeance will be exacted from them, for the day of the resurrection is the day of separation and justice, even as God says: "We shall place scales of justice for the day of the resurrection; not one soul will be treated unjustly" (Q 21.47).[65]

In this section, Baghawī continues by noting the meaning of the following dream symbols: entering paradise, eating or taking the fruit of Paradise, giving its fruit to another, entering Hell, or partaking of Hell's food or drink. It is thus that he proceeds for the duration of his commentary. And by the time he finishes, he has ended up citing just about the entirety of the contents of a dream manual the size of Ibn Qutaybah's. Like the authors of the dream manuals, Baghawī also occasionally spices up his presentation with anecdotes, almost invariably accounts of remarkable feats of interpretation executed by Ibn Sīrīn.

There can be no doubt that Baghawī is drawing on one or more earlier dream manuals. It is not, however, entirely clear what his source or sources may have been. His work is most strongly parallel to that of Ibn Qutaybah, however. There are, nonetheless, enough differences to suggest that he was not making use of that work directly. Perhaps he had access to the major source that stood behind Ibn Qutaybah's work, the dream manual of Kirmānī. Or perhaps he had made use of a dream manual that had itself drawn on Ibn Qutaybah's text. Whatever the case, the parallels between the two works are still strong enough that any future edition of Ibn Qutaybah's dream manual would have to make use of Baghawī's testimony.

In Baghawī's work, the line between dream manual and commentary on prophetic traditions is not firmly drawn. In terms of the author's stated purposes, the work should be considered an exposition of prophetic traditions on dreams. In terms of its contents, however, it contains nearly all the materials that would be found in a dream manual. It is probably this fact more than any other that caused this chapter of his work to be transmitted separately, as if it were a self-contained dream manual. This phenomenon can be seen in one of the manuscripts preserved in the Topkapı.[66] This manuscript is a miscellany on dreams. It begins with a beautifully written copy of the famous dream manual of Sālimī (fl. ca. 800/1398).[67] It concludes with a poem on the meaning of dreams in which one sees the Koran.[68] Inserted between these two works is the so-called *Kitāb al-ru'yā* (Book of Dreams) of Baghawī. What might at first glance appear to be a dream manual is in fact only a copy of his chapter on dreams from his commentary on the prophetic traditions. And yet, because its contents and format so closely resemble what is found in Muslim oneirocritic works, its cataloger took it to be an otherwise unknown dream manual by the famous scholar. In the end, it must be concluded, it is not too difficult to turn a collection of prophetic traditions on dreams into a dream manual.

DREAM MANUALS AND THEIR READERS: THE CASE OF ANDALUSIA

The scholars of prophetic traditions in the Umayyad period were concerned that the materials they transmit be authentic. To ensure such authenticity, they devised the institution of the isnād. Traditions had to be provided with a chain of authorities or isnād that linked their latest recipient to the persons who had first put them into circulation. (I heard it from x, who heard it from y, who heard it from z, that the prophet said. . . .) As one might well imagine, with the passage of time these isnāds could become unwieldy. With the transition from a primarily oral to a primarily written form of transmission, additional problems were introduced. Imagine, if you will, an author who compiles a book of traditions in, say, 150 A.H. Each tradition included in the book would be provided with its own chain of authorities. What happens when the author transmits the book to his students? It is a question now of transmitting a collection of traditions, rather than individual traditions. Do his students "update" each of their teacher's isnāds, so that they themselves are now listed as the latest recipients of the traditions? One does, indeed, sometimes encounter this phenomenon. A more common procedure, however, is for the students to preface their teacher's compilation with a short note specifying when and how they received the work. When, in turn, these students transmit the work to their own students, their own students will note in the preface when and how they received the work. These prefatory remarks after a few generations will themselves begin to resemble isnāds, or perhaps better, meta-isnāds. They are chains of authorities meant to guarantee the transmission of complete works from authorized teachers to authorized pupils—hence their name in Arabic, "riwāyahs," from a root meaning "to pass on or transmit."

In time riwāyahs could become detached from the prefaces of the works to which they belonged. One finds, for example, authors who provide in the introductions to their own works lists of all the earlier sources on which they relied. To assure their readers that they were authorized to transmit those earlier works, they could provide for each title its riwāyah. Alternatively, scholars might compile a sort of *curriculum vitae* in which they list all of the works they had studied, as well as all of the riwāyahs for those works. Such a dossier was generally known in Arabic as a *Fihris* or *Fahrasah* (both derived from the Persian word *Fihrist*, meaning "catalog" or "list"), or alternatively as a *bārnāmeh* ("account book"). Many of these dossiers are extant, and some have been published. Although intended by their authors to certify the authenticity of written works, riwāyahs can provide modern researchers with data for an analysis of the transmission of knowledge among the ulema. Not unlike the circulation cards used in modern libraries, they provide lists of the people who had taken an interest in a work and specify when they had expressed their interest in that work. They tell us who checked out a book and when, if you will.

Many early Muslim dream manuals are provided with riwāyahs. Kirmānī's dream manual is known to have been transmitted in this fashion. Riwāyahs for it are found in Qayrawānī's *Mumatti*ᶜ as well as in other works.[69] Some have also been preserved for Ibn Qutaybah's dream manual. One can be found in the Jerusalem manuscript of the work; others are found in Qayrawānī's *Mumatti*ᶜ and elsewhere.[70] Two manuscripts of Maᶜāfirī's oneirocritic poem are provided with riwāyahs. Similarly, one of Qayrawānī's shorter dream manuals was thus transmitted. There are also riwāyahs extant for many of the works utilized by Qayrawānī in his *Mumatti*ᶜ: the dream manuals of Ibn al-Mughīrah, Nuᶜaym b. Ḥammād, and others. Yet other riwāyahs are preserved for oneirocritic works that are no longer extant.[71] An analysis of the riwāyahs of the early Muslim dream manuals can be quite useful. It will be recalled from chapters 1 and 2 that often such works could be dated only on the basis of their riwāyahs. A detailed study of the riwāyahs of the dream manuals can also offer occasional surprises. For instance, from its riwāyahs we know that the first person to whom Maᶜāfirī taught his dream manual was Abū Ḥafṣ ᶜUmar b. ᶜIrāk (d. 388/998). From another riwāyah we know that this same person had at one time read a copy of Ibn Qutaybah's dream manual.[72] It would thus seem that this Ibn ᶜIrāk had something of a special interest in the study of dream manuals.

A list of names in a riwāyah by itself tells us little. It is only when these names are accompanied by a well-developed biographical tradition that they can be made to yield significant information. In short, a riwāyah is valuable if and only if the transmitters it lists are known. The extent to which this is the case, however, varies from region to region and from period to period. Qayrawānī, for instance, had included in the introduction to his *Mumattiᶜ* a list of the dream manuals on which he had relied, as well as the riwāyahs that certified that he was authorized to transmit those works. Unfortunately, nearly all of the figures mentioned in his riwāyahs are unknown to the biographical tradition. The situation is quite the opposite in the case of fifth- and sixth-century Andalusia—thanks largely to the labors of Ibn Khayr and Ibn Bashkuwāl. The former was the author of an extensive dossier; the latter, of an exquisitely detailed biographical dictionary, one that treats many of the scholars mentioned in Ibn Khayr's dossier. Through this dossier and this biographical dictionary, researchers have access both to riwāyahs for dream manuals and to a well-developed biographical tradition. So extensive is the evidence that it allows us to analyze in some detail how dream lore was transmitted among the ulema of Andalusia. It offers, in short, a rare glimpse into the role of dream interpretation in the intellectual lives of the ulema.

Ibn Khayr was born in 502/1108 in Seville.[73] Over the course of his life, he studied with teachers throughout nearly the whole of Andalusia—not only in Seville, but also in Cordova, Almería, Malaga, Granada, and so on. He, in turn, had many students of his own. It is said that he kept a series of ten notebooks, each of thirty pages, in which he listed the names of those who had studied with him. Eventually, Ibn Khayr was appointed as prayer leader of a mosque in Cordova, and it was in that city that he died in 575/1179. Ibn Khayr is best remembered today for his sole surviving work, a dossier of the books he had learned from his teachers. For each book he studied, Ibn Khayr provides a full riwāyah that lists the person or persons from whom he received it and the chain of transmitters that linked his own teacher of the work to its original author. Ibn Khayr's scholarly interests encompassed nearly all of the subjects current among the ulema of his day: the Koranic sciences, works of or about prophetic traditions, biographies of the prophet, jurisprudence, grammar, lexicography, poetry—and dream interpretation.

The data that Ibn Khayr provides in his dossier can be analyzed in some detail, largely because the majority of the Andalusian scholars he mentions are also treated in the biographical tradition on the ulema of Andalusia. In this regard, especially valuable is a work written by Ibn Bashkuwāl. This Andalusian religious scholar was born in Cordova in 495/1101. He was educated first by his father and then by other notable scholars in Seville. In fact, he could count among his teachers most of the same persons with whom Ibn Khayr had studied. After a short stint as a judge, he gave up his administrative career to devote himself to learning, dying in 578/1183 at the age of 83. The most famous of Ibn Bashkuwāl's extant works is his *Kitāb al-ṣilah fī ta'rīkh a'immat al-Andalus wa-ᶜulamā'ihim wa-muḥaddithīhim wa-fuḍalā'ihim wa-udabā'ihim* (A Continuation, On the History of the Religious Leaders of Andalusia, Treating Religious Scholars, Transmitters of Prophetic Traditions, Notables, and Litterateurs),[74] a biographical dictionary in which he chronicles the lives of some 1,400 religious scholars who flourished in Andalusia during the fifth and sixth centuries of the Muslim era.

In his dossier, Ibn Khayr records that he had studied a total of five different dream manuals.[75] (See Table 4.1 on page 126 for a graphic representation of the riwāyahs of these texts.) Among the works he had studied were three, by now ancient texts: the dream manuals of Kirmānī, Nuᶜaym b. Ḥammād, and Ibn Qutaybah. The latter he had studied on three separate occasions, with two different teachers. Ibn Khayr also studied a number of more recent works. One was written by an eastern author, Abū Dharr al-Harawī (d. 434/1042); the other, a massive commentary on the dream manual of Kirmānī, by an Andalusian scholar, Abū ᶜAbd Allāh b. al-Ḥadhdhā' (d. 416/1025). The latter Ibn Khayr studied on two separate occasions, with two different teachers. With whom did Ibn Khayr study these dream manuals? And who had been responsible for transmitting them?

Ibn Khayr received one copy of each of his five dream manuals from Abū Muḥammad b. ᶜAttāb (d. 520/1126),[76] a famous Cordovan religious scholar and a scion of one of that city's well-known scholarly families. As for Abū Muḥammad, he had studied these texts under a number of his own teachers. The works of Kirmānī and Nuᶜaym b. Ḥammād, he learned from his father, Abū ᶜAbd Allāh b. ᶜAttāb (d. 462/1069), a judge in Cordova and Toledo and a man considered by his contemporaries to be one of the greatest living Mālikī jurists.

As for Nuᶜaym b. Ḥammād's dream manual, this Abū ᶜAbd Allāh received from Abū Bakr b. Aḥmad (d. 406/1015), another Cordovan religious scholar. As for this Abū Bakr,[77] he learned the work from Ismāᶜīl b. Badr (d. 385/995), a scholar of prophetic traditions in Saragossa. Ibn Badr, for his part, had studied it with Abū ᶜAbd Allāh b. Waḍḍāḥ al-Marwānī (d. 287/900),[78] a famous Andalusian scholar of prophetic traditions who had traveled widely in the east in search of teachers. Among the teachers with whom Ibn Waḍḍāḥ studied while in Egypt was the famous jurist and transmitter of prophetic traditions, Ḥarmalah b. Yaḥyā (d. 243/857),[79] a figure well known both as a student of Shāfiᶜī and as a teacher of such notables as Muslim and Ibn Mājah. It was under Ḥarmalah b. Yaḥyā that Ibn Waḍḍāḥ studied the dream manual of Nuᶜaym. Ḥarmalah, in turn, had studied the text with its author.

It was also from his father that Abū Muḥammad b. ᶜAttāb received Kirmānī's dream manual. This text his father had studied with the Mālikī jurist Abū al-Qāsim b. Yaḥyā (d. 405/1014), a native of Toledo who settled in Cordova, where he was the prayer leader of a mosque.[80] One of Ibn Yaḥyā's teachers was the Cordovan

TABLE 4.1
The Dream Manuals Read by Ibn Khayr

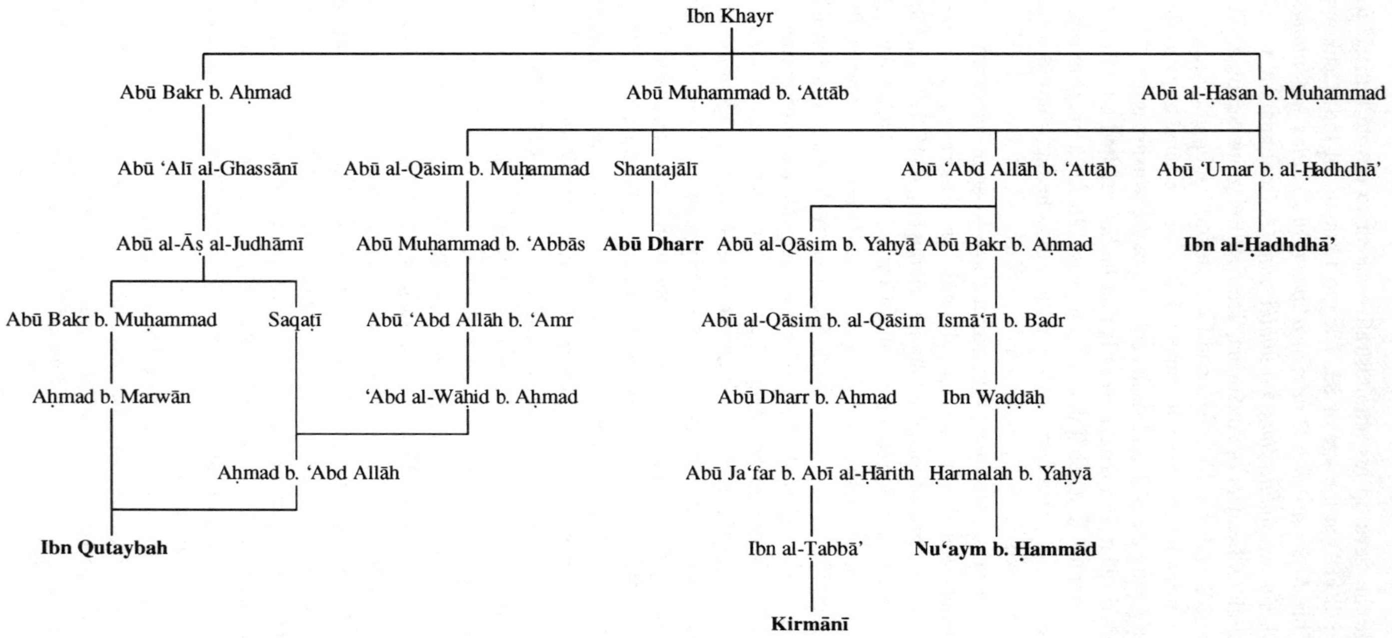

scholar of prophetic traditions Abū al-Qāsim b. al-Qāsim (d. 353/964).[81] As a young man, the latter had traveled extensively in the eastern parts of the Islamic world, studying prophetic traditions in Iraq, Syria, and the Yemen. While abroad, the year 324/935 found him in Baghdad studying with Abū Dharr b. Aḥmad.[82] It was from him that he received Kirmānī's dream manual. Little is known of Abū Dharr, other than that he had been a teacher of prophetic traditions in Baghdad. One source, however, refers to him rather enigmatically as *ṣāhib ᶜibārat al-ruʾyā* (lit. "the master of the interpretation of dreams"),[83] an expression that probably means that he had himself been the author of a work on dreams. Regardless, Abū Dharr had studied the work of Kirmānī with a Ḥarrānian scholar of prophetic traditions, Abū Jaᶜfar Muḥammad b. Abī al-Ḥārith al-Wāsiṭī (d. ca. 243/857).[84] As for Wāsiṭī, he had received Kirmānī's dream manual from the famous scholar of prophetic traditions Ibn al-Ṭabbāᶜ (d. ca. 214/829),[85] who had himself journeyed to Kirmān to study the work with its author.

It was also with Abū Muḥammad b. ᶜAttāb that Ibn Khayr studied the dream manual of Ibn Qutaybah. This work Abū Muḥammad transmitted from Abū al-Qāsim b. Muḥammad (d. 469/1076).[86] The latter was a well-known scholar of prophetic traditions who had in his youth studied in many parts of North Africa as well as in Mecca. He appears to have lived mostly in Toledo. It was there that he studied Ibn Qutaybah's dream manual with Abū Muḥammad b. ᶜAbbās (d. 438/1046).[87] As for this Abū Muḥammad, he was a director of prayer and preacher in one of that city's mosques. He, for his part, had received the work from Abū ᶜAbd Allāh b. ᶜAmr (d. 370/980), a native of Toledo who had studied in his home town and in Cordova.[88] As for Ibn ᶜAmr, he had studied the work with no less an authority than the grandson of Ibn Qutaybah, ᶜAbd al-Wāḥid b. Aḥmad. This text the latter had received from his own father, Aḥmad b. ᶜAbd Allāh (d. 320/932), one of the son's of Ibn Qutaybah.[89] As for Aḥmad, he was a Mālikī jurist who was for a time the chief judge of Egypt. It is said that he had memorized the whole corpus of his father's writings, including no doubt his father's dream manual.

It was also with Abū Muḥammad b. ᶜAttāb that Ibn Khayr studied the dream manual of Abū Dharr al-Harawī (d. 434/1042). As for Abū Muḥammad, he had studied the text under Abū Muḥammad al-Shantajālī (d. 436/1044).[90] The latter apparently spent most of the early part of his life in Cordova. In 391/1000, however, he traveled east, spending approximately forty years as a student in Mecca. There he studied with many of the famous ulema of his time. Among his teachers in Mecca was Abū Dharr al-Harawī himself. Coincidentally, while in Mecca Shantajālī was also a student of Kharkūshī.[91] Regardless, upon Shantajālī's return to Andalusia (ca. 400/1009), he transmitted to his students many of the works he had learned while abroad. Ibn Khayr records, in particular, that among these was Kharkūshī's famous biography of the prophet (*Sharaf al-nabī*),[92] which, like Abū Dharr's dream manual, was transmitted to Ibn Khayr from Shantajālī by Abū Muḥammad b. ᶜAttāb.

The final dream manual that Ibn Khayr studied under Abū Muḥammad b. ᶜAttāb is Abū ᶜAbd Allāh b. al-Ḥadhdhāᵓ's (d. 416/1025) massive commentary on the dream manual of Kirmānī. Ibn al-Ḥadhdhāᵓ was a resident of Cordova,[93] although he had spent a great deal of time in the eastern parts of the Islamic world. He was considered by some of his contemporaries to have been the most learned Mālikī jurist of the day. It is recorded that his own son used to say of him: "My father was thoroughly versed in prophetic traditions, jurisprudence, and dream interpretation." Among those whom he authorized to teach his dream manual was this same son, Abū ᶜUmar b. al-Ḥadhdhāᵓ (d. 467/1074).[94] The latter also lived in Cordova, although during his life he resided in most of the more prominent Andalusian cities, even acting as a judge for a while in Toledo. Abū ᶜUmar was not himself possessed of a great reputation for learning. It was primarily as a transmitter of his father's works that he was remembered. Regardless, it was from him that Abū Muḥammad b. ᶜAttāb received his copy of Ibn al-Ḥadhdhāᵓ's dream manual, a work that he then transmitted to Ibn Khayr. A second copy of this text was conveyed to Ibn Khayr by Abū al-Ḥasan b. Muḥammad (d. 532/1137).[95] This person was "one of the great sheikhs of Cordova" and a specialist in the history of the ulema of Andalusia. He was also one of the students of Abū ᶜUmar, and to him, also, Abū ᶜUmar had taught his father's dream manual.

Finally, as for the dream manual of Ibn Qutaybah, this work Ibn Khayr studied three times. As seen above, he studied it once with Abū Muḥammad b. ᶜAttāb. On two other occasions he studied it with Abū Bakr b. Aḥmad (d. 542/1147), a prominent scholar of prophetic traditions from Seville.[96] This Abū Bakr was one of the students of Abū ᶜAlī al-Ghassānī (d. 498/1104),[97] under whom he studied the dream manual of Ibn Qutaybah. Ghassānī was considered by some to be the chief scholar of prophetic traditions in his day in Cordova. He was also a student of Abū al-ᶜĀṣ al-Judhāmī (d. 447/1055), from whom he received the dream manual of Ibn Qutaybah. This Judhāmī was a native of Cordova. He had studied in his home town, as well as in other Andalusian cities. In 381/991 he went east to make the pilgrimage and to study, mostly in Mecca, Egypt, and Qayrawān. It was while abroad that he studied the dream manual of Ibn Qutaybah. This he did on two different occasions. While in Mecca, he studied the text with Abū al-Qāsim al-Saqaṭī (d. 406/1015).[98] This person, about whom little is known, seems to have studied and taught prophetic traditions in both Baghdad and Mecca. Among his pupils he could count not only Judhāmī, but also Abū Dharr al-Harawī, as seen above, himself the author of a dream manual. As for Saqaṭī, he transmitted Ibn Qutaybah's dream manual from Aḥmad b. ᶜAbd Allāh, the son of Ibn Qutaybah. Judhāmī also studied the dream manual of Ibn Qutaybah while he was living in Egypt. The teacher from whom he received the work was the scholar of prophetic traditions, Abū Bakr b. Muḥammad (d. 385/995).[99] He, in turn, was transmitting it from the famous Mālikī jurist Aḥmad b. Marwān (d. after 330/941), who had studied the text with Ibn Qutaybah himself.[100]

Based on the data provided by Ibn Khayr, it is possible to reconstruct in some detail a small portion of the transmission-history of five early Muslim dream manuals, to follow these works from the time they were put into circulation until the time they came to be studied by Ibn Khayr, and most important, to ascertain the identity of those responsible for transmitting them. It is possible to see how, in many instances, these dream manuals were handed down in family circles, how, in many cases, these works were capable of traversing the geographical limits of the Muslim world. Indeed, one should note the ease with which they were able to pass from one end of the Muslim world to the other. As for the persons responsible for transmitting these dream manuals, they were all members of the ulema—in many cases, as we have seen, ones quite famous, not only as scholars of prophetic traditions, but also judges, jurists, and so on. While one must keep in mind the risks of extrapolating from Andalusian evidence to the situation of the ulema as a whole, the evidence of Ibn Khayr suggests that dream interpretation was not only an important aspect of the intellectual concerns of the ulema, but also a sharᶜī discipline. Indeed, the same persons reading dream manuals were also reading literature more readily recognized by modern researchers as sharᶜī. The three scholars who had taught Ibn Khayr his five dream manuals, for instance, had all also taught him other sorts of sharᶜī literature. They had, for example, all also been responsible for transmitting to him copies of the most famous biography of Muḥammad, that by Ibn Hishām—a quintessentially sharᶜī work.[101] In Andalusia, at least, dream interpretation was a sharᶜī discipline, one avidly pursued by the ulema.

THE DIARY OF A ḤANBALĪ INTERPRETER OF DREAMS

The early Muslim dream manuals provide little information on the lives of their authors. Indeed, in these works it is only on very rare occasions that their authors speak in their own voices. So also, the various biographical sources that speak about these authors are quite limited as to the sorts of information they convey. In most instances, what we learn amounts to little more than a person's name, the names of his teachers and students, the date of his death, and maybe, if we're lucky, a few anecdotes about him. It is not from dream manuals or from biographical notices on their authors that one can glimpse something of the role of dream interpretation in the day-to-day life of the ulema. For this we must turn to other sources.

One of the rare autobiographical narratives to survive from the early Muslim period comes from the pen of Ibn al-Bannāʾ (d. 471/1078), a famous Ḥanbalī jurist who is also known to have composed a commentary on the work of Kirmānī.[102] Notwithstanding the loss of his commentary, we know far more about Ibn al-Bannāʾ as a dream interpreter than we do about any of the authors of the early Muslim dream manuals. For this we have to thank George Makdisi, who discovered in Damascus an autograph fragment of Ibn al-Bannāʾ's diary.[103] This fragment covers about one year of its author's life. It was almost certainly never intended for publication. Who but Ibn al-Bannāʾ would have been interested in notes on his financial affairs: "The bill was paid up to the end of Thursday, the 14th of Jumādā II of the year 461. He still has (coming to him the price of) 8 *riṭl*s of (roasted pumpkin?) seeds." Ibn al-Bannāʾ's diary is fascinating not only for its insights into the lives of the ulema of Baghdad, but also for the light it sheds on the concrete realities of dream interpretation in the lives of the ulema. If Ibn Khayr has provided our most detailed picture of the circulation of dream manuals among the ulema, Ibn al-Bannāʾ offers our most vivid glimpse into the life of a religious scholar who was interested in dreams.

Though it covers but a year of its author's life, Ibn al-Bannāʾ's diary contains accounts of approximately twenty-five dreams. On average, Ibn al-Bannāʾ or one of his acquaintances has a dream of note once every fortnight. Some dreams are had by the author himself. Others are seen by members of his family or by his friends, most of whom were themselves members of the ulema. Some dreams involve the dramatic appearance of loved ones who had passed away. These loved ones show themselves after their deaths to convey information about their state in the other world or to provide warnings to family members. Two such dreams are especially interesting, as they were seen by Ibn al-Bannāʾ's son.

> My son Abū Naṣr—may God favor him—had seen his grandfather in his dream, on a night when I had been to visit his tomb. My son said: "Grandfather said to me: 'Your father, the sheikh, was at my place; he recited verses from the Koran and visited my tomb. I rejoiced in his company, but I was not able to speak to him or to make any reply. May God, on my behalf, make his recompense good!'"[104]

> On Saturday, my son Abū Naṣr informed me that he saw his grandfather in his sleep, and asked him: "What has God done with you?" His grandfather answered: "He did not call me to account, but simply admitted me into Paradise." My son continued: "So I said to him: 'You used to pray: "O God! unite my soul with the souls of the saints!" Has God answered your prayer?' He replied: 'Yes; He has placed my soul with the souls of the prophets—peace be upon them!'"[105]

While dreams like these do not need to be interpreted, other dreams are symbolic in nature and demand interpretation. In his diary, Ibn al-Bannāʾ records a great many such dreams. Some are his own; others are his friends'. He usually recounts, first, the full narrative of the dream, specifying also who had seen it. He then records how he himself interpreted the dream, almost always providing his reasons for his interpretation—usually, by elucidating the symbolic meaning of the component parts of the dream.

> On the night of Tuesday, at daybreak, Abū ᶜAlī al-Ṣābūnī informed me that he had dreamt as though he were reading the Koranic suras Luqmān and Sajdah, and that I learned them from him, and that he saw me, and that I recited them, and that he marveled at my learning them, at the pressing of my lips against them, and at my reliance upon them. I interpreted this as meaning that I would attain the age of 74 years, which is equivalent to the number of verses in the two suras.[106]

Actually, the number of verses in these suras is only sixty-four. Regardless, this dream must have made quite an impact on the author and his family. Ibn al-Bannāʾ records that throughout the next night the members of his family repeatedly dreamed that they were there while the first dream had been narrated and interpreted, and that they looked on and proclaimed "That is a beautiful age to which to live: another thirty or so years."

Some of the dreams that Ibn al-Bannāʾ interprets are not his own. They had been seen by his colleagues among the ulema, by his own students, or by members of their families. Occasionally the circumstances of the dream-consultation are mentioned. We sometimes see these people show up at his door in the morning and recount their dreams to him. At other times they come to his house in the middle of the night. Or sometimes they mention their dreams at the study circles he ran in the local mosques. In the majority of instances, however, the dreams that Ibn al-Bannāʾ interprets are his own.

Many of Ibn al-Bannāʾ's dreams touch on contemporary political and theological debates. Some concern the renegade Ḥanbalī jurist Ibn ᶜAqīl, who was at the time being persecuted by his fellow Ḥanbalīs for having taken an interest in Muᶜtazilī thought. One dream, in particular, is interpreted by Ibn al-Bannāʾ as meaning that he himself would be the first to issue a legal ruling against the infidelity, deviation, and reprobation of this atheist and devil.[107] On one occasion, Ibn al-Bannāʾ specifically asks God to show him a dream concerning Ibn ᶜAqīl, a dream that would "confirm my suspicions or remove them."[108] (God confirmed his suspicions.) Many dreams also concern the confused political situation of Baghdad at the time, the wars and rumors of war with regard to the Seljuk Alp Arslān[109] and the fate of the wazir Ibn Jahīr.[110]

Perhaps the most interesting political dream is one had by Ibn al-Bannāʾ himself.[111] In it, he sees a recently deceased teacher accompanied by a great crowd. Ibn al-Bannāʾ asks the crowd where they are going. They reply: "To the Caliph." Ibn al-Bannāʾ comes forward to greet his teacher and sees that he is dressed in fine clothing. He then notices that his teacher's feet are unshod, and asks: "Master, are you walking barefoot?" To this he receives the reply: "Yes, this is the way to walk when one is going to complain against oppression." Or something to that effect, for Ibn al-Bannāʾ could not on waking remember the exact wording of his teacher's response. Regardless, this dream must have struck terror into Ibn al-Bannāʾ's heart, for within a few days he dispatched an account of it to the caliph himself. Ibn al-Bannāʾ includes in his diary the text of his rather lengthy letter.[112] He opens his missive with four well-known prophetic traditions:

> Ibn Sīrīn heard it from Abū Hurayrah that the prophet said: "The dream of the Muslim is one forty-sixth part of prophecy."
>
> ᶜUbādah b. al-Ṣāmit related that the prophet said: "The dream of the Muslim is one of the seventy parts of prophecy."
>
> ᶜĀʾishah said that Muḥammad's first revelation came in a true dream.
>
> Ibn Sīrīn heard it from Abū Hurayrah [that the prophet said]: "In the end times the dream of the Muslim will scarcely ever be false; and he whose dreams are most true is he whose speech is most true."

Having established the authority of dreams, he explains to the caliph why his ominous dream indicates that the dead are disturbed in their graves. He then gently reminds the caliph of his duties to look after the interests of religion, suggesting, not so subtly, that injustice and corruption are rampant and that it is the caliph's duty to clean things up.

Ibn al-Bannāʾ's dream and the letter it occasioned point up in a dramatic fashion just how seriously Ibn al-Bannāʾ and his contemporaries among the ulema took their dreams. While it is difficult to draw any general conclusions from the dream narratives that Ibn al-Bannāʾ records in his diary, they do suggest, at a minimum, that the ulema took a lively interest in the interpretation of their dreams. It should be noted in general, too, that Ibn al-Bannāʾ's work as an interpreter of dreams was restricted to acting as a consultant for people in his own social circles. We do not see him sitting in the mosque after Friday prayers interpreting the dreams of the common folk. In short, it was not toothless old women, but stolid Ḥanbalī ulema who were asking him to interpret their dreams. For these ulema, at least, dream interpretation was a legitimate religious pursuit, one of the sharᶜī disciplines.

CONCLUSIONS

The first volume of Fuat Sezgin's history of Arabic literature treats what can only be described as the orthodox or sharᶜī disciplines. It is concerned with such genres as Koranic commentary, prophetic traditions, history, law, and dogmatic theology. Later volumes were reserved for other types of literature, all more or less respectable—poetry, astronomy, medicine, arithmetic, and so on. There is no need to belabor Sezgin's disregard of divinatory literature. Let us imagine, however, that a second edition of his work were to be prepared. Let us further imagine that this second edition were to include a treatment of divinatory literature. In which volume of this revised edition should dream interpretation be treated? Would it belong in an entirely new volume devoted specifically to the various types of divinatory literature produced by early Muslims? Or should it be included elsewhere in the work, perhaps even in volume one? The arguments of this chapter suggest that this imaginary revision of Sezgin's work would have to consider dream interpretation in conjunction with the other sharᶜī disciplines, and thus, that the only legitimate place for its treatment would be volume one, where it would be considered alongside Koranic commentary, accounts of Muḥammad's life, juridical handbooks, and the like. In short, dream interpretation falls not at the periphery, but at the center of the concerns of the ulema.

In the fourth century A.H., there arose in Baṣrah a mysterious group of Ismāᶜīlīs who styled themselves the Brethren of Purity. It was they who composed the set of fifty-two tractates that together make up the *Epistles of the Brethren of Purity*, a work that in its entirety comprises a veritable encyclopedia of the premodern intellectual disciplines. Among the epistles of the Brethren was one that treats of the classification of these disciplines.[113] These they divided into three groups: the preparatory disciplines, the disciplines that are sharᶜī and based on authorities, and the authentic philosophic disciplines. In light of the arguments of the present chapter, it is interesting to note where the techniques of divination fell among the disciplines.

Most types of divination the Brethren subsumed under the heading of the preparatory disciplines, where they hold court alongside such things as reading, writing, and arithmetic, the study of magic, talismans, and alchemy, or bookkeeping, agriculture, and animal husbandry. One type of divination alone did not fall under this heading. The Brethren identified a total of six sharᶜī disciplines. Not surprisingly, the first five of these are: the study of the text of the Koran, the study of its interpretation, the study of prophetic traditions and their transmission, the study of religious law, and the study of spirituality. As for the sixth and final sharᶜī discipline, this the Brethren identified as dream interpretation. Of the divinatory techniques cultivated by early medieval Muslims, the Brethren considered dream interpretation alone to be a sharᶜī discipline. Based on the arguments of the present chapter, it was with every justification that the Brethren so classified it.

Nor were the Brethren alone in classifying dream interpretation as a sharᶜī discipline. Something similar was suggested by the great historian and jurist Ibn Khaldūn. He, too, categorized dream interpretation as nothing less than "one of the sharᶜī disciplines,"[114] one "luminous with the light of prophecy."[115] He, too, recalled the words of the prophet, who said both that "the true dream is one of the forty-six parts of prophecy" and that when he was gone "there would remain naught of glad tidings, except for the true dream, which the good man sees or which is seen for him."[116] It was thus that Ibn Khaldūn treated dream interpretation alongside other, more readily recognized sharᶜī disciplines, while at the same time carefully differentiating it from other forms of divination. Again, based on the arguments presented in this chapter, it was with every justification that Ibn Khaldūn so classified it.

Why did the ulema express such a lively interest in the interpretation of their dreams? The short answer is that they had no choice. There was an oneirocritic imperative in the foundational documents of their religion. The need to interpret dreams was mandated by scripture (properly interpreted) and by the dictates of the prophet. But perhaps this interest in dream interpretation is really nothing remarkable. It is, after all, difficult to find a single religion or culture in the whole of premodern Afro-Eurasia in which it was not recognized that the occult could be discerned through dreams.[117] What would be remarkable is the existence of a religion or culture that did not express such an interest, one that was roundly hostile to the very possibility that the divine might chose to communicate through dreams. There was in fact such a group. The Christians of late antiquity. While late antique Christians looked askance at the interpretation of dreams, a Christian tradition of dream interpretation would in time arise. This Christian oneirocritic tradition was not, however, autochthonous. It arose on Muslim soil. As for the rise of this Christian form of dream interpretation, its earnest and lively dialogue with the Muslim oneirocritic tradition, and the social contexts in which this dialogue took place, these are the subjects of the next chapter.

CHAPTER FIVE

DREAM INTERPRETATION, HELLENISM, AND NON-MUSLIMS

Muslim oneirocrits did not disregard earlier, non-Muslim forms of dream interpretation. Similarly, non-Muslims did not ignore Muslim oneirocritic techniques. Beginning already in the fourth century A.H., the Muslim oneirocritic tradition began to traverse some of the cultural and religious boundaries of the Near East. This chapter investigates how this happened. A full examination of how and why the Muslim oneirocritic tradition became an object of concern to non-Muslims is a complex topic, and I attempt to convey some sense of its complexity in the concluding portions of this chapter. Here, however, I have undertaken to follow in detail just one of its trajectories, one that can be traced in some detail given the surviving evidence. In this regard, of particular concern are two Christian dream manuals, both composed in and around the fourth century A.H. The first is in Greek and is of Byzantine provenance—the work generally known as the oneirocriticon of Ps. Achmet. The second was composed in Arabic by Bar Bahlūl, a Nestorian Christian from Iraq.

While Ps. Achmet and Bar Bahlūl were not the first Christians to take an interest in dreams, they were the first to compose dream manuals. Furthermore and notwithstanding the diverse provenance of these two works, both contain features that suggest that their authors made use of Muslim sources. Is it the case that these texts drew on the Muslim oneirocritic tradition? And if so, what sources were used? And more important, how were those sources used? Now that something is known about the early Muslim tradition of dream interpretation, solid answers to these questions can at last be offered. An analysis of these two dream manuals should not stop at an examination of their sources and their authors' strategies for appropriating those sources. It is also necessary to investigate the social contexts in which they were produced, and the roles that those contexts played in determining why their authors sought to make use of Muslim sources. These, then, are the subjects to which the present chapter is devoted.

To understand how and why Ps. Achmet and Bar Bahlūl went about appropriating Muslim sources, it is necessary, first, to examine briefly how dreams had traditionally been understood by Christians, particularly those of the eastern Mediterranean. To capture the full diversity of earlier Christian approaches to this subject would be an immense topic and one quite beyond the scope of the present study. It is, in fact, a topic that has already attracted not a little scholarly attention.[1] Here I am concerned with just one aspect of this topic, how earlier Christians approached the subject of dream interpretation. The authors of our two dream manuals did not exist in a historical vacuum. They were heirs to a long tradition of reflection on dream interpretation. If we are to understand why they approached the subject as they did, it is necessary to contextualize their works against this earlier tradition of reflection. It is only thus that the full significance and indeed novelty of their respective works can become clear.

DREAM INTERPRETATION AND THE CHRISTIANS OF LATE ANTIQUITY

The year 620 A.D. found Muḥammad being persecuted at the hands of the Meccans. So harsh had the situation become that he and his community would shortly be forced to relocate to Medina. The year 620 was also a difficult one for the Christians of Syro-Palestine. For almost two decades they had been living under the Persian occupation, and it would be some years yet before the emperor would be able to expulse the occupying armies. Meanwhile, in the monasteries of Syro-Palestine life continued much as it had before the occupation. One of these monasteries was that of Mar Sabas, located a day's walk from Jerusalem. It was there in or around 620 that a certain Antiochus compiled a handbook for the monastic life.[2] Drawing upon centuries of monastic wisdom, Antiochus wrote down in an orderly fashion everything that a monk might need to know about sin, temptation, and virtue.

Among the topics Antiochus thought worthy of discussion was the proper role of dreams in the life of a monk.[3] This topic he could not pass over in silence, for there are some, he notes with horror, "who put their faith in dreams and have thereby caused themselves to deviate from the straight path." Antiochus is adamant—dreams are dangerous. "They are nothing but the images and simulacra of a mind led astray, the sport of wicked demons." In support of this opinion, Antiochus can find much in the Bible, which he dutifully cites. Does not Jude state that "dreamers defile the flesh, deny the powers, and blaspheme the glories" (8)? Does not the preacher condemn dreams as the source of a multitude of temptation (Eccl 5.3, 7)? Does not Sirach state:

> Dreams deceive the stupid. . . . Like one who runs after shadows or chases the wind is the man who clings to his dreams. What truth is there in a lie?

> Prophecies, omens, and dreams are vain, for dreams have deceived many and have caused the downfall of those who hope in them.[4]

Clearly there is much in the Bible to cast doubt on the validity of dreams. There is, thus, little need for Antiochus to be so duplicitous in citing its testimony. Jude's dreamers, he neglects to note, are merely metaphorical; and in citing Sirach, he fortuitously skips over the part where some dreams are said to be sent by God (34.6). These omissions notwithstanding, Antiochus goes on to offer advice on prayer. That his monastic readers might escape the danger of dreams, he bids them to have recourse to prophylactic prayer. In particular, as they lay on their bed before sleep, they should ask God to protect their souls and give flight to error. They are to pray not for good or true dreams, but for a "mind enlightened by the light of the knowledge of the Gospel."

Although roundly hostile to dreams, even Antiochus has to admit that not all dreams are demonic. There are, he grants, some that come from God. He grudgingly concedes that Job, in particular, had once mentioned them (33.14–16). How should one respond to such divine dreams? Remarkably, Antiochus suggests that even these should be rejected by his monastic brethren:

> You, my beloved, ought not believe or consent to [such] dreams. Even if, as is likely, it is a question of a dream sent to you via divine revelation, let us heed it not. . . . If we do this, we shall not cause God to be angry; rather, he will receive us, insofar as we have fearfully guarded the treasure that he had entrusted to us.

To illustrate further how an excessive interest in dreams can lead one astray, Antiochus concludes his discourse with a monitory example, "one among many old or new," he assures his readers, that he might have cited. There was once, he says, a monk who dwelt at Mt. Sinai. This monk was renowned for his virtuous life and for many years had lived as a solitary. During this time the devil began to toy with him. To gain his trust, the devil first revealed to him many true dreams. Having induced him to believe in dreams, he then showed him a dream in which the martyrs, apostles, and Christians were mired in filth, while Moses, the prophets, and the Jews, were residing in light. Immediately, the monk arose and went to Palestine where he converted to Judaism. He married a Jewish woman and spent the remaining years of his life as a polemicist for Judaism. All his fellow monks lamented, Antiochus writes, for here was a model of virtue, one who had grown gray while living the ascetic life, who yet defiled himself in the end by blaspheming Christ—and all because he had been induced to believe in his dreams. In the final analysis, Antiochus can only cite Christ's admonition (Lk 12.39) to keep on one's guard in that one knows not at what hour the thief comes.

Antiochus' discourse on dreams is one of the fullest to survive from the pen of a late antique Christian. For all that, it is not particularly unusual. Most of its themes were, in fact, thoroughly traditional. Even its monitory example had long been in circulation among the eastern monastic communities. Although Antiochus presented himself as having seen the events he describes take place—"this [monk's downfall] I myself observed, as did many of the other monks. . . . When I and some other pious monks saw this we lamented greatly"—this was simply not the case. The anecdote had already enjoyed a long life in the Christian east.[5] It was, moreover, also known to western monastic readers, thanks to Cassian's having included it in his *Conferences*.[6] It may be that Antiochus was simply being dishonest, or, what is more likely, careless—the whole of the example, including the passages in which the narrator speaks in the first person, may well have been lifted whole from a prior source. Whatever the case, the wide circulation of this anecdote points up just how thoroughly traditional Antiochus' understanding of dreams was, how very nearly it approached what Gilbert Dagron has termed "the permanent position of the church" on the subject of dreams and their interpretation.[7]

As a general rule, the Christians of late antiquity did not much care for dream interpretation. At times they dismiss the practice as a silly but basically harmless form of feminine superstition. It is the sort of thing toyed with by "nurses" when they play with children, the sort of thing to which the apostle Paul was referring when he spoke of "oldwives' tattle" (I Tim 4.7).[8] It is the stuff of dream-vendors (ὀνειροπῶλαι) and dream-hucksters (ὀνειροκάπηλοι).[9] It is similar to what is done by those who overly allegorize Scripture, attempting to find significance where there is none.[10] This understanding of dream interpretation as a relatively harmless superstition is, however, the minority view. Far more commonly the interpretation of dreams is condemned in harsher terms. It is a practice that the pagans invented.[11] It makes use of devilish forces.[12] It is totally inappropriate for Christians, even for nurses and oldwives.

Taking as his text Matthew 25.41 ("Away from me, evildoers, into the eternal fire that has been prepared for the devil and his angels") and pointing straight at his congregation, one late antique preacher proclaims that this verse applies to them, for they themselves are companions of the devil and his angels.[13] How does the preacher know this? They associate, he says, with magicians, diviners, enchanters, wizards, sorcerers, and astrologers. Worse yet, he notes, they consort with those who claim to be able to tell them the meaning of their dreams. To fraternize with such as these, he argues, is to disassociate oneself from God and forfeit one's status as a Christian. In the end, the preacher must conclude that those who do so are running a terrible risk: "traveling with the demons mentioned by Christ into that same unquenchable fire." To this preacher's mind, dream interpretation was something far worse than a harmless form of superstition. It was, instead, a dangerous form of devilish magic—and he leaves little doubt as to whether good Christians should take an interest in it. This preacher's understanding of dream interpretation is not unusual. It is also encountered in the writings of the early Christian apologists.[14] It is a theme in the texts of monastic and ascetically oriented authors.[15] It is a subject on which preachers spoke at length. Indeed, it is in the sermons of these preachers that one can best catch the strain of moral outrage occasioned by dream interpretation.

The Psalmist had said: "God is our refuge and strength" (46.1). Taking this text as his theme, another preacher asks his congregation to consider whether God is really their refuge.[16] He notes that if they are troubled by an enemy, the first thing they do is seek the aid of a human patron. He observes that if their children are sick, they immediately run to those who know occult chants or to those who make amulets. It is, indeed, only as a last resort that they think of consulting a doctor—and even then, it is a human doctor rather than he who is able to give the true medicaments. In much the same fashion, the preacher points out, if someone has a dream that seems in the least significant, the first thing the dreamer does on waking is run to the interpreter of dreams. In the end, the preacher must conclude, his congregants are calling God their refuge with their mouths, while with their actions they are drawing on the devilish and vain aid of those who are unable to provide aid.

Commenting on Psalm 106.35 ("But they mingled with the nations, and learned their practices"), another preacher proclaims that this prophecy has been fulfilled among his congregation,[17] for they have begun to devote themselves to Jewish and pagan myths and genealogies, to divination and astrology, to drugs and to amulets. They are hanging lamps near sacred springs and there practicing superstitious ablutions. These same Christians, he continues, observe lucky days and years, omens, and the sounds of birds. The final crime for which he has to condemn them: their attempt to divine the unknown through the interpretation of their dreams.

> Those who do such things, how can they be considered Christians? How can they be so bold as to call themselves Christians? They are worse than the pagans and yet they dare to approach the divine mysteries!?

Once again, dream interpretation is condemned by assimilating it to other, more recognized forms of magic and divination, and as such it falls under the more general admonition for Christians to "regard not spells and divinations, [which] is communion with Satan."[18]

While one might think the preachers' words harsh, their words are the only weapons they have. In the end, they can do little more than exhort their congregations. The case was otherwise with the Christian emperors, who were able to enshrine their very similar understanding of dream interpretation in the judicial codes and to back up their understanding with legal sanctions. One emperor, for instance, condemns to the torture horse and the iron claws anyone in his retinue found practicing divination.[19] Falling under the ban are readily recognized malefactors (wizards, magicians, soothsayers, diviners, augurs, astrologers). He also includes, however, "anyone who hides their divination under the guise of interpreting dreams."

The single most compelling piece of evidence for the dislike of dream interpretation among the Christians of late antiquity is not the sermons of preachers or the legislation of emperors. It is, instead, the undeniable fact that these Christians were hardly avid composers of dream manuals. Late antique dream manuals are unknown to the Latin, Coptic, and Syriac Christian traditions. As for the Greek tradition, there were perhaps in circulation two short dream keys.[20] Such texts are difficult to date and the precise relations among the extant examples have yet to be established with certainty. Nonetheless, there are some who date to late antiquity the alphabetic dream key of Ps. Daniel and the versified dream key attributed to the Persian magus Astrampsychus. If, in fact, these two texts were composed by late antique Christians, it is interesting to note that their authors were unwilling to take responsibility for them, but chose instead to put them into circulation pseudonymously. In any case, these are brief dream keys, not fully developed dream manuals. To the extent of our present knowledge, it was not until the early Middle Ages that the first full-length Christian dream manuals appeared, works comparable to the dream manual of Artemidorus or to the Muslim texts considered in this study. Of these, there were two, one in Greek, the other in Arabic. It is to the former that I now turn.

THE DREAM MANUAL OF PS. ACHMET

While we do not know precisely when the so-called oneirocriticon of Ps. Achmet was written,[21] a number of considerations converge to suggest some rough estimates. Because the text mentions Maʾmūn,[22] it must have appeared after 813 A.D., the year that caliph began his reign. Things are less certain when it comes to the work's latest possible date. Two pieces of evidence provide our only clues. First, while the earliest manuscripts of the oneirocriticon stem from the thirteenth century A.D., there is a manuscript of Artemidorus that bears two marginalia derived from the oneirocriticon. These marginalia have been dated on paleographic grounds to the eleventh century. Accordingly, the oneirocriticon must date from the eleventh century or earlier.[23] Second, there is an abbreviated version of the oneirocriticon. Its earliest copy has also been dated on paleographic grounds to the eleventh century—more precisely, to ca. 1075.[24] Accordingly, the oneirocriticon must have appeared before this date.[25] Granted the soundness of the paleographic judgments at issue, a matter in which I must bow to wiser heads, the oneirocriticon can be dated to sometime between the early ninth and the eleventh centuries. And even if it were to turn out that these paleographic judgments are less than sound, there can be no doubt that the oneirocriticon was written before 1176 A.D., the year in which it was translated into Latin.[26]

Little is known about the provenance of the oneirocriticon. While its compiler chose to remain anonymous, it is clear that he was a Christian. This is borne out by the contents of the text, in particular its use of Christian Scripture. Moreover, it is probable that its compiler lived not under Muslim rule, but in Byzantium. This can be inferred from what is known about the decline of Greek among the Christians living under Islam. While comprehensive studies are lacking, the situation in Palestine has been well analyzed by Sidney H. Griffith, who concludes "that from the ninth century onward one is hardpressed to name many compositions of any significance in Greek to come from Palestine."[27] Cyril Mango, too, has come to a similar conclusion: "In the course of the ninth century the practice of Greek all but died out in Palestine and Syria."[28] If the situation of Syro-Palestine was typical, that the oneirocriticon's compiler chose to write in Greek strongly suggests that he stemmed from regions still under Byzantine control. Moreover, even if there may have been some elite Christians under Muslim rule still capable of reading and writing Greek, that the compiler wrote in Greek suggests that he was writing for an audience able to read Greek, and such an audience would have been hard to come by among the Christians under Muslim rule.

The only place in the oneirocriticon where its compiler speaks in his own voice is his preface.[29] Everything else in the work is presented as the fruits of his labors as a compiler. Further, it is in his preface that he reveals his literary persona. He presents himself as a dream interpreter working for his "master." He has labored long, he claims, for his master, seeking an accurate understanding of dreams. During his studies, he discovered that the best interpreters were the Indians, Persians, and Egyptians. Such sages, he says, after discovering the truth about dreams, set down their findings in writing. It is from these writings that he claims to have compiled his work, arranging his materials by subject and listing for each type of dream symbol the opinions of the three oneirocritic traditions. This method, he hopes, will help his master learn the truth and thereby put to the test this most wonderful of sciences "through which the issue of the future is foreknown." This and this alone the compiler chooses to "reveal" about himself.

Following his prefatory remarks, the compiler begins immediately to cite his sources. These he presents in large blocks, interjecting his own voice only to provide titles to signify a change of subject or a change of source. He opens with three descriptions of the nature of dream interpretation. These are taken, he claims, from the writings of Syrbacham the dream interpreter of the king of India, Baram the interpreter of the Sasanian king of Persia, and Tarphan the interpreter of the king of Egypt. Of the three, Syrbacham's discourse is the longest and the only one explicitly Christian.[30] Syrbacham opens by roundly proclaiming: "The interpretation of dreams is great wisdom. It is prophecy that God proclaims as a glad tidings for all." To support these claims, he appeals first to Christ's words that "I and my Father will come to those who love me and will make our dwelling in them" (Jn 14.23). This, he asserts, is fulfilled when God sends dreams. Syrbacham next appeals to the examples of Joseph, Mary's husband, as well as of Daniel and the other prophets, all of whom received information from God in their dreams. It is, indeed, the testimony of these that assures us that "the seeing of dreams is for all people a type of divine information, which makes known to them all things, regardless of whether they are good or bad." Syrbacham then turns to considerations of method. One ought not think, he says, that a dream means the same thing for each person. The interpretation of a dream varies in accordance with the status of the person who sees it: it means one thing for the king, another for the poor, one thing for women, another for men, and so on. The meaning of a dream can also vary with the time of the year in which it is seen. For these reasons, he argues, it is necessary that the interpreter be "wise and learned in many subjects" and possessed of an ever-vigilant divine fear. Moreover, the interpreter must recognize that God sends dreams not just to the righteous: even as he provides sustenance for those who deny and blaspheme him, so also he sends dreams to the wicked. Syrbacham concludes: "Now, by the power of the holy Trinity, who is without beginning or division, I begin my interpretations."

The opening discourse of the Sasanian Baram is concerned with a different set of problems.[31] It is basically an attempt to show that dream interpretation is better than astrology. Through the interpretation of dreams, Baram proclaims, one is able to discover "great knowledge and foreknowledge." Furthermore, the interpretation of dreams—provided that the interpreter is skilled—requires far less labor than astrology. This is because astrology is toilsome, prone to error, wearisome, and demanding of much time. Also problematic: astrologers are often at variance with one another over how to read the signs. Contrariwise, we are assured, the interpretation of dreams is wholly unambiguous. As for the qualities that should be had by the interpreter: "He who wishes to pursue a knowledge of this [subject] should have a subtle mind and a love for the lords of the stars." Like Syrbacham, Baram closes by stating his intention to commence his interpretations.

The third discourse comes from Tarphan the Egyptian.[32] He proclaims that he has found what all the kings of Egypt sought with regard to the interpretation of dreams—accuracy. He announces himself the greatest living interpreter and states that he gained his experience by working for the Pharaoh, who was wont to have many dreams. Because the Pharaoh loved the gods, they would show him through dreams everything that was to befall him. These dreams Tarphan would interpret, and always accurately. Indeed, it was only through his mediation, Tarphan claims, that the Pharaoh was able to have knowledge of the future. Like Syrbacham and Baram, Tarphan closes with a transition to his dream manual proper, declaring that he will include everything discovered by himself, as well as by the ancient Pharaohs[33] and their wise men. In short, he will treat "everything that it is possible for men to see" in their dreams.

The remaining portions of the oneirocriticon consist of what purport to be extended citations from the dream lore of the Indians, Persians, and Egyptians.[34] Presumably we are meant to believe that the compiler derived his materials from works by Syrbacham, Baram, and Tarphan. This is not, however, explicitly stated.

The remaining three hundred or so chapters are simply ascribed to the respective communities:

> From the Indians—The Interpretation of the Resurrection
> From the Persians—The Interpretation of the Resurrection
> From the Egyptians—The Interpretation of the Resurrection
> [and so on . . .]

The compiler organizes his treatise by subject. Each type of dream symbol usually receives three treatments, once by each of the three communities. Some topics, however, are treated in combined chapters, most commonly "Persians and Egyptians," but sometimes "Indians, Persians, and Egyptians." Interspersed among these formalized interpretations are thirteen anecdotes. These recount consultations in which someone (often Ma᾿mūn) consults an interpreter (usually someone called Sereim; once someone called Achmet the son of Sereim), tells him of a dream, and receives its proper interpretation. The following is typical:

> There was once a certain man who pretended to be his own master. To test the dream interpreter Sereim, he went to him and said: "I dreamt that I drank the whole of the Tigris river." He replied: "You didn't dream this. It's impossible." This the man acknowledged: "You're right. It wasn't I who had this dream but my master who sent me." Sereim replied: "When you go back you'll find that he has died." Even as he predicted, so it happened.[35]

There can be little doubt that these anecdotes are an attempt to invoke the authority of the "founder" of the Muslim tradition of dream interpretation, Muḥammad b. Sīrīn.

There is much about the oneirocriticon to suggest that its compiler had access to Muslim sources, not least its anecdotes. Unfortunately, most research on the oneirocriticon has taken it for granted that its compiler claimed to be an Arab interpreter of dreams named Achmet or Achmet the son of Sereim. This is not the case. As seen above, the compiler of the oneirocriticon chose to remain anonymous. This point must be emphasized. The contents of the text simply do not support the conclusion that its compiler claimed to be this Achmet. To be sure, in the body of the text there occur anecdotes about this Achmet's marvelous feats of dream interpretation. Markedly absent, however, is any attempt to identify the Achmet about whom stories are told with the compiler of the text as a whole. The ascription of the oneirocriticon to Achmet seems to be based solely on the work's titles. The manuscripts of the oneirocriticon transmit it under a wide variety of different titles, some of which are variants on the following: *The Oneirocriticon Composed by Achmet the Son of Sereim, the Dream Interpreter of the Caliph Mamoun.* This seems to be a scribal extrapolation from the work's contents. It must be emphasized, however: nowhere in the oneirocriticon does its compiler present himself as this Achmet, not even in his preface, where alone he speaks in his own voice.[36]

Early debates on the oneirocriticon's sources took it for granted that its compiler presented himself as an Arab interpreter of dreams named Achmet or Achmet the son of Sereim. Not surprisingly, therefore, these early debates were primarily concerned to determine whether this Achmet was a historical person or whether the name "Achmet" was rather a nom de plume utilized by someone modeling himself on Muḥammad b. Sīrīn. One opinion had it that the compiler was making no attempt to appropriate the legacy of Ibn Sīrīn, that the text was in fact written by someone attached to the court of Maʾmūn, and that this person bore the name "Achmet." Perhaps the most prominent exponent of this view was the text's editor, Franz Drexl.[37] He suggests that the mysterious Achmet was a Greek Christian attached to the court of Maʾmūn. This should not be surprising, Drexl opines, for it is well known that Maʾmūn was interested in all things Greek and made little distinction between matters Christian and Muslim. Moreover, this Achmet—who is, I might add, otherwise unknown—was probably educated in Byzantium and only later came to "his homeland" (that is, Baghdad). Drexl was not the only one to adopt a position along these lines. The basic authenticity of the work has also been accepted by other researchers.[38]

Others have argued that there was a conscious attempt by the compiler to associate his work with Muḥammad b. Sīrīn. Probably the first to advocate this thesis was the British orientalist N. Bland,[39] who argued that the work cannot have been written by the historical Ibn Sīrīn: not only did Ibn Sīrīn die a full century before Maʾmūn, but also the text was written not by a Muslim but by a Christian. "Besides this," he assures us, "the arrangement, as well as the whole character of the composition, is far from oriental." If the text was not by a Muslim, who then wrote it? Bland suggests that it was originally written in Greek by a Christian, though perhaps making use of Arabic sources, and that it was the anonymous compiler of the text who ascribed it to Ibn Sīrīn. Bland goes on to propose that one of the oneirocriticon's sources may have been the Arabic dream manual entitled *Khabar al-Maʾmūnī* (lit. "Maʾmūn's Account")—hence the oneirocriticon's references to dreams of Maʾmūn. It is a question here of the dream manual of Abū Ṭālib ʿAbd al-Salām b. Ḥasan al-Maʾmūnī (d. ca. 383/993). His dream manual is not extant, but was mentioned by a number of later authors.[40] Bland is quite mistaken, however. The *Khabar al-Maʾmūnī* derives its name not from its accounts of the caliph Maʾmūn's dreams, but from its author's name. Regardless, Bland's understanding of the oneirocriticon has become fairly common, especially among more recent researchers, although there are numerous variations as to the specific identity of the person who adopted "Achmet" as a pseudonym.[41]

As for the oneirocriticon's sources, we need not discuss in detail the numerous suggestions that have been offered. In those cases where the suggestions of

Bland are not being followed, more often than not they consist of rather a motley parade of hypotheses lacking foundations. And the certainty with which the hypotheses are put forward usually increases in direct proportion to the hypothesizer's innocence of matters Arabic and Islamic. To give just a single example, one recent researcher has suggested that the oneirocriticon's compiler may have used a wide variety of Muslim sources: not only the dream manual of Maᵓmūnī (à la Bland), but also Ibn Saᶜd's *Ṭabaqāt* (one of the first popular Muslim "dream-books"), as well as the dream manuals of Muḥammad b. Maḥmūd al-Āmulī and Ibn Shāhīn.[42] The only problems with these suggestions: Ibn Saᶜd's *Ṭabaqāt* was not a dream manual, but a biographical dictionary; Āmulī flourished in the fourteenth century; Ibn Shāhīn, in the fifteenth.

Did the oneirocriticon use Arabic sources? And if so, which ones? These seemingly simple questions have not yet received satisfactory answers. If many researchers are agreed that there must be some use of Muslim sources, they are far from unanimous as to the identity of those sources or how they are being used. Gilbert Dagron has aptly summarized the current state of the question: "If all specialists . . . agree today in recognizing in the *Oneirocriticon* a Byzantine work influenced by Islam, no one has yet elucidated the complex problem of its borrowings from the Arabic literature of the ninth and tenth centuries."[43]

The Oneirocriticon's Sources

Before turning to the details, let me summarize what I think to be the relation between the oneirocriticon and the early Muslim tradition of dream interpretation. There can be no doubt that the compiler of the work made use of Muslim sources in Arabic. This can be demonstrated in a number of different ways. The order in which he treats dream symbols is nearly identical to what is found in most early Muslim dream manuals. The contents of his dream manual—or at least parts of it, as shall be seen—are a very nearly literal version of what is found in the early Muslim dream manuals. Many of the oneirocriticon's thirteen anecdotes, as well, are fairly literal, if somewhat expanded versions of anecdotes found in Muslim texts. It is not yet possible to identify the oneirocriticon's major source or sources, however. None of the extant, early Muslim dream manuals was among them. But even if we do not have his sources, given the homogeneity of the Muslim oneirocritic tradition, it is nonetheless patent that the compiler of the oneirocriticon was drawing on one or more Muslim works and that he made use of them in written form.

Consider, first, the order in which the oneirocriticon treats the objects appearing in dreams. Early Muslim dream manuals follow one of two patterns. The rarer one is found in the dream manual of Ibn Sīnā and is derived from the order in which Artemidorus interpreted dreams in the first two books of his dream manual. The other appears to be peculiar to the Muslim tradition. It is widespread, being found in many different texts with only slight variations. We can distinguish six different parts to this organizational pattern:

1. Dreams of things to do with religion.
2. Dreams of the sun, moon, and stars.
3. Dreams of things to do with human beings.
4. Dreams of features of the landscape and of the climate.
5. Dreams of animate objects.
6. Dreams of various types of nonhuman living creatures.

The oneirocriticon is organized in a parallel fashion. The parallels between it and the early Muslim dream manuals are laid out in Tables 5.1 and 5.2, which compare the organization of the oneirocriticon with that of Ibn Qutaybah's dream manual and the first of Qayrawānī's shorter dream manuals. The left-hand columns present the sequence of chapters in the dream manuals of Ibn Qutaybah and Qayrawānī; the right-hand columns, the corresponding sequence of chapters in the oneirocriticon. It can readily be seen that the structure of the oneirocriticon follows closely the traditional Muslim organization. Differences are few. On the one hand, a few of the categories of dream symbols appearing in the Muslim dream manuals are not treated: dreams of God, the Koran, and mountains, for instance. On the other hand, a few of the chapters appear out of order. These "misplaced" chapters are marked in Tables 5.1 and 5.2 through the use of bold type. Aside from these differences, in terms of its overall structure, the oneirocriticon treats of nearly the same dream symbols as the Muslim texts and in nearly the same order. Such parallels can hardly be coincidental. They suggest, rather, that the oneirocriticon had access to Muslim written sources. This is not to say that it made use of the dream manual of Qayrawānī or Ibn Qutaybah. The pattern at issue is far too common to justify such a conclusion.

Not only does the structure of the oneirocriticon parallel that found in the Muslim dream manuals, there are also many extremely close verbal parallels. These parallels are so extensive that it is impossible to provide more than a few examples, ones already familiar from chapter 3. Consider, first, dreams of the resurrection. The oneirocriticon offers the following:

> If someone sees in a dream the resurrection of the dead, in whatever place he sees in the dream the resurrection of the dead, in that place justice will be accomplished. If in that place [the inhabitants] are unjust, they will be punished. If they are being treated unjustly, quickly they will receive retribution, for in the resurrection God alone is the just judge.[44]

Compare this with the dream manuals of Ibn Qutaybah, Kharkūshī, and Qayrawānī.

> Whoever sees the resurrection happen in a place, justice will be spread in that place for its people if they are being oppressed, and against them,

TABLE 5.1
The Sequence of Chapters in Ibn Qutaybah and Ps. Achmet

Topic	Ibn Qutaybah	Ps. Achmet
God	1	—
resurrection, Paradise, Hell, angels	2–3	5–10
heaven	4	8
prophets	5	11
Ka'bah, *qiblah*	6	—
to become a believer	7	12
to change one's name	8	—
Koran, prayer, building mosques	9	—
judges	10	15
things related to judges	11	16–17
faith	12	13–14
sun, moon, stars	13	166–69
man and his members	14	18–102
marriage, divorce, birth, corpses	15–16	124–32
earth, buildings	17	142–43
hills, mountains	18	—
rain, moisture, etc.	19	170–84
drinks	20	185–86, 195–96
trees, fruit, plants	21	197–207
seeds	22	209–12
large tents, hair-cloth tents, etc.	23	—
clothing	24	156–57, 215–29
horses	25	230–33
weapons	26	155
jewelry	27	245, 255–58
fire, etc.	28	158–59
clouds, rain, etc.	29	162–63, 170–73
flying, jumping	30	160–61
horses, nags, etc., mules, asses, camels	31–34	230–35
bulls, cows	35	256–57
sheep, rams, goats	36–37	240
beasts of prey	38	270–74
elephants, buffalo, pigs	39	268–69, 279
insects	40	295–97
lions	41	267
birds	42	284–94
water-birds and others	43	299
scorpions, snakes, reptiles	44	281, 283, 300
occupations	45	—
oddities	46	—

TABLE 5.2
The Sequence of Chapters in Qayrawānī and Ps. Achmet

Topic	Qayrawānī	Ps. Achmet
God	1	—
resurrection, Paradise, Hell, angels	2	5–9
angels, heavens, flying	3	10
prophets and companions	4	11
Ka'bah, prayer, fasting, call to prayer	5	—
Koran	6	—
sultan, judge, measure, balance	7	15–17
sun, moon, stars	8	166–69
wounds, bodily members	9	18–107
man (young and old), marriage, divorce	10	124–30
sickness, death agony, death, corpses	11	131–32
wood, throne, bedstead, doors, thrones, minbars, coffins	12	—
earth, villages, cities, estates, buildings	13	142–43, 146, 148
mountains, ascent, descent	14	—
clouds, rain, wind	15	162–71
thunder, earthquakes, eclipse	16	145
seas, rivers, entering the bath, waters, washing, ablution, boats	17	174–84
drinking, drunkenness, teat, breast, emesis	18	185–86, 195–96
gardens, trees, fruits, sowing, seeds	19	197–213
pelts, clothing, rugs, linen, cotton, wool, hair	20	156–57, 215–29
armor, swords, all types of weapons	21	155
gold, silver, seal-rings, jewels, pearls	22	245, 255–58
fire, smoke, mirage, dust particles in the air	23	158–59
horses, mules, asses	24	230–33
camels, cows, sheep	25	234–37
lions, elephants, beasts of prey	26	267–74
birds, fish, eggs	27	284–94
snakes, scorpions, insects	28	283, 295–97
interpretive principles	29	—
collection of oddities	30	—

if they are oppressors—for the day of the resurrection is the day of separation [of good from evil] and of retribution and judgment. For God said: "We shall place scales of justice for the day of the resurrection; not one soul will be treated unjustly" (Q 21.47).[45]

Whoever sees in his dream that the resurrection has occurred in a place, justice will be spread in that place for its people and they will avenge themselves against those who oppress them there and those who are being oppressed will be victorious, for that day is the day of separation and the day of justice.[46]

Whoever sees the resurrection happen, justice will be spread in the place in which he sees that it happens; if in it there are those who are oppressed, they will be victorious; if they are oppressors, [God] will avenge himself on them and their affair will be separated. For God says: "The day of separation is the time appointed for them all" (Q 44.40).[47]

Or again, consider the oneirocriticon's treatment of dreams of the planets:

Aphrodite is the queen.
Hermes is the chief scribe.
Ares is the king's minister of war.
Zeus is the one in charge of the king's treasure, estates, and gold.
Chronos is his chief punisher and discipliner.[48]

These symbols Ibn Qutaybah, Sijistānī, Qayrawānī, and Ibn Sīnā interpret as follows:

Venus is the king's wife.
Mercury is his scribe.
Mars is his minister of war.
Jupiter is his minister of finance.
Saturn is his minister of justice.[49]

Venus is the king's wife.
Mars is his minister of war.
Mercury is his scribe.
Jupiter is his minister of finance and his judge.
Saturn is his minister of justice.
It is also said that Jupiter is the king's minister of irrigation.[50]

Venus is the king's wife.
Mercury is his scribe.
Mars is his minister of war.
Jupiter is his minister of finance.
Saturn is his minister of justice.[51]

Venus is the king's wife.
Mercury is his scribe.
Mars is his minister of war.
Jupiter is [his minister] of finance.
Saturn is [his chief] of police and overseer of prisons or the one in charge of punishments.[52]

As can readily be seen, there are no substantive differences between the oneirocriticon and these Muslim texts. As for dreams of the resurrection, to appropriate his Muslim source or sources all the oneirocriticon's compiler had to do was change a Koranic verse into a theological platitude. As for dreams of the planets, there are no significant variants at all, even as to the order in which the five symbols are presented. Again, such parallels can hardly be coincidental. They suggest, rather, that the compiler had access to Muslim written sources.

If one lays out the parallels for the whole of the oneirocriticon a distinct pattern emerges. Parallels between it and the early Muslim dream manuals are found only in those sections that present the interpretations of the Indians, or in some cases in those sections that present combined sets of interpretations. Oddly enough, in the oneirocriticon it is precisely these chapters that display the influence of the Christian tradition: they alone contain citations of biblical verses; they alone treat of religious subjects that are specific to Christianity. Another interesting feature that emerges only in a full collation is that the parallels between the oneirocriticon and the early Muslim dream manuals are most often found only at the very beginning of the Indian chapters, where the basic meaning of the dream symbol is presented. As for the oneirocriticon's many permutations on these basic dream symbols, they are seldom paralleled in the Muslim texts. There are a number of possible explanations for this. The compiler of the oneirocriticon may have used a source that itself contained these additional permutations, or contrariwise, the compiler may himself have been expanding on the basic data of his Muslim source. It is not yet possible to determine which of these explanations is the more likely. What is certain is that the compiler of the oneirocriticon did, in fact, draw on Muslim sources for the basic data included in his Indian chapters.

As for the thirteen anecdotes found in the oneirocriticon, I have thus far been able to find parallels in Muslim texts for about half of these. The oneirocriticon, for instance, offers the following anecdote:

> The caliph Mamoun saw in a dream that he was in the most great temple in Mecca, that is, the tent of Abraham. He went forth to the upper part, where the throne is, and urinated in the two corners; in the same fashion, he also urinated in the two lower corners outside the temple. As he was amazed at this greatest of sins, he sent an intimate friend to the oneirocrit Sereim, and this, that the dream might be interpreted for him [as if it were his own]. The oneirocrit Sereim spoke to him, saying: "You did not see this, for you are not of the blood of the caliph; for this reason, I shall not interpret it." The caliph then summoned Sereim and made him swear that he would not reveal the interpretation of the dream. Sereim responded: "The four corners of the temple, in which you urinated—these signify four children. The two of the upper part, where the throne is—these are two successors to your throne and authority. The two of the

> lower part—these are two offspring who will not possess your authority and throne."[53]

A similar tradition is found in Muslim sources:

> Ismāʿīl b. Abī Ḥakīm said: "I dreamt that ʿAbd al-Malik urinated four times in the prayer niche of the Messenger of God's mosque." I asked Ibn al-Musayyib about this and he said: "If your dream is true, four caliphs shall stand in it."[54]

> Ismāʿīl b. Abī Ḥakīm said: A man said: "I saw in a dream that ʿAbd al-Malik b. Marwān was urinating in the prayer niche of the mosque of the prophet, and this, four times. I mentioned that to Saʿīd b. al-Musayyib and he said: 'If your dream is true, there shall arise from his loins four caliphs.'"[55]

> Marwān b. al-Ḥakam dreamt that he was urinating in the prayer niche. He reported his dream to Saʿīd b. al-Musayyib, who replied: "Verily, you shall beget caliphs."[56]

> It is reported that Marwān b. al-Ḥakam saw in his dream that he was urinating in the prayer niche. He told his dream to Saʿīd b. al-Musayyib, who replied: "Truly you shall beget caliphs." Another version has it that ʿAbd al-Malik b. Marwān was urinating in the prayer niche four times and that they asked Saʿīd b. al-Musayyib about this and he replied: "Four of the children of your loins shall reign." The last of these was Hishām.[57]

The anecdote concerns a caliph who dreamed that he urinated four times in the Kaʿbah or some other famous mosque, the dream signifying the status of his four sons. In the oneirocriticon, the caliph in question is Maʾmūn. This version is historical nonsense—none of Maʾmūn's sons reigned after him and Ibn Sīrīn *alias* Achmet was not Maʾmūn's contemporary. The Muslim versions ascribe this dream to the Umayyad caliph ʿAbd al-Malik (or his father) and names the interpreter as Ibn al-Musayyib, who was indeed a contemporary of that caliph. Moreover, in the Muslim versions, the dream fits the historical context well, for it is indeed the case that four of ʿAbd al-Malik's sons held the caliphate after their father's death. Regardless, the oneirocriticon's anecdote, even if historical nonsense, is clearly a version of traditions circulating in Muslim circles. The same holds for many of the other anecdotes as well.

In sum, did the oneirocriticon have access to Muslim sources? The cumulative weight of the evidence necessitates, I think, a positive answer to this question. There can be no doubt that the anonymous compiler of the oneirocriticon made use of Muslim sources. If so, which ones? This, unfortunately, is a question that cannot yet be answered, for none of the extant, early Muslim dream manuals was his source. While it is clear that the oneirocriticon had access to Muslim sources, many questions remain. What of the materials in his Indian chapters that are without parallel in the Muslim tradition? Are these of the compiler's own invention, or were they included in his source? Even more problematically, what sources, if any, underlie the Persian and Egyptian chapters? Were these materials derived from an earlier source or sources,[58] or were they of the compiler's own invention? And if they were of his own invention, might it not be in these chapters, themselves so un-Christian, that he expresses his own views as to the nature of dream interpretation? None of these questions can yet be answered.

The Context of the Oneirocriticon

While questions concerning the oneirocriticon remain, it is possible to speculate about the context in which its anonymous compiler wrote and, in particular, about the place of his work in the broader process by means of which aspects of Muslim high culture were transmitted in the early Middle Ages to the Christians of Byzantium. Researchers are now beginning to understand the extent of what was shared by the Christians of Byzantium and the Muslims of the Near East. As might well be imagined, much that was common was a result of a shared Near Eastern cultural background. The medicine of Muslim doctors, for instance, was very like that of Byzantine doctors, for the simple reason that they read the same authoritative ancient books: Galen and Hippocrates said the same thing whether they spoke in Greek or a halting Arabic. Umayyad palaces were architecturally like Byzantine palaces, as both drew on a common repository of Near Eastern techniques of construction. But a common origin was not the only reason Byzantines and Muslims shared so much. It is now beginning to be recognized that Byzantines and Muslims were separated from one another by a border that was permeable to cultural exchange. That such exchange might flow from the "elder" Byzantines to the "younger" Muslims is not surprising, especially given the extent to which Muslims actively strove to appropriate the cultural resources of the Hellenic past and equally recognized that such resources might be gotten from the Byzantines. Less well known is the inverse of this process: the gradual transferal of cultural resources from Muslims to Byzantines. Consider, first, material culture.

The early Middle Ages witnessed Byzantines appropriating select aspects of Muslim material culture.[59] The influence of the Muslims can be discerned in many different contexts: monumental construction techniques and automata;[60] textile decorations and fashions in clothing;[61] decorative work in ceramics, tiles, and enamels;[62] and even in the use of "pseudo-Kufic" calligraphy to adorn the facades of buildings—an ornamental script, itself nonsensical, meant to imitate the monumental calligraphy of the Muslims.[63] Not all aspects of material culture were shared, however. According to Oleg Grabar, Muslim influences were most keenly felt in the art of the court, as opposed to contexts more strictly religious. Nor, he argues, was it equally easy at all times for Byzantines to draw on Muslim resources:

their influence seems to have been most strongly felt between the ninth and the twelfth centuries, when Byzantium "felt strong enough to incorporate such exotic themes," in contrast to the later centuries of political decline, when there was a need to draw firmer boundaries and cultivate "an unadulterated Christian art."[64]

Even as Byzantines could appropriate select aspects of Muslim material culture, they were equally able to draw on aspects of Muslim high culture, including parts of the Arabic literary tradition. Regardless, it must be emphasized that here also Byzantine intellectuals exercised selective appropriation. Many if not most types of Arabic literature were of little interest to them. Although some knowledge of Muslim theology was occasionally able to traverse the Byzantine-Muslim border,[65] as a whole these were not subjects of interest. As for philosophy, I know of no evidence to suggest that Byzantine intellectuals engaged Muslims on these subjects, certainly nothing comparable to the situation of medieval western Christendom. Arabic belles-lettres, as well, appear to have left little mark, with the notable exception of an eleventh-century work based on the *Kalīlah wa-ḍimnah.*[66] All such subjects, although widely cultivated by Muslims, seem to have had little effect on Byzantines. And yet, if the theology, philosophy, and belles-lettres of Muslims did not interest Byzantines, the situation was far otherwise with the Hellenic sciences.

Already by the eleventh century A.D., we find Byzantines beginning to take an interest in the Hellenic sciences as they were being advanced by Muslims. As for the specific subjects of interest, astronomy and astrology seem to have been paramount, with some evidence that Muslim advances in medicine and divination were beginning to be appropriated as well.[67] As for divination, although early translations are unknown, a number of works were translated from Arabic into Greek in the thirteenth century: one on celestial omens, the other on geomancy.[68] As for medicine, one thinks in particular of the work of the shadowy Symeon Seth (fl. 11th century A.D.), himself the translator of the *Kalīlah wa-ḍimnah.*[69] As for astronomy, beginning also in the eleventh and twelve centuries, Muslim advances begin to be echoed in Byzantine works—first in a number of anonymous compilations and then in a complete translation of a work from Arabic.[70] The field in which Byzantines were most active in appropriating the labors of Muslims was not astronomy, but astrology.[71] In this regard, beginning already by ca. 1000 A.D., numerous works were translated directly from Arabic into Greek. Among these: treatises of Abū Maᶜshar[72] and his disciple Shādhān, a work by Ps. Ptolemy and a commentary on that work by Aḥmad b. Yūsuf, as well as the enormous compilation of Aḥmad the Persian, his *Introduction to the Foundations of Astrology*. It is these sorts of works more than any others that were able to traverse the cultural and religious boundary separating Byzantines and Muslims.

Christian intellectuals of Byzantium could appropriate Muslim scientific works because such works were not doctrinally Muslim. In each instance, Byzantines appropriated the works of Muslim authors who were themselves appropriating and developing in creative ways the resources of an earlier and largely shared Hellenic intellectual tradition. In short, Byzantine and Muslim scientists were engaged in a shared discourse concerning a shared Hellenic past. And it was this shared Hellenic past that more than anything else facilitated the passage of high cultural resources from the Muslim cultural sphere to that of Byzantium. While certainty is lacking, it is reasonable to contextualize the oneirocriticon in this broader process whereby Muslim scientific works were being appropriated by Byzantines. The oneirocriticon would thus represent yet another instance of Byzantines and Muslims engaged in an earnest and lively debate over the shared resources of a common past. That the oneirocriticon revives a Hellenic (that is, pagan) divinatory technique, which hitherto Christians had roundly condemned, is not too surprising: it is very like what happened in the case of astrology, itself a discipline routinely condemned by patristic authorities.[73] For these authorities, astrology, like dream divination, was associated with pagan practice and was thus to be avoided. Of course, by the Byzantine period the pagan threat had receded into the shadows of a distant past. And perhaps it was precisely for this reason that Christians, with the aid of Muslims, were able once again to examine the benefits that the divinatory disciplines of Hellenic antiquity offered their practitioners.

Toward the end of the middle ages, the great Muslim jurist and historian Ibn Khaldūn set himself to describe the ebb and flow of the rational sciences in history.[74] Discovered by the Greeks, these sciences were bequeathed to the people of Rome. When the rulers of the latter adopted Christianity, he says, they forswore the pursuit of the Hellenic sciences, as required by their religious laws. Fortunately or even providentially, Ibn Khaldūn opines, the works of the Greeks continued to be preserved in the libraries of Rome (now Byzantium, the new Rome)—until the fullness of time, when "God brought Islam." When the Arabs decided to become versed in the Hellenic sciences, they sent to the Byzantine emperor, who conveyed to them the works preserved in his libraries, as well as translators to turn those works into Arabic. And it was only thus that a portion of this material was preserved. Writing in the fourteenth century, Ibn Khaldūn notes with marvel that some say the Hellenic sciences have recently come to be cultivated by the Franks (that is, the Europeans). Although he has heard rumors to this effect, he seems understandably disinclined to believe them. That the people of the new Rome might have continued to cultivate the Hellenic sciences, let alone that the Muslims themselves might have played a role in the revival of the Hellenic sciences among them—of such things Ibn Khaldūn had heard not even rumors.

BAR BAHLŪL'S *BOOK OF SIGNS*

Bar Bahlūl was an Iraqi Nestorian who flourished in the fourth century A.H. Until recently he was remembered primarily for his magnificent, multivolume *Syriac-Arabic Lexicon*.[75] His legacy began to be reinterpreted in the early 1970s, however, when Fuat Sezgin discovered in Istanbul an unknown work by him, his *Kitāb al-dalāʾil* or *Book of Signs*.[76] This work is not unlike an old-fashioned almanac, and among the subjects it treats: dream interpretation. Indeed, the last and longest of its chapters is a self-contained dream manual, one that comprises roughly one-eighth of the work's total length. It must be admitted that very little is known about Bar Bahlūl. There is no source that preserves a connected account of his life. What can be known must be inferred from scattered bits of information preserved in a number of Muslim and Christian sources.

It is fairly certain that Bar Bahlūl was a native of the region in and around Takrīt, to the north of Baghdad. This is suggested by passages in his lexicon where he deals with dialectical usages, some of which are introduced with the lemma: "according to our usage in Takrīt"[77] Further, a Muslim biographical dictionary gives Bar Bahlūl the names *al-Awānī* and *al-Ṭīrhānī*.[78] The former is a reference to Awānā, a small city located to the north of Baghdad, about halfway to Takrīt; the latter, to Ṭīrhān, the administrative district in which Takrīt was located.[79] Bar Bahlūl's connections to the region of Ṭīrhān are further suggested by other passages in his lexicon, where he defines words "according to our usage in Ṭīrhān."[80]

If Bar Bahlūl was a native of the region around Takrīt, at some point he must have made his way to Baghdad. This can be inferred from a marginal comment found in some of the manuscripts of his lexicon. This identifies the work as "the lexicon of Bar Bahlūl . . . which he wrote in Arsacian Babylon, the town of strength, the city of peace," that is, in Baghdad.[81] It is also suggested by an account in the work of the historian Mārī b. Sulaymān, where Bar Bahlūl is portrayed as active in Baghdad in 963 A.D.[82] It was then that he played a role in the events surrounding the election of ᶜAbdīshūᶜ as catholicus of the Nestorians. This passage is doubly significant in that it offers the only incontrovertible date for the events of Bar Bahlūl's life.

It is probable that Bar Bahlūl was a doctor by profession. A notice in a Muslim biographical dictionary portrays him as a translator of medical texts.[83] Bar Bahlūl's lexicon contains, moreover, a great many entries on medical terms and evinces a wide familiarity with contemporary and ancient medical works in Greek, Arabic, and Syriac.[84] That he was a doctor is also suggested by a number of passages in his lexicon that show him in personal contact with the medical authorities of his day: among these, the famous Sinān b. Thābit (d. 331/943),[85] a Harranian pagan who converted to Islam and served as doctor to a number of caliphs, as well as a certain Byzantine doctor (*al-ṭabīb al-rūmī*) by the name of Ibn Sīnā (not to be confused with the philosopher).[86] This much and little more is known of the life of Bar Bahlūl.

Bar Bahlūl on Dreams and Their Interpretation

As suggested above, Bar Bahlūl's *Book of Signs* is not unlike an old-fashioned almanac. It provides lists of various types of useful information, much related in some fashion to the calendar. As the author himself—rather poorly—describes the contents and purpose of the work:

> The benefit in this book is great whether one be at home or abroad, for it gives indications of the festivals of the nations, the dhakārīn of the Christians (that is, the days of prayer in which they remember the martyrs, apostles, their deceased katholikoi, and their saints), the divisions of the year, when it is hot and when it is cold, when one should plant trees, cereals, greens, and aromatics.[87]

Bar Bahlūl then suggests that such information is indispensable, especially in those parts of the world where one does not have access to experts on the stars and the seasons or to the many books that explain the finer points of agriculture and chronography. According to its author, the work's final selling point is its usefulness for those who do a lot of traveling. The massive amount of information it contains alleviates them from the need to ask questions and, in particular, from having to consult the officials in charge of the markets in foreign parts.

Much of Bar Bahlūl's *Book of Signs* is concerned with calendrical matters: how time is reckoned by the Armenians, Copts, Harranians, Indians, Jews, Muslims, Persians, and so on; when the various festivals are celebrated by the members of these communities; how to convert dates from one system to another. At the same time, a sizable portion of the text is concerned with matters not strictly calendrical: the different poisons and their effects, how to pick out good slaves and horses, basic medical advice, and so on. In this regard, a number of types of divination are discussed: what days are auspicious or inauspicious, basic astrological knowledge, how to take omens from weather phenomena, as well as physiognomy and dream interpretation. This last subject is treated in the final and longest chapter of the *Book of Signs*.[88]

Bar Bahlūl's chapter on dream interpretation is divided into two portions of unequal length. The first, its introduction, is rather short.[89] Bar Bahlūl opens with a general statement of the importance of dream interpretation: it is an exalted science, one "acknowledged by the adherents of all religions," notwithstanding that the physicians of old ascribed dreams to imbalances in the humors or preoccupations of the thoughts. He continues with an eightfold typology of dreams:

> The four types of dreams that arise from an imbalance of the humors.
> That arising from the preoccupations of one's thoughts.
> That in which a person's own soul speaks.
> That which the angel of dreams sends as glad tidings or warning.
> That arising from having eaten the wrong sorts of food.

This typology Bar Bahlūl explicitly ascribes to the Suryānīyūn, a name used throughout the *Book of Signs* to refer to the sages and scholars of the Syriac Christian tradition, but especially those who had been interested in the Hellenic scientific tradition.

Following this typology of dreams, Bar Bahlūl treats the general nature of dreams and their interpretation.[90] He does not claim to be writing in his own voice here, but to be recording what "they say." He begins by noting that the true dream is a portion of revelation (*waḥy*) and a forty-sixth part of prophecy (*nubūwah*). He then discusses the sorts of persons who have the truest dreams, the times of the year or day in which the truest dreams are seen, and how a person should sleep to have true dreams. Still continuing with his record of the opinions of these anonymous persons, Bar Bahlūl next offers counsel on the proper behavior of dreamers and dream interpreters: you must only tell your dream to learned friends (that they might give it a good interpretation, for often it happens that the outcome of a dream follows its interpretation); you must not mention your dream if its contents are disturbing; you must studiously avoid misreporting your dream, whether by adding to it or by omitting parts. The final section of his introduction treats the various methods for interpreting dreams: how the meaning of a dream varies with the status of the dreamer, how its meaning can sometimes be transferred from the dreamer to another, and how such things as verses (*āyāt*), revealed words (*kalām munzal*), well-known proverbs, verses of poetry, and etymology, can sometimes provide the clues for interpreting the meaning of a dream.

The second part of Bar Bahlūl's chapter consists of a dream manual proper—a list of dream symbols and of what those symbols mean.[91] The format of Bar Bahlūl's presentation is not dissimilar to that of the early Muslim dream manuals, although it is as a whole more laconic than those texts, with the possible exception of Sijistānī's. To illustrate the extreme brevity with which Bar Bahlūl writes, consider his first category of dream symbols, dreams of God:

> Whoever sees God in a place, justice, happiness, joy, and good pervaded that place, for God's is this world and the next; his face, mercy; his turning away, a warning about sins; his gift in the dream, affliction and trial via calamity and sickness; and [sometimes] his exhortation and his censure; and if the man see him with him on a couch, repentance and his sympathy for him and testing and examination.

Seeking to present as much information as he can as briefly as he can, it is thus that Bar Bahlūl proceeds for the duration of his text. As he passes from one set of symbols to the next, he follows an order already familiar from the early Muslim dream manuals, presenting, first, dreams of a religious nature (God, the resurrection, Paradise, hell, heaven, the Kaᶜbah, and so on) and only then dreams concerned with the things of this world. In the course of his exposition, Bar Bahlūl cites no sources. There are, however, a handful of occasions where authorities are mentioned, either by name or by allusion: "they say" (four times), "Ibn Sīrīn says" (three times), "from the prophet" (once).[92] On no occasion does Bar Bahlūl provide anything like the anecdotes so often encountered in Muslim dream manuals, nor does he cite proof texts.

Bar Bahlūl's Sources and Strategies as a Compiler

The manner in which Bar Bahlūl treats dream interpretation suggests that he may have made use of Muslim sources. A number of parallels have already been suggested above. It should also be noted that Bar Bahlūl deals with many dreams that are specifically Muslim in character. He interprets dreams of the festival of al-Mawsim.[93] He speaks of dreams of the Ka^{c}bah.[94] He is interested in prayer leaders.[95] If someone dreams that his five fingers are extended, this signifies his prayers.[96] (It is the Muslims, not the Christians, that have five daily prayers.) Ritual ablution also comes in for mention.[97] Such passages speak prima facie for a Muslim influence on Bar Bahlūl. Is it the case that Bar Bahlūl used Muslim sources? If so, what were those sources and how did he go about appropriating them?[98]

Now that something is known about the early Muslim tradition of dream interpretation it is possible to be precise as to the identity of Bar Bahlūl's sources and his manner of using them. Before turning to the details, however, let me summarize what is at issue. Bar Bahlūl's main source was none other than the dream manual of Ibn Qutaybah. This is clear both from the structure of his dream manual and from the specific interpretations that he assigns to the individual dream symbols. Indeed, so closely does Bar Bahlūl follow his source that his chapter on dreams must be considered as basically an abridgment of Ibn Qutaybah's dream manual. Nonetheless, as will be argued, Bar Bahlūl was deliberately crafting his source, seeking to make of it a work that was neither Muslim nor Christian, but one that was generically monotheistic, and thus usable by Muslims, Jews, and Christians alike.

Consider, first, the structure of Bar Bahlūl's chapter on dreams. He divides his dream symbols into forty-one classes. As can be seen from Table 5.3, he treats these symbols in almost exactly the same order as Ibn Qutaybah: indeed, his is far closer to Ibn Qutaybah's order of presentation than to that of any other early Muslim dream manual. Only one chapter in Ibn Qutaybah's work is lacking (the ninth, on reading the Koran, the call to prayer, and building a mosque) and a few of Ibn Qutaybah's chapters are combined. Other than these few variants, Bar Bahlūl's dream manual is structured in a manner identical to Ibn Qutaybah's.

Second, Bar Bahlūl treats the symbols within each chapter in an order much the same as Ibn Qutaybah. The parallels are too extensive to cite in detail. The data presented in Table 5.4 (p. 161) can serve to represent the text as a whole. This table presents the first twenty-five dream symbols from their respective chapters on dreams of the occupations. As can be seen, with few exceptions the order in which the symbols are treated is the same. As for the four differences between the texts (set in bold in Table 5.4), three probably result from scribal errors: *mujabbir* versus *makhbaz*, *qaṣṣār* versus *qaṭṭān*, *yadhra*^{c} versus *yarza*^{c}, all words easily confused in the Arabic script. The only major difference is Bar Bahlūl's

TABLE 5.3
The Sequence of Chapters in Ibn Qutaybah and Bar Bahlūl

Topic	Ibn Qutaybah	Bar Bahlūl
God	1	1
resurrection, Paradise, Hell, angels	2–3	2–3
heaven	4	4
prophets	5	5
Ka'bah, *qiblah*	6	6
to become a believer	7	7
to change one's name	8	7
Koran, prayer, building mosques	9	—
judges	10	8
things related to judges	11	8
faith	12	9
sun, moon, stars	13	10
man and his members	14	11
marriage, divorce, birth, corpses	15–16	12–13
earth, buildings	17	14
hills, mountains	18	15
rain, moisture, etc.	19	16
drinks	20	17
trees, fruit, plants	21	18
seeds	22	18
large tents, hair-cloth tents, etc.	23	19
clothing	24	20
horses	25	21
weapons	26	22
jewelry	27	23
fire, etc.	28	24
clouds, rain, etc.	29	25
flying, jumping	30	26
horses, nags, etc., mules, asses, camels	31–34	27–30
bulls, cows	35	31
sheep, rams, goats	36–37	32–33
beasts of prey	38	33
elephants, buffalo, pigs	39	34
insects	40	35
lions	41	36
birds	42	37
water-birds and others	43	38
scorpions, snakes, reptiles	44	39
occupations	45	40
oddities	46	41

inclusion of the interpretation of dreams of a washerman (*ghassāl*). But even this is not without a basis in his source. This can be seen from the full texts:

> Ibn Qutaybah: The fuller (*qaṣṣār*) is a man from whose hand there proceeds the alms of men, or a man who alleviates troubles, for dirt in clothes is sins and cares.
>
> Bar Bahlūl: The cottonworker (*qaṭṭān*) is a man from whose hand there proceeds alms, and a washerman (*ghassāl*) alleviates troubles, for dirt in clothes is sins or cares.

Ibn Qutaybah had given two interpretations for the dream of a fuller: it is either a man who gives alms or a man who gets rid of troubles. Bar Bahlūl's exemplar must have been corrupt, reading cottonworker (*qaṭṭān*) for fuller (*qaṣṣār*). For this reason, the analogy being posited in the second interpretation made little sense. By adding washerman (*ghassāl*), Bar Bahlūl thus emended his exemplar in accordance with the sense of the analogy.

Third, Bar Bahlūl's dependence on Ibn Qutaybah is perhaps most clearly seen in the wording of their respective texts. Again, as the parallels are quite extensive I cite just a single example. Table 5.5 (p. 162) presents the texts of their respective chapters on dreams of camels. Laying out the texts in parallel columns shows clearly both the extent of the parallels and the extent to which Bar Bahlūl is summarizing his source. Roughly half of Ibn Qutaybah's text is present in Bar Bahlūl's. And what he has adopted, he has adopted nearly verbatim. His main editorial intrusion is that of omitting materials. There seems to be nothing about the materials that are omitted to account for their noninclusion: it would appear that Bar Bahlūl simply adopted what he considered to be the main permutations on dreams of camels. Page after page, the same sorts of parallels are found, with topics being treated in exactly the same order and often in exactly the same words. This factor, in conjunction with the two considered above, makes it clear beyond doubt that Bar Bahlūl was drawing on the dream manual of Ibn Qutaybah, that Bar Bahlūl's dream manual was an abridgement of Ibn Qutaybah's.

It might be easy to conclude that Bar Bahlūl is a fine example of the proverbial blind copyist. This general impression is not justified, however. Bar Bahlūl may be a copyist but he is also an editor, and he is exercising editorial discretion where he thinks it needed. While he may make no attempt to rewrite his source, he does fastidiously attempt to extract from it what is essential, while at the same time discarding its dross. In the end, it must be concluded that Bar Bahlūl was fairly successful. He was able to preserve the substance of Ibn Qutaybah's dream manual, while discarding roughly 80 percent of its surplusage. In this regard, he had different strategies for trimming what he considered his source's excesses.

Bar Bahlūl's most common strategy is that seen in Table 5.5. A single dream symbol may occasion a number of different permutations in his source: a camel,

TABLE 5.4
Ibn Qutaybah and Bar Bahlūl on Occupations

Item	Ibn Qutaybah	Bar Bahlūl
1	ironsmith	ironsmith
2	**bonesetter (*mujabbir*)**	**bakery (*makhbaz*)**
3	maker of scales	maker of scales
4	polisher	polisher
5	maker of armor	maker of armor
6	goldsmith	goldsmith
7	dyer	dyer
8	doctor	doctor
9	**fuller (*qaṣṣār*)**	**cottonworker (*qaṭṭān*)**
10	—	**washerman**
11	tailor	tailor
12	weaver	weaver
13	**measure (*yadhraʿ*) earth/mountain**	**sow (*yazraʿ*) earth/mountain**
14	to twist thread	to twist thread
15	shoemaker	shoemaker
16	working with an awl	working with an awl
17	maker of sandals	maker of sandals
18	sandal	sandal
19	bed	bed
20	potter	potter
21	glazier	glazier
22	maker of lamps	maker of lamps
23	maker of saddles	maker of saddles
24	coppersmith	coppersmith
25	carpenter	carpenter

to dismount a camel, to fight with a camel, to milk a camel and have blood come out, to eat a camel's flesh, and so on. He is able to compress his source by not appropriating all of its permutations. A second strategy for Bar Bahlūl is to omit those parts of his source where proof texts are cited. When Ibn Qutaybah cites, for example, a verse of poetry to justify his linkage of a dream symbol and its meaning, Bar Bahlūl simply omits such materials: in effect, he shears off Ibn Qutaybah's footnotes. Yet another of Bar Bahlūl's strategies is to leave off his source's anecdotal narratives. While most he simply omitted, some he paraphrased, keeping the concluding oneirocritic lesson and discarding the narrative framework in which that lesson had been presented.

The final and most effective strategy through which Bar Bahlūl was able to abbreviate his source without affecting its substance was, quite simply, to leave off Ibn Qutaybah's lengthy and somewhat randomly structured introduction. (It will be recalled that the introduction to Ibn Qutaybah's dream manual took up nearly half the total length of that work.) Ibn Qutaybah's introduction Bar Bahlūl

TABLE 5.5
Ibn Qutaybah and Bar Bahlūl on Camels

Ibn Qutaybah	Bar Bahlūl
al-ba'īr al-majhūl li-man ra'ā annahu rakiba 'alayhi wa-huwa yasīru bihi safar.	al-ba'īr al-majhūl li-man ra'ā annahu rākibuhu wa-huwa yasīru bihi safar.
fa-in kānat najīban fa-huwa safar ba'īd.	fa-in kāna najīban fa-huwa safar ba'īd.
fa-in taḥawwala 'anhu aṣābahu ḥuzn.	
wa-in nazala 'anhu mariḍa thumma shufiya.	wa-in nazala 'anhu mariḍa thumma shufiya.
fa-in qātala ba'īran nāza'a rajulan.	
fa-in malaka ibilan kathīrah waliya walāyah 'alā al-nās.	
fa-in kānat al-ibil 'irāban kānū 'araban.	
wa-in kānat bakhātī kānū 'ajaman.	
fa-in ra'ā annahu yaḥlubu ibilan aṣāba mālan wa-sulṭānan.	fa-in ra'ā annahu yaḥlubu ibilan aṣāba mālan min sulṭān.
fa-in ḥalabahā daman kāna al-māl ḥarāman.	
fa-in aṣāba nāqah aṣāba imra'ah.	wa-in aṣāba nāqah aṣāba imra'ah.
wa-man akala laḥm ba'īr aw nāqah aṣābahu maraḍ.	wa-man akala min laḥm ba'īr aw nāqah aṣābahu maraḍ.
fa-in aṣāba min luḥūmihā min ghayr akl aṣāba mālan min al-sabab alladhī tunsab ilayhi al-ibil fī tilka al-ru'yā.	
fa-in ra'ā anna ba'īran nuḥira wa-qusima laḥmuhu māta rajul zakhm [*sic*] fī dhālika al-mawḍi' wa-qusima māluhu.	wa-in ra'ā anna ba'īran dhubiḥa wa-qusima laḥmuhu māta rajul 'aẓīm ḍakhm wa-qusima māluhu.
fa-in ra'ā anna ba'īran majhūlan yatba'uhu aṣābahu hamm wa-ḥuzn.	
fa-in ra'ā jamā'at ibil dakhalat arḍan dakhalahā 'adūw wa-rubbamā kāna dhālika saylan wa-rubbamā kāna awjā'an.	fa-in ra'ā anna ibilan jamā'atan dakhalat baladan dakhalahu 'adūw wa-rubbamā kāna saylan wa-rubbamā kāna awjā'an.
wa-julūd al-ibil mawārīth.	wa-julūd al-ibil mawārīth.
wa-kadhālika al-jild min kull dābbah mīrāth mā yunsab ilayhi tilka al-dābbah fī al-ta'wīl.	wa-kadhālika min kull dābbah mīrāth mimmā tunsab ilayhi al-dābbah.

simply discarded. While what he substituted in its place bears a slight resemblance to Ibn Qutaybah's work, its themes are general enough and verbal parallels are to such an extent lacking that it is difficult to conclude that it was drawn from Ibn Qutaybah. About a third of it is, in fact, specifically ascribed to the Suryānīyūn. Regardless, Bar Bahlūl here also must have been using a source of Muslim provenance, for most of his introduction's themes are typically Muslim, being found in nearly every early Muslim dream manual. Bar Bahlūl, it will be recalled, even alluded to the well-known prophetic tradition that states that the true dream is one of the forty-six parts of prophecy. Once again, however, Bar Bahlūl's main goal in his introduction was to summarize to the greatest extent possible: each phrase of his introduction would have been developed in detail in a more expansive Muslim dream manual. It is for this reason that many parts of his introduction are so laconic as to be nearly unintelligible: judging from the two extant copies of the introduction, it must have been difficult also for the medieval scribes who copied it.[99] In general, then, Bar Bahlūl's strategies as a compiler in his introduction are not dissimilar to the strategies he employed throughout his dream manual: to present the substance of the discipline in the shortest amount of space.

In his dream manual, there is only one passage that might indicate that Bar Bahlūl's religious convictions affected his strategies as a compiler. It will be recalled that he omitted the whole of Ibn Qutaybah's chapter on dreams of the Koran, the call to prayer, and the building of mosques. It is imprudent, however, to suppose that such materials were removed as a result of Bar Bahlūl's Christian sensibilities. He was not out to craft a Christian dream manual. There is not one passage in his chapter on dreams that is explicitly Christian: no Bible verses are cited, for example, nor are any specifically Christian dream symbols interpreted. If it was not a Christian dream manual that he was crafting, what sort of dream manual was it? Let me suggest that Bar Bahlūl's goal as a compiler was to create from Ibn Qutaybah's dream manual a text that was generically monotheistic, one that would have been usable by Muslims, Jews, and Christians alike. To accomplish this purpose, the first thing he did was take from his source everything that smacked of the culture of the ulema and their theological methodology: prophetic traditions and the beloved isnād both fall by the wayside. Bar Bahlūl next removed from his source nearly all discussion of specifically Muslim dream symbols. A few were kept, but not many. When Bar Bahlūl was done, Ibn Qutaybah had come to speak a different language. His was no longer a Muslim text for Muslims, but one that was largely generic: neither Muslim, nor Christian, but simply monotheistic. This may sound familiar. It will be recalled from chapter 2, that Ḥunayn b. Isḥāq had also endeavored to craft a very similar type of work from the dream manual of Artemidorus. On leaving the hands of these Christian editors, Artemidorus had been disabused of his paganism, while Ibn Qutaybah had been made to forget Islam. Both of their dream manuals had come, instead, to speak the language of generic monotheism.

The Context of the Book of Signs

Bar Bahlūl's strategies as a compiler in his chapter on dreams accord well with the overall ambience of the *Book of Signs*. Throughout the work, Bar Bahlūl moves with apparent ease among the sources of Hellenic antiquity, freely making use of authorities like Democritus, Galen, Hippocrates, and Aristotle.[100] His use of religious authors, be they Christian or Muslim, is more circumspect. The only Christian author he cites is Ḥunayn b. Isḥāq.[101] And yet, it is not one of Ḥunayn's theological works that is at issue, but his thoroughly Hellenic investigation of tides.

Among Bar Bahlūl's Muslim authorities were doctors and philosophers such as Ibn Rabbān al-Ṭabarī (d. 250/864), Kindī (d. 256/870), and Rāzī (d. ca. 313/925),[102] as well as more specifically religious authorities. In the latter case, however, he appeals to these authorities only on nonreligious topics: Ibn ᶜAbbās (d. 68/687) and Ibn ᶜArābī (230/844)[103] on calendrical matters, and Ibn Qutaybah (d. 276/889) on weather and astronomy.[104] The same general pattern holds when Bar Bahlūl appeals to authorities in a more anonymous fashion: what is said by the ancients, by ancient and reliable books, by Arabs, doctors, and Greeks, by pagans (*ḥunafāʾ*), philosophers, and the poets of the Arabs.[105] Even as Bar Bahlūl's chapter on dreams spoke the language of generic monotheism, so also did the *Book of Signs* as a whole.

The overall ambience of Bar Bahlūl's work can tell us something about the context in which it was produced and the audience for which it was intended. We are dealing with a work firmly situated in the midst of what has been called the renaissance of Islam or, more properly, I think, the Greco-Arabic renaissance.[106] Lasting from the mid-ninth to the mid-eleventh century, this period witnessed the wholesale conveyance of the Hellenic philosophic and scientific tradition to the lettered elite of the Muslim world. It was a period in which subjects such as astronomy, mathematics, physics, medicine, alchemy, logic, and philosophy were being studied by select members of most of the religious groups making up the population of the Muslim empire. What united the participants in this renaissance was not a shared religion, but a shared interest in the legacy of Hellenism. And it was as heirs to this legacy that the participants in this renaissance formed a distinct class of intellectuals, marked off over against other classes of intellectuals, especially the more strictly religious.

The most significant cultural barriers for the participants in this Greco-Arabic renaissance were not those between the various religious communities making up the Muslim empire, but those that clove the religious communities themselves. This is especially clear in the case of dream interpretation. Ibn Sīnā (a Muslim and a philosopher) adapted the dream manual of Artemidorus (a pagan) to forge an understanding of dream interpretation at variance with that of his sharīᶜah-minded contemporaries. But Ibn Sīnā did not read Artemidorus in the original. He had access to that text only in the version of Ḥunayn b. Isḥāq (a Christian and a philosopher), who in crafting his translation had taught the master to speak the language of generic monotheism, a language intelligible to Muslims, Jews, and Christians alike. Similarly, Bar Bahlūl (a Christian and a philosopher) rewrote his major source, the dream manual of Ibn Qutaybah (a largely sharīᶜah-minded work) to make it speak the language of generic monotheism, a language intelligible not just to Christians, but to the philosophically sophisticated as a whole, be they Christians, Muslims, Jews, or pagans. It was not religious boundaries that occasioned difficulties for Ibn Sīnā, Bar Bahlūl, and Ḥunayn. All three had far more in common with each other than any of them had with someone like Qayrawānī or the curmudgeonly Antiochus the monk. That which they shared: a common interest in the legacy of Hellenism.

Bar Bahlūl was not the only Christian to write about dream interpretation during the Greco-Arabic renaissance. Among his contemporaries to take an interest in this subject was also Abū Sahl ᶜĪsā b. Yaḥyā al-Jurjānī (d. 401/1010), a Christian doctor from Baghdad, famous as much for his abilities as an Arabic stylist as for having been the teacher of Ibn Sīnā. While Jurjānī's dream manual does not appear to have survived, we know that it was composed not for a Christian audience, but for a Muslim patron, Muḥammad b. Maᵓmūn Khwārizmshāh.[107] Judging from what is known of its author and later reception, this dream manual must have been not too dissimilar to Bar Bahlūl's: a dream manual written by a philosophically sophisticated Christian for an audience that included Muslims and non-Muslims. It may also have been Christians like Bar Bahlūl and Jurjānī who were responsible for putting into circulation a number of pseudepigraphic dream manuals ascribed to the famous personages of Hellenic antiquity: Porphyry, Euclid, Ptolemy, Aristotle, Plato, and so on.[108] While not one of these works appears any longer to be extant, it is tempting to situate them in the midst of the Greco-Arabic renaissance, alongside the oneirocritic labors of Bar Bahlūl, Jurjānī, and Ḥunayn.

CONCLUSIONS

Ps. Achmet and Bar Bahlūl were the first Christians to write dream manuals. As has been argued, however, neither started from scratch. Both set out, instead, to adapt earlier Muslim works on the subject. While we do not know the identity of Ps. Achmet's sources, it is clear that he used works not unlike the extant, early Muslim dream manuals. As for Bar Bahlūl, his major source was the dream manual of Ibn Qutaybah. Notwithstanding that the authors of these dream manuals lived and worked in different contexts, one in Byzantium, the other under Islam, they were able to engage Muslim sources on the basis of a shared interest in the legacy of Hellenism. Ps. Achmet worked in a milieu in which Muslim innovations in the Hellenic sciences had begun to traverse the Byzantine-Muslim border, while Bar Bahlūl worked in the midst of the Greco-Arabic renaissance, a movement wherein Muslims, Christians, Jews, and others were actively engaged with the Hellenic rational traditions. In both instances, these Christians could appropriate the Muslim oneirocritic tradition because of a shared interest in Hellenism. In the final analysis, both Ps. Achmet and Bar Bahlūl could use Muslim sources because both Muslims and Christians were in dialogue with a tradition more ancient than their own.

In this chapter I have undertaken to examine how the Muslim oneirocritic tradition was appropriated by two Christian dream interpreters in the early medieval Near East. The trajectory I have traced is but one that might have been followed. These two Christians were not alone in appropriating Muslim sources on the interpretation of dreams. Other echoes are heard at other times and in other places, and even among other religious communities. It is beyond the scope of this study to investigate these other echoes in detail. Much basic research must be undertaken before a general history of dream interpretation in the early medieval Near East can be written. Here I am content to suggest some of the paths such research will need to follow.

Bar Bahlūl was an arabophone Christian who lived among Muslims. There were other Christians living among Muslims or on the marches who also made creative use of the Muslim oneirocritic tradition. The work of Jurjānī has already been mentioned. The medieval Armenians, as well, developed a lively tradition of dream interpretation, and many of their works on dreams were written with the aid of Muslim sources: there are even medieval Armenian dream manuals ascribed to Ibn Sīrīn.[109] In much the same fashion, Syriac speaking Christians in the Near East cultivated an oneirocritic tradition that made use of Muslim sources. Among the most famous Syrian Christians to turn his attention to this subject was Bar Hebraeus, the great thirteenth-century polymath. His dream manual is no longer extant; it is thus impossible to determine whether it drew on Muslim sources.[110] There is, however, at least one extant dream manual in Syriac, and in it the influence of Muslim sources is ubiquitous.[111] Being anonymous and preserved in but a single late manuscript, this work is difficult to date and contextualize. It is significant, nonetheless, suggesting as it does that Syriac speaking Christians, too, were able to draw on Muslim sources to craft an oneirocritic tradition of their own, a process that has continued into more recent times, to judge from the existence of a similar tradition in neo-Syriac.[112]

If Christians writing in Arabic, Syriac, and Armenian could use Muslim works on dreams, it is perhaps not surprising that Jews living among Muslims could do so as well. The task of classifying the various fragments of the Cairo Geniza began in 1901. One of those involved in this process was Hartwig Hirschfeld. Within a year of beginning his work, he announced to the Thirteenth International Congress of Orientalists that among the Geniza fragments were to be found a number of Muslim dream manuals in Arabic, works that had been copied by Jewish scribes in the Hebrew script.[113] If Ibn Sīrīn could learn Armenian, it is not too remarkable to find him clothed in Hebrew garb, for among these new texts was a תפסיר אלמנאמאת לאבן סירין or *Tafsīr al-manāmāt li-Ibn Sīrīn* (The Exegesis of Dreams according to Ibn Sīrīn). Nor was this the only Muslim dream manual in Hebrew guise: "I have found hitherto in the same collection not less than *eight* other fragments, all in different sizes and writing." If a single year's research could turn up this many texts, how many more might be known today? It is difficult to say. To the best of my knowledge this is not a subject to which modern Geniza specialists have turned their attention. The Cairo Geniza is not alone is offering evidence for the influence of Muslim works on the Jewish tradition of dream interpretation. The same can be said for Jewish works preserved only in Latin, among which should probably be counted the so-called *Liber Zachelis in solutione sompniorum*, seemingly a work by or ascribed to the famous Jewish astrologer, Sahl b. Bishr (d. ca. 235/850).[114] It is also widely accepted that the famous dream manual of Solomon ben Jacob Almoli, a sixteenth-century Turkish Jew, made extensive use of Muslim sources.[115] This work circulated widely, not only in its original Hebrew and Aramaic, but also in a Yiddish version, one that was and remains a classic among the Ashkenazi.

The strongest echoes of the Muslim oneirocritic tradition among non-Muslims are found not in the east, but among the Christians of the medieval Latin west. The vast majority of these echoes are faint, taking place only at second hand, mostly through a Latin version of the oneirocriticon of Ps. Achmet. For this version we have to thank Leo Tuscus. Resident in the large Pisan colony in Constantinople in the second half of the twelfth century A.D. were two brothers, masters Hugo Eterianus and Leo Tuscus. One day Hugo had a dream. In it he saw the Byzantine emperor mounted on a horse and surrounded by a crowd of Latin sages. The emperor was reading a book, but suddenly, ignoring those present, he interrupted his reading to address Hugo. The dream troubled the brothers, for they were unable to discern its meaning. It was not until later that subsequent events were able to elucidate it, showing that the dream had signified that the emperor would put an end to an important theological controversy, only after having read one of Hugo's books. Regardless, the dream piqued Leo's interest, with the result that he translated into Latin the most famous of Greek works on dreams, Ps. Achmet's oneirocriticon.[116]

Leo's translation inaugurated a new stage in the afterlife of the Muslim tradition of dream interpretation among Christians. Although the oneirocriticon was often copied by the Greeks, it was among western Christians that it would see its widest circulation and influence. Once accessible in Latin, the oneirocriticon enjoyed a huge and immediate success. Its influence was felt, first, in a number of original Latin compositions on dreams and divination. Perhaps the most famous of these was the *Liber thesauri occulti* of Pascalis Romanus, another westerner living in twelfth-century Constantinople.[117] About a century later, Leo's version of the oneirocriticon was used by the anonymous compiler of the *Expositio somniorum*.[118] And again, the fourteenth-century William of Aragon made extensive use of it in his *De pronosticatione sompniorum*,[119] and following William, the fifteenth-century Venancius of Moerbeke, in his *De presagiis futurorum*.[120] In addition to such original compositions, the oneirocriticon was also widely circulated in vernacular versions.[121] No less than three medieval French versions are extant (Anglo-Norman, continental French, and Ile de France Middle French), all of which were apparently translated from Leo Tuscus' Latin version.[122] Leo's text also formed the basis for a sixteenth-century Italian version made by Tricassio da Cesesari, and it was at about the same time that yet another

Latin version was undertaken by John Leunclavius. From these two versions, yet other vernacular renderings were made: another French translation from the Italian, as well as a German and still another French translation from Leunclavius' version. Lastly, we must not forget the late medieval Czech dream manuals, some of which made use of the oneirocriticon.[123] All in all, a good showing, and one that would not have been possible apart from the earlier labors of men like Ps. Achmet and Bar Bahlūl, Christians willing to engage the Muslim oneirocritic tradition on the basis of a shared interest in the legacy of Hellenism.

Conclusions

Marshall G. S. Hodgson once found himself in a terminological quandary. It would be problematic to call Maimonides an Islamic philosopher. He was, after all, not a Muslim, but a Jew. Yet, Hodgson sensed, Maimonides' philosophic concerns were as much Muslim as Jewish. The problems for which he sought answers were often those with which Muslim philosophers struggled. The authoritative sources at his disposal were often identical to those of Muslim philosophers. Moreover, he was thoroughly conversant with Muslim philosophic works. If it were impossible to call Maimonides an Islamic philosopher, Hodgson wondered whether it might not be possible to call him an "Islamicate" philosopher. To call him this would mean not that he was an adherent to Islam, but simply that "he was . . . a writer in the philosophic tradition of Islamdom."[1] While this tradition was distinct to the world of Islam, it was not distinct to Muslims. It was, in short, a tradition in which both Muslims and non-Muslims participated.

While philosophy for Hodgson was the quintessential Islamicate discourse,[2] it was not the only one. There was also an Islamicate medicine, literature, art, and architecture. All such discourses were carried on in fashions distinct to the world of Islam. Even so, all were discourses in which both Muslims and non-Muslims participated. Thus, for Hodgson, to speak of Islamicate civilization is to speak of a "*culture* . . . which has been historically distinctive of Islamdom" and "which has been naturally shared in by both Muslims and non-Muslims"—if not by all non-Muslims, at least by those "who participate at all fully in the society of Islamdom."[3] Hodgson's qualification is important, for many non-Muslims did not participate. They continued to live in ways that predated the rise of Islam. It was not these who participated in Islamicate civilization, but only those willing to live "socially within the sphere of the Muslim culture," acting as "integral and contributory participants."[4]

At stake in Hodgson's quandary was an issue of great moment: how to identify the boundaries of Islamic civilization. For Hodgson, historians of that civilization cannot restrict themselves to the contributions of Muslims, but must also study those of non-Muslims. One cannot understand, for instance, the Islamicate philosophic tradition if one restricts oneself to folks like Kindī, Fārābī, and Ibn Sīnā. To understand this tradition, one has to study much that is not strictly speaking Islamic. One has to understand how non-Muslims were contributory participants to this discourse: how they mediated pre-Islamic philosophic traditions. One has, also, to examine how non-Muslims were integral participants: in short, what Muslims and non-Muslims shared and contested. Only within this broader framework can one contextualize the labors of the Muslim philosophers and identify the boundaries of their discourse—a discourse that was not just Islamic, but also Islamicate.

DREAM INTERPRETATION AS AN ISLAMICATE DISCOURSE

Dream interpretation, like philosophy, was an Islamicate discourse. In its formative period, it had been based wholly on the foundations of prophetic monotheism. In seeking to ground their interest in dreams, early oneirocrits like Kirmānī, Ibn Qutaybah, and Sijistānī looked to the authorities of prophetic monotheism, not to pre-Islamic Greece, Persia, or India. By the end of the fourth century A.H., however, new sources had become available. Among these, the most important by far was Ḥunayn's version of Artemidorus. Ḥunayn taught Artemidorus Arabic. He also disabused the master of his religious sensibilities. Although the Artemidorus of history was a polytheist, on leaving Ḥunayn's hands he had been converted. While he did not become a Christian, he did become a generic monotheist. Despite Ḥunayn's efforts to rectify, clean up, and otherwise sanitize this, the most famous Hellenic dream manual, later Muslims still gave this work a varied reception, one that was integrally linked to the increasing complexity of the Muslim intelligentsia, which had fractured into a number of rival cultural orientations. These two factors, the varied reception of Artemidorus and the emergence of rival cultural orientations, together caused the Muslim tradition of dream interpretation to fracture.

From the remains and debris of the earlier, unified tradition there arose no less than four competing legacies. At one extreme stood Qayrawānī, heir to the formative period. Like earlier oneirocrits, he sought to ground the interpretation of dreams in a prophetic past. At the other extreme stood Ibn Sīnā, who derisively cast aside the Muslim tradition of dream interpretation, replacing it with a vision of the discipline modeled on his Hellenic forebear, Artemidorus as adapted by Ḥunayn. Between these two stood Dīnawarī and Kharkūshī. The former was open to the use of non-Muslim authorities. Although the core of his dream manual was derived from Muslim sources, he was eager to flesh out that core with non-Muslim traditions. While his major new, non-Muslim source was Ḥunayn's Artemidorus, he also made use of the authorities of ancient Persia and India, and even of the labors of contemporary Jews and Christians. The dream manual of

Kharkūshī, on the other hand, although derived from Dīnawarī's, presented a very different vision of the discipline. While Kharkūshī took most of his material from Dīnawarī, he was unwilling to let Dīnawarī's non-Muslim sources retain their ascription. Some he adopted without reference to their provenance. Others, in particular Artemidorus, he ascribed innocuously to the ancients. New sources and new cultural orientations, thus, combined to fracture the Muslim tradition of dream interpretation. It must be emphasized, however: this fracturing would have been impossible without non-Muslims, not least, Ḥunayn, the Christian responsible for mediating Artemidorus. To borrow Hodgson's terminology, Ḥunayn was a contributory participant in the Islamicate discourse on dreams.

If Ḥunayn was a contributory participant, Bar Bahlūl was—in Hodgson's terminology—an integral participant. His dream manual was an abridgment of Ibn Qutaybah's. Yet, while Bar Bahlūl was a copyist, he was not uncritical. In abridging his source, he crafted from it a dream manual that was neither Muslim nor Christian, but, like Ḥunayn's Artemidorus, generically monotheistic. He accomplished this by omitting everything smacking of the ulema and their methods of argumentation. What remained was the core of his source: its long list of dream symbols, a list now denuded of its specifically Muslim elements. The Islamicate discourse on dreams has only begun to be examined here. Other paths of investigation lie open. Enough has been seen, though, to support the proposition that one cannot understand the cultural discourses of the world of Islam if one ignores the contributions of the non-Muslims who flourished under Islam and in dialogue with it.

DREAM INTERPRETATION AS AN ECUMENIC DISCOURSE

In seeking to understand the venture of Islam, Hodgson was concerned with more than Islamicate civilization. Although that civilization was an intelligible field, it was such only in terms of something broader. That something was nothing less than Afro-Eurasia as a whole or as he often called it, with Toynbee, the ecumene. In that the ecumene was the context in which the venture of Islam transpired, it served Hodgson as a canvas on which to paint Islamicate civilization.

> The various regions [of the ecumene] had their own traditions. . . . But all these lesser historical wholes were imperfect wholes. They were secondary groupings. . . . The whole of the Afro-Eurasian zone is the only context large enough to provide a framework for answering the more general and more basic historical questions that can arise.[5]

While Hodgson's Islamicate thesis has been influential within Islamic studies, its effects have been less commonly felt in other disciplines—not so his approach to the ecumene. One researcher finds in it nothing less than the foundation for the first truly global approach to world history.[6] Another sees in it a model for understanding hemispheric integration during the Middle Ages.[7] Yet another finds in it reason to push back the emergence of the world system into the premodern period.[8] In each instance, what these researchers find intriguing is Hodgson's notion that regional developments must be situated against the ecumene as a whole, in other words, that "all the parts are also shaped by—and can only be adequately understood in relation to—their participation in the whole and their relations with other parts."[9]

In part as a response to Hodgson, there has been much recent work on cross-cultural exchange in the premodern ecumene. Much has focused on technological innovations. The diffusion of agricultural innovations in the early Islamic period, for instance, has been well analyzed by Andrew M. Watson.[10] At issue are some twenty crops that first appear in the Muslim world in the early Middle Ages. These crops had diverse points of origins: some were domesticated in East Asia; others, in Africa. Most, however, were diffused to the Muslim world from India. In time, largely via the Muslim world, many of these innovations also made their way to western Christendom. Watson's account illustrates vividly how technological innovations passed with ease from one end of the ecumene to the other. Similar studies of the diffusion of technological innovations have been undertaken by others.[11] While these other researchers dealt with different types of technology, the conclusions of one can stand for all. After examining such matters as the diffusion to medieval Europe of windmill technology from Tibet and blowguns from Malaya, this researcher was forced to conclude that "it is an objective fact that, despite difficult communication, mankind in the Old World . . . has long lived in a more unified realm of discourse than we have been prepared to admit."[12]

Technological innovations were not alone in being diffused. Cultural innovations, too, could traverse regional boundaries—sometimes with amazing speed. A case in point: the concept of zero, arguably the most important mathematical innovation ever.[13] By the sixth century A.D., the zero sign was in use in India, where it was probably invented. By the eighth century, it had come to China. By the late eighth century, it had found its way to the eastern Muslim world, whence it spread by the ninth to North Africa and Spain, thence to western Christendom. It is first attested in the tenth century in Christian Spain and by the twelfth was coming into use elsewhere in Europe. Within a few centuries of its invention, thus, this innovation had traversed the limits of the ecumene, from China to western Christendom. The diffusion of yet other cultural innovations is beginning to attract the attention of researchers. Particularly intriguing is what we are beginning to learn about the ability of cultural innovations enshrined in literary form to traverse regional boundaries. Given the wealth of surviving evidence, perhaps the most dramatic instance of this phenomenon is astronomy and astrology. Thanks to the work of David Pingree, it is now possible "to illustrate the incredible facility with which these sciences, which serve as an example for other systems of knowledge, were transmitted from one civilization to another."[14]

With regard to astronomy and astrology, at least, it is possible to trace in some detail the peregrinations of texts throughout the premodern ecumene.

The world of Islam played an important role in the mediation of both technological and cultural innovations to the Christians of the Mediterranean. Examples have been noted above: agricultural innovations, for instance, or the concept of zero. Indeed, its role in mediating such innovations is inscribed in the very etymology of terms like *sugar* (< *sukkar*), *cotton* (< *quṭun*), *orange* (< *nāranj*), *lemon* (< *laymūn*), *spinach* (< *isbānakh*) or even the word *zero* (< *ṣifr*). Yet other instances are known. More particularly, there are numerous examples of its mediation of cultural innovations to the northeastern portions of the Mediterranean, to the regions ruled by Byzantium. A number of examples were discussed in the previous chapter. Yet another, vivid instance is provided by Dimitri Gutas's recent study of the Greco-Arabic translation movement. After tracing the transmission of Hellenic philosophy and science into Arabic in the early centuries of the Muslim era, Gutas concludes "that scientific and philosophical thought are international, not bound to a specific language and culture."[15] In this case, nearly the whole of Hellenic philosophy and science, such as it had been known in late antiquity, was mediated to the world of Islam. This is a story that is not unfamiliar. The most intriguing aspect of Gutas's work touches the effects of the Greco-Arabic translation movement on the "first Byzantine humanism." Gutas was able to conclude, in fact, that the translation movement directly stimulated the renewal of the Hellenic sciences in ninth-century Byzantium.

As the above examples suggest, the world of Islam mediated innovations in two ways, both by absorbing regional innovations and by transmitting innovations to other regions. In the present study, a similar pattern has been uncovered. Regional materials were absorbed into the Islamicate discourse on dreams: not just Hellenic materials but also lore from India and ancient Persia. Dream lore was also diffused beyond its regional confines. Indeed, already by the fourth century A.H. the Muslim discourse on dreams had begun to traverse the boundaries of the ecumene. It would be an immense project to analyze the full extent to which non-Muslims beyond Islam's borders appropriated Muslim oneirocritic labors. In this study, I have examined in detail just one instance: the work of Ps. Achmet. Although the identity of this work's sources remains unclear, there is no doubt that it made use of Muslim texts. Further, while it enjoyed a wide circulation in Byzantium, it was not there that it had its greatest impact. Once translated into Latin, it became a source for a number of important Latin compositions. It was also translated many times into the vernaculars of western Christendom. We do not know who compiled this work. Having completed his task, however, his labors became the foundation for an extensive western Christian discourse on dreams. Here, at any rate, is a dramatic example of an Islamicate discourse diffused beyond the regional confines of the world of Islam.

Though not as well documented as Pingree's examples of astronomy and astrology or Gutas's work on the Hellenic sciences, the Islamicate discourse on dreams, too, was able both to absorb regional lore and transmit its own materials beyond the regional confines of the world of Islam. By attending to its Islamicate context, it is hoped that this study has been able to understand the Islamic discourse on dreams more fully. By attending to its ecumenic context, it is hoped that this study has been able to shed light on the Islamicate discourse on dreams. The cultural discourses of the world of Islam were not *sui generis*. They were enmeshed in a context that predated the rise of Islam. They were also able to pass beyond the borders of the world of Islam. It is only by understanding the broader context of Islamicate cultural discourses that researchers can begin to understand them fully. In short, if it is useful to view the Islamic through the prism of the Islamicate, so also, the Islamicate can be viewed with profit from the perspective of the ecumenic.

APPENDIX

EARLY MUSLIM DREAM MANUALS

In this appendix, I offer what I hope is a fairly comprehensive account of those Muslim dream manuals written before the year 500 A.H. Included are extant texts, as well as those that are no longer extant. It should be noted that the inclusion of a work here is not to be taken as an assertion of its authenticity; some of these texts are surely pseudepigraphic, and in this regard, the cautionary comments expressed on pp. 38–39 should be recalled. As for the authors of the following texts, I do not provide full biographical information on them. I generally offer simply their name (given in full, if they are not well known) and their date of death (estimated where necessary), as well as a reference either to a standard work of biography or to an entry in a medieval biographical dictionary (preferably one whose editor has provided references to parallels in other sources). There are a number of types of oneiric literature that I have made no efforts to include here: (1) works on dreams that do not treat specifically of dream divination; (2) dream manuals circulating in the early Islamic period but ascribed to pre-Islamic figures; and (3) dream manuals written by non-Muslims living under Islam. In a number of cases, it was difficult to determine exactly when some of these works were written. Regardless, if it seemed likely that they appeared before 500 A.H. I have included them, noting where necessary any controversy as to their dating.

SECOND CENTURY

1. Ibn Sīrīn (d. 110/728). Responsible for putting dream lore into circulation, but not the author of a dream manual. See pp. 19–25.
2. Jaᶜfar al-Ṣādiq (d. 148/765). A work on dream interpretation is first ascribed to him by Tiflīsī (d. ca. 600/1203). See Tiflīsī *Kāmil* 25, and cf. Ibn Shāhīn *Ishārāt* 3, Ḥājjī Khalīfah *Kashf* 1:466, Riyādīzādeh *Asmāʾ* 113, and Bağdatlı *Hadīyah* 1:251. While dream manuals

ascribed to Jaʿfar al-Ṣādiq are occasionally encountered in manuscript form, not one that I have examined has any claim to authenticity.

3. Ibn Isḥāq (d. 151/768). Riyāḍīzādeh (*Asmāʾ* 106) ascribed to a certain Ibn Isḥāq a work entitled *Taʿbīr al-ruʾyā*. It is not clear to whom he is referring, but it may be a reference to the famous Muḥammad b. Isḥāq (d. 151/768). Contrariwise, it could be a reference to Ḥunayn b. Isḥāq's translation of Artemidorus.
4. Ismāʿīl b. Mūsā b. Jaʿfar (fl. latter half of the 2nd c. A.H.). Ṭūsī (*Fihrist* 41) ascribed to him a *Kitāb al-ruʾyā*. Ṭabarsī *Dār al-salām* 1:36 noted that he himself had seen this work. He further specified that it was merely a section (*juzʾ*) of a larger work, that it contained just a few akhbār, and that it was far from complete. For Ismāʿīl, see Kaḥḥālah *Muʿjam* 1:382.
5. Kirmānī (fl. latter half of the 2nd c. A.H.). Author of what may be the earliest Muslim dream manual (*al-Dustūr fī al-taʿbīr*). See pp. 25–26.
6. Jābir b. Ḥayyān (fl. end of 2nd c. A.H.). Ascribed to him is a work entitled *al-Irshād fī al-taʿbīr*. It is first mentioned in the dream manual of Tiflīsī (d. ca. 600/1203). See Tiflīsī *Kāmil* 25, and cf. Ibn Shāhīn *Ishārāt* 3 (who frequently cites the text), Ḥājjī Khalīfah *Kashf* 1:69, 1:416, Riyāḍīzādeh *Asmāʾ* 42, Ṭabarsī *Dar al-salām* 1:35, and Bağdatlı *Hadīyah* 1:249.

THIRD CENTURY

7. Ibn al-Mughīrah (fl. early 3rd c. A.H.). Full name: ʿAbd al-Raḥmān b. al-Mughīrah al-Ḥarāmī. An akhbār-based dream manual. Fragments can be found in Qayrawānī's *Mumattiʿ*. See pp. 22 and 55.
8. Misʿadah b. Yasaʿ (fl. early 3rd c. A.H.). Full name: Misʿadah b. Yasaʿ b. F.y.d. An akhbār-based dream manual. Fragments can be found in Qayrawānī's *Mumattiʿ*. See pp. 21 and 56. Misʿadah's work also seems to have been known to Abū Nuʿaym (*Ḥilyah* 2:276–77).
9. ʿĪsā b. Dīnār (d. 212/827). Full name: Abū Muḥammad ʿĪsā b. Dīnār al-Qurṭubī. His dream manual (*Kitāb Ibn Sīrīn*) was used by Qayrawānī in his *Mumattiʿ*. See pp. 22 and 56. For ʿĪsā b. Dīnār, see Dhahabī *Siyar* 10:439–40.
10. Zarrād al-Kūfī (d. 224/838). Full name: Abū ʿAlī al-Ḥasan b. Maḥbūb al-Zarrād (or al-Sarrād) al-Kūfī. Bağdatlı (*Hadīyah* 1:266) ascribed to him a *Taʿbīr al-ruʾyā*. For Zarrād al-Kūfī, see Kaḥḥālah *Muʿjam* 1:580.

11. Madāʾinī (d. 225/839). His *Kitāb Ibn Sīrīn* is mentioned in a number of sources. See p. 22.
12. Nuʿaym b. Ḥammād (d. 228/842). An akhbār-based dream manual. Fragments are found in Qayrawānī's *Mumattiʿ*. See pp. 21 and 55–56.
13. Ibn Ḥabīb (d. 238/852). Full name: Abū Marwān ʿAbd al-Malik b. Ḥabīb al-Sulamī. An akhbār-based dream manual. Fragments can be found in Qayrawānī's *Mumattiʿ*. See pp. 22 and 55. For Ibn Ḥabīb, see Dhahabī *Siyar* 12:102–7.
14. Ṣābūnī (fl. mid-3rd c. A.H.). Full name: Muḥammad b. Aḥmad b. Ibrāhīm Abū al-Faḍl al-Kūfī known as al-Ṣābūnī. Date of death is unknown, but judging from a riwāyah given by Ṭūsī he must have lived in the mid-third c. A.H. (*Fihrist* 379–80). His dream manual (*Kitāb taʿbīr al-ruʾyā*) was mentioned by Najāshī *Fihrist* 265 and Ṭabarsī *Dar al-salām* 1:35.
15. ʿAlī al-Ẓāhirī (d. 252/866). Full name: Abū al-Qāsim ʿAlī b. Muḥammad b. al-Shāh al-Ẓāhirī al-Baghdādī. Ibn al-Nadīm (*Fihrist* 170) ascribed to him a *Kitāb al-ruʾyā*. Cf. Bağdatlı *Hadīyah* 1:637. For ʿAlī al-Ẓāhirī, see Kaḥḥālah *Muʿjam* 2:507.
16. Abū Maʿshar al-Balkhī (d. 272/885). Ibn al-Nadīm (*Fihrist* 336) ascribed to him a *Kitāb al-tafsīr al-manāmāt min al-nujūm*. Cf. Bağdatlı *Hadīyah* 1:251.
17. Barqī (d. 274/887 or 280/893). Full name: Abū Jaʿfar Aḥmad b. Muḥammad b. Khālid al-Barqī. One of the chapters of his *Kitāb al-maḥāsin* treated of dreams (and presumably their interpretation). See Ibn al-Nadīm *Fihrist* 277, Ṭūsī *Fihrist* 30, Yāqūt, *Udabāʾ* 1:432, Ṭabarsī *Dār al-salām* 1:35, and Bağdatlı *Hadīyah* 1:67. Some fragments can be found in Majlisī (*Biḥār* 61:151–233 *passim*) and Ṭabarsī (*Dār al-salām passim*). For Barqī, see *Encyclopedia of Islam*, 2nd ed., S:127–28.
18. Ṣaymarī (d. 275/888). Full name: Abū ʿAnbas Muḥammad b. Isḥāq al-Ṣaymarī al-Kūfī al-Baghdādī. His *Kitāb tafsīr al-ruʾyā* is first mentioned by Ibn al-Nadīm (*Fihrist* 169). It is also mentioned in Bağdatlı *Hadīyah* 2:19 and Yāqūt *Udabāʾ* 6:2422. For Ṣaymarī, see Yāqūt *Udabāʾ* 6:2420–24.
19. Ibn Qutaybah (d. 276/889). The earliest extant Muslim dream manual. See pp. 27–34.
20. Thaqafī (d. 283/896). Full name: Ibrāhīm b. Muḥammad b. Saʿīd al-Kūfī al-Thaqafī. Ṭūsī (*Fihrist* 17) ascribed to him a *Kitāb al-ruʾyā*. Cf. Ṭabarsī *Dār al-salām* 1:35. For Thaqafī, see Kaḥḥālah *Muʿjam* 1:63.

FOURTH CENTURY

21. Abū Jaʿfar al-Ṭabarī (d. 310/923). Yāqūt (*Udabāʿ* 6:2462) ascribed to him a ḥadīth-based dream manual, entitled *Kitāb fī ʿibārat al-ruʾyā*, a work left unfinished at its author's death.
22. Ayyāshī (d. 320/932). Full name: Abū Naṣr Muḥammad b. Masʿūd al-Ayyāshī. Ṭūsī (*Fihrist* 317) ascribed to him a *Kitab al-ruʾyā*. Cf. Najāshī *Fihrist* 248 and Ṭabarsī *Dār al-salām* 1:35. For Ayyāshī, see Kaḥḥālah *Muʿjam* 3:714–15.
23. ʿUqaylī (d. 322/933). Full name: Abū Jaʿfar Muḥammad b. ʿAmr b. Mūsā b. Ḥammād al-ʿUqaylī. His dream manual was used by Qayrawānī in his *Mumattiʿ*. See p. 56. For ʿUqaylī, see Dhahabī *Siyar* 15:236–39.
24. Kulaynī (d. 329/940). Full name: Abū Jaʿfar Muḥammad b. Yaʿqūb al-Kulaynī. Ṭūsī (*Fihrist* 327) ascribed to him a *Kitāb taʿbīr al-ruʾyā*, cf. Ṭabarsī *Dār al-salām* 1:35 and Bağdatlı *Hadīyah* 2:35. Fragments in Majlisī (*Bihār* 61:151–233 *passim*) and Ṭabarsī (*Dār al-salām passim*). For Kulaynī, see Kaḥḥālah *Muʿjam* 3:775–76.
25. Dawlābī (fl. first half of the 4th c. A.H.). Full name: ʿAlī b. ʿAbd al-ʿAzīz b. Muḥammad al-Dawlābī al-Baghdādī. Ibn al-Nadīm (*Fihrist* 292) ascribed to him an *ʿIbārat al-ruʾyā*. Cf. Bağdatlı *Hadīyah* 5:678. For Dawlābī, see Kaḥḥālah *Muʿjam* 2:459.
26. Ibn Aṣfahbad (fl. first half of the 4th c. A.H.). Full name: Abū ʿAbbās Aḥmad b. Aṣfahbad al-Qummī. Ṭūsī (*Fihrist* 24) ascribed to him a *Kitāb fī taʿbīr al-ruʾyā*. Judging from its riwāyah as preserved by Ṭūsī, Ibn Aṣfahbad flourished in the first half of the fourth century A.H.: the text was first transmitted by Abū al-Qāsim al-Qummī (d. ca. 368/978), on whom, see Ṭusī *Fihrist* 78. Ṭusī also recorded that some think that this work was actually written by Kulaynī—an opinion he rejects. Cf. Ṭabarsī *Dār al-salām* 1:35.
27. Maʿāfirī (fl. mid-4th c. A.H.). The earliest known dream manual in verse. See pp. 37–38.
28. Ibrāhīm b. Bakkūs (fl. mid-4th c. A.H.). A Muslim doctor who studied with Yaḥyā b. ʿAdī. His dream manual was mentioned by Ibn al-Nadīm (*Fihrist* 378). For Ibrāhīm, see Ibn Abī Uṣaybiʿah *ʿUyūn* 329, as well as Bağdatlı *Hadīyah* 1:7 and Kaḥḥālah *Muʿjam* 1:17.
29. Ismāʿīl b. Ashʿath al-Muʿabbir (d. 360/970). His dream manual was one of Tiflīsī's (d. ca. 600/1203) sources. See Tiflīsī *Kāmil* 25, cf. Ibn Shāhīn *Ishārāt* 3 (who frequently cites the text also), Ḥājjī Khalīfah *Kashf* 1:416, Ṭabarsī *Dar al-salām* 1:35, and Bağdatlı *Hadīyah* 1:208. For his *vita*, see Kaḥḥālah *Muʿjam* 1:359.

30. Abū Sulaymān al-Sijistānī (fl. second half of the 4th c. A.H.). Full name: Abū Sulaymān Muḥammad b. Ṭāhir al-Manṭiqī al-Sijistānī. Ibn al-Nadīm (*Fihrist* 378) ascribed to him a dream manual entitled *Fī al-indhārāt al-nawmīyah*. Cf. Ibn Abī Uṣaybiᶜah *ᶜUyūn* 428. For Abū Sulaymān al-Sijistānī, see Kaḥḥālah *Muᶜjam* 3:363.
31. ᶜĀmirī (d. 381/922). Full name: Abū al-Ḥasan Muḥammad b. Yūsuf al-ᶜĀmirī. A work on what appears to be dream divination (*al-Tabṣīr li-wujūh al-taᶜbīr*) was mentioned by the author in the introduction to another of his works. See ᶜĀmirī *Amad* 54.
32. Maᵓmūnī (d. ca. 383/993). Full name: Abū Ṭālib ᶜAbd al-Salām b. Ḥasan al-Maᵓmūnī. His dream manual (*Kanz al-ruᵓyā*) was used by Tiflīsī (d. ca. 600/1203). See Tiflīsī *Kāmil* 25, cf. Ibn Shāhīn *Ishārāt* 3, Ḥājjī Khalīfah *Kashf* 2:1517, Ṭabarsī *Dar al-salām* 1:35, and Bağdatlı *Hadīyah* 1:569. For Maᵓmūnī, see Kaḥḥālah *Muᶜjam* 2:146.
33. Ibn Daqqāq (d. 392/1001). Full name: Abū Bakr Muḥammad b. Muḥammad b. Jaᶜfar al-Shāfiᶜī. Ḥājjī Khalīfah (*Kashf* 2:1300) ascribed to him a dream manual (*Fawāᵓid al-farāᵓid*), cf. Ṭāshkubrīzādeh *Miftāḥ* 1:336. For Ibn Daqqāq, see Kaḥḥālah *Muᶜjam* 3:634.
34. Dīnawarī (wr. 399/1008). See pp. 59–64.
35. Sijistānī (d. 399/1008). See pp. 34–37.
36. Khallāl (fl. late 4th c. A.H.). Full name: al-Ḥasan b. al-Ḥusayn al-Khallāl al-Sijistānī. Author of a biographical dictionary of dream interpreters and a dream manual. See pp. 17–19.

FIFTH CENTURY

37. Kharkūshī (d. 407/1016). See pp. 64–69.
38. Ibn al-Ḥadhdhāᵓ (d. 416/1025). Full name: Abū ᶜAbd Allāh Muḥammad b. Yaḥyā al-Tamīmī al-Qurṭubī al-Mālikī. Author of a massive commentary on the dream manual of Kirmānī. See p. 26. For Ibn al-Ḥadhdhāᵓ, see Ibn Bashkuwāl *Ṣilah* 2:478–80.
39. Qayrawānī (fl. early fifth cen. A.H.). Author of four dream manuals. See pp. 51–59.
40. Ibn Sīnā (d. 428/1037). See pp. 69–76.
41. Jaᶜfar b. Muḥammad (d. 432/1040). Full name: Jaᶜfar b. Muḥammad b. al-Muᶜtaz al-Mustaghfirī. Ascribed to him is a *Kitāb al-manāmāt*. For this work and its author, see Ibn Quṭlūbughā *Tāj* 147.
42. Abū Dharr al-Harawī (d. 434/1042). Full name: Abū Dharr ᶜAbd b. Aḥmad also known as Ibn al-Sammāk al-Anṣārī al-Khurasānī al-Harawī. Author of a *Kitāb al-ruᵓyā wa-l-manāmāt*. There is a

riwāyah for this work in Ibn Khayr *Fahrasah* 267, 286. Cf. Qāḍī ᶜIyāḍ *Tartīb* 4:698. For Abū Dharr, see Dhahabī *Siyar* 17:554–63.

43. Ibn al-Bannāᵓ (d. 471/1078). Full name: Abū ᶜAlī al-Ḥasan b. Aḥmad al-Baghdādī al-Ḥanbalī. Author of a commentary on the dream manual of Kirmānī (*Sharḥ kitāb al-Kirmānī fī al-taᶜbīr*). See pp. 26, 129–32.
44. ᶜAbdūs (490/1096). Full name: Abū al-Fatḥ ᶜAbdūs b. ᶜAbd Allāh al-Rudhbārī. His dream manual (*Bayān al-taᶜbīr*) was used by Tiflīsī (d. ca. 600/1203). See Tiflīsī *Kāmil* 24, cf. Ibn Shāhīn *Ishārāt* 3, Ḥājjī Khalīfah *Kashf* 1:260, 1:416, Ṭabarsī *Dar al-salām* 1:35, and Bağdatlı *Hadīyah* 1:644. For ᶜAbdūs, see Dhahabī *Siyar* 19:97–98.

UNIDENTIFIED AUTHORS

45. Fīryānī. Ibn al-Nadīm (*Fihrist* 378) ascribed to a certain Fīryānī a *Kitāb taᶜbīr al-ruᵓyā*. His dream manual must predate ca. 385/995, the date of Ibn al-Nadīm's death. Perhaps the *Fihrist* has not accurately transmitted the name, in which case it may be a question here of the famous jurist Firyābī (d. 301/913), on whom, see Dhahabī *Siyar* 14:96–106.
46. Abū al-Ḥasan ᶜAlī b. Muḥammad b. al-ᶜAbbās b. F.sāb.kh.s. (fl. ante 450/1058). Najāshī (*Fihrist* 191) ascribed to him a *Kitāb al-manāmāt*, which he had seen in a copy written in the author's own hand. Cf. Ṭabarsī *Dār al-salām* 1:35. It is not known when this oneirocrit lived, but he must have flourished before 450/1058, the date of Najāshī's death.
47. Khabbāz. Full name: Muḥammad b. Ḥammād al-Rāzī al-Khabbāz. Toward the end of the 4th c. A.H., Khallāl (on whom, see p. 18) ascribed to him a dream manual.
48. Abū Bakr al-Mawṣilī. Mentioned by Qayrawānī as the author of a work on dreams. See p. 56.
49. Abū Ṭalḥah. Qayrawānī made reference to a *Kitāb Abī Ṭalḥah* in the riwāyah of Hishām. See p. 56.
50. Jāḥiẓ b. Isḥāq. His work on dreams was one of Tiflīsī's sources (d. ca. 600/1203). See Tiflīsī *Kāmil* 24, and cf. Ṭabarsī *Dar al-salām* 1:35. Given Tiflīsī's dates, this work may predate 500 A.H.
51. Fakhrī (vocalization uncertain). Tiflīsī (*Kāmil* 24) ascribed to him a work entitled *Īḍāḥ al-taᶜbīr*. Once again, it may predate 500 A.H. Cf. Riyāḍīzādeh *Asmāᵓ* 75 and Ṭabarsī *Dar al-salām* 1:36.
52. Ṭāmūsī. Tiflīsī (*Kāmil* 24) referred to a dream manual by this otherwise unidentified person. Once again, it may predate 500 A.H.

53. Khālid Iṣfahānī. Tiflīsī (*Kāmil* 24) referred to a dream manual (*Minhāj al-taᶜbīr*) by this person. Once again, it may predate 500 A.H. Cf. Ṭabarsī *Dar al-salām* 1:36.
54. Muḥammad Sāhūnah. Tiflīsī (*Kāmil* 24) referred to a dream manual (entitled *Wajīz*) by this person. There is some confusion as to the spelling of his name, for Ibn Shāhīn *Ishārāt* 3 referred to him as Muḥammad b. Shāmawayh, while Ḥājjī Khalīfah *Kashf* 2:2002 mentioned a certain *al-Wajīz fī al-taᶜbīr* by Muḥammad b. Shāhuwayh. Cf. Üniv. Ktp. F645.1, ff. 1a-212b, 679/1280, which contains a Persian dream manual entitled *Kitāb al-taᶜbīr* (fol. 5a) or *Kitāb taᶜbīr-nāmeh* (fol. 1a), ascribed to a certain Abū al-Ḥasan ᶜAlī b. Aḥmad al-Ṭabarī also known as Shāhūwayh.
55. Dārī. Full name: Abū ᶜAlī al-Ḥusayn b. al-Ḥasan b. Ibrāhīm al-Khalīlī al-Dārī. He flourished between ca. 400/1009 and 635/1237. See my "Some Notes on the Dream Manual of al-Dārī," *Rivista degli studi orientali* 70 (1996): 47–52.

ANONYMOUS WORKS

56. *Kitāb taᶜbīr al-ruʾyā li-ahl al-bayt.* A work mentioned by Ibn al-Nadīm *Fihrist* 378, who specified that it was *laṭīf* ("a good read"). It must predate ca. 385/995, the date of Ibn al-Nadīm's death.
57. *Kitāb taᶜbīr al-ruʾyā ᶜalā madhāhib ahl al-bayt.* A work mentioned by Ibn al-Nadīm *Fihrist* 378. It also must predate ca. 385/995.
58. *Jumal al-dalāʾil.* Tiflīsī *Kāmil* 24, cf. Ibn Shāhīn *Ishārāt* 3. This and the remaining works are all anonymous dream manuals first mentioned in Tiflīsī's (d. ca. 600/1203) list of sources. Any of these works may predate 500 A.H.
59. *Kāfī al-ruʾyā.* Tiflīsī *Kāmil* 24, cf. Ṭabarsī *Dār al-salām* 1:36, Ibn Shāhīn *Ishārāt* 3, and Ḥājjī Khalīfah *Kashf* 2:1376.
60. *Muqarmiṭ al-ruʾyā.* Tiflīsī *Kāmil* 24, cf. Ḥājjī Khalīfah *Kashf* 2:1805. Ibn Shāhīn *Ishārāt* 3, as well, mentioned a certain *Kitāb m.q.r al-ruʾyā.*
61. *Tuḥfat al-mulūk.* Tiflīsī *Kāmil* 24, cf. Ibn Shāhīn *Ishārāt* 3.
62. *Muqaddimat al-taᶜbīr.* Tiflīsī *Kāmil* 24, cf. Ibn Shāhīn *Ishārāt* 3. Ṭabarsī *Dār al-salām* 1:36, as well, mentioned a certain *Kitāb mutaqaddim al-taᶜbīr.*
63. *Ḥaqāʾiq al-ruʾyā.* Tiflīsī *Kāmil* 24, cf. Ḥājjī Khalīfah *Kashf* 1:672, Ibn Shāhīn *Ishārāt* 3, and Ṭabarsī *Dār al-salām* 1:36.

NOTES

INTRODUCTION

1. The absence of divinatory literature from Sezgin's work has puzzled others. R. Lemay has trenchantly suggested that it results from Sezgin having organized his history in such a way as to highlight the triumph of the "'authentic' sciences in the course of the development of Islam" and vaunt the merits of those "whose writings appeared to him to anticipate the accomplishments of modern science" ("L'Islam historique et les sciences occultes," *Bulletin d'études orientales* 44 [1992]: 21).

2. "Arabça, türkçe, farsça yazma eserlerin ilimlere göre tasnifi," *Islâm tetkikleri enstitüsü dergisi* 2 (1958): 201–8, with an introductory paragraph by Fuat Sezgin.

3. See Toufic Fahd, *Artemidorus: Le livre des songes* (Damascus: Institut français de Damas, 1964), xxii.

4. *La divination arabe: Études religieuses, sociologiques et folkloriques sur le milieu natif de l'Islam* (Leiden: E. J. Brill, 1966).

5. Ibid., 331–63.

6. Prior to Fahd's labors, little was known of the Muslim oneirocritic tradition. Earlier studies were based on European mss. collections, usually on just one or two mss. The limited number of sources utilized lent these studies a lack of perspective. The more important include: N. Bland, "On the Muhammedan Science of Tâbír, or Interpretation of Dreams," *Journal of the Royal Asiatic Society* 16 (1856): 118–71; M. Steinschneider, "Ibn Shahin und Ibn Sirin: Zur Literatur der Oneirokritik," *Zeitschrift der deutschen morgenländischen Gesellschaft* 17 (1863): 227–44; and P. Schwarz, "Traum und Traumdeutung nach ᶜAbdalġanī an-Nābulusī," *Zeitschrift der deutschen morgenländischen Gesellschaft* 67 (1913): 473–93.

7. *Divinatione arabe*, 330.

8. To my knowledge, since Fahd's study there has appeared only one additional, scholarly investigation of the early Muslim oneirocritic tradition: M. J. Kister, "The Interpretation of Dreams: An Unknown Manuscript of Ibn Qutayba's *ᶜIbārat al-Ruʾyā*," *Israel Oriental Studies* 4 (1974): 67–103. There have been, however, a number of studies on Muslim dreams and dreamers in general. Most of these are cited in the Bibliography. Note especially the fine contributions of Jonathan G. Katz, Leah Kinberg, and Annemarie Schimmel (with some materials on dream interpretation proper, but for the early period dependent on Fahd).

9. I derive these numbers from Fuat Sezgin, *Geschichte des arabischen Schriftums*, Bd. 1 (Leiden: E. J. Brill, 1967), 25–39.

10. A. Abdel Daïm, *L'oniromancie arabe d'après Ibn Sîrîn* (Damascus: Presses Universitaires, 1958).

11. See, for example, the introduction to ᶜAbd al-Raḥmān al-Jūzū's edition of Dārī's *Muntakhab al-kalām fī tafsīr al-aḥlām* (Beirut: Dār Maktabat al-ḥayāt, n.d.).

12. Muhammad M. al-Akili, *Ibn Seerïn's Dictionary of Dreams according to Islāmic Inner Traditions* (Philadelphia: Pearl Publishing House, 1992), a compilation based primarily on the dream manuals of Dārī (wr. between ca. 400H and 635H) and Nābulsī (d. 1143H).

13. "The Future of Dreams: From Freud to Artemidorus," *Past and Present* 113 (1986): 3–37.

14. Ibid., 33–35.

15. Marc Bloch, *The Historian's Craft* (New York: Vintage Books, 1953), 26 (slightly adapted).

16. An edition of Ḥunayn's version Artemidorus' dream manual has been prepared by Toufic Fahd. See above at note 3.

17. Abū Nuᶜaym *Ḥilyah* 9:146. The term *zanādiqah* has here been translated as "Manicheans." It should be noted that this same word can also refer to atheist materialists in general. Its sense here is not entirely certain.

CHAPTER ONE. FROM ANECDOTE TO FORMALISM

1. We know little about this person. Apart from the summaries of his biographical dictionary (see next note), the only other references to him that I have encountered are a passage on dreams ascribed to him in the *Mukhtaṣar* of al-Shaykh al-ᶜAmīd, fol. 12a (Ism. Saib Sincer 4501.1), giving his name as al-Ḥasan b. al-Ḥusayn al-Khallāl al-Sijistānī al-Muᶜabbir, and a citation of "one of the books of Khallāl" in the dream manual of Sijistānī, fol. 11a–b (Üniv. Ktp. A4437). Independent notices on him are seemingly lacking in the biographical tradition. Ḥājjī Khalīfah knew his biographical dictionary (*Kashf* 2:1107), but was dependent on an intermediate source, most likely Dīnawarī (see next note). Bağdatlı likewise knew the work (*Hadīyah* 1:275), but wrongly ascribed it to Abū Muḥammad al-Ḥasan b. Muḥammad al-Baghdādī (d. 439H).

2. It is Dīnawarī (on whom, see pp. 59–64) that was responsible for outlining the history of the text presented here (fol. 39b–40b [Chester Beatty 3569]). All other summaries of Khallāl's dictionary are dependent on Dīnawarī's abbreviation. These include Nābulsī *Ta*ʿ*ṭīr* 2:355–59; Ibn Ghannām (d. 674H), *al-Mu*ʿ*allim* ʿ*alā ḥurūf al-mu*ʿ*jam*, fol. 9a (Ayasofya 1730); Ibn al-Daqqāq (fl. early 8th c. A.H.), *al-Ḥikam wa-l-ghāyāt fī ta*ʿ*bīr al-manāmāt*, fol. 280b (Reisülküttâb Mustafa Ef. 449); al-Bakrī (fl. 666H), *al-Mu*ʿ*tabir fī* ʿ*ilm al-ta*ʿ*bīr* (in Persian), fol. 7b (Amcazâde Hüseyin Paşa 273).

3. See Jean Lecerf, "The Dream in Popular Culture: Arab and Islamic," in *The Dream and Human Societies*, eds. G. E. von Grunebaum and Roger Caillois (Berkeley and Los Angeles: University of California Press, 1966), 368–70.

4. Toufic Fahd, *La divination arabe: Études religieuses, sociologiques et folkloriques sur le milieu natif de l'Islam* (Leiden: E. J. Brill, 1966), 342, is probably mistaken in making this one person into two, Muḥammad b. Ḥammād al-Rāzī and al-Khabbāz. No instances of this list that I have examined in mss. form insert a *wāw* before the name *al-Khabbāz*.

5. On this work, see pp. 47–51.

6. On Ibn Sīrīn, see Ibn Saʿd *Ṭabaqāt* 7:143–54, Ibn Khayyāṭ *Ṭabaqāt* 360, id. *Ta*ʾ*rīkh* 267, Ibn Ḥanbal *Zuhd* 371–74, Abū Nuʿaym *Ḥilyah* 2:263–82, Ibn al-Nadīm *Fihrist* 378, Khaṭīb al-Baghdādī *Ta*ʾ*rīkh Baghdād* 5:331–38, Ibn Qutaybah *Ma*ʿ*ārif* 309, 442–43, Dhahabī *Tadhkirah* 1:77–78, id. *Siyar* 4:606–22, id. ʿ*Ibar* 1:135–36, Ibn Ḥajar *Tahdhīb* 5:139–41, Ṣafadī *Wāfī* 3:146, Ibn Khallikān *Wafayāt* 4:181–83, Ibn ʿImād *Shadharāt* 1:138–39.

7. Ṭabarī *Ta*ʾ*rīkh* 3:377.

8. Apart from the testimony of Khallāl, the only other relatively early reference to such a text seems to be that found in Ibn al-Nadīm (d. ca. 385H), *Fihrist* 378.

9. Key in this regard are the testimonies of the dream manuals of Qayrawānī (fl. early 5th c. A.H.) and Dārī (wr. between ca. 400H and 635H). Both texts contain extensive lists of sources; neither knew of a dream manual ascribed to Ibn Sīrīn. For Qayrawānī's sources, see pp. 55–56. For Dārī's, see my "Some Notes on the Dream Manual of al-Dārī," *Rivista degli studi orientali* 70 (1996): 47–52.

10. Ṭāshkubrīzādeh *Miftāḥ* 1:336 and Qayrawānī *Mumatti*ʿ, fol. 6a16 (Carullah 1571).

11. Ibn Khaldūn *Ta*ʾ*rīkh* 1:529.

12. Ibn Khallikān *Wafayāt* 4:182.

13. Dhahabī *Siyar* 4:618.

14. Ibn Ḥanbal *Musnad* 2:269, Ibn Mājah *Sunan* 2:1285, 1289, 1294, Muslim *Ṣaḥīḥ* 15:20–21, Abū Dāwūd *Sunan* 4:304–5, Nasāʾī *Sunan* 4:390, Tirmidhī *Jāmi*ʿ 4:532, 541–42, Bukhārī *Ṣaḥīḥ* 9:47–48, Dārimī *Sunan* 2:168, ʿAbd al-Razzāq *Muṣannaf* 11:211–12, Ibn Abī Shaybah *Muṣannaf* 7:242, Bayhaqī *Jāmi*ʿ 9:56–58, Baghawī *Sharḥ* 12:208–9, as well as the dream manuals of Kharkūshī,

fol. 55a and 1b (Top. A3175) and Ibn Qutaybah, fol. 182a (Ism. Saib Sincer I 4501.2). There are sometimes, however, variants in the form of its transmission: one occasionally finds it divided into its component pieces, each of which is separately transmitted.

15. See his *Muslim Tradition: Studies in Chronology, Provenance, and Authorship of Early Ḥadīth* (Cambridge: Cambridge University Press, 1983), as well as his "Early Islamic Society as Reflected in Its Use of Isnads," *Le muséon* 107 (1994): 151–94. Juynboll is building on foundations laid by Joseph Schact in *The Origins of Muhammadan Jurisprudence* (Oxford: Clarendon Press, 1950), 171–75. Juynboll has not gone unchallenged: see Michael Cook, "Eschatology and the Dating of Early Traditions," *Princeton Papers in Near Eastern Studies* 1 (1992): 23–47, and Harald Motzki, "*Quo vadis Ḥadīṯ*-Forschung? Eine kritische Untersuchungen von G. H. A. Juynboll: 'Nāfiᶜ the *Mawlā* of Ibn ᶜUmar, and His Position in Muslim *Ḥadīṯ* Literature,'" *Der Islam* 73 (1996): 40–80.

16. "Early Islamic Society," 155.

17. Fahd, *Divination arabe*, 313–15.

18. On him and his *Mumattiᶜ*'s sources, see pp. 55–56.

19. See, for example, Ibn al-Nadīm *Fihrist* 117, Yāqūt *Udabāʾ* 4:1858, Bağdatlı *Hadīyah* 1:670, id. *Īḍāḥ* 1:38 (the author's name wrongly given as al-M.d.y.nī).

20. Ibn Qutaybah *apud* Ibn ᶜImād *Shadharāt* 1:139.

21. Dīnawarī, fols. 45b–46a (Chester Beatty 3569), Kharkūshī, fol. 8a (Top. A3175), Dārī *Muntakhab* 68–69.

22. Qayrawānī *Mumattiᶜ*, fol. 6a17–19 (Carullah 1571). al-Layth b. Saᶜd died in 175H. On him, see, for example, Dhahabī *Siyar* 8:136–63. Yaḥyā b. ᶜAbd Allāh was one of his students.

23. On him, see, for example, Ibn Saᶜd *Ṭabaqāt* 5:89-113, Ibn Khayyāṭ *Ṭabaqāt* 425, Abū Nuᶜaym *Ḥilyah* 2:161–75, Ibn Ḥajar *Tahdhīb* 2:335–38, Dhahabī *Tadhkirah* 1:54–55, id. *Siyar* 4:217–46.

24. Ibn Saᶜd *Ṭabaqāt* 5:93.

25. Ibid., 5:93–95. Cf. the derivative version in Dhahabī *Siyar* 4:235–37.

26. Paris ms. ar. 2758.2, ff. 5b–51b, 1015H, contains, as per its introduction, a *mukhtaṣar* of the dream manual of Abū Isḥāq (ms.: Isḥār) al-Kirmānī written by a certain Muḥammad b. ᶜAlī b. Ḥusayn al-Ṣiqillī al-Andalusī shahīr bi-l-Ḥājj al-Shāṭibī (ms.: al-Shāṭib). This work is not a *mukhtaṣar* of Kirmānī: among his sources, the author mentions (fol. 5b16) a variety of works written by later authors. Hacı Mahmud Ef. 6234, 137 ff., without date, entitled *Taᶜbīr al-ruʾyā li-l-fāḍil al-Kirmānī*, is, in fact, a portion of the dream manual of Dīnawarī.

27. *al-Dustūr fī al-taᶜbīr*: Ḥājjī Khalīfah *Kashf* 1:755. *Kitāb taᶜbīr al-ruʾyā*: Ibn al-Nadīm *Fihrist* 378, Ḥājjī Khalīfah *Kashf* 2:1405. *Kitāb al-Kirmānī fī al-taᶜbīr*: Yāqūt *Udabāʾ* 6:2615. *Kitāb al-ᶜibārah*: Ibn Khayr *Fahrasah* 266.

28. Kirmānī: Ibn al-Nadīm *Fihrist* 378, Ibn Khayr *Fahrasah* 266, Ibn Khaldūn *Taʾrīkh* 1:529, Yāqūt *Udabāʾ* 6:2615. Ibrāhīm al-Kirmānī: Ḥājjī Khalīfah

Kashf 1:755, Tiflīsī *Kāmil* 24, Ibn Shāhīn *Ishārāt* 3. Abū Isḥāq al-Kirmānī: Ḥājjī Khalīfah *Kashf* 1:97, 2:1405.

29. Khallāl *Ṭabaqāt apud* Nābulsī *Taᶜṭīr* 2:357, Ps. Ibn Sīrīn *Nasamah*, fol. 19a (Fâtih 5300.1), Dārī *Muntakhab* 68 (as well as its introduction, as restored in my "Some Notes," 50), Qayrawānī *Mumattiᶜ*, fol. 16b (Carullah 1571), and Sijistānī, fol. 11a (Üniv. Ktp. A4437). Ibn Qutaybah identified him as the son of ᶜAbd al-Malik. This is the reading of the Jerusalem ms. (see p. 188 n. 49) at fol. 17a, but the text may be corrupt, for the Ankara ms. (see p. 189 nn. 50, 51) reads ᶜAbd Allāh.

30. G. Makdisi ("Autograph Diary of an Eleventh-Century Historian of Baghdād," *Bulletin of the School of Oriental and African Studies* 18 [1956]: 20 n. 6) errs in identifying Kirmānī as Abū Muḥammad (or Abū ᶜAbd Allāh) Ḥarb b. Ismāᶜīl al-Kirmānī (d. 288H). Bayard Dodge, tr., *The Fihrist of al-Nadim: A Tenth-Century Survey of Muslim Culture*, 2 vols., Records of Civilization: Sources and Studies, no. 83 (New York: Columbia University Press, 1970), 2:1027, states that Kirmānī also wrote a book on the Hebrew patriarchs. He seems to be misunderstanding Ḥājjī Khalīfah *Kashf* 2:1405, where the patriarchs are mentioned in a description of Kirmānī's dream manual.

31. See Sijistānī, fol. 11a–b (Üniv. Ktp. A4437); al-Shaykh al-ᶜAmīd *Mukhtaṣar*, fol. 17a (Ism. Saib Sincer I 4501.1); Kharkūshī, fol. 27a (Top. A3175), adding that Kirmānī came to al-Mahdī from al-Sīrjān; Dīnawarī, fol. 63a–b (Chester Beatty 3569), likewise that he came from al-Sīrjān, noting also that the caliph then ordered Kirmānī to write a book on dream interpretation; Dārī *Muntakhab* 144, dependent on Kharkūshī; Ps. Ibn Sīrīn *Nasamah*, fol. 19a–b (Fâtih 5300.1).

32. See Kharkūshī, fol. 33b (Top. A3175); Dārī *Muntakhab* 179, dependent on Kharkūshī; Dīnawarī, fol. 92b (Chester Beatty 3569); Ps. Ibn Sīrīn *Nasamah*, fol. 24a (Fâtih 5300.1).

33. Another tradition recorded in Mizzī *Ishārah*, fol. 12b (Top. A3166.1) has an account by Kirmānī of an event taking place "in the days of Hārūn al-Rashīd."

34. For an account of how these riwāyahs functioned in the transmission of early Arabic literature, see pp. 122–23.

35. Ibn Ḥajar *Tahdhīb* 1:157, Khaṭīb al-Baghdādī *Taᵓrīkh Baghdād* 6:332–33.

36. Ibn Khayr *Fahrasah* 266.

37. Qayrawānī *Mumattiᶜ*, fol. 16a (Carullah 1571).

38. For the fullest version, cited here, see Dīnawarī, fol. 46a (Chester Beatty 3569). Cf. also Dārī *Muntakhab* 68, Ḥājjī Khalīfah *Kashf* 2:1405, Qayrawānī *Mumattiᶜ*, fol. 16b (Carullah 1571), Kharkūshī, fol. 8a (Top. A3175), Sālimī *Ishārah*, fol. 2a (Chester Beatty 3711), the anonymous *Kitāb taᶜbīr al-ruᵓyā* (fol. 1b) in Üniv. Ktp. A3077, and the *Khvābguzārī*, 62 (ed. Afshār).

39. Ḥājjī Khalīfah *Kashf* 2:1405. A similar report in found in the *Khvābguzārī*, 62 (ed. Afshār), and in the anonymous *Kitāb taᶜbīr al-ruᵓyā* (fol. 1b) in Üniv. Ktp. A3077.

40. Ḥājjī Khalīfah *Kashf* 2:1405: *akhadha al-taʾwīl . . . ^{c}an Sa^{c}īd b. al-Musayyib wa-^{c}an Ibn Sīrīn.* The *ṣuḥuf Ibrāhīm* are mentioned at Q 53.36, 87.19, without implying that they are on dreams. For the "pages of Abraham," see Jāḥiẓ *Ḥayawān* 1:98 and Ṭabarī *Tafsīr* 11:532–33, 12:549. For the books of Daniel, see Ṭabarī *Taʾrīkh* 5:477. A certain *qawl* of Daniel is mentioned as a source by Tiflīsī *Kāmil* 25. Similarly, Ibn Shāhīn names as one of his sources a work entitled *al-Uṣūl* written by Daniel (*Ishārāt* 3), giving likewise many citations of this text. Cf. Ḥājjī Khalīfah *Kashf* 1:113, 416, who mentions an *Uṣūl* and *Uṣūl al-ta^{c}bīr* by Daniel.

41. For Ibn Qutaybah's and Ma^{c}āfirī's use of Kirmānī, see pp. 33 and 38. For Qayrawānī's, see p. 55. For Sālimī's, in addition to the many quotations in his text, cf. Ḥājjī Khalīfah *Kashf* 1:97, who says that Sālimī's work was founded on Kirmānī's. For Tiflīsī's use of Kirmānī, see *Kāmil* 25. For Ibn Shāhīn's, see *Ishārāt* 3.

42. Ibn Khaldūn *Taʾrīkh* 1:529.

43. I can think of only two other cases where this happens, both times the commentary being on a dream manual in verse. ^{c}Abd Allāh b. ^{c}Abd al-Raḥmān al-Ḥanbalī (wr. 1212H) composed a commentary on Nābulsī's (d. 1143H) *al-^{c}Abīr fī al-ta^{c}bīr*, entitled *al-Nafḥ al-^{c}aṭīr fī sharḥ al-^{c}abīr* (autograph in Cairo VI^{2}, 178 [141], 118 ff., 1212H). Similarly, Zayn al-Dīn al-Munawī (d. 1031H) composed a fascinating commentary on Ibn al-Wardī's (d. 729H) *al-Alfīyah fī al-ta^{c}bīr*, entitled *al-Fuyūḍ al-ilāhīyah fī sharḥ al-alfīyah al-wardīyah* (extant in numerous copies, e.g., University of California Library, ms. ar. 10, 124 ff., undated, and Princeton, Yah. 3280, 156 ff., undated).

44. See Qāḍī ^{c}Iyāḍ *Tartīb* 8:7, 6:134, Ibn Khayr *Fahrasah* 267, Ḥājjī Khalīfah *Kashf* 1:246, Riyādīzādeh *Asmāʾ* 2:63, Yāqūt *Udabāʾ* 6:2676.

45. Yāqūt *Udabāʾ* 6:2676.

46. Ibn Rajab *Dhayl* 1:35. The same author compiled a work on *The Dreams Seen by the Imām Aḥmad* (b. Ḥanbal), see ibid.

47. On him, see G. Lecomte, *Ibn Qutayba (mort en 276/889): L'homme, son ouvres, ses idées* (Damascus: Institut français de Damas, 1965). Also useful is Yūsuf ^{c}Alī Ṭawīl's introduction to his edition of Ibn Qutaybah's *^{c}Uyūn al-akhbār.* Primary sources include: Ibn al-Nadīm *Fihrist* 85–86, Khaṭīb al-Baghdādī *Taʾrīkh Baghdād* 10:170–71, Ibn Kathīr *Bidāyah* 11:52, Ṣafadī *Wāfī* 17:607–9, Ibn Khallikān *Wafayāt* 3:42–44, Ibn Ḥajar *Lisān* 3:357–59, Dhahabī *Mīzān* 2:503, id. *Tadhkirah* 2:633, id. *^{c}Ibar* 2:62, id. *Siyar* 13:296–302.

48. Marshall G. S. Hodgson, *The Venture of Islam: Conscience and History in a World Civilization*, 3 vols. (Chicago: University of Chicago Press, 1974), 1:461.

49. Yahuda ms. ar. 196, copied in 845H in Damascus and consisting of 67 folios of a delicate, vocalized *naskhī*. The work is variously titled *^{c}Ibārat al-ruʾyā* (fols. 67a, 1a) or *Ta^{c}bīr al-ruʾyā* (fols. 1a–b, 67a). This manuscript was

discovered by M. J. Kister ("The Interpretation of Dreams: An Unknown Manuscript of Ibn Qutayba's *ᶜIbārat al-Ruᵓyā*," *Israel Oriental Studies* 4 [1974]: 67–103).

50. Is. Saib Sincer I, 4501.2, ff. 180a–217b, discovered by Fahd (*Divination arabe*, 350). While the ms. is not dated, Fahd thought it "assez ancien." It is written in a clear *naskhī* and has been fairly well preserved, but stands in need of being rebound.

51. The Ankara manuscript contains only the first half of Ibn Qutaybah's text, corresponding to fols. 1-25 of the Jerusalem manuscript. Judging from its *fihrist*, this manuscript as originally copied did not contain the latter half of the text. This manuscript is also lacking a half-dozen or so pages from its end, corresponding to fols. 23a1–25a11 of the Jerusalem manuscript. As for the Jerusalem manuscript, Kister ("Interpretation of Dreams," 69) has correctly identified a number of lacunae in its introduction, some lengthy. There are, in addition, a great many smaller ones that he did not note: for example, at fol. 3b11ff., 7a4ff., 8b2ff., corresponding to Ankara fol. 186b6ff., 191a12ff., and 193a4ff. The manuscripts, moreover, do not present identical recensions of the text. The Ankara manuscript in particular is sometimes only a paraphrase of what is found in the Jerusalem manuscript, while at other times it simply omits parts of the text. Such omissions are especially frequent in the section (Jer. fols. 8b15–22b15) where Ibn Qutaybah transmits his large collection of anecdotes (see p. 31).

52. See Dhahabī *Siyar* 13:297, Ibn al-Nadīm *Fihrist* 378, Ṣafadī *Wāfī* 17:609 (*Kitāb al-waḥsh wa-l-ruᵓyā*, a corruption of *Kitāb al-waḥsh wa-Kitāb al-ruᵓyā*), Abū Ṭayyib al-Lughawī *Marātib* 85, Zurqānī *Sharḥ* 7:173, Ibn Khayr *Fahrasah* 266–67.

53. "Ibn Ḳutayba, Abū Muḥammad b. ᶜAbd Allāh b. Muslim al-Dīnawarī," *Encyclopedia of Islam*, 2nd ed. (1971), 3:845.

54. *Divination arabe*, 317.

55. Ibn Qutaybah *ᶜUyūn* 1:49.

56. Such a work was known to Ibn al-Nadīm (*Fihrist* 378), as well as to Maᶜāfirī (fl. mid-fourth c. A.H.), on whom, see pp. 37–38. Such a work was also used in the early fifth century A.H. by Qayrawānī. For Qayrawānī and his sources, see pp. 55–56. His many direct citations from the work are, moreover, paralleled in the text preserved in the Jerusalem and Ankara manuscripts.

57. For example, Isḥāq b. Rāhawayh (Jer. fol. 11b, 17a, 20a), see Lecomte, *Ibn Qutayba*, 52–53; Abū Ḥātim Sahl b. Muḥammad (Jer. fol. 14b, 17b, 20a, 23a, 3b, 4b), ibid., 50; Muḥammad b. ᶜUbayd (Jer. fol. 1b), ibid., 53; Muḥammad b. Ziyād (Jer. fol. 1b), ibid., 55; Ḥusayn b. Ḥasan al-Marwazī (Jer. fol. 2b), ibid., 64; and Ibn Qutaybah's own father (Jer. fol. 20b13).

58. Jer. fol. 1b.

59. Lecomte, *Ibn Qutayba*, 12.

60. Ibn Khayr *Fahrasah* 1:266–67.

61. Jer. fols. 1–25.
62. Jer. fols. 1b6–2b11.
63. Jer. fol. 2a2–4.
64. Jer. fol. 2a15–2b4.
65. There follows an erudite digression (Jer. fols. 2b11-4a10) on the difference between spirit (*rūḥ*) and soul (*nafs*). It should be noted that there is a lengthy lacuna at fol. 3a10—it can be filled from the Ankara manuscript, beginning at fol. 184a6.
66. Jer. fols. 4a10–8b15.
67. Jer. fols. 4a10–5a8. The end of this section is lacking in the Jerusalem ms. It can be supplied from the Ankara manuscript (fol. 188b4–8).
68. Jer. fol. 5a4-5.
69. This passage is lacking in the Jerusalem manuscript. It can be supplied from the Ankara manuscript (fols. 188b9–189a8).
70. Jer. fol. 5a8–5b14.
71. Jer. fols. 5b14–6a8.
72. For this prophetic tradition, see, for example, Ibn Abī Shaybah *Muṣannaf* 4:439 and ᶜAbd al-Razzāq *Muṣannaf* 4:444.
73. Jer. fols. 6a8–7b8.
74. Jer. fols. 7b8–8a7.
75. Jer. fol. 8a7–8b6.
76. Jer. fol. 8b6–11.
77. Jer. fol. 8b11–15.
78. Jer. fols. 8b15–22b15.
79. Jer. fol. 16b1-9, 16b9–12.
80. Jer. fols. 23a1–25a11.
81. Jer. fol. 24b9–14.
82. Jer. fols. 25a–67a.
83. Jer. fol. 28b6–7.
84. Jer. fol. 28b7–9.
85. Jer. fol. 28b11–12.
86. Jer. fol. 17a4–8.
87. Dārī named Ibn Qutaybah as one of his sources in his introduction, restored to the printed text in my "Some Notes," 50. For Qayrawānī, see pp. 51–59.
88. For Bar Bahlūl's use of Ibn Qutaybah's dream manual, see pp. 158–63.
89. The dream manual of Maᶜāfirī, on which, see pp. 37–38. Ibn Qutaybah's dream manual was also used by the anonymous dream manual found in Üniv. Ktp. A3077.
90. On him, see Clifford Edmund Bosworth, *The History of the Saffarids of Sistan and the Maliks of Nimruz (247/861 to 949/1542–43)*, Columbia Lectures on Iranian Studies, no. 8 (Costa Mesa, Calif., and New York: Mazda Publishers in association with Bibliotheca Persica, 1994), 301–39.

91. Ibid., 302, 329.

92. Ẓāhirīyah *maj.* 92.15, cited in Fuat Sezgin, *Geschichte des arabischen Schriftums*, Bd. 1 (Leiden: E. J. Brill, 1967), 217.

93. Bosworth, *Saffarids of Sistan*, 329–31.

94. Ibid., 333–34.

95. Ṣafadī *Wāfī* 13:365.

96. Top. A3158, 75 ff., 781H, entitled *Kitāb ta^cbīr al-ru^ɔyā* and ascribed to Abū Aḥmad Khalaf b. Aḥmad al-Amīr al-Sijistānī; Üniv. Ktp. A4437, 58 ff., 883H, entitled *Kitāb ta^cbīr uṣūl al-ru^ɔyā* and ascribed to Abū Aḥmad Khalaf b. Aḥmad al-Sijistānī. The latter's cover page bears the following, below its title and ascription: *allafahu bi-rasm khizānat al-amīr al-kabīr al-akhaṣṣ al-muḥtaram al-iṣfahsallār ḥusām al-dunyā wa-l-dīn Ibrāhīm b. Sharvīn al-malakī al-kāmilī.* I am unable to identify this person. While Fahd (*Divination arabe*, 354) knew both the Istanbul University and Topkapı manuscripts, he ascribed the work to an unknown Abū al-^cAbbās Aḥmad b. Khalaf b. Aḥmad al-Sijistānī. It is likely that Fahd was relying on the testimony of Ḥājjī Khalīfah (*Kashf* 1:375) for the form of the name. Fahd (*Divination arabe*, 354) also referred to a Turkish translation of Sijistānī's text, citing Ayasofya 1734.1, ff. 1–79, 986H, Hacı Mahmud Ef. 6240.4, an anonymous lithograph, with no date of publication, and Atıf Ef. 1977, anonymous, copied in 1137H (according to Fahd). I was unable to gain access to the latter library. The catalogue of that library (*Defter-i Kütüphane-i Atıf Efendi* [Istanbul: n.p., 1310/1893]) lists the manuscript under *Ṭibb* (as it does all other dream manuals) and gives it the title: *Mukhtaṣar ta^cbīr-nāmeh al-musammā bi-Tuḥfat al-mulūk*. I was able to examine the first two texts cited by Fahd. The Ayasofya manuscript bears on its title page *Kitāb ta^cbīr-nāmeh* and ascribes the work to Ibn Sīrīn. Its cover, however, has in a second hand (writing in pencil) *Tuḥfat al-mulūk*, the same being found at the end of the text (fol. 78b). Hacı Mahmud Ef. 6240.4, too, is entitled *Tuḥfat al-mulūk*, but is transmitted anonymously. A comparison of the Turkish and Arabic texts shows that it is not a question of a translation of Sijistānī's dream manual, but of a wholly different text.

97. Princeton, Yah. 938, 61 ff., 892H, lacking title and ascription; Çorum 3094, 61 ff., undated, lacking ascription and entitled *Tahdhīb fī ^cilm al-ru^ɔyā*; and Esad Ef. 1832, 72 ff., 749H, bearing on its title page (*manu secunda*): *Kitāb fīhi ta^cbīr al-ru^ɔyā li-Ibn Sīrīn wa-ta^cbīr āḥar li-^cAlī b. Abī Ṭālib al-Tanūkhī al-Qayrawānī wa-fīhi shay^ɔ min al-uṣūl*. (*al-Tanūkhī al-Qayrawānī* are written by a third hand). This ms. now contains only Sijistānī's work. To further complicate matters, a fourth hand has written on the title page *marqūm bi-Tuḥfat al-mulūk*.

98. There is a ms. in Qum (Mar^cashī Najafī Library 5937, 82 ff., undated) entitled *Tuḥfat al-mulūk*, ascribed to Abū al-^cAbbās Aḥmad b. Khalaf b. ^cAbbās al-Sijistānī, and consisting of 59 chapters. I was unable to examine this manuscript. The catalog of Sayyid Aḥmad Ḥusaynī (*Fihrist-i Kitābkhānah-i ^cUmūmī-i Ḥaẓrat-i Āyat Allāh al-^cuẓmā Najafī Mar^cashī*, 20 vols. [Qum: Mar^cashī Library,

1975–1991]) provides only a very brief description of the manuscript. That the manuscript contains a Persian translation of Sijistānī's dream manual must thus be considered provisional. The similarity of the author's name and of the *incipit* of the first chapter (as given by Ḥusaynī) is, however, striking. This Persian dream manual was apparently known to Ḥājjī Khalīfah (*Kashf* 1:375), who refers to a dream manual in 59 chapters, entitled *Tuḥfat al-mulūk*, a *mukhtaṣar* by Abū al-ᶜAbbās Aḥmad b. Khalaf b. Aḥmad al-Sijistānī.

99. In the biographical dictionary of Ṣafadī (*Wāfī* 13:365), we read that Sijistānī "also had a book on the interpretation of dreams that he named *Tuḥfat al-mulūk*." This title is probably to be preferred to the other, more generic titles under which it is transmitted.

100. Unless otherwise noted, Sijistānī's work is cited from Üniv. Ktp. A4437.

101. Fols. 1b–2a.

102. Traces of this system can still be found in Esad Ef. 1832.

103. Fols. 3b–4a.

104. Fols. 4a–5a.

105. Fol. 5a–b.

106. Fol. 6a–b.

107. Fols. 6b–13a.

108. Fols. 13b–57b.

109. Fols. 14b–15a.

110. Here citing Esad Ef. 1832 (fol. 18b), which agrees with Top. A3158. Üniv. Ktp. 4437 is abbreviated at this point.

111. There is one exception: at fol. 55a-b Sijistānī cites some anecdotes about dreams interpreted for Nebuchadnezzar by the prophet Daniel.

112. He occasionally cites a Koranic verse to support his interpretations; more rarely, an authority: Daniel (fol. 26a15), Ibn Sīrīn (fol. 26a16), Kirmānī (fol. 49b8 and 13).

113. Three manuscripts are known: Köpr. 1202, 18 ff., copied in 981H by a certain Abū al-Faḍl Muḥammad al-Aᶜraj, entitled *Urjūzah fī taᶜbīr al-ruʾyā ᶜalā ṣifat khalq al-insān*, and ascribed to Abū al-Ḥasan ᶜAlī b. Abī al-Sakan al-Maᶜāfirī al-Mufassir; Top. A3162.1, ff.1a–20a, copied in 920H by the same scribe and ascribed to Abū al-Ḥasan ᶜAlī b. al-Sakan al-Maᶜāfirī al-Mufassir, with the title: *Urjūzah fī taᶜbīr al-ruʾyā ᶜalā ṣifat khalq al-insān fī jamīᶜ aᶜḍāʾihi min al-raʾs ilā taḥtā al-qadim*; and University of Riyadh 1713.2, ff. 2-23, 1157H (see Ṣāliḥ Sulaymān Ḥājjī, *Fihris makhṭūṭāt Jāmiᶜat al-Riyāḍ: 3. al-aᶜmāl al-ᶜāmmah / al-falsafah* [Riyadh: Jāmiᶜat al-Riyāḍ, 1399/1979], 34–35). Maᶜāfirī's poem made little impact on later readers; the only independent reference to it seems to be Ḥājjī Khalīfah *Kashf* 1:62, where mention is made of an *Urjūzah fī taᶜbīr al-ruʾyā ᶜalā ṣifat khalq al-insān li-l-shaykh Abī al-Ḥasan ᶜAlī b. al-Sakan al-Maᶜāfirī*. Although Ṭabarsī (*Dār al-salām* 1:35) references Maᶜāfirī's work (*Urjūzah fī al-taᶜbīr li-ᶜAlī b. al-Sakan al-Maᶜāfirī*), he was dependent on Ḥājjī Khalīfah.

114. This can be inferred from the riwāyahs preserved in the Top. and Köpr. manuscripts, according to which the work was first transmitted by Abū Ḥafṣ ʿUmar b. ʿIrāk (d. 388H; see Dhahabī *Tadhkirah* 3:1020).

115. Köpr. fol. 2a.

116. Köpr. fol. 17b–18a. Ibn Sīrīn and Kirmānī were also both invoked once by name in the body of Maʿāfirī's dream manual (Köpr. fol. 7b6–7).

117. Köpr. fol. 7a4.

118. Köpr. fol. 8b8–9.

119. Köpr. fol. 2b9.

120. Köpr. fol. 13a7.

121. Among these is the dream manual of Jaʿfar al-Ṣādiq (d. 148H), a work apparently first mentioned in Tiflīsī's (d. 629H) dream manual (*Kāmil* 25). One occasionally encounters dream manuals ascribed to Jaʿfar al-Ṣādiq in manuscript form. None that I have examined has any claim to authenticity. The *Taʿbīr-nāmeh* of Jaʿfar al-Ṣādiq in Üniv. Ktp. A4646, 336 pp., 1171H, for example, is only an acephalous copy of the dream manual of Ibn Shāhīn. Another example is the dream manual ascribed to Jābir b. Ḥayyān (fl. late 2nd c. A.H.), and perhaps also that ascribed to Abū Maʿshar al-Balkhī (d. 272H). The former was apparently first mentioned by Tiflīsī (*Kāmil* 25). The latter has a higher probability of being authentic, being first mentioned by Ibn al-Nadīm (*Fihrist* 336).

122. The *Kitāb al-ruʾyā* or *Kitāb taʿbīr al-ruʾyā* ascribed to Abū Jaʿfar al-Barqī (d. ca. 274H) is an example of this phenomenon. Later authors describe this text as free-standing (e.g., Ṭūsī *Fihrist* 39, Yāqūt *ʿUdabāʾ* 1:432, Bağdatlı *Hadīyah* 1:67). It was originally a chapter in his *Kitāb al-maḥāsin* (as noted, e.g., by Ibn al-Nadīm [*Fihrist* 277]).

123. This is especially the case with a number of works from the fourth century A.H.—for example, Abū al-Ḥasan al-ʿĀmirī's (d. 381H) *al-Tabṣīr li-wujūh al-taʿbīr* and Abū Sulaymān al-Sijistānī's (d. ca. 375H) *Fī al-indhārāt al-nawmīyah.*

124. With two exceptions: fragments of dream manuals by Abū Jaʿfar al-Kulaynī (d. 329H) and Ismāʿīl b. Ashʿath (d. 360H) are cited by Majlisī (*Bihār* 61:151–233 *passim*) and Ṭabarsī (*Dār al-salām passim*).

125. Hodgson, *Venture*, 1:461.

126. Such as, for example, the sources utilized by Qayrawānī (see pp. 55–56). Others are mentioned in the Appendix.

CHAPTER TWO. THE FRACTURING OF THE TRADITION

1. For an overview, see *The Venture of Islam: Conscience and History in a World Civilization*, 3 vols. (Chicago: University of Chicago Press, 1974), 1:238–39.

2. "The Sharʿī Islamic Vision" (ibid., 1:315–58).

3. Ibid., 1:238.

4. "Muslim Personal Piety: Confrontations with History and with Selfhood, *c*. 750-945" (ibid., 1:359-409).

5. Ibid., 1:402.

6. "Adab: The Bloom of Arabic Literary Culture *c*. 813–945" (ibid., 1:444–72).

7. "Speculation: Falsafah and Kalām *c*. 750–945" (ibid., 1:410–43).

8. For a nuanced presentation of alternative forms of adab, see Tarif Khalidi, *Arabic Historical Thought in the Classical Period*, Cambridge Studies in Islamic Civilization (Cambridge: Cambridge University Press, 1994), 83–130.

9. *Adīb*s such as those studied by Joel L. Kraemer in *Humanism in the Renaissance of Islam: The Cultural Revival during the Buyid Age*, 2nd ed. (Leiden: E. J. Brill, 1992).

10. The standard edition is that of Roger A. Pack, *Artemidori Daldiani onirocriticon libri V* (Leipzig: Teubner, 1963). An English version of Pack's edition has been prepared by Robert J. White, *The Interpretation of Dreams: Oneirocritica by Artemidorus*, 2nd ed. (Torrance, Calif.: Original Books, 1990).

11. On him, see Ibn al-Nadīm *Fihrist* 352–53, Bayhaqī *Taʾrīkh* 16–18, Ibn al-Qifṭī *Taʾrīkh* 171–77, Ibn Juljul *Ṭabaqāt* 68–72, Ibn Ṣāʿid *Ṭabaqāt* 36–37, Ibn Abī ʿUṣaybiʿah *ʿUyūn* 258–74.

12. It is nearly certain that Ḥunayn did the translation. See, for example, Ibn al-Nadīm (*Fihrist* 378), who states that Ḥunayn translated the five books of Artemidorus. There has been some debate on the point, however. See Manfred Ullmann, "War Hunain der Übersetzer von Artemidors Traumbuch?" *Die Welt des Islams*, n.s. 13 (1971): 204–11, and Toufic Fahd's response, "Ḥunayn Ibn Isḥāq est-il le traducteur des *Oneirocritica* d'Artémidore d'Éphèse?" *Arabica* 21 (1974): 270–84.

13. *Artemidorus: Le livre des songes* (Damascus: Institut français de Damas, 1964). An "edition" has also been prepared by ʿAbd al-Munʿim al-Ḥifnī (*Kitāb taʿbīr al-ruʾyā, awwal wa-ahamm al-kutub fī tafsīr al-aḥlām* [Cairo: Dār al-Rashād, 1991]), who had access to the text only through Fahd's edition, which he freely rewrites.

14. See especially the studies of Gerald M. Browne, Anthony Breen, André Miquel, Roger A. Pack, Elisabeth Schmitt, and Franz Rosenthal—cited in the Bibliography.

15. Cited by Franz Rosenthal, *The Classical Heritage in Islam*, trans. Emile and Jenny Marmorstein (1975; London: Routledge, 1992), 27, from Ibn al-Maṭrān's *Bustān al-aṭibbāʾ* according to a manuscript in the Army Medical Library in Cleveland, Ohio.

16. Cf. G. Strohmaier, "Die griechischen Götter in einer christlich-arabischen Übersetzung: Zum Traumbuch des Artemidor in der Version des Ḥunain ibn Isḥāḳ," in *Die Araber in der alten Welt*, eds. F. Altheim and R. Stiehl, Bd. 5.1 (Berlin: de Gruyter, 1968), 127–62.

17. Gr. 17.5/Ar. 33.12.

18. Gr. 15.20/Ar. 31.10.
19. Gr. 202.1/Ar. 364.3.
20. Gr. 19.7/Ar. 37.2.
21. Respectively, Gr. 14.15/Ar. 29.3–4 and Gr. 158.6/Ar. 286.14.
22. Gr. 160.7/Ar. 287.10.
23. Gr. 160.13/Ar. 288.4.
24. Gr. 15.4–5.
25. Ar. 30.2–3.
26. Gr. 163.7–11.
27. Ar. 293.6–9.
28. Gr. 175.22.
29. Ar. 316.3–4.
30. Strohmaier, "Traumbuch des Artemidor," 139. Cf. Fahd, *Artemidorus*, xvii n. 3.
31. Gr. 168.7–8.
32. Ar. 301.9–12.
33. Gr. 78.11/Ar. 144.9–10.
34. Gr. 155.24/Ar. 282.8.
35. Rosenthal, *Classical Heritage*, 13.
36. Ibid., 11.
37. Ibn Khaldūn *Taʾrīkh* 1:530. Cf. Bağdatlı, who knew Qayrawānī's *Mumattiᶜ* under three titles: *al-Mumtaniᶜ fī al-taᶜbīr* (*Īḍāḥ* 2:554), *al-Ishārah fī taᶜbīr al-ruʾyā* (*Īḍāḥ* 1:85), and *al-Mumattiᶜ fī taᶜbīr al-ruʾyā* (*Hadīyah* 2:471).
38. Among the works I have consulted: Dabbāgh *Maᶜālim* and Kinānī *Takmīl*. The Mālikī biographical tradition, too, is silent on Qayrawānī, including Qāḍī ᶜIyāḍ *Tartīb*, Ibn Farhūn *Dībāj*, Bābā al-Tunbuktī *Nayl*, and Muḥammad b. Muḥammad Makhlūf, *Shajarat al-nūr al-zakīyah fī ṭabaqāt al-Mālikīyah*, 2 vols. in 1 (Beirut: Dār al-Kutub al-ᶜArabīyah, n.d.).
39. Neither Sezgin, Brockelmann, nor Kaḥḥālah have notices on him. Toufic Fahd (*La divination arabe: Études religieuses, sociologiques et folkloriques sur le milieu natif de l'Islam* [Leiden: E. J. Brill, 1966], 350) knew the above passage from Ibn Khaldūn, but was unable to provide information about Qayrawānī.
40. From the first (on whom, see, Qāḍī ᶜIyāḍ *Tartīb* 7:243–52) he received the dream manual of Kirmānī, the *Ṣaḥīḥ* of Bukhārī, the *Musnad* of Nasāᶜī, and the *Jāmiᶜ* of Ibn ᶜUyaynah. From the second (on whom, see Qāḍī ᶜIyāḍ *Tartīb* 7:260–61) he received the *Jāmiᶜ* of Ibn Wahb. Qayrawānī named other teachers whom I have been unable to identify. He received four works from a certain Abū ᶜAbd Allāh Muḥammad b. Manṣūr b. ᶜAbd Allāh al-Tustarī: the *kitāb* of Ibn al-Mughīrah (a dream manual), the *Kitāb al-manāmāt* of Ibn Abī Dunyā, the *kitāb* of Ibn Qutaybah (his dream manual), and the *kitāb* of Misᶜadah (a dream manual). He also received a copy of Kirmānī's dream manual from a certain Abū Mūsā ᶜĪsā b. Manṣūr al-Qurashī.

41. Fol. 169b (Qayrawānī's *Mumatti^{c}* is cited from Carullah 1571, on which, see p. 197 n. 60).

42. See below, in the descriptions of the manuscripts of his dream manuals. There is some evidence to suggest that he also bore the *nisbah al-Tanūkhī*, but it is far from conclusive. Esad Ef. 1832, 72 ff., 749H, bears on its title page: *Kitāb fīhi ta^{c}bīr al-ruʾyā li-Ibn Sīrīn wa-ta^{c}bīr ākhar li ^{c}Alī b. Abī Ṭālib al-Tanūkhī al-Qayrawānī*, The latter text is no longer found in the manuscript. It should be noted, however, that the words *al-Tanūkhī al-Qayrawānī* are written by a later hand.

43. For example, fol. 17b13.

44. That found in Ḥasanīyah 5596, on which, see p. 197 n. 58

45. In particular, while in Mecca Qayrawānī received from Abū Dharr a number of traditions (*Mumatti^{c}*, fol. 33b). For Abū Dharr, see, for example, Qāḍī ^{c}Iyāḍ *Tartīb* 7:229–33. Abū Dharr was himself the author of a dream manual. Ibn Khayr supplies a riwāyah for the text (*Fahrasat* 267) and it is mentioned by Qāḍī ^{c}Iyāḍ (*Tartīb* 7:233).

46. Dhahabī *Siyar* 8:86, in his entry on Mālik.

47. Ibn Abī ^{c}Uṣaybi^{c}ah *^{c}Uyūn* 20.

48. Ḥājjī Khalīfah, too, may have known one of these shorter works. See *Kashf* 2:1405.

49. Reşit Ef. 1003.17, ff. 302b–319a, undated. The inc. gives the author's name as Abū al-Ḥasan ^{c}Alī b. Sa^{c}īd al-Khawlānī known as Ibn al-Qaṣṣār al-Qayrawānī. Top. A1458.3, ff. 126a–154b, 868H, with a lacuna in chapter 28, from ff. 149b–150a. The inc. ascribes the text to Abū al-Ḥasan ^{c}Alī b. Sa^{c}īd al-Khawlānī known as Ibn al-Qaṣṣār al-Qayrawānī. It is from this latter manuscript that I cite the present work.

50. Bibliothèque nationale, ar. 2746, 44 ff., undated. The inc. specifies as its author: Abū al-Ḥasan ^{c}Alī b. Sa^{c}īd al-Khawlānī known as Ibn al-Qaṣṣār.

51. Ḥasanīyah 4536, 30 ff., 1159H, with much worm damage. The inc. ascribes the text to Abū al-Ḥasan ^{c}Alī b. Sa^{c}d al-Khaff (!) known as Ibn al-Qaṣṣār al-Qayrawānī.

52. Biblioteca Ambrosiana E201.7, ff. 111a–129a, 1050H, ascribed to Abū al-Ḥasan ^{c}Alī b. Sa^{c}īd al-J.zlānī known as Ibn al-Qaṣṣār al-Qayrawānī.

53. Fol. 127b2–3.

54. On whom, see p. 55.

55. Fol. 128b9–10.

56. Vat. ar. 1304.2, ff. 174a–198a, undated, ascribed (fol. 174b) to Abū al-Ḥasan ^{c}Alī b. Sa^{c}īd al-Khawlānī. Giorgio Levi della Vida (*Elenco dei manoscritti arabi islamici della Biblioteca Vaticana: Vaticani, Barberiniani, Borgiani, Rossiani*, Studi e Testi, no. 67 [Vatican City: Biblioteca Apostolica Vaticana, 1935], 199) suggests that there is another copy in Tübingen manuscript ar. 200, in this being followed by Fahd (*Divination arabe*, 343, no. 60). This is not correct. The latter manuscript is a *mukhtaṣar* of Kharkūshī's dream manual (see p. 201 n. 121).

57. I was not able to examine Cairo š 57, 45 ff., 1255H. Judging from the catalog (Fuʾād Sayyid, *Fihrist al-makhṭūṭāt: Nashrah bi-l-makhṭūṭāt allatī iqtanathā al-dār min sanat 1936–1955*, 3 vols. [Cairo: Dār al-Kutub, 1961–63], 1:243), this manuscript may contain another copy of the text. The incipit appears to be identical, though Sayyid gives only its first six, rather generic words. The work is said to be entitled *Kitāb fī taʿbīr al-ruʾyā* and ascribed to Abū al-Ḥasan ʿAlī b. Saʿīd al-Khawlānī al-Qaṣṣār. The only problem: it is said to consist of sixty not fifty-eight chapters.

58. Ḥasanīyah 5596, 57 ff., undated, entitled (*manu secunda*): *Kitāb taʿbīr al-ruʾyā li-l-Qayrawānī*. Following the riwāyah, the author's name is given as Abū al-Ḥasan ʿAlī b. Abī Ṭālib. The copyist of the manuscript received the work in 513 from Abū al-Ḥasan ʿAlī b. al-Muslim b. Muḥammad b. al-Fatḥ b. ʿAlī al-Sulamī (d. 533H, see Dhahabī *Siyar* 20:31–34).

59. Fol. 10a–b.

60. Carullah 1571, 194 ff., 1049H (see fol. 99b), entitled *Kitāb al-mumattiʿ fī taʿbīr al-ruʾyā*, ascribed to Abū al-Ḥasan ʿAlī b. Saʿīd al-Khawlānī known as Ibn al-Qaṣṣār al-Qayrawānī.

61. Lacunae include: beginning of the index; end of ch. 4 to beginning of ch. 6; end of ch. 10, beginning of ch. 11; end of ch. 18, beginning of ch. 19; end of ch. 19, beginning of ch. 20; middle portions of ch. 20; almost all of ch. 25, beginning of ch. 26; end of the text is lacking, breaking off in *faṣl* 11 of *bāb* 32 (the index states that the work originally had 32 chapters).

62. Hekimoğlu Ali Paşa 590, 343 ff., undated, beginning and end lacking, a compilation of earlier dream manuals, including the *Mumattiʿ*, from which an enormous number of quotations are taken. Bağdatlı Vehbi Ef. 941, 121 ff., 1005H, acephalous, a *mukhtaṣar* of the *Mumattiʿ*.

63. Fols. 2b–16b.

64. Note in particular Qayrawānī's reference to him as *dhawī al-ijtihād* (fol. 2b6–7).

65. Riwāyahs for all three are found at fols. 15b–16a, two for the dream manual of Kirmānī. Ibn Abī Dunyā's text is not a dream manual, but a collection of *akhbār* on dreams of the dead. It has been well served by its editor, Leah Kinberg: *Ibn Abī al-Dunyā: Morality in the Guise of Dreams: A Critical Edition of* Kitāb al-Manām *with Introduction*, Islamic Philosophy, Theology and Science: Texts and Studies, no. 18 (Leiden: E. J. Brill, 1994).

66. Fol. 15b.

67. A certain Abū al-Qāsim ʿAbd al-Raḥmān b. al-Mughīrah b. ʿAbd al-Raḥmān al-Ḥizāmī al-Madanī al-Asadī was known to Ibn Ḥajar, but he did not know the date of his death (*Tahdhīb* 3:422–23), though his father is known to have died in 180H (Dhahabī *Siyar* 8:167).

68. On him, see Ibn Ḥajar *Tahdhīb* 6:12–13.

69. On him, see, Dhahabī *Siyar* 12:102–7 and Ibn Farhūn *Dībāj* 154–56.

70. Entitled: *al-Duhūr wa-taṣārīf al-umūr*. See, for example, fols. 31a [x 2] and 92b.

71. For example, fols. 50a, 50b, 95a, where it is called, simply, *Jāmiʿ*.

72. On him, see, for example, Khaṭīb al-Baghdādī *Taʾrīkh Baghdād* 13: 306–14, Ibn al-Jawzī *Muntaẓam* 11:149, Ibn Ḥajar *Tahdhīb* 5:635–38, and Ibn al-ʿImād *Shadharāt* 2:66–67.

73. Ibn Khayr *Fahrasat* 267, specifying that it was a work in three parts.

74. Dhahabī *Mīzān* 4:97–98, Ibn Ḥajar *Lisān* 6:22–23.

75. Fol. 15b. Qayrawānī < Abū ʿAbd Allāh al-Tustarī (see above) < Abū Bakr Muḥammad b. Ibrāhīm al-Muqriʾ al-Iṣbahānī (d. 381H: Dhahabī *Siyar* 16:398–402) < Aḥmad b. ʿUmayr (ms.: ʿUmar) b. Yūsuf b. Mūsā b. Jawṣā al-Dimashqī (d. 320H: Dhahabī *Siyar* 15:15–21) < Abū ʿAbd al-Raḥmān Zakarīyā b. Yaḥyā (d. 289H: Ibn Ḥajar *Tahdhīb* 2:197–98) < Abū ʿAbd Allāh Muḥammad b. Ḥātim al-Sarḥī al-Muʾaddib < Misʿadah b. al-Yasaʿ b. F.y.d.

76. See, for example, fol. 98b.

77. Misʿadah's work seems also to have been used by Abū Nuʿaym (*Ḥilyah* 2:276–77).

78. Fol. 12b.

79. On him, see, for example, Dhahabī *Siyar* 10:439–40.

80. For example, fol. 6a–b [x 5].

81. For example, fols. 61a and 82b. On him, see, for example, Dhahabī *Siyar* 15:236–39.

82. Fol. 23b.

83. Fols. 58a, 82a [x 2], 70b.

84. For example, fols. 92a and 50a.

85. Fol. 63a.

86. Fols. 2b–3a.

87. See the discussion of this tradition below at pp. 109–115.

88. Fols. 11b–15b.

89. He cites this tradition (fol. 12a) from "the book of Nuʿaym [b. Ḥammād]."

90. Fol. 6a–b.

91. Fols. 4b–5b.

92. Fol. 4a5–6.

93. For example, Cairo VI^2, 176 [493], 229 ff., 740H; Dār Ṣaddām 598, 360 ff., undated; Qarawīyīn 1292, 202 ff., undated; Hekimoğlu 593, 300 ff., 1110H; Lâleli 1658, 517 ff., 861H; Ayasofya 2006, 361 ff., 926H; Yeni Câmi 699, 227 ff., 691H; Top., A3171, 340 ff., undated; Chester Beatty 3569, 437 ff., 694H; Chester Beatty 5379, 372 ff., 826H. Recently an edition was prepared by Fahmī Saʿd, *Kitāb al-taʿbir fī al-ruʾyā aw al-Qādirī fī al-taʿbīr*, 2 vols. (Beirut: ʿĀlam al-Kutub, 1997). As this edition is basically a printed manuscript, in what follows I have had recourse to the text through Chester Beatty 3569.

94. It was used by Dārī in his *Muntakhab al-kalām fī taʿbīr al-manām* (see my "Some Notes," 50) and Nābulsī in his *Taʿṭīr al-anām fī taʿbīr al-manām* (see 2:349–50, as well as 2:355–59). Ayasofya 1704, 209 ff., 786H, contains an anonymous *mukhtaṣar*, entitled *Kitāb al-taḥbīr fī ʿilm al-taʿbīr mukhtaṣar al-Qādirī . . . taʾlīf . . . Abī Saʿd Naṣr b. Yaʿqūb b. Ibrāhīm al-Dīnawarī.* As the author explains (fol. 1b), he summarizes Dīnawarī in the first twenty-nine chapters of his work, while in chapter 30 "from others works written on this subject" he adds what is lacking. There is also an anonymous dream manual in Üniv. Ktp. A6233, 183 ff., 1147H, entitled *Kitāb al-tanwīr fī ruʾyā al-taʿbīr* and bearing in its margins scholia ascribed to Artemidorus, Christians, Byzantines, Jews, and Jāmāsb. These scholia seem to have been taken from Dīnawarī.

95. For an exemplar, see Ayasofya 1718, 314 ff., undated.

96. *Yatīmah* 4:357–60. The notice in Ṣafadī's *Wāfī* is derived from Thaʿālibī. The volume of Ṣafadī's biographical dictionary in which Dīnawarī's biography is contained has not yet been published in the edition being prepared by the Orient-Institut. I have relied on a transcription of the relevant portion of the Topkapı manuscript, graciously supplied by Professor Angelica Neuwirth.

97. For the date, see M. Abu Bakr Ṣiddīque, *A Critical Study of Abu Mansur al-Thaʿalibi's Contribution to Arabic Literature* (Dhaka: Sultana Prokashoni, 1991), 144.

98. Thaʿālibī *Yatīmah* 4:358.

99. Ibid., 4:358, suggesting that his work on stones was dedicated to Sijistānī.

100. Ibid., 4:358–60.

101. Ibid., citing his *Rawāʾiʿ al-tawjīhāt fī badāʾiʿ al-tashbīhāt.*

102. Entitled, respectively, *Thimār al-uns fī tashbīhāt al-furs* and *Rawāʾiʿ al-tawjīhāt fī badāʾiʿ al-tashbīhāt*. For these works, see ibid., 4:357–58, Ḥājjī Khalīfah *Kashf* 1:523, 1:914, and Bağdatlı *Hadīyah* 2:490. A paragraph from the introduction of the latter is cited in Thaʿālibī *Yatīmah* 4:358.

103. Thaʿālibī *Yatīmah* 4:358. This same text was known to Ibn Ṭāwūs. See Etan Kohlberg, *A Medieval Muslim Scholar at Work: Ibn Ṭāwūs and His Library*, Islamic Philosophy, Theology and Science: Texts and Studies, vol. 12 (Leiden: E. J. Brill, 1992), 203.

104. Entitled, *Ḥuqqat al-jawāhir fī al-mafākhir*. For this work, see Thaʿālibī *Yatīmah* 4:358.

105. In his *Kitāb al-jamāhir fī maʿrifat al-jawāhir* (Hyderabad: Maṭbaʿat Jamʿīyat Dāʾirat al-Maʿārif al-ʿUthmānīyah, 1355/1936). On this text, see Mohammed Jahia Haschmi, *Die Quellen des Steinbuches des Bērūnī* (Bonn: C. Schulze, 1935), and G. C. Anawati, "The Kitāb al-Jāmahir [*sic*] fī Maʿrifah al-Jawāhir of al-Bīrūnī," in *Al-Bīrūnī Commemorative Volume*, ed. Hakim Mohammed Said (Karachi: The Times Press, 1979), 437–53.

106. Fols. 1b–3a.
107. Fols. 29a–40b.
108. Fols. 29a, 30a.
109. Fols. 31b–32a, 32b.
110. Fol. 33a.
111. Fol. 30a–b.
112. Fol. 34b: *muᶜabbirūn min naṣārā al-rūm.*
113. Fols. 30a, 30b, 38b–39b.
114. Fol. 30a–b.
115. Occasionally he is encountered with the *kunyā* Abū Saᶜīd.
116. Dhahabī *Siyar* 17:256–57, id. *Tadhkirah* 3:1066–67, id. *ᶜIbar* 3:98–99, Subkī *Ṭabaqāt* 5:222–23, as well as 4:369, Khaṭīb al-Baghdādī *Taʾrīkh Baghdād* 10:432, Samᶜānī *Ansāb* 2:350–51, Ṣafadī *Wāfī* 19:199–200, Yāqūt *Buldān* 2:360–61, Ibn al-ᶜImād *Shadharāt* 3:184–85, Bağdatlı *Hadīyah* 2:625, Fārisī *Siyāq* 47a–b, Ṣarīfīnī *Muntakhab* 94b, Ibn ᶜAsākir *Tabyīn* 233-36, Ibn Athīr *Lubāb* 1:353–54, Sibṭ b. al-Jawzī *Mirʾāt* 300–301, Asnawī *Ṭabaqāt* 1:477.
117. For this work, usually entitled *Tahdhīb al-asrār fī ṭabaqāt al-akhyār*, see, for example, Ḥājjī Khalīfah *Kashf* 1:514 and Bağdatlı *Hadīyah* 1:625, cf. Samᶜānī *Ansāb* 2:351, who mentions a work by Kharkūshī *fī siyar al-ᶜubbād wa-l-zuhhād*, and Ṣafadī *Wāfī* 19:200, who mentions a work *fī zuhd*. For an exemplar, see Şehid Ali Paşa 1157, 231 ff., 863H. A. J. Arberry has published a brief description of this work ("Khargūshī's Manual of Ṣufism," *Bulletin of the School of Oriental and African Studies* 9 [1937/9]: 345–49). He notes its derivative character and that it is transmitted by a disciple of a disciple of Kharkūshī and has suffered interpolation.
118. Entitled: *Sharaf al-Muṣṭafā*. For an exemplar, see Staatsbibliothek 9571, 313 ff., 447H. This text was mentioned by Ḥājjī Khalīfah *Kashf* 2:1045, who notes that it was in eight volumes and suggests that it is identical with another work ascribed to Kharkūshī, his *Sharaf al-nubūwah*. Cf. the notice in Bağdatlı *Hadīyah* 1:625. It may be that this text is identical with another work of Kharkūshī on *dalāʾil al-nubūwah* mentioned, for example, in Fārisī *Siyāq* 47a, Samᶜānī *Ansāb* 2:351, Yāqūt *Buldān* 2:361, Dhahabī *Siyar* 17:256, and Ṣafadī *Wāfī* 19:200. Kharkūshī's life of the prophet is also preserved in Persian translation: Muḥammad Rawshan, ed., *Sharaf al-nabī* (Teheran: Intishārāt-i Bābāk, 1982).
119. The *tafsīr* is mentioned in Ṣafadī *Wāfī* 19:200, Dhahabī *Siyar* 17:256 and *Tadhkirah* 3:1066–67. His other works include one entitled *Shiᶜār al-Ṣāliḥīn* or perhaps *Shaᶜāʾir al-Ṣāliḥīn*, and a text called *al-Lawāmiᶜ*. For the former, see Ḥājjī Khalīfah *Kashf* 2:1047 and Bağdatlı *Hadīyah* 1:625. The latter is mentioned in Ḥājjī Khalīfah *Kashf* 2:1569 and Bağdatlı *Hadīyah* 1:625.
120. There are at least twenty-five extant copies of this text. Among these: Top. A3176, 125 ff., 944H; Top. A3175, 109 ff., undated; Ayasofya 1688, 263 ff., undated; Beşir Ağa 348, 258 ff., 1123H; Cairo VI², 174 [33], 202 ff., 1068H; Cairo

š 65, 128 ff., 825H; Mingana 1922 [618], 223 ff., 980H; Qarawīyīn 1290, 242 ff., undated; Vat. ar. 1304.8, ff. 230–314, 944H. In what follows I have used Top. A3175.

121. Dārī's dream manual is a *mukhtaṣar* of Kharkūshī's (for this work, written between ca. 400H and 635H, and its use of Kharkūshī, see my "Some Notes," 51–52). There is an anonymous *mukhtaṣar* of Kharkūshī's dream manual in Ayasofya 1731.2, ff. 5b–179b, 841H, Üniv. Ktp. A2889, 121 ff., 1138H, Tübingen manuscript ar. 200, and probably Çorum 3098, 90 ff., undated. Ibn Shāhīn (d. 872H), too, used it *(Ishārāt* 3). And finally, there is in the Dār Ṣaddām a manuscript (1997.2) entitled *Sharḥ risālah al-Wāᶜiẓ fī taᶜbīr al-ruᵓyā*. Usāmah Nāṣir al-Naqshabandī ("Makhṭūṭāt taᶜbīr al-ruᵓyā wa-tafsīr al-aḥlām fī Dār Ṣaddām li-l-Makhṭūṭāt," *al-Mawrid* 20/2 [1992]: 146), described this work, consisting of 101 pages, as follows: "It is a commentary on the epistle of dream interpretation written by Abū Saᶜd ᶜAbd al-Malik d. Abī ᶜUthmān al-Wāᶜiẓ [scil. Kharkūshī]. It contains prophetic traditions on the subject of dreams and the proper conduct of dreamers. The commentator cites some of his information from the *Kitāb al-ruᵓyā* written by Sijistānī."

122. Fol. 1b.

123. Fols. 1b–5a.

124. Fol. 1b15–19.

125. Fols. 3b–4a.

126. Fol. 4a5–9.

127. Fols. 4b6–5a3.

128. Fols. 5a–6b.

129. For Abū ᶜUbayd Muḥammad b. Ḥassān al-Busrī, see, for example, Sulamī *Ṭabaqāt* 147, 176, 192, 228, Abū Nuᶜaym *Ḥilyah* 10:318, as well as Fuat Sezgin, *Geschichte des arabischen Schriftums*, Bd. 1 (Leiden: E. J. Brill, 1967), 642.

130. Fol. 6b13–19, from the chapter on dreams of God.

131. Fol. 16a12–13, from the chapter on prayer.

132. Fol. 23b17–19, from the chapter on the resurrection.

133. Fol. 56b1–3.

134. Fol. 56b9–10.

135. Fol. 97b3.

136. *On*. 3.56 (ar. 421.3–12).

137. *On*. 3.56 (ar. 420.3–7).

138. *On*. 1.66 (ar. 133.7–10).

139. Soheil M. Afnan, *Avicenna: His Life and Works* (London: G. Allen and Unwin, 1958).

140. A small portion has been published and translated into English: Mohd. Abdul Muid Khan, "A Unique Treatise on the Interpretation of Dreams," in *Avicenna Commemoration Volume* (Calcutta: Iran Society, 1956), 255–307; "Kitabu Taᶜbir-Ir-Ruya of Abu ᶜAli B. Sina," *Indo-Iranica* 9 (1956): 43–57.

141. Gar. 930, 90 ff., 892H; British Library, manuscript ar. 978.44 (add. 16,659), ff. 519b–547a, 1091H; Bağdalı Veh. Ef. 1488.12, ff. 154b–172b, undated; Esat Ef. 3774.6, ff. 90b–131b, 973H. Unless otherwise stated, I cite the text from Gar. 930.

142. Raza 541, ff. 373b-502a, 1291H; 1789, ff. 39b–122b, 1256H. See Imtiyaz Ali Arshi, *Catalogue of the Arabic Manuscripts in Raza Library, Rampur*, 6 vols. to date (Rampur: Raza Library Trust, 1963–), 5:470–71. Khan used two manuscripts in the Asafiyah: *maj.* no. 41, 133 pp., undated, and *nair.* no. 283, 86 pp., undated. Yahya Mahdavi, *Bibliographie d'Ibn Sīnā* (Teheran: n.p., 1954), 59, notes another copy in "Ben II, 787." He also lists three copies in Teheran (Majlis-i Shūrā-yi Islāmī Library 756, 1859.10; Millī Malik Library 2020.1) and one in Mashhad (Āstān-i Quds-i Raẓavī Library). A final copy, in private possession, was used by Muhammad al-Hashimi in his "On Avicenna's Taᶜbīr al-Ruʾyā," Ph.D. Dissertation, London School of Oriental and African Studies, 1948.

143. Fols. 2b–3b (damaged portions supplemented from the British Library ms.) While Ibn Sīnā does not identify his patron, Khwansārī (*Rawḍāt* 244) suggests that it was ᶜAlā al-Dawlah. Although he cites no source, his suggestion is not unreasonable, for Ibn Sīnā was closely connected with ᶜAlā al-Dawlah's court for the last fourteen years of his life (see William E. Gohlman, *The Life of Ibn Sina* [Albany: State University of New York Press, 1974], 57–89).

144. Sec. 1–2 (fols. 7a–9b). There is a lacuna between fols. 9b and 10a (end of Sec. 2 and beginning of Sec. 3). I have supplemented from the British Library manuscript. For the discussion of a passage in the introduction, see S. Pines, "The Arabic Recension of *Parva Naturalia* and the Philosophical Doctrine concerning Veridical Dreams according to *al-Risāla al-Manāmiyya* and Other Sources," *Israel Oriental Studies* 4 (1974): 104–53.

145. Sec. 3 (fol. 10a–b).

146. Secs. 4-5 (fols. 10b–13a).

147. Sec. 6-7 (fols. 13a–15b).

148. Fol. 16a7–8.

149. Sec. 8 (fols. 15b–18a).

150. The reading *al-ṣābiʾah* is conjectural.

151. The manuscripts vary in their transmission of the name of the entity or entities recognized by the Zoroastrians. These I have identified with the Aməša Spəntas or Amahra Spandān—the six Holy Immortal Ones who together with Ahura Mazdā comprise the divine heptad of Zoroastrianism. The Princeton manuscript reads: *m.s.yā wa-sh.b.n.dān*. The British Library manuscript reads: *m.shā sh.b.n.dān*. Thus also the two Turkish manuscripts.

152. Fol. 17a3–5.

153. Sec. 9 (fols. 18a–19a).

154. Sec. 10 (fols. 19a–20b).

155. Sec. 11 (fols. 20b–23b).

156. Sec. 12 (fol. 24a–b).

157. Ibn Sīnā closes this portion of his introduction with a discussion of allegorical dreams. (secs. 14–16, fols. 25b–31b), showing that a dream's meaning can vary with the dreamer's identity.

158. Fol. 32a3–4.

159. Sec. 17 (fols. 31b–32a).

160. Fol. 31b12–33.

161. Fol. 36a14.

162. Secs. 30-37 (fols. 41b–46b).

163. Fols. 42b13–43a1.

164. This is suggested by Sec. 36 (fol. 45a), which presents a discussion of the species (*jins*), genus (*nawᶜ*), and type (*tabᶜ*) of dreams, a discussion paralleled in the dream manual of Ibn Qutaybah (Jer. fols. 23b10–24a15), but not, seemingly, found in other texts.

165. Sec. 39 (fol. 47a–b).

166. Secs. 40–129 (fols. 47b–90b).

167. Fol. 16a7–8.

168. Among these: the dream manuals of Sālimī (d. 800H), Chester Beatty 3711, 86 ff., 898H; Ibn Shāhīn (d. 872H), published, see bibliography; and Sawdī (d. 932H), Top. A3177, 159 ff., 995H. Lesser known works include the dream manuals of Maqdisī (d. 697H), Top. A3168, 172 ff., 741H, and Ibn Rāshid (fl. ca. 731H), Ḥasanīyah 451, 160 ff., undated.

169. For example, Shihāb al-Dīn Aḥmad b. Abī Bakr al-Shādhilī's collection of dreams had by the "shaykh of shaykhs" Abū al-Ḥasan ᶜAlī b. ᶜUmar al-Qurashī al-Shādhilī al-Umawī al-Yamanī (Şehid Ali Paşa 1357.7, ff. 120b–273a, without date).

170. For instance, Abarqūhī's dream manual (wr. 763H), for which, see, for example, Fâtih 3651, 177 ff., 882H.

CHAPTER THREE. HOMOGENEITY AND IMITATION

1. Cic. *de div*. 2.130.
2. See Q 12.44 and 21.5.
3. Ibn Qutaybah, fol. 181b (Ism. Saib Sincer I 4501).
4. Cic. *de div*. 1.109–10.
5. Ibid., 1.118.
6. Sijistānī, fols. 4a–5a (Üniv. Ktp. A4437).
7. Fol. 2a (Yah. 196).
8. On dreams of Muḥammad, see Muṣṭafā Aḥmad al-Zarqā, "Man raᵓānī fa-qad raᵓā al-ḥaqq fa-inna al-shayṭān lā yatamaththalu bī," *al-Durūs al-Ḥasanīyah* (1986), 121–30; F. Krenkow, "The Appearance of the Prophet in Dreams," *Journal of the Royal Asiatic Society* (1912): 77–99, with a response by I. Goldziher, "The

Appearance of the Prophet in Dreams," *Journal of the Royal Asiatic Society* (1912): 503–6. Cf. also Fritz Meier, "Eine Auferstehung Mohammeds bei Suyūṭī," *Der Islam* 62 (1985): 20–58.

9. Fol. 24b (Yah. 196).

10. For the context of this tradition, see Ibn Saᶜd *Ṭabaqāt* 2:167.

11. Dreams are also called *manām/manāmāt*, a word derived from a root meaning "to sleep." The *manām* and the *ru*ᵓ*yā* are distinguished in the dream manuals from dreams that do not bear significance. These latter are usually called *ḥulm/aḥlām* or *aḍghāth al-aḥlām*.

12. I here follow the typology of Macrobius' *Commentary on the Dream of Scipio* 1.3.2 and 1.3.8. This typology is not original to Macrobius. He draws on a long tradition. For his sources, see Steven F. Kruger, *Dreaming in the Middle Ages*, Cambridge Studies in Medieval Literature, no. 14 (Cambridge: Cambridge University Press, 1992), 17–43, and Caes Blum, *Studies in the Dream-Book of Artemidorus* (Uppsala: Almqvist & Wiksells, 1936), 57–60.

13. See, for example, the tradition ascribed to ᶜĀᵓishah (Ṭabarī *Ta*ᵓ*rīkh* 2:298): "The Messenger of God's first experience of revelation (*waḥy*) took place in a true dream." Another tradition has it that Muḥammad's initial encounter with Gabriel took place while he was asleep (*wa-anā nā*ᵓ*im*), and that when it was over Muḥammad "awoke from sleep" (Ṭabarī *Ta*ᵓ*rīkh* 2:301).

14. Ibn Qutaybah, fol. 28b (Yah. 196).

15. Dīnawarī, fol. 347b (Chester Beatty 3569).

16. Ibn Qutaybah, fol. 25b (Yah. 196).

17. Dīnawarī, fol. 345b (Chester Beatty 3569).

18. Closely connected with this technical term are two synonyms: *ta*ᵓ*wīl* and *tafsīr*, both of which mean "exegesis" and are commonly thus used with reference to the Koran.

19. See the authorities cited by Ibn Manẓūr (*Lisān* 6:203).

20. Qayrawānī, *Mumattiᶜ*, fol. 73a (Carullah 1571).

21. Ibid.

22. Dīnawarī, fol. 98b (Chester Beatty 3569).

23. Kharkūshī, fol. 35a (Top. A3175).

24. Qayrawānī, *Mumattiᶜ* fol. 73b (Carullah 1571).

25. Ibid.

26. ᶜUmar al-Khayyām *Taᶜbīr* 34.

27. Fol. 59a–b (Yah. 196).

28. *Collected Papers*, eds. Charles Hartshorne and Paul Weiss, 8 vols. (Cambridge: Harvard University Press, 1931–60), 2:634.

29. "Unlimited Semiosis and Drift: Pragmaticism vs. 'Pragmatism,'" in *The Limits of Interpretation* (Bloomington/Indianapolis: Indiana University Press, 1994), 27.

30. "Unlimited Semiosis and Drift," 23–43; cf. his "Overinterpreting Texts," in *Interpretation and Overinterpretation* (Cambridge: Cambridge University Press, 1992), 45–66.

31. *Mumatti*ᶜ, fol. 182a (Carullah 1571).

32. Leah Kinberg, "The Legitimation of the Madhāhib through Dreams," *Arabica* 32 (1985): 47-79; cf. her "Literal Dreams and Prophetic *Ḥadīṯs* in Classical Islam: A Comparison of Two Ways of Legitimation," *Der Islam* 70 (1993): 279–300.

33. Leah Kinberg, "The Standardization of Quran Readings: The Testimonial Value of Dreams," in *Proceedings of the Colloquium on Arabic Grammar, Budapest . . . 1991*, ed. K. Dévényi (Budapest: Eötvös Loránd University Chair for Arabic Studies, 1991), 223–38.

34. Two famous works in this regard are the *Kitāb al-manāmāt* of Ibn Abī Dunyā (d. 281H), on eschatology (Leah Kinberg, ed., *Ibn Abī al-Dunyā: Morality in the Guise of Dreams: A Critical Edition of* Kitāb al-Manām *with Introduction*, Islamic Philosophy, Theology and Science: Texts and Studies, no. 18 [Leiden: E. J. Brill, 1994]), and the work of Dāraquṭnī (385H), on the permissibility of visions of God (Mabrūk Ismāᶜīl Mabrūk, ed., *Ruʾyat Allāh jalla wa-ᶜalā* [Cairo: Maktabat al-Qurʾān, n.d.]).

35. Notable early examples include works by Kindī and Fārābī, see Toufic Fahd, *La divination arabe: Études religieuses, sociologiques et folkloriques sur le milieu natif de l'Islam* (Leiden: E. J. Brill, 1966), 345 (no. 66) and 337 (no. 35).

36. See, for example, ibid., 331 (no. 6), 353–54 (no. 111), and H. Corbin, "The Visionary Dream in Islamic Spirituality," in *The Dream and Human Societies*, eds. G. E. von Grunebaum and Roger Caillois (Berkeley and Los Angeles: University of California Press, 1966), 381–408.

37. Jonathan G. Katz, "Visionary Experience, Autobiography, and Sainthood in North African Islam," *Princeton Papers in Near Eastern Studies* 1 (1992): 95.

38. See, for example, the texts discussed by Katz in his "Visionary Experience," as well as Eerik Nael Dickinson, "The Development of Early Muslim Ḥadīth Criticism: The *Taqdima* of Ibn Abī Ḥātim al-Rāzī (d. 327/938)," Ph.D. Dissertation, Yale University, 1992, 88–94, on how dreams are used "to demonstrate divine approbation for the critics" of prophetic traditions.

39. I have had access to this text through Hacı Mahmud Ef. 1893, 47 ff., 1192H, entitled *Risālah fī ruʾyā Sayyidī ᶜAbd Allāh b. Abī Jamrah*. For Ibn Abī Jamrah, see also Katz, "Visionary Experience," 89–92, and Fahd, *Divinatione arabe*, 332–33 (no. 12).

40. *Divinatione arabe*, 330–67.

41. This is how Fahd defined the terms when called to task by Brunschvig. See his "L'oniromancie orientale et ses repercussions sur l'oniromancie de l'occident

medieval," in *Oriente e occidente nel Medioevo: Filosofia e scienze*, eds. M. C. Hernandez et al., Accademia Nazionale dei Lincei: Atti dei covegni, vol. 13 (Rome: Accademia Nazionale dei Lincei, 1971), 372.

42. Fol. 59a (Yah. 196).

43. Fol. 45a (Üniv. Ktp. A4437).

44. Sijistānī is a bit confused. The Koranic text in question states that it was the Egyptians, not the Israelites, who were punished by the plague of frogs.

45. Fol. 182a–b (Carullah 1571).

46. Fol. 151a–b (Top. A1458.3).

47. Fol. 184a (Vat. 1304.2).

48. Fol. 347a–b (Chester Beatty 3569).

49. See *on*. 2.15 (Ar. 239).

50. It reads: "A certain Jew dreamt that frogs left the land. He went to an interpreter and asked him about this. He said: This is good news for the people of the land, for punishment will be lifted from the people of the land because of [their] prayers and supplications. God says in the Torah: Pharaoh summoned Moses and Aaron . . . and said to them: Intercede with God for me that he might turn away the frogs from me and my people. When Moses and Aaron left the presence of the cursed Pharaoh, Moses called on God concerning the frogs that he had brought upon Pharaoh. And God did as Moses asked. The frogs departed from the houses, residences, and estates."

51. O*n*. 2.15 (Ar. 239): "Artemidorus said: A slave saw in a dream that he seized a frog. He was put in charge of everything in his master's house. This is because the spring from which he took the frog signifies the house of the man; the frogs [signify] those in the house; and the hunting of frogs, his subduing [of the master of the house]."

52. Fol. 66a (Top. A3175).

53. Fol. 59a (Yah. 196).

54. Fol. 45a (Üniv. Ktp. A4437).

55. Fol. 182a–b (Carullah 1571).

56. Fol. 184a (Vat. 1304.2).

57. Fols. 345b–346a (Chester Beatty 3569).

58. Fol. 66a (Top. A3175).

59. Kirmānī *apud* Ibn Shāhīn *Ishārāt* 306.

60. Fol. 59a (Yah. 196).

61. For a parallel tradition, see Jāḥiẓ *Ḥayawān* 4:157: "There is a saying of the muḥaddiths: 'Among the most exalted of what God created are the snake, the crayfish, and the fish.'"

62. Fol. 45a (Üniv. Ktp. A4437).

63. Reading *khalqan* for *ḥaqqah.*

64. "To dream of acquiring a crayfish or possessing it or taking it means that [the dreamer] will acquire a friend or meet someone who has the same char-

acter and nature [as the crayfish]. He will get from [this person] kindness and tribulation according to the good and evil that he received from the crayfish."

65. Fol. 182b (Carullah 1571).
66. Fol. 184a (Vat. 1304.2).
67. Fol. 346a (Chester Beatty 3569).
68. Fol. 66a (Top. A3175).
69. Kirmānī *apud* Ibn Shāhīn *Ishārāt* 305.
70. Fol. 25b (Yah. 196).
71. Fol. 24a (Top. A3175).
72. *Mumatti*ᶜ, fol. 19b (Carullah 1571) and the first of his shorter dream manuals, fol. 129a–b (Top. A1458.3).
73. Fol. 435a–b (Chester Beatty 3569).
74. Respectively, fol. 14b (Üniv. Ktp. A4437) and fol. 177a (Vat. 1304.2).
75. A monstrous beast that will mark the faces of believers and unbelievers.
76. A certain Jew who will come in the last days.
77. Fol. 24a (Top. A3175).
78. Respectively, fol. 19b (Carullah 1571) and fol. 129a–b (Top. A1458.3).
79. Fol. 435a–b (Chester Beatty 3569).
80. Fol. 24a (Top. A3175).
81. Respectively, fol. 19b (Carullah 1571) and fol. 435a–b (Chester Beatty 3569).
82. Fol. 435a–b (Chester Beatty 3569): "If he sees that on that day he is standing in the presence of God, [the punishment will be] harsher and more powerful and quicker. If he sees the graves and they are split open and the dead come forth from them, justice will be spread there. . . . If he sees that he is alone on the Day of Assembly, he is an oppressor, for [God] said: 'Assemble those who have wrought oppression and their wives' (Q 37.22). If he sees that he is in the resurrection, he will undertake a journey. If he sees the resurrection and he is at war, his people will be victorious over the enemy."
83. Fol. 24a (Top. A3175).
84. Fol. 19b (Carullah 1571), suggesting that a dream of the resurrection is "glad tidings for a man or a warning for him, depending on what he sees in sleep of good or fear and so on."
85. Fol. 435a–b (Chester Beatty 3569): "A man dreamt that the resurrection had occurred, that he was surrounded by cows and bulls and sheep, and that they were butting him, saying: 'Give us our due, for you have wronged us.' The man awoke and reported his dream to an interpreter who said: 'I don't think that this in actual fact will happen to you. Rather, the dream is meant to censure you. Thus, take care that you do what is good.'"
86. Fol. 24a (Top. A3175): "If he sees that the resurrection has happened and that he is watching its events and then he sees them cease and the world return to its [former] state, this signifies that oppression will follow on justice for

a people, none of whom are expecting oppression. It is said that this dream signifies that the one who has it is occupied in the pursuit of enmity or is a perpetrator of acts of disobedience, delaying repentance or resolute in dishonesty—as God said: 'If they were brought back, they would return to what has been forbidden them; verily they are liars' (Q 6.28)."

87. Fol. 28b (Yah. 196).

88. Fol. 15b (Üniv. Ktp. A4437).

89. Fol. 41b (Carullah 1571).

90. Fol. 176b (Vat. 1304.2).

91. Fol. 230a (Chester Beatty 3569).

92. Fol. 70b (Top. A3175).

93. Fol. 89a–b (Gar 930).

94. See Toufic Fahd, "Les corps des métiers au IVe/Xe siècle à Baġdād d'après le chapitre XII d'*al-Qādirī fī-t-ta^{c}bīr* de Dīnawarī," *Journal of the Social and Economic History of the Orient* 8 (1965): 186–212.

95. Fol. 60a (Yah. 196).

96. Kirmānī *apud* Ibn Shāhīn *Ishārāt* 340.

97. Fol. 186a (Carullah 1571).

98. Fol. 47a (Üniv. Ktp. A4437).

99. Fol. 195b (Chester Beatty 3569).

100. Fol. 58a (Top. A3175).

101. Fols. 77b–78a (Gar 930).

102. Fol. 192b (Vat. 1304.2).

103. See, for example, Sijistānī, fol. 47a (Üniv. Ktp. A4437) and the *Mumatti^{c}* of Qayrawānī, fol. 186b (Carullah 1571).

104. Fol. 60a (Yah. 196).

105. Kirmānī *apud* Ibn Shāhīn *Ishārāt* 338.

106. Fol. 47a (Üniv. Ktp. A4437).

107. Fol. 78a (Gar. 930).

108. Fol. 184a (Carullah 1571).

109. Fol. 192b (Vat. 1304.2).

110. Fol. 189a (Chester Beatty 3569).

111. Fol. 57a (Top. A3175): "A tailor is a man who unites men in what is good, whose blessing encompasses both the noble and the despised."

112. Fol. 189a (Chester Beatty 3569), cf. Kharkūshī, fol. 57a (Top. A3175).

113. Fol. 189a (Chester Beatty 3569). The first suggests that if you dream that you are sewing for yourself, this means that you "are a man with an upright religion, who is concerned about the situation of your soul." The second notes that dreams of sewing for one's wife means that evil and cares will befall the dreamer.

114. Fol. 57a (Top. A3175): "If he sees that he is sewing for himself, he himself will make the world upright in religion. . . . If he sees that he is sewing the clothing of a woman, there will befall him something shameful."

115. Fol. 60a (Yah. 196).

116. Reading *yuzīl* for *yuzayyin*.
117. Kirmānī *apud* Ibn Shāhīn *Ishārāt* 338.
118. Deleting *wa* before *ashghāl*.
119. Fol. 47a (Üniv. Ktp. A4437).
120. Fol. 199a (Chester Beatty 3569).
121. Qayrawānī, *Mumatti*[c], fol. 186b (Carullah 1571).
122. Qayrawānī, *Shorter Dream Manual II*, fol. 192b (Vat. 1304.2).
123. Kharkūshī, fol. 56a (Top. A3175).
124. Dārī flourished between ca. 400 A.H. and 635 A.H. For his dream manual's use Kharkūshī, see my "Some Notes on the Dream Manual of al-Dārī," *Rivista degli studi orientali* 70 (1996): 51–52.
125. Marshall G. S. Hodgson, *The Venture of Islam: Conscience and History in a World Civilization*, 3 vols. (Chicago: University of Chicago Press, 1974), 1:457.

CHAPTER FOUR. DREAM INTERPRETATION AND ORTHODOXY

1. Tarif Khalidi, *Arabic Historical Thought in the Classical Period*, Cambridge Studies in Islamic Civilization (Cambridge: Cambridge University Press, 1994), 7.
2. Toufic Fahd, *La divination arabe: Études religieuses, sociologiques et folkloriques sur le milieu natif de l'Islam* (Leiden: E. J. Brill, 1966), 257–58.
3. See, for example, Ibn Kathīr *Tafsīr* 4:202-3.
4. Fol. 2a (Yah. 196).
5. Fol. 2b (Carullah 1571).
6. Fol. 127b (Top. A1458.3).
7. Fol. 174b (Vat. 1304.2).
8. Fol. 1b (Chester Beatty 3569).
9. Fol. 2a (Top. A3175).
10. Fol. 1b (Üniv. Ktp. A4437).
11. Q 7.57, 27.63.
12. Q 25.22, 57.12, cf. 39.17.
13. Q 11.74, 11.69, 29.31, cf. 3.126, 8.10.
14. Q 25.48, 2.97, 16.89, 102, 27.2.
15. Q 46.12.
16. Ṭabarī *Jāmi*[c] *al-bayān* 6:577–82.
17. Ibid., 6:577.
18. Traditions 2-5, 9, 14–15, 23–24, and 40.
19. Tradition 2.
20. Traditions 1, 6–8, 17–22, 25.
21. Tradition 7.
22. Traditions 10–12, here citing number 11.
23. Tradition 13, cf. 38.
24. Tradition 16.

25. Ṭabarī *Jāmi*[c] *al-bayān* 6:581.
26. Ibid.
27. Yāqūt *Udabā*[c] 6:2462.
28. Ibid.
29. Muqātil b. Sulaymān, *Tafsīr*, fol. 170a (Top. A74/1).
30. [c]Abd al-Razzāq *Tafsīr* 2:296.
31. On him, see Fuat Sezgin, *Geschichte des arabischen Schriftums*, Bd. 1 (Leiden: E. J. Brill, 1967), 41.
32. Huwwārī *Tafsīr* 2:200–1.
33. Baghawī *Tafsīr* 2:360.
34. Ibn al-Jawzī *Zād al-masīr* 4:34.
35. Ibn Aṭīyah *Muḥarrar* 9:62–63.
36. Bukhārī *Ṣaḥīḥ* 9:37–58.
37. Muslim *Ṣaḥīḥ* 15:16–35.
38. Ibn Mājah *Sunan* 2:1286–94.
39. Abū Dāwūd *Sunan* 4:304–6.
40. Tirmidhī *Jāmi*[c] 4:532–43.
41. Nasā[c]ī *Sunan* 4:382–92.
42. [c]Abd al-Razzāq *Muṣannaf* 11:211–16.
43. Ibn Abī Shaybah *Muṣannaf* 7:230–46.
44. Dārimī *Sunan* 2:165–75.
45. Bukhārī *Ṣaḥīḥ* 9:37.
46. Ibid., 9:38–39.
47. Ibid., 9:39.
48. Ibid.
49. Ibid., 9:39–40.
50. Ibid., 9:40.
51. Ibid., 9:40–41.
52. For an overview, see Ibn Kathīr *Tafsīr* 4:534-38, with parallels to Bukhārī's tradition.
53. Bukhārī *Ṣaḥīḥ* 9:41–42.
54. Ibid., 9:42–43.
55. Ibid., 9:43–44.
56. Ibid.
57. Ibid., 9:44–45.
58. Ibid., 9:45.
59. Ibid., 9:45–58.
60. Ibid., 9:51.
61. Ibid., 9:47–48.
62. Ibid., 9:54, 54–55, 55–58.
63. Baghawī *Sharḥ* 12:202–53.
64. Ibid., 12:216–17.

65. Ibid., 12:233–34.

66. Top. A3165. For this manuscript see Fehmı Edhem Karatay, *Topkapı Sarayı Müzesi Arapça yazmalar kataloğu*, 4 vols. (Istanbul: Millî Eğitim Bakanlığı Yayınları, 1962–66), 3:887, who suggests that it was copied in 804H. The manuscript, however, seems not to bear scribal colophons or other indications of date.

67. That is, his *al-Ishārah ᶜilā ᶜilm al-ibārah* (ff. 1b–151a). Note that the title page falsely ascribes the work to Kharkūshī.

68. This poem is attributed by Karatay (*Arapça yazmalar*, 3:887) to "Ẓahīr [*sic*] ad-Dīn b. Aḥmad." It is, in fact, an excerpt of the dream manual of Ibn Ghannām (d. 674H), his *Durrat al-aḥlām fī taᶜbīr al-ruʾyā*. This work is extant in a great many copies. I know of about fifty. Among these: Princeton, Yah. 3886, 45 ff., 833H, and Yozgat 788.1, ff. 1a–52a, undated.

69. Including the *Fahrasah* of Ibn Khayr, for which, see p. 124.

70. For instance, again, in the *Fahrasah* of Ibn Khayr.

71. Many of these are mentioned in the Appendix.

72. The Jerusalem manuscript lists Ibn ᶜIrāk as one of its transmitters.

73. On him, see Dhahabī *Siyar* 21:85–86 (with parallels cited by the editor).

74. Ibn Bashkuwāl considered his work a continuation (hence its name) of Ibn al-Faraḍī's (d. 403H) *Taʾrīkh al-ᶜulamāʾ wa-l-ruwāt li-l-ᶜilm bi-l-Andalus*.

75. *Fahrasah* 1:266–67.

76. Ibn Bashkuwāl *Ṣilah* 1:332–33.

77. Ibid., 1:103.

78. Dhahabī *Siyar* 13:445–46.

79. Ibid., 11:389–91.

80. Ibn Bashkuwāl *Ṣilah* 1:160–61.

81. Dhahabī *Siyar* 16:110, Ibn al-Faraḍī *Taʾrīkh* 2:128–30.

82. The date is found in Ibn Khayr; for Abū Dharr, see Khaṭīb al-Baghdādī *Taʾrīkh Baghdād* 1:315–16.

83. Khaṭīb al-Baghdādī *Taʾrīkh Baghdād* 1:315.

84. Ibn Ḥajar *Tahdhīb* 5:70, who notes that he was sometimes called Abū ᶜAbd Allāh rather than Abū Jaᶜfar.

85. Ibid., 1:157. Ibn Khayr says that Abū Jaᶜfar received Kirmānī's dream manual from Ibn al-Ṭabbāᶜ in 278H. This cannot be correct. Abū Jaᶜfar would already have been dead. Either there is a textual error in Ibn Khayr's dossier or a link has fallen out of the riwāyah.

86. Ibn Bashkuwāl *Ṣilah* 1:154–57.

87. Ibid., 1:316–17.

88. Ibn al-Faraḍī *Taʾrīkh* 2:83–84.

89. Dhahabī *Siyar* 14:565–66.

90. Ibn Bashkuwāl *Ṣilah* 1:263–65.

91. Ibid., 1:264.

92. Ibn Khayr *Fahrasah* 1:289.
93. Ibn Bashkuwāl *Ṣilah* 2:478–80.
94. Ibid., 1:65–66.
95. Ibid., 2:649–50.
96. Ibid., 2:557–58.
97. Ibid., 1:141–43.
98. Dhahabı *Siyar* 17:236–37.
99. Ibid., 16:462.
100. Ibid., 15:427–28.
101. *Fahrasah* 1:233.4, 233.10–11, 235.14.
102. For this commentary, see chapter 1. Ibn al-Bannāʾ is also known to have compiled a work on dreams in which Ibn Ḥanbal appeared after his death. On this work, see the introduction to Makdisi's edition and translation of his diary, cited below.
103. G. Makdisi, ed. and tr., "Autograph Diary of an Eleventh-Century Historian of Baghdād," *Bulletin of the School of Oriental and African Studies* 18 (1956): 9–31, 239–60; 19 (1957): 13–48, 281–303, 426–43.
104. Num. 73.
105. Num. 107.
106. Num. 69.
107. Num. 99. Cf. Nums. 42, 44.
108. Num. 89.
109. Num. 7.
110. Num. 53.
111. Num. 128.
112. Num. 130.
113. *Rasāʾil ikhwān al-ṣafāʾ* 1:258–75.
114. Ibn Khaldūn *Taʾrīkh* 1:526.
115. Ibid., 1:530.
116. Ibid., 1:526.
117. One of the few attempts to treat dream interpretation in premodern Afro-Eurasia as a whole is A.-M. Esnoud et al., *Les songes et leur interprétation*, Sources orientales, vol. 2 (Paris: Éditions du Seuil, 1959). Among the cultures treated: the Egyptians, Babylonians, and Hittites, the peoples of Canaan and Israel, the Arabs and Persians, the Altaic peoples (Turkic, Mongolian, and Tungusic), the Kurds, the Indians, the Cambodians, the Chinese, and the Japanese.

CHAPTER FIVE. DREAM INTERPRETATION, HELLENISM, AND NON-MUSLIMS

1. See, for example, Patricia Cox Miller, *Dreams in Late Antiquity: Studies in the Imagination of a Culture* (Princeton: Princeton University Press, 1994)

and Gilbert Dagron, "Rêver de Dieu et parler de soi: Le rêve et son interprétation d'après les sources byzantines," in *I sogni nel medioevo*, ed. Tullio Gregory, Lessico intellettuale Europeo, no. 35 (Rome: Edizioni dell'Ateneo, 1985), 37–55. For the Latin tradition, see Jacqueline Amat, *Songes et visions: L'au-dela dans la littérature latine tardive* (Paris: Études Augustiniennes, 1985) and Martine Dulaey, *Le rêve dans la vie et la pensée de saint Augustin* (Paris: Études Augustiniennes, 1973).

2. *Pandecta scripturae sacrae* (Patrologia graeca [hereafter = PG] 89:1415–1849).

3. *hom.* 84 (PG 89:1687–92).

4. A conflation of Sirach 34.1, 2–3, 5–7.

5. See F. Halkin, *Bibliotheca hagiographica graeca*, 3rd ed. (Brussels: Société des Bollandistes, 1957), 1448s.

6. Jo. Cas. *coll.* 2.8 (Patrologia latina 95:535–36). For its *Nachleben* in the west, see Lynn Thorndike, *A History of Magic and Experimental Science*, 8 vols. (New York: Macmillan, 1923–58), 2:299.

7. "Rêver de Dieu et parler de soi," 40.

8. Gr. Nyss. *Eun.* 6.4. See also his *virg.* 3, where attention to portents, dreams, omens, and the like, are all described as a mark of foolishness.

9. Bas. *ep.* 211.

10. This linkage of hyperallegory and dream interpretation seems to have been a topos. See, for example, Gr. Naz. *or.* 45.12 (he situates his exegesis between a manner that is lowly and Jewish and one that is excessively contemplative, the latter being like τὸ ὀνειροκριτικόν); Bas. *hex.* 9.1 (those who "do not admit the common sense of Scripture" are "like the interpreters of dreams"); Gr. Nyss. *Eun.* 6.4 (not taking Scripture at face value is like what the dream interpreters do); Chrys. *fr. Job* (PG 64:520: "To interpret in a spiritual manner this list of animals [in Job 1.3] is not only like the procedures of dream interpretation but superfluous as well"). Cf. Maren Neihoff, "A Dream Which Is Not Interpreted Is Like a Letter Which Is Not Read," *Journal of Semitic Studies* 43 (1992): 58–84.

11. See, for example, Clem. *str.* 1.16 (the pagan Telmessians invented dream divination). The same was believed by Ps. Nonnos (Sebastian Brock, ed., *The Syriac Version of the Pseudo-Nonnos Mythological Scholia*, University of Cambridge Oriental Publications, no. 20 [Cambridge: Cambridge University Press, 1971], 116).

12. See, for example, Cyr. H. *catech.* 19.8 (dreams or evil spirits lead people astray, causing them to perform pagan rituals) and Thdt. *qu. in Dt.* 12 (PG 80:420) (on how and why God lets demons effect prophecies and miracles).

13. Eus. Al. *serm.* 21.4 (PG 86:423).

14. See, for example, Just. *1 apol.* 1.14 (demons use dreams and magic to deceive the believers); Athenag. *leg.* 27 (demons use dreams to lead astray the

ignorant, especially so as to give rise to idolatry); Tat. *or.* 18 (through dreams demons induce people to do things, and this, so as to ape the true God). Cf. Clem. *prot.* 1.2 (dream interpretation is a form of pagan madness).

15. See Jo. Clim. *scal.* 3 (PG 88:669–72), Gr. Nyss. *vir.* 13 (on those ascetics who put more faith in the illusions of their dreams than in the teachings of the Gospel), and Thdt. *h.e.* 4.10.

16. Bas. *hom. in psal.* 45 (PG 29:417). Cf. Jo. D. *parall.* at PG 95:1429C.

17. Ps.Chrys. *pseud.* 7 (PG 59:559).

18. Ephrem the Syrian, *On Admonition and Repentance* 13 (Nicene and Post-Nicene Fathers, ed. P. Schaff et al., II, 13:334).

19. *CT* 9.16.6, cf. *CJ* 9.18.7.

20. For an overview, see Giulio Guidorizzi, ed., *Pseudo-Niceforo: Libro dei sogni*, Koinonia, no. 5 (Naples: Associazione di studi tardoantichi, 1980), 7–26, as well as Steven M. Oberhelman, "Prolegomena to the Byzantine *Oneirokritika*," *Byzantion* 50 (1980): 487–503. I have not had access to G. Calofonos, "Byzantine Oneiromancy," M. Phil. Thesis, Birmingham, 1994. Translations of the Greek dream keys are available in Karl Brackertz, tr., *Die Volks-Traumbücher des byzantinischen Mittelalters* (Munich: C. H. Beck, 1993).

21. The standard edition: Franx X. Drexl, *Achmetis Oneirocriticon* (Leipzig: Teubner, 1925). Translations include: Steven M. Oberhelman, *The Oneirocriticon of Achmet: A Medieval Greek and Arabic Treatise on the Interpretation of Dreams* (Lubbock: Texas Tech University Press, 1991), and Karl Brackertz, *Das Traumbuch des Achmet ben Sirin* (Munich: Beck, 1986).

22. For example, *Achmetis Oneirocriticon* 29.19–30.10.

23. This argument was put into general circulation by Steven M. Oberhelman, "Two Marginal Notes from Achmet in the cod. Laurent. Plut. 87, 8," *Byzantinische Zeitschrift* 74 (1981): 326–27. It had, however, been suggested earlier by Toufic Fahd, "L'oniromancie orientale et ses répercussions sur l'oniromancie de l'occident médiéval," in *Oriente e occidente nel Medioevo: Filosofia e scienze*, eds. M. C. Hernandez, et al., Accademia Nazionale dei Lincei: Atti dei covegni, vol. 13 (Rome: Accademia Nazionale dei Lincei, 1971), 365.

24. Gabriel Rochefort, "Une anthologie grecque du XIe siècle: Le *Parisinus suppl. gr.* 690," *Scriptorium* 4 (1950): 5–6.

25. This argument for dating the oneirocriticon was first put forward, I think, by Daria Gigli, "Gli onirocritici del cod. Paris. suppl. gr. 690," *Prometheus* 4 (1978): 79–80.

26. For Leo Tuscus and his translation, see p. 167. Cf. S. Collin-Roset, ed., "Le *Liber thesauri occulti* de Pascalis Romanus (un traité d'interprétation des songes du XIIe siècle)," *Archives d'histoire doctrinale et littéraire du moyen âge* 30 (1963): 134, who argues that the oneirocriticon must already have appeared by 1165.

27. "Byzantium and the Christians in the World of Islam: Constantinople and the Church in the Holy Land in the Ninth Century," *Medieval Encounters* 3

(1997): 245. On this same subject, see his "The Monks of Palestine and the Growth of Christian Literature in Arabic," *The Muslim World* 78 (1988): 1–28.

28. "Greek Culture in Palestine after the Arab Conquest," in *Scritture, libri e testi nelle aree provinciali di Bisanzio*, ed. Guglielmo Cavallo et al., 2 vols. (Spoleto: Centro Italiano di studi sull'alto medioevo, 1991), 1:151.

29. *Achmetis Oneirocriticon* 1.3–14.

30. Ibid., 1.15–2.24.

31. Ibid., 2.26–3.11.

32. Ibid., 3.13–24.

33. Ibid., 3.22: οἱ ἀρχαῖοι φαραωνῖται. The translation is uncertain. The only other occurrence of the word appears to be that found in the Ps.Jo. D. *hom.* 5 (PG 96:653A) where φαραωνίτην ἄνακτα refers to the Pharaoh himself.

34. *Achmetis Oneirocriticon* 240.6-241.26 returns to theoretical matters. It is not clear whether it is original or a later addition. See Gigli, "Paris. suppl. gr. 690," 81.

35. *Achmetis Oneirocriticon* 137.23–29.

36. Over a century ago, N. Bland ("On the Muhammedan Science of Tâbír, or Interpretation of Dreams," *Journal of the Royal Asiatic Society* 16 [1856]: 169–71) pointed out that the name Achmet seems to have been "prefixed to the work without much authority to justify its use." He notes that the Latin translation of Leo Tuscus (see p. 167) does not have this ascription; that of the Greek mss. on which the *editio princeps* was based only one had in a later hand "Achmetes"; and that the Latin translation of Leunclavius (see p. 168) ascribes the work to Apomazares (that is, Abū Maᶜshar).

37. *Achmets Traumbuch: Einleitung und Probe eines kritischen Textes* (Freising: F. P. Datterer, 1909), 1–5.

38. C.-E. Ruelle, "La clef des songes d'Achmet Abou-Mazar: Fragment inédit et bonnes variantes," *Revue des études grecques* 7 (1894): 350; Otto Gotthardt, *Über die Traumbücher des Mittelalters*, Königliches Luthergymnasium zu Eisleben, Progr. Nr. 334 (Eisleben: Ernst Schneider, 1912), 2–4; Lynn Thorndike, *History of Magic*, 2:292, n. 3.

39. Bland, "Muhammedan Science of Tâbír," 169–71.

40. See, for example, Ibn Shāhīn *Ishārāt* 3, Ḥājjī Khalīfah *Kashf* 2:1517, Bağdatlı *Hadīyah* 1:569, and Tiflīsī *Kāmil* 25.

41. Hans-Georg Beck, *Geschichte der byzantinischen Volksliteratur*, Byzantinisches Handbuch, Teil 2, Bd. 3 (Munich: C. H. Beck, 1971), 203; Karl Brackertz, *Traumbuch des Achmet*, 10–11; Steven M. Oberhelman, *Oneirocriticon of Achmet*, 12–13; Fahd, "L'oniromancie orientale," 363–68.

42. Oberhelman, *Oneirocriticon of Achmet*, 16–17.

43. Dagron, "Rêver de Dieu et parler de soi," 49.

44. *Achmetis Oneirocriticon* 3.26–4.2.

45. Ibn Qutaybah, fol. 25b (Yah. 196).

46. Kharkūshī, fol. 24a (Top. A3175).
47. Qayrawānī, *Mumatti*^{c}, fol. 19b (Carullah 1571).
48. *Achmetis Oneirocriticon* 129.13–17.
49. Ibn Qutaybah, fol. 28b (Yah. 196).
50. Sijistānī, fol. 15b (Üniv. Ktp. A4437).
51. Qayrawānī, *Mumatti*^{c}, fol. 41b (Carullah 1571).
52. Ibn Sīnā, fol. 89a–b (Gar. 930), citing the opinion of the Arabs.
53. *Achmetis Oneirocriticon* 29.19–30.10.
54. Qayrawānī, *Mumatti*^{c}, fol. 73a (Carullah 1571), citing Ibn Ḥabīb (< Wāqidī).
55. Ibn Sa^{c}d *Ṭabaqāt* 5:93 (< Wāqidī). Cf. parallel in Dhahabī *Siyar* 4:236.
56. Dīnawarī, fol. 99a (Chester Beatty 3569).
57. Kharkūshī, fol. 35a14–17 (Top. A3175). Cf. parallel in Dārī *Muntakhab* 184.

58. Guidorizzi (*Libro dei sogni*, 18, n. 41) suggests that there is little evidence that Artemidorus was among the oneirocriticon's direct sources. To the contrary, Oberhelman (*Oneirocriticon of Achmet*, 18–19) has argued for its extensive use of Artemidorus. This is a subject that needs to be reexamined.

59. Oleg Grabar, "Islamic Influence on Byzantine Art," *Oxford Dictionary of Byzantium* (1991), 2:1018–19.

60. André Grabar, *L'art de la fin de l'antiquité et du moyen âge*, 3 vols. (Paris: Collège de France, 1984), 1:286.

61. N. P. Kondakov, "Les costumes orientaux à la cour byzantine," *Byzantion* 1 (1924): 7–49, esp. 15-17 for clothing *à la mode sarrasine*.

62. Timothy E. Gregory, "Ceramics," *Oxford Dictionary of Byzantium* (1991), 1:400; id., "Sgraffito Ware," *Oxford Dictionary of Byzantium* (1991), 3:1886.

63. R. Ettinghausen, "Kufesque in Byzantine Greece, the Latin West and the Muslim World," *A Colloquium in Memory of George Carpenter Miles (1904–1975)* (New York: American Numismatic Society, 1976), 28–47.

64. Grabar, "Islamic Influence," 1019. Very much the opposite has been observed vis-à-vis the influx of Arab astronomical knowledge, which reached its apogee only at the end of the Byzantine era. See Joseph Mogenet, "L'influence de l'astronomie arabe à Byzance du IXe au XIVe siècle," in *Colloques d'histoire des sciences, I (1972) et II (1973): I. Résistance et ouverture aux découvertes et aux théories scientifiques dans le passé*, Université de Louvain, Receueil de travaux d'histoire et de philologie, 6th series, fasc. 9 (Louvain: Éditions Nauwelaerts, 1976), 45–55.

65. The most obvious example is a ninth-century refutation of the Koran by Nicetas of Byzantium (PG 105:669–806), who had direct access to the Arabic text of the Koran.

66. See Beck, *Geschichte der byzantinischen Volksliteratur*, 41–44, and Lars Olaf Sjöberg, ed., *Stephanites und Ichnelates: Überlieferungsgeschichte und Text*, Acta Universitatis Upsaliensis: Studia Graeca Upsaliensia, no. 2 (Stockholm: Almqvist & Wiksells, 1962).

67. See, for example, Alexander P. Kazhdan and Ann Wharton Epstein, *Change in Byzantine Culture in the Eleventh and Twelfth Centuries*, The Transformation of the Classical Heritage, no. 7 (Berkeley: University of California Press, 1985), 149–50.

68. See David Pingree, *From Astral Omens to Astrology from Babylon to Bīkāner*, Serie orientale roma, 78 (Rome: Istituto italiano per l'Africa e l'oriente, 1997), 76–77.

69. This Symeon was probably of eastern origin, perhaps from Antioch. See Beck, *Geschichte der byzantinischen Volksliteratur*, 41–42; Alexander P. Kazhdan, "Seth, Symeon," *Oxford Dictionary of Byzantium* (1991), 3:1882–83. For Arabic astrological lore in Symeon's work, see Mogenet, "Astronomie arabe à Byzance," 49.

70. In addition to Mogenet's "Astronomie arabe à Byzance," see his "Une scholie inédite du Vat. gr. 1594 sur les rapports entre l'astronomie arabe et Byzance," *Osiris* 14 (1962): 198–221, as well as A. Tihon, "L'Astronomie Byzantine (du Ve au XVe siècle)," *Byzantion* 51 (1981): 603–24; O. Neugebauer, "Commentary on the Astronomical Treatise Par. gr. 2425," *Mémoires de l'Académie Royale de Belgique, Cl. des lettres* 59.4 (1969): 5–45; and Paul Kunitzsch, "Die arabische Herkunft von zwei Sternverzeichnissen in cod. Vat. gr. 1056," *Zeitschrift der deutschen morgenländischen Gesellschaft* 120 (1970): 281–87; and the introduction to Alexander Jones, *An Eleventh-Century Manual of Arabo-Byzantine Astronomy*, Corpus des astronomes byzantins, no. 3 (Amsterdam: Gieben, 1987).

71. For an overview, see David Pingree and Alexander P. Kazhdan, "Astrology," *Oxford Dictionary of Byzantium* (1991), 1:215–18, as well as Pingree, *From Astral Omens to Astrology*, 63–77.

72. David Pingree, ed., *Albumasaris de revolutionibus nativitatum* (Leipzig: Teubner, 1968), translated from Arabic into Greek ca. 1000 and from Greek into Latin in the thirteenth century. See also Herbert Hunger, *Die hochsprachliche profane Literatur der Byzantiner*, 2 vols., Byzantinisches Handbuch, Teil 5, Bd. 2 (Munich: C. H. Beck, 1978), 234–35.

73. Tamsyn Barton, *Ancient Astrology*, Sciences of Antiquity (London: Routledge, 1994), 64–85, and U. Riedinger, *Die heilige Schrift im Kampf der griechischen Kirche gegen die Astrologie von Origenes bis Johannes von Damaskos* (Innsbruck: Universitätverlag, 1956).

74. Ibn Khaldūn *Ta'rīkh* 1:531–35.

75. R. Duval, ed., *Lexicon Syriacum*, 3 vols. (Paris: e Reipublica typographao, 1888–1901).

76. Sezgin knew two manuscripts, only one complete: Hekimoğlu Ali Paşa 572.1, ff. 1a–291a, 556H, and Fâtih 5411.4, ff. 113a–136b, 688H. For another, Vat. ar. 1304.7, see my "New Light on the Textual Tradition of Bar Bahlūl's *Book of Signs*," *Le muséon* 112 (1999): 227-30. The *Book of Signs* has been edited by Yūsuf Ḥabbī, *Kitāb al-dalā'il li-l-Ḥasan b. al-Bahlūl* (Kuwait: Manshūrāt Ma'had

al-Makhṭūṭāt al-ᶜArabīyah, 1987). Ḥabbī also published portions of it as articles (see the Bibliography). For a facsimile edition, see Fuat Sezgin, *The Book of Indications (Kitāb al-Dalāʾil) by al-Ḥasan ibn al-Bahlūl (Tenth Century* A.D.*)*, Publications of the Institute for the History of Arabic-Islamic Science, C10 (Frankfurt am Main: Institut für Geschichte der Arabisch-Islamischen Wissenschaften, 1985). I cite the *Book of Signs* from Ḥabbī's edition.

77. Duval, *Lexicon Syriacum*, x, xxv.

78. Ibn Abī ᶜUṣaybiᶜah *ᶜUyūn* 158, reading *al-Ṭīrhānī* for *al-Ṭ.b.rhānī*. But cf. Yāqūt *Buldān* 5:223, where it is said that al-Ṭ.b.rhān is in the district of Mawṣil.

79. For Awānā, see Yāqūt *Buldān* 1:274 and Samᶜānī *Ansāb* 1:225. Alternatively, it may here be a question of the village of Awānā located in Beth Nuhadre, beyond Mawṣil, on which, see G. Hoffman, *Auszüge aus syrischen Akten persischer Märtyrer*, Abhandlugen für die Kunde des Morgenlandes, Bd. 7.3 (Leipzig: F. A. Brockhaus, 1880), 211. For Ṭīrhān, see Guy Le Strange, *Lands of the Eastern Caliphate* (Cambridge: Cambridge University Press, 1905), 34.

80. Duval, *Lexicon Syriacum*, x, xxv.

81. Ibid., xi.

82. Henricus Gismondi, ed., *Maris Amri et Slibae de patriarchis nestorianorum commentaria: Pars prior, Maris textus arabicus* (Rome: Excudebat C. de Luigi, 1899), 101.

83. Ibn Abī ᶜUṣaybiᶜah *ᶜUyūn* 158, concerning Bar Bahlūl's translation of the *Little Kunnāshah* of John the son of Serapion (fl. 9th c. A.D.). It should also be noted that this John is frequently cited as an authority in Bar Bahlūl's lexicon. See Duval, *Lexicon Syriacum*, xx-xxi.

84. See Duval, *Lexicon Syriacum*, xiii-xxiv.

85. Ibid., xxiv. For Sinān b. Thābit, see Ibn Abī ᶜUṣaybiᶜah *ᶜUyūn* 300–304.

86. Duval, *Lexicon Syriacum*, xix.

87. *Dalāʾil*, 56.

88. Ibid., 382–439.

89. Ibid., 382–85.

90. Ibid., 384.

91. Ibid., 385–439.

92. "They say" at ibid., 393, 396, 399, 412; Ibn Sīrīn at 396, 411, 414; the Prophet at 400.

93. Ibid., 390.

94. Ibid., 386–87.

95. Ibid., 388.

96. Ibid., 392.

97. Ibid., 400.

98. This a subject I have treated in brief elsewhere: "The Sources of Ibn Bahlūl's Chapter on Dream Divination," *Studia patristica*, vol. 33 (Louvain: Peeters Press, 1996), 553–57.

99. See my "New Light," 227–30.

100. Democritus at *Dalā'il* 57; Galen at 58, 189; Hippocrates at 63–5; Aristotle at 67.

101. Ibid., 72–5.

102. Ibn Rabbān and Kindī at ibid., 324, 128; Rāzī (used anonymously) on physiognomy (see discussion by Ḥabbī at 199).

103. Abū ʿAbd Allāh Muḥammad b. Ziyād b. al-ʿArābī (Dhahabī *Siyar* 10:687–88).

104. Ibn ʿAbbās at *Dalā'il* 195; Ibn al-ʿArābī at 178, 187, 197, 201, 203, 205–6, 208, 210, 214; Ibn Qutaybah at 59, 60, 97, 145, 175, 187.

105. Ancients at ibid., 85, 162; ancient and reliable books at 168; Arabs at 61, 67, 86, 121, 127; doctors at 325; Greeks at 89; pagans at 73; philosophers at 328; poets of the Arabs at 88–89, 112–13, 121–22, 127, 137.

106. See, e.g., the discussion in Joel Kraemer, *Humanism in the Renaissance of Islam: The Cultural Revival during the Buyid Age*, 2nd edition (Leiden: E. J. Brill, 1992), 2–10.

107. Ibn Abī ʿUṣaybiʿah *ʿUyūn* 432–3; Ṭāshkubrīzādeh *Miftāḥ* 1:336; Ḥājjī Khalīfah *Kashf* 2:1498 and 1:416; Bağdatlı *Hadīyah* 1:806.

108. For the dream manual of Porphyry, see Ibn al-Nadīm *Fihrist* 378. For the dream manuals of Euclid, Ptolemy, Aristotle, and Plato, see Ḥājjī Khalīfah *Kashf* 1:417.

109. The Armenian oneirocritic tradition has not to my knowledge been studied. For one Armenian dream book translated from Arabic, see Jacobus Dashian, *Catalog der armenischen Handscriften in der Mechitharisten-Bibliothek zu Wien*, in *Haupt-Catalog der armenischen Handscriften*, Bd. 1, Bk. 2 (Vienna: Mechitharisten-Buchdruckerel, 1895), 56. That there are Armenian works ascribed to Ibn Sīrīn is something I was told by Professor Peter S. Cowe.

110. See Anton Baumstark, *Geschichte der syrischen Literatur* (Bonn: A. Marcus und E. Webers Verlag, 1922), 318.

111. G. Furlani, ed., "Une clef des songes en syriaque," *Revue de l'orient chrétien*, 3rd series, 2 (1920/21): 118–44, 225–48. Cf. Franx X. Drexl "Achmet und das syrische Traumbuch des Cod. syr. or. 4434 des Brit. Mus.," *Byzantinische Zeitschrift* 30 (1929/30): 110–13.

112. Furlani, "Clef des songes," 118.

113. See his "Die arabischen Fragmente der Cairo-Genizah zu Cambridge," in *Verhandlungen des XIII. internationalen Orientalisten-Kongresses, Hamburg September 1902* (Leiden: E. J. Brill, 1904), 306–8, as well as his "The Arabic Portion of the Cairo Genizah at Cambridge," *Jewish Quarterly Review* 15 (1902–3): 167–81.

114. See Fahd, "Oniromancie orientale," 370-71.

115. See, for example, Joshua Trachtenberg, *Jewish Magic and Superstition: A Study in Folk Religion* (New York: Behrman's Jewish Book House, 1939), 237–38. For a translation, see Yaakov Elman, *Dream Interpretation from Classical Jewish Sources* (Hoboken: Ktav, 1998).

116. These events are described in Leo's introduction to his translation. For the passage in question, see Charles H. Haskin, "Leo Tuscus," *Byzantinische Zeitschrift* 24 (1923/24): 45–47, and id., "Leo Tuscus," *The English Historical Review* 33 (1918): 492–96. For Hugo and Leo, see Antoine Dondaine, "Hugues Éthérien et Léon Toscan." *Archives d'histoire doctrinale et littéraire du moyen âge* 19 (1952): 67–134.

117. For an edition and study, see Collin-Roset, "*Liber thesauri occulti,*" (cited above). As argued by Collin-Roset (p. 133–34), while part of Romanus' Ps. Achmet-citations come from Leo's version, part appear to have been original translations on the part of Romanus.

118. See Thorndike, *History of Magic*, 2:297–300.

119. See R. A. Pack, ed., "De pronosticatione sompniorum Libellus Guillelmo de Aragonia adscriptus," *Archives d'histoire doctrinale et littéraire du moyen âge* 33 (1966): 237–93; for its use of Achmet, see esp. 247.

120. See R. A. Pack, ed., "A Treatise on Prognostications by Venancius of Moerbeke," *Archives d'histoire doctrinale et littéraire du moyen âge* 43 (1976): 311–22.

121. For a brief history and bibliography of the early editions and translations of the oneirocriticon, see Drexl, *Einleitung*, 6–9, and Ruelle, "Achmet Abou-Mazar," 305–7.

122. See M. G. Glover, "Critical Edition of the Middle French Version of Achmet ibn Sirin's Oneiromancy Found in MS. Français 1317 folios 51r–106v, Paris, Bibliothèque Nationale, entitled (cy commence la table des) Exposicions et significacions des songes par Daniel et autres exposez," Ph.D. dissertation, London, Birkbeck College, 1992.

123. F. V. Vykoukal, *O snech a vykladech snu: Kulturni obrazek* (Prague: F. Simacek, 1898). I am dependent on Gotthardt's summary, *Traumbücher des Mittelalters*, 1–2.

CONCLUSIONS

1. *The Venture of Islam: Conscience and History in a World Civilization*, 3 vols. (Chicago: University of Chicago Press, 1974), 1:59–60. Hodgson adopted the term "Islamdom," because he found expressions like "Islamic world" to be inaccurate: "If there is to be an 'Islamic world,' this can only be in the future" (ibid., 1:58).

2. Ibid., 1:411–12. Cf. his discussion of philosophy in "The Interrelations of Societies in History," in *Rethinking World History: Essays on Europe, Islam, and World History*, ed. Edmund Burke III (Cambridge: Cambridge University Press, 1993), 14.

3. Hodgson, *Venture*, 1:58.

4. Ibid., 1:90.

5. Hodgson, "Interrelations of Societies," 17.

6. Edmund Burke III, "Marshall G. S. Hodgson and the Hemispheric Interregional Approach to World History," *Journal of World History* 6 (1995): 237–50; id., "Islamic History as World History: Marshall G. S. Hodgson and The Venture of Islam," in *Rethinking World History*, 301–28; id., "Marshall G. S. Hodgson and World History," ix–xxi.

7. Jerry H. Bentley , "Hemispheric Integration, 500–1500 C.E.," *Journal of World History* 9 (1998): 237–54. Cf. his *Old World Encounters: Cross-Cultural Contacts and Exchanges in Premodern Times* (New York: Oxford University Press, 1993).

8. Andre Gunder Frank, "A Plea for World System History," *Journal of World History* 2 (1991): 1–28; id. "The Thirteenth-Century World System: A Review Essay," *Journal of World History* 1 (1990): 249–56.

9. Frank, "Plea for World System History," 1.

10. *Agricultural Innovation in the Early Islamic World: The Diffusion of Crops and Farming Techniques, 700–1100*, Cambridge Studies in Islamic Civilization (Cambridge: Cambridge University Press, 1983), 77–83.

11. Notable examples include Lynda Shaffer, "Southernization," *Journal of World History* 5 (1994): 1–21; Arnold Pacey, *Technology in World Civilization: A Thousand Year History* (Oxford: Blackwell, 1990); P. Huard, "Sciences et techniques de l'Eurasie," *Bulletin de la société des études indo-chinoises*, 2nd series, vol. 15 (1950), 111–48; and Lynn White, *Medieval Technology and Social Change* (Oxford: Oxford University Press, 1962); id., "Tibet, India, and Malaya as Sources of Western Medieval Technology," *The American Historical Review* 65 (1960): 515–26; id., "Technology and Invention in the Middle Ages," *Speculum* 15 (1940): 141–59.

12. White, "Tibet, India, and Malaya," 526.

13. See Georges Ifrah, *From One to Zero: A Universal History of Numbers*, trans. Lowell Bair (New York: Viking Penguin, 1985), 428–89.

14. *From Astral Omens to Astrology from Babylon to Bīkāner*, Serie orientale Roma, vol. 78 (Rome: Istituto italiano per l'Africa e l'oriente, 1997), 9.

15. *Greek Thought, Arabic Culture: The Graeco-Arabic Translation Movement in Baghdad and Early ʿAbbāsid Society (2nd–4th/8th–10th centuries)* (London: Routledge, 1998), 192.

BIBLIOGRAPHY

ᶜAbd al-Razzāq *Muṣannaf* = Abū Bakr ᶜAbd al-Razzāq b. Hammām al-Sanᶜānī. *al-Muṣannaf.* 12 vols. Ed. Ḥabīb al-Raḥmān al-Aᶜẓamī. Second Printing. Beirut: al-Maktab al-Islāmī, 1983.

ᶜAbd al-Razzāq *Tafsīr* = Id. *Tafsīr al-Qurʾān.* 4 vols. Ed. Muṣṭafā Muslim Muḥammad. Riyadh: Maktabat al-Rushd, 1989.

Abū Dāwūd *Sunan* = Abū Dāwūd Sulaymān b. al-Ashᶜath al-Sijistānī al-Azdī. *Sunan.* 4 vols. Ed. Muḥammad Muḥyī al-Dīn ᶜAbd al-Ḥamīd. Beirut: Dār Iḥyāʾ al-Sunnah al-Nabawīyah, n.d.

Abū Nuᶜaym *Ḥilyah* = Abū Nuᶜaym Aḥmad b. ᶜAbd Allāh al-Iṣfahānī. *Ḥilyat al-awliyāʾ wa-ṭabaqāt al-aṣfiyāʾ.* 10 vols. Beirut: Dār al-Fikr, n.d.

Abū Ṭayyib al-Lughawī *Marātib* = Abū Ṭayyib ᶜAbd al-Wāḥid b. ᶜAlī al-Lughawī al-Ḥalabī. *Marātib al-naḥwīyīn.* Ed. Muḥammad Abū al-Faḍl Ibrāhīm. Cairo: Maktabat Nahḍāt Miṣr wa-Maṭbaᶜatihā, 1955.

Afnan, Soheil M. *Avicenna: His Life and Works.* London: G. Allen and Unwin, 1958.

al-Akili, Muhammad M. *Ibn Seerīn's Dictionary of Dreams accord to Islāmic Inner Traditions.* Philadelphia: Pearl Publishing House, 1992.

Amat, Jacqueline. *Songes et visions: L'au-delà dans la littérature latine tardive.* Paris: Études Augustiniennes, 1985.

ᶜĀmirī *Amad* = Abū al-Ḥasan Muḥammad b. Yūsuf al-ᶜĀmirī. *Kitāb al-amad ᶜalā al-abad.* Ed. and trans. K. Everett Rowson. *A Muslim Philosopher on the Soul and Its Fate: al-ᶜĀmirī's Kitāb al-amad ᶜalā l-abad.* American Oriental Series, vol. 70. New Haven: American Oriental Society, 1988.

Anawati, G. C. "The Kitāb al-Jāmahir [*sic*] fī Maᶜrifah al-Jawāhir of al-Bīrūnī." In *Al-Bīrūnī Commemorative Volume.* Ed. Hakim Mohammed Said. Karachi: The Times Press, 1979. 437–53.

Arberry, A. J. "Khargūshī's Manual of Ṣufism." *Bulletin of the School of Oriental and African Studies* 9 (1937/39): 345–49.

Arshi, Imtiyaz Ali. *Catalogue of the Arabic Manuscripts in Raza Library, Rampur.* 6 vols. to date. Rampur: Raza Library Trust, 1963–.

Asnawī *Ṭabaqāt* = Jamāl al-Dīn ᶜAbd al-Raḥīm b. al-Ḥasan al-Asnawī. *Ṭabaqāt al-Shāfiᶜīyah.* 2 vols. Ed. ᶜAbd Allāh al-Jubūrī. Baghdad: Maṭbaᶜat al-Irshād, 1970–71.

Bābā al-Tunbuktī *Nayl* = Abū al-ᶜAbbās Aḥmad b. Aḥmad. *Nayl al-ibtihāj bi-taṭrīz al-dībāj*. In the margin of Ibn Farḥūn *Dībāj* (see below).

Bağdatlı *Hadīyah* = Bağdatlı İsmail Paşa. *Hadīyat al-ᶜārifīn asmāʾ al-muʾallifīn wa-āthār al-muṣannifīn min kashf al-ẓunūn ᶜan asāmī al-kutub wa-l-funūn*. 2 vols. Eds. Mahmud Kemal İnal and Avni Aktuç. Beirut: Dār al-Kutub al-ᶜIlmīyah, 1992.

Bağdatlı *Īḍāḥ* = Id. *Īḍāḥ al-maknūn fī al-dhayl ᶜalā kashf al-ẓunūn*. 2 vols. Eds. Şerefettin Yaltkaya and Kilisli Rifat Bilge. Beirut: Dār al-Kutub al-ᶜIlmīyah, 1992.

Baghawī *Sharḥ* = Abū Muḥammad al-Ḥusayn b. Masᶜūd al-Baghawī. *Sharḥ al-sunnah*. 16 vols. Eds. Shuᶜayb al-Arnāʾūṭ et al. Beirut: al-Maktab al-Islāmī, 1971–83.

Baghawī *Tafsīr* = Id. *Tafsīr al-Baghawī al-musammā Maᶜālim al-tanzīl*. 4 vols. Eds. Khālid ᶜAbd al-Raḥmān and Marwān Suwār al-ᶜUk. Beirut: Dār al-Maᶜrifah, 1987.

Bar Bahlūl *Dalāʾil* = al-Ḥasan b. al-Bahlūl. *Kitāb al-dalāʾil li-l-Ḥasan b. al-Bahlūl*. Ed. Yūsuf Ḥabbī. Kuwait: Manshūrāt Maᶜhad al-Makhṭūṭāt al-ᶜArabīyah, 1987.

Barton, Tamsyn. *Ancient Astrology*. Sciences of Antiquity. London: Routledge, 1994.

Baumstark, Anton. *Geschichte der syrischen Literatur*. Bonn: A. Marcus und E. Webers Verlag, 1922.

Bausani, A. "I sogni nell'Islam." In *I sogni del medioevo*. Ed. Tullio Gregory. Lessico intellettuale europeo, no. 35. Rome: Edizioni dell'Ateneo, 1985. 25–36.

Bayhaqī *Dalāʾil* = Abū Bakr Aḥmad b. al-Ḥusayn al-Bayhaqī. *Dalāʾil al-nubūwah wa-maᶜrifat aḥwāl ṣāḥib al-sharīᶜah*. 7 vols. Ed. ᶜAbd al-Muᶜṭī Qalᶜajī. Beirut: Dār al-Kutub al-ᶜIlmīyah, 1988.

Bayhaqī *Jāmiᶜ* = Id. *al-Jāmiᶜ li-shuᶜab al-īmān*. 10 vols. Ed. ᶜAbd al-ᶜAlī ᶜAbd al-Ḥamīd Ḥāmid. Bombay: al-Dār al-Salafīyah, 1986-90.

Bayhaqī *Taʾrīkh* = Abū al-Ḥasan ᶜAlī b. Zayd al-Bayhaqī. *Taʾrīkh ḥukamāʾ al-Islām*. Ed. Muḥammad Kurd ᶜAlī. Damascus: Maṭbūᶜāt al-Majmaᶜ al-ᶜIlmī al-ᶜArabī, 1946.

Beck, Hans-Georg. *Geschichte der byzantinischen Volksliteratur*. Byzantinisches Handbuch, Teil 2, Bd. 3. Munich: C. H. Beck, 1971.

Bentley, Jerry H. "Hemispheric Integration, 500–1500 C.E." *Journal of World History* 9 (1998): 237–54.

———. *Old World Encounters: Cross-Cultural Contacts and Exchanges in Pre-Modern Times*. New York: Oxford University Press, 1993.

al-Bīrūnī, Abū al-Rayhān Muḥammad b. Aḥmad al-Bīrūnī. *Kitāb al-jamāhir fī maᶜrifat al-jawāhir*. Hyderabad: Maṭbaᶜat Jamᶜīyat Dāʾirat al-Maᶜārif al-ᶜUthmānīyah, 1355/1936.

Bland, N. "On the Muhammedan Science of Tâbír, or Interpretation of Dreams." *Journal of the Royal Asiatic Society* 16 (1856): 118–71.

Bloch, Marc. *The Historian's Craft*. New York: Vintage Books, 1953.

Blum, Claes. *Studies in the Dream Book of Artemidorus: Inaugural Dissertation*. Uppsala: Almqvist & Wiksells, 1936.

Bosworth, Clifford Edmund. *The History of the Saffarids of Sistan and the Maliks of Nimruz* (247/861 to 949/1542–3). Columbia Lectures on Iranian Studies, no. 8. Costa Mesa, Calif., and New York: Mazda Publishers in association with Bibliotheca Persica, 1994.

Brackertz, Karl, trans. *Die Volks-Traumbücher des byzantinischen Mittelalters*. Munich: C. H. Beck, 1993.

———, trans. *Das Traumbuch des Achmet ben Sirin*. Munich: C. H. Beck, 1986.

Breen, A. "Observations on the Arabic Translation of Artemidorus, Book I." *Le muséon* 101 (1988): 179–81.

Brock, Sebastian, ed. and trans. *The Syriac Version of the Pseudo-Nonnos Mythological Scholia.* University of Cambridge Oriental Publications, no. 20. Cambridge: Cambridge University Press, 1971.

Browne, Gerald M. "Ad Artemidorum Arabum II." *Le muséon* 103 (1990): 267–82.

———. "Ad Artemidorum Arabum." *Le muséon* 97 (1984): 207–20.

Bukhārī *Ṣaḥīḥ* = Muḥammad b. Ismāʿīl al-Bukhārī. *al-Jāmiʿ al-Ṣaḥīḥ.* 9 vols. in 3. Ed. Aḥmad Muḥammad Shākir. Beirut: Dār al-Jīl, n.d.

Burke, Edmund, III. "Marshall G. S. Hodgson and the Hemispheric Interregional Approach to World History." *Journal of World History* 6 (1995): 237–50.

———. "Islamic History as World History: Marshall G. S. Hodgson and The Venture of Islam." In *Rethinking World History: Essays on Europe, Islam, and World History.* Cambridge: Cambridge University Press, 1993. 301–28.

———. "Marshall G. S. Hodgson and World History." In *Rethinking World History: Essays on Europe, Islam, and World History.* Cambridge: Cambridge University Press, 1993. ix–xxi.

Calofonos, G. "Byzantine Oneiromancy." M. Phil. Thesis. Birmingham, 1994.

Collin-Roset, S., ed. "Le *Liber thesauri occulti* de Pascalis Romanus (un traité d'interprétation des songes du XIIᵉ siècle)." *Archives d'histoire doctrinale et littéraire du moyen âge* 30 (1963): 111–98.

Cook, Michael. "Eschatology and the Dating of Early Traditions." *Princeton Papers in Near Eastern Studies* 1 (1992): 23–47.

Corbin, H. "The Visionary Dream in Islamic Spirituality." In *The Dream and Human Societies.* Eds. G. E. von Grunebaum and Roger Caillois. Berkeley and Los Angeles: University of California Press, 1966. 381–408.

Dabbāgh *Maʿālim* = ʿAbd al-Raḥmān b. Muḥammad al-Dabbāgh. *Maʿālim al-īmān fī maʿrifat ahl al-Qayrawān.* 4 vols. in 2. Tunis: Matbaʿah al-ʿArabīyah al-Tunisīyah, 1320/1902.

Dagron, Gilbert. "Rêver de Dieu et parler de soi: Le rêve et son interprétation d'après les sources byzantines." In *I sogni nel medioevo.* Ed. Tullio Gregory. Lessico intellettuale Europeo, no. 35. Rome: Edizioni dell'Ateneo, 1985. 37–55.

Daïm, A. Abdel. *L'oniromancie arabe d'après Ibn Sîrîn.* Damascus: Presses Universitaires, 1958.

al-Dāraquṭnī, Abū al-Ḥasan ʿAlī b. ʿUmar. *Ruʾyat Allāh jalla wa-ʿalā.* Ed. Mabrūk Ismāʿīl Mabrūk. Cairo: Maktabat al-Qurʾān, n.d.

Dārī *Muntakhab* = Abū ʿAlī al-Ḥusayn b. al-Ḥasan al-Khalīlī al-Dārī. *al-Imām Muḥammad b. Sīrīn: Muntakhab al-kalām fī tafsīr al-aḥlām.* Ed. ʿAbd al-Raḥmān al-Jūzū. Beirut: Dār Maktabat al-Ḥayāt, n.d.

Dārimī *Sunan* = ʿAbd Allāh b. ʿAbd al-Raḥmān al-Dārimī al-Samarqandī. *Sunan.* 2 vols. Eds. Fawwāz Aḥmad Zamarlī and Khālid al-Sabʿ al-ʿAlamī. Beirut: Dār al-Kitāb al-ʿArabī, 1987.

Dashian, Jacobus. *Catalog der armenischen Handschriften in der Mechitharisten-Bibliothek zu Wien.* In *Hauptcatalog der armenischen Handscriften*, Bd. 1.2. Vienna: Mechitharisten-Buchdruckerel, 1895.

Defter-i Kütüphane-i Atıf Efendi. Istanbul: n.p., 1893.

Dhahabī *ᶜIbar* = Abū ᶜAbd Allāh Muḥammad b. Aḥmad al-Dhahabī. *al-ᶜIbar fī khabar man ghabar*. 5 vols. Eds. Fuʾād Sayyid and Ṣalāḥ al-Dīn al-Munajjid. 2nd ed. Kuwait: Matbaᶜat Ḥukūmat al-Kuwait, 1984.

Dhahabī *Mīzān* = Id. *Mīzān al-iᶜtidāl fī naqd al-rijāl*. Ed. ᶜAlī Muḥammad al-Bajāwī. 4 vols. Beirut: Dār al-Fikr, n.d.

Dhahabī *Siyar* = Id. *Siyar aᶜlām al-nubalāʾ*. 25 vols. Eds. Shuᶜayb al-Arnāʾūṭ et al. 10th printing. Beirut: Muʾassasat al-Risālah, 1994.

Dhahabī *Tadhkirah* = Id. *Tadhkirat al-ḥuffāẓ*. 4 vols. Beirut: Dār al-Kutub al-ᶜIlmīyah, n.d.

Dickinson, Eerik Nael. "The Development of Early Muslim Ḥadīth Criticism: The *Taqdima* of Ibn Abī Ḥātim al-Rāzī (d. 327/938)." Ph.D. Dissertation. Yale University, 1992.

al-Dīnawarī, Abū Saᶜd Naṣr b. Yaᶜqūb. *Kitāb al-taᶜbīr fī al-ruʾyā aw al-Qādirī fī al-taᶜbīr*. 2 vols. Ed. Fahmī Saᶜd. Beirut: ᶜĀlam al-Kutub, 1997.

Dodge, Bayard, trans. *The Fihrist of al-Nadim: A Tenth-Century Survey of Muslim Culture*. 2 vols. Records of Civilization: Sources and Studies, no. 83. New York: Columbia University Press, 1970.

Dondaine, Antoine. "Hugues Éthérien et Léon Toscan." *Archives d'histoire doctrinale et littéraire du moyen âge* 19 (1952): 67–134.

Drexl, Franz X. "Achmet und das syrische Traumbuch des Cod. syr. or. 4434 des Brit. Mus." *Byzantinische Zeitschrift* 30 (1929/30): 110–13.

———, ed. *Achmetis Oneirocriticon*. Leipzig: Teubner, 1925.

———. *Achmets Traumbuch: Einleitung und Probe eines kritischen Textes*. Freising: F. P. Datterer, 1909.

Dulaey, Martine. *Le rêve dans la vie et la pensée de saint Augustin*. Paris: Études Augustiniennes, 1973.

Duval, R., ed. *Lexicon Syriacum*. 3 vols. Paris: e Reipublica typographao, 1888–1901.

Eco, Umberto. "Unlimited Semiosis and Drift: Pragmaticism vs. 'Pragmatism.'" In *The Limits of Interpretation*. Bloomington and Indianapolis: Indiana University Press, 1994. 23–43.

———. *Interpretation and Overinterpretation*. Cambridge: Cambridge University Press, 1992.

Elman, Yaakov, trans. *Dream Interpretation from Classical Jewish Sources*. Hoboken: Ktav, 1998.

Esnoud, A.-M., et al. *Les songes et leur interprétation*. Paris: Éditions du Seuil, 1959.

Ettinghausen, R. "Kufesque in Byzantine Greece, the Latin West and the Muslim World." In *A Colloquium in Memory of George Carpenter Miles (1904– 1975)*. New York: American Numismatic Society, 1976. 28–47.

Fahd, Toufic. "Ḥunayn Ibn Isḥāq est-il le traducteur des *Oneirocritica* d'Artémidore d'Éphèse?" *Arabica* 21 (1974): 270–84.

———. "L'oniromancie orientale et ses répercussions sur l'oniromancie de l'occident médiéval." In *Oriente e occidente nel Medioevo: Filosofia e scienze*. Eds. M. C. Hernandez, et al. Accademia Nazionale dei Lincei: Atti dei convegni, vol. 13. Rome: Accademia Nazionale dei Lincei, 1971. 347–71.

———. *La divination arabe: Études religieuses, sociologiques et folkloriques sur le milieu natif de l'Islam*. Leiden: E. J. Brill, 1966.

———. "Les corps des métiers au IVᵉ/Xᵉ siècle à Baġdād d'après le chapitre XII d'al-Qādirī fī-t-taᶜbīr de Dīnawarī." *Journal of the Social and Economic History of the Orient* 8 (1965): 186–212.

———, ed. *Artemidorus: Le livre des songes*. Damascus: Institut français de Damas, 1964.

Fārisī *Siyāq* = ᶜAbd al-Ghāfir b. Ismāᶜīl al-Fārisī. *Kitāb al-siyāq li-ta'rīkh Nīsābūr*. Fascimile edition in Richard N. Frye. *The Histories of Nishapur*. Harvard Oriental Series, vol. 45. Cambridge: Harvard University Press, 1965.

Frank, Andre Gunder. "A Plea for World System History." *Journal of World History* 2 (1991): 1–28.

———. "The Thirteenth-Century World System: A Review Essay." *Journal of World History* 1 (1990): 249–56.

Furlani, G. "Une clef des songes en syriaque." *Revue de l'orient chrétien*, 3rd series, 2 (1920/21): 118–44, 225–48.

Gigli, Daria. "Gli onirocritici del cod. Paris. suppl. gr. 690." *Prometheus* 4 (1978): 65–86.

Gismondi, Henricus, ed. *Maris Amri et Slibae de patriarchis nestorianorum commentaria: Pars prior, Maris textus arabicus*. Rome: Excudebat C. de Luigi, 1899.

Glover, M. G. "Critical Edition of the Middle French Version of Achmet ibn Sirin's Oneiromancy Found in MS. Français 1317 folios 51r-106v, Paris, Bibliothèque Nationale, entitled (cy commence la table des) Exposicions et significacions des songes par Daniel et autres exposez." Ph.D. Dissertation. London, Birkbeck College, 1992.

Gohlman, William E. *The Life of Ibn Sina*. Albany: State University of New York Press, 1974.

Goldziher, I. "The Appearance of the Prophet in Dreams." *Journal of the Royal Asiatic Society* (1912): 503–6.

Gotthardt, Otto. *Über die Traumbücher des Mittelalters*. Königliches Luthergymnasium zu Eisleben, Progr. Nr. 334. Eisleben: Ernst Schneider, 1912.

Grabar, André. *L'art de la fin de l'antiquité et du moyen âge*. 3 vols. Paris: Collège de France, 1968.

Grabar, Oleg. "Islamic Influence on Byzantine Art." *Oxford Dictionary of Byzantium* (1991), 2:1018–19.

———. *The Formation of Islamic Art*. Revised edition. New Haven: Yale University Press, 1987.

Gregory, Timothy E. "Ceramics." *Oxford Dictionary of Byzantium* (1991), 1:399–400.

———. "Sgraffito Ware." *Oxford Dictionary of Byzantium* (1991), 3:1886.

Griffith, Sidney H. "Byzantium and the Christians in the World of Islam: Constantinople and the Church in the Holy Land in the Ninth Century." *Medieval Encounters* 3 (1997): 231–65.

———. "The Monks of Palestine and the Growth of Christian Literature in Arabic." *The Muslim World* 78 (1988): 1–28.

Guidorizzi, Giulio, ed. *Pseudo-Niceforo: Libro dei sogni*. Koinonia, no. 5. Naples: Associazione di studi tardoantichi, 1980.

Gutas, Dimitri. *Greek Thought, Arabic Culture: The Graeco-Arabic Translation Movement in Baghdad and Early ᶜAbbāsid Society (2nd–4th/8th–10th centuries)*. London: Routledge, 1998.

Ḥabbī, Yūsuf. "Les sources du *Livre des Signes* d'al-Ḥasan Ibn Bahlūl." In *Actes du deuxième congrès international d'études arabes chrétiennes*. Ed. Khalil Samir. Orientalia christiana analecta, vol. 226. Rome: Pont. Institutum studiorum orientalium, 1986. 193–203.

———, ed. "al-Āthār al-ᶜalwīyah li-l-Ḥasan b. al-Bahlūl." *Majallat al-majmaᶜ al-ᶜilmī al-ᶜIrāqī: Hay'at al-lughah al-suryānīyah* 8 (1984): 165–95.

———, ed. "Taᶜbīr al-ru'yā li-l-Ḥasan b. al-Bahlūl." *Majallat al-mawrid* 13 (1984): 127–62.

———, ed. "Dalā'il al-aᶜyād wa-l-aṣwām li-l-Ḥasan b. al-Bahlūl." *Majallat al-majmaᶜ al-ᶜilmī al-ᶜIrāqī: Hay'at al-lughah al-suryānīyah* 7 (1983): 206–34.

Ḥājjī, Ṣāliḥ Sulaymān. *Fihris makhṭūṭāt Jāmiᶜat al-Riyāḍ: 3. al-aᶜmāl al-ᶜāmmah / al-falsafah.* Riyadh: Jāmiᶜat al-Riyāḍ, 1399/1979.

Ḥājjī Khalīfah *Kashf* = Ḥājjī Khalīfah Muṣṭafā b. ᶜAbd Allāh commonly known as Kātib Çelebi. *Kashf al-ẓunūn ᶜan asāmī al-kutub wa-l-funūn.* 2 vols. Eds. Şerefettin Yaltkaya and Kilisli Rifat Bilge. Beirut: Dār al-Kutub al-ᶜIlmīyah, 1992.

Halkin, F. *Bibliotheca hagiographica graeca*, 3rd ed. Brussels: Société des Bollandistes, 1957.

Haschmi, Mohammed Jahia. *Die Quellen des Steinbuches des Bērūnī.* Bonn: C. Schulze, 1935.

al-Hashimi, Muhammad. "On Avicenna's Taᶜbīr al-Ru'yā." Ph.D. Dissertation. London School of Oriental and African Studies, 1948.

Haskins, Charles H. "Leo Tuscus." *Byzantinische Zeitschrift* 24 (1923/24): 43–47.

———. "Leo Tuscus." *The English Historical Review* 33 (1918): 492–96.

al-Ḥifnī, ᶜAbd al-Munᶜim, ed. *Arṭimīdūrus al-Ifsī: Kitāb taᶜbīr al-ru'yā, awwal wa-ahamm al-kutub fī tafsīr al-aḥlām.* Cairo: Dār al-Rashād, 1991.

Hirschfeld, Hartwig. "Die arabischen Fragmente der Cairo-Genizah zu Cambridge." In *Verhandlungen des XIII. internationalen Orientalisten-Kongresses, Hamburg September 1902.* Leiden: E. J. Brill, 1904. 306–8.

———. "The Arabic Portion of the Cairo Genizah at Cambridge." *Jewish Quarterly Review* 15 (1902/3): 167–81.

Hodgson, Marshall G. S. "The Interrelations of Societies in History." In *Rethinking World History: Essays on Europe, Islam, and World History.* Ed. Edmund Burke III. Cambridge: Cambridge University Press, 1993. 3-28.

———. *The Venture of Islam: Conscience and History in a World Civilization.* 3 vols. Chicago: University of Chicago Press, 1974.

———. "Hemispheric Interregional History as an Approach to World History." *Cahiers d'histoire mondiale* 1 (1954): 715–23.

Hoffman, G. *Auszüge aus syrischen Akten persischer Märtyrer.* Abhandlungen für die Kunde des Morgenlandes, Bd. 7.3. Leipzig: F. A. Brockhaus, 1880.

Huard, P. "Sciences et techniques de l'Eurasie." *Bulletin de la société des études indo-chinoises.* 2nd series, 15 (1950): 111–48.

Hunger, Herbert. *Die hochsprachliche profane Literatur der Byzantiner.* 2 vols. Byzantinisches Handbuch, Teil 5, Bd. 2. Munich: C. H. Beck, 1978.

Ḥusaynī, Sayyid Aḥmad, et al. *Fihrist-i Kitābkhānah-i ᶜUmūmī-i Ḥaẓrat-i Āyat Allāh al-ᶜuẓmā Najafī Marᶜashī.* 20 vols. Qum: Marᶜashī Library, 1975–91.

Huwwārī *Tafsīr* = Hūd b. Muḥakkam al-Huwwārī. *Tafsīr Kitāb Allāh al-ᶜAzīz.* 4 vols. Ed. Bālḥājj bin Saᶜīd Sharīfī. Beirut: Dār al-Gharb al-Islāmī, 1990.

Ibn Abī Shaybah *Muṣannaf* = Abū Bakr ᶜAbd Allāh b. Muḥammad al-ᶜAbsī al-Kūfī. *al-Muṣannaf fī al-aḥādīth wa-l-āthār.* Ed. Saᶜīd al-Laḥām. 9 vols. Beirut: Dār al-Fikr, 1994.

Ibn Abī ᶜUṣaybiᶜah *ᶜUyūn* = Abū al-ᶜAbbās Aḥmad b. al-Qāsim al-Saᶜdī al-Khazrajī. *ᶜUyūn al-anbāʾ fī ṭabaqāt al-aṭibbāʾ*. Ed. Nizār Riḍā. Beirut: Dār Maktabat al-Ḥayāh, n.d.

Ibn ᶜAsākir *Tabyīn* = Abū al-Qāsim ᶜAlī b. al-Ḥasan b. Hibat Allāh b. ᶜAsākir al-Dimashqī. *Tabyīn kadhib al-muftarī fī-mā nusiba ilā al-imām Abī al-Ḥasan al-Ashᶜarī*. Beirut: Dār al-Kutub al-ᶜArabīyah, 1979.

Ibn al-Athīr *Kāmil* = Abū al-Ḥasan ᶜAlī b. Muḥammad al-Shaybānī. *al-Kāmil fī al-taʾrīkh*. 13 vols. 7th printing. Beirut: Dār Ṣādir, 1995.

Ibn al-Athīr *Lubāb* = Id. *al-Lubāb fī tahdhīb al-ansāb*. 3 vols. in 2. Cairo: Maktabat al-Quds, 1356–57/1937–38.

Ibn Aṭīyah *Muḥarrar* = Abū Muḥammad ᶜAbd al-Ḥaqq b. Ghālib al-Gharnāṭī. *al-Muḥarrar al-wajīz fī tafsīr al-Kitāb al-ᶜAzīz*. 16 vols. in 8. Ed. al-Majlis al-ᶜIlmī bi-Fās. Rabat: al-Mamlakah al-Maghribīyah, Wizārat al-Awqāf wa-l-Shuʾūn al-Islāmīyah, 1975–91.

Ibn Bashkuwāl *Ṣilah* = Abū al-Qāsim Khalaf b. ᶜAbd al-Malik al-maᶜrūf bi-Ibn Bashkuwāl. *Kitāb al-ṣilah fī taʾrīkh aʾimmat al-Andalus wa-ᶜulamāʾihim wa-muḥaddithīhim wa-fuqahāʾihim wa-udabāʾihim*. 2 vols. Ed. ᶜIzzat al-ᶜAṭṭār al-Ḥusaynī. 2nd printing. Cairo: Maktabat al-Khānjī, 1994.

Ibn Faraḍī *Taʾrīkh* = Abū al-Walīd ᶜAbd Allāh b. Muḥammad al-Azdī. *Taʾrīkh al-ᶜulamāʾ wa-l-ruwāt li-l-ᶜilm bi-l-Andalus*. 2 vols. Ed. ᶜIzzat al-ᶜAṭṭār al-Ḥusaynī. 2nd printing. Cairo: Maṭbaᶜat al-Khanjī, 1988.

Ibn Farḥūn *Dībāj* = Burhān al-Dīn Ibrāhīm b. ᶜAlī b. Muḥammad b. Farḥūn al-Yaᶜmarī. *al-Dībāj al-mudhahhab fī maᶜrifat aᶜyān ᶜulamāʾ al-madhhab*. Ed. ᶜAbbās b. ᶜAbd al-Salām b. Shaqrūn. Cairo: n.p., 1351/1932.

Ibn Ḥajar *Lisān* = Abū al-Faḍl Aḥmad b. ᶜAlī b. Ḥajar al-ᶜAsqalānī. *Lisān al-mīzān*. 7 vols. 2nd printing. Beirut: Shirkat ᶜAlāʾ al-Dīn, 1971.

Ibn Ḥajar *Tahdhīb* = Id. *Tahdhīb al-tahdhīb*. 6 vols. Beirut: Dār Iḥyāʾ al-Turāth al-ᶜArabī, 1991.

Ibn Ḥanbal *Musnad* = Abū ᶜAbd Allāh Aḥmad b. Muḥammad b. Ḥanbal al-Shaybānī. *al-Musnad*. 6 vols. Beirut: al-Maktab al-Islāmī / Dār Ṣādir, 1969.

Ibn Ḥanbal *Zuhd* = Id. *al-Zuhd*. 2nd printing. Beirut: Dār al-Kutub al-ᶜIlmīyah, 1994.

Ibn al-ᶜImād *Shadharāt* = Abū al-Falāḥ ᶜAbd al-Ḥayy b. Aḥmad al-maᶜrūf bi-Ibn al-ᶜImād al-Ḥanbalī. *Shadharāt al-dhahab fī akhbār man dhahab*. 8 vols. in 4. Beirut: Dār al-Āfāq al-Jadīdah, n.d.

Ibn al-Jawzī *Muntaẓam* = Abū al-Faraj ᶜAbd al-Raḥmān b. ᶜAlī b. Muḥammad b. al-Jawzī. *al-Muntaẓam fī taʾrīkh al-mulūk wa-l-umam*. 19 vols. in 17. Eds. Muḥammad ᶜAbd al-Qādir ᶜAṭā and Muṣṭafā ᶜAbd al-Qādir ᶜAṭā. Beirut: Dār al-Kutub al-ᶜIlmīyah, 1992.

Ibn al-Jawzī *Zād al-masīr* = Id. *Zād al-masīr fī ᶜilm al-tafsīr*. 8 vols. Ed. Aḥmad Shams al-Dīn. Beirut: Dār al-Kutub al-ᶜIlmīyah, 1994.

Ibn Juljul *Ṭabaqāt* = Abū Dāwūd Sulaymān b. Ḥassān al-Andalusī. *Ṭabaqāt al-aṭibbāʾ wa-l-ḥukamāʾ*. Ed. Fuʾād Sayyid. Cairo: Imprimerie de l'Institut Français d'Archéologie Orientale, 1955.

Ibn Kathīr *Bidāyah* = Abū al-Fidāʾ Ismāᶜīl b. ᶜUmar b. Kathīr al-Dimashqī. *al-Bidāyah wa-l-nihāyah*. 14 vols. in 7. Eds. Aḥmad Abū Mulḥim et al. Cairo: Dār al-Dayyān li-l-Turāth, 1988.

Ibn Kathīr *Tafsīr* = Id. *Tafsīr al-Qur'ān al-ʿAẓīm*. 4 vols. Beirut: Dār al-Jīl, 1991.

Ibn Khaldūn *Ta'rīkh* = ʿAbd al-Raḥmān b. Muḥammad b. Khaldūn al-Ḥaḍramī. *Ta'rīkh Ibn Khaldūn al-musammā Kitāb al-ʿibar wa-dīwān al-mubtadā wa-l-khabar fī ayyām al-ʿarab wa-l-ʿajam wa-l-barbar wa-man ʿāṣamahum min dawā al-sulṭān al-akbar*. 7 vols. Beirut: Dār al-Kutub al-ʿIlmīyah, 1992.

Ibn Khallikān *Wafayāt* = Aḥmad b. Muḥammad b. Abī Bakr b. Khallikān. *Wafayāt al-aʿyān wa-anbā' abnā' al-zamān*. 8 vols. Ed. Iḥsān ʿAbbās. Beirut: Dār Ṣādir, 1978.

Ibn Khayr *Fahrasah* = Abū Bakr Muḥammad b. Khayr al-Ishbılı. *Fahrasat mā rawāh ʿan shuyūkhihi min al-dawāwīn al-muṣannaf fī ḍurūb al-ʿilm wa-anwāʿ al-maʿārif*. 2 vols. Ed. Franciscus Cordera and J. Ribera Tarrago. Saragossa: In typ. fratrum Comas, 1894–95.

Ibn Khayyāṭ *Ta'rīkh* = Abū ʿAmr Khalīfah b. Khayyāṭ al-ʿUṣfurī. *Ta'rīkh*. Ed. Suhayl Zakkār. Beirut: Dār al-Fikr, 1993.

Ibn Khayyāṭ *Ṭabaqāt* = Id. *Kitāb al-ṭabaqāt*. Ed. Suhayl Zakkār. Beirut: Dār al-Fikr, 1993.

Ibn Mājah *Sunan* = Abū ʿAbd Allāh Muḥammad b. Yazīd al-Qazwīnī. *al-Sunan*. 2 vols. Ed. Muḥammad Fu'ād ʿAbd al-Bāqī. Cairo: Dār Ihyā' al-Kutub al-ʿArabīyah, 1952-53.

Ibn Manẓūr *Lisān* = Abū al-Faḍl Muḥammad b. Mukarram b. Manẓūr. *Lisān al-ʿarab*. 20 vols. in 6. Cairo: Būlāq, 1300–1308/1882–90.

Ibn al-Nadīm *Fihrist* = Abū al-Faraj Muḥammad b. Abī Yaʿqūb Isḥāq al-Warrāq al-Baghdādī. *Kitāb al-fihrist li-l-Nadīm*. Ed. Riḍā Tajaddud. n.l.: n.p., n.d.

Ibn al-Qifṭī *Ta'rīkh* = Abū al-Ḥasan ʿAlī b. Yūsuf al-Qifṭī. *Ta'rīkh al-ḥukamā'*. Ed. Julius Lippert. Leipzig: Dieterich'sche Verlagsbuchhandlung, 1903.

Ibn Qutaybah *Maʿārif* = Abū Muḥammad ʿAbd Allāh b. Muslim b. Qutaybah al-Dīnawarī al-Marwazī. *Kitāb al-maʿārif*. Ed. Saroite Okacha. United Arab Republic: Ministère de la culture et de l'orientation nationale, 1960.

Ibn Qutaybah *ʿUyūn* = Id. *ʿUyūn al-akhbār*. 4 vols. in 2. Ed. Yūsuf ʿAlī Ṭawīl. Beirut: Dār al-Kutub al-ʿIlmīyah, n.d.

Ibn Quṭlūbughā *Tāj* = Abū al-Fidā' Zayn al-Dīn Qāsim b. Quṭlūbughā al-Sūdūnī. *Tāj al-tarājim*. Ed. Muḥammad Khayr Yūsuf. Damascus: Dār al-Qalam, 1992.

Ibn Rajab *Dhayl* = Abū al-Faraj ʿAbd al-Raḥmān b. Aḥmad al-Ḥanbalī. *Kitāb al-dhayl ʿalā ṭabaqāt al-ḥanābilah*. 2 vols. Beirut: Dār al-Maʿrifah, n.d.

Ibn Saʿd *Ṭabaqāt* = Abū ʿAbd Allāh Aḥmad b. Saʿd al-Baṣrī. *al-Ṭabaqāt al-kubrā*. 9 vols. Ed. Muḥammad ʿAbd al-Qādir ʿAṭā. Beirut: Dār al-Kutub al-ʿIlmīyah, 1990.

Ibn Ṣāʿid *Ṭabaqāt* = Abū al-Qāsim Ṣāʿid b. Aḥmad al-Andalusī. *Kitāb al-Ṭabaqāt al-umam*. Ed. Louis Cheikho. Beirut: Imprimerie Catholique, 1912.

Ibn Shāhīn *Ishārāt* = Jars al-Dīn Khalīl b. Shāhīn al-Ẓāhirī. *Kitāb al-ishārāt fī ʿilm al-ʿibārāt*. In the margin of vol. 2 of Nābulsī's *Taʿṭīr* (see below).

Ifrah, Georges. *From One to Zero: A Universal History of Numbers*. Trans. Lowell Bair. New York: Viking Penguin, 1985.

Jāḥiẓ *Ḥayawān* = Abū ʿUthmān ʿAmr b. Baḥr al-Jāḥiẓ. *Kitāb al-ḥayawān*. 8 vols. Ed. ʿAbd al-Salām Muḥammad Hārūn. Beirut: Dār al-Fikr, 1988.

Jones, Alexander, ed. *An Eleventh-Century Manual of Arabo-Byzantine Astronomy*. Corpus des astronomes byzantins, no. 3. Amsterdam: Gieben, 1987.

Juynboll, G. H. A. "Early Islamic Society as Reflected in Its Use of Isnads." *Le muséon* 107 (1994): 151–94.

———. *Muslim Tradition: Studies in Chronology, Provenance, and Authorship of Early Ḥadīth*. Cambridge: Cambridge University Press, 1983.

Kaḥḥālah *Mu*ᶜ*jam* = ᶜUmar Riḍā Kaḥḥālah. *Mu*ᶜ*jam al-mu*ᵓ*allifīn*. 4 vols. Beirut: Muᵓassasat al-Risālah, 1414/1993.

Karatay, Fehmı Edhem. *Topkapı Sarayı Müzesi Arapça yazmalar kataloğu*, 4 vols. Istanbul: Millî Eğitim Bakanlığı Yayınları, 1962-66.

Katz, Jonathan G. "An Egyptian Sufi Interprets His Dreams: ᶜAbd al-Wahhāb al-Shaᶜrānī, 1493–1565." *Religion* 27 (1997): 7–24.

———. *Dreams, Sufism and Sainthood: The Visionary Career of Muhammad al-Zawāwī*. Leiden: E. J. Brill, 1996.

———. "Visionary Experience, Autobiography, and Sainthood in North African Islam." *Princeton Papers in Near Eastern Studies* 1 (1992): 85–118.

Kazhdan, Alexander P. "Seth, Symeon." *Oxford Dictionary of Byzantium* (1991), 3:1882–83.

———, and Ann Wharton Epstein. *Change in Byzantine Culture in the Eleventh and Twelfth Centuries*. The Transformation of the Classical Heritage, no. 7. Berkeley: University of California Press, 1985.

Khalidi, Tarif. *Arabic Historical Thought in the Classical Period*. Cambridge Studies in Islamic Civilization. Cambridge: Cambridge University Press, 1994.

Khan, Mohd. Abdul Muid. "A Unique Treatise on the Interpretation of Dreams." In *Avicenna Commemoration Volume*. Calcutta: Iran Society, 1956. 255–307.

———. "Kitabu Taᶜbir-Ir-Ruya of Abu ᶜAli B. Sina." *Indo-Iranica* 9 (1956): 43–57.

Kharkūshī, Abū Saᶜd ᶜAbd al-Malik b. Abī ᶜUthmān Muḥammad al-Wāᶜiẓ. *Sharaf al-nabī* (Persian). Ed. Muḥammad Rawshan. Teheran: Intishārāt-i Bābāk, 1982.

Khaṭīb al-Baghdādī *Ta*ᵓ*rīkh Baghdād* = Abū Bakr Aḥmad b. ᶜAlī al-Khaṭīb al-Baghdādī. *Ta*ᵓ*rīkh Baghdād*. 14 vols. Beirut: Dār al-Kutub al-ᶜIlmīyah, n.d.

Khvābguzārī = *Khvābguzārī*. Ed. Īrāj Afshār. Teheran: n.p., 1983.

Khwansārī *Rawḍāt* = Muḥammad Bāqir b. Zayn al-ᶜĀbidīn. *Rawḍāt al-jannāt*. Teheran, 1888.

Kinānī *Takmīl* = Muḥammad b. Ṣāliḥ ᶜĪsā al-Kinānī al-Qayrawānī. *Takmīl al-ṣulaḥā*ᵓ *wa-l-a*ᶜ*yān li-ma*ᶜ*ālim al-īmān fī awliyā*ᵓ *al-Qayrawān*. Ed. Muḥammad al-ᶜInnābī. Tunis: al-Maktabah al-ᶜAtīqah, 1970.

Kinberg, Leah. *Ibn Abī al-Dunyā: Morality in the Guise of Dreams: A Critical Edition of* Kitāb al-Manām *with Introduction*. Islamic Philosophy, Theology and Science: Texts and Studies, no. 18. Leiden: E. J. Brill, 1994.

———. "Literal Dreams and Prophetic *Ḥadīṯs* in Classical Islam: A Comparison of Two Ways of Legitimization." *Der Islam* 70 (1993): 279–300.

———. "The Standardization of Quran Readings: The Testimonial Value of Dreams." In *Proceedings of the Colloquium on Arabic Grammar, Budapest . . . 1991*. Ed. K. Dévényi. Budapest: Eötvös Loránd University Chair for Arabic Studies, 1991. 223–38.

———. "The Legitimization of the *Madhāhib* through Dreams." *Arabica* 32 (1985): 47–79.

Kister, M. J. "The Interpretation of Dreams: An Unknown Manuscript of Ibn Qutayba's ᶜ*Ibārat al-Ru*ᵓ*yā*." *Israel Oriental Studies* 4 (1974): 67–103.

Kohlberg, Etan. *A Medieval Muslim Scholar at Work: Ibn Ṭāwūs and His Library*. Islamic Philosophy, Theology and Science: Texts and Studies, no. 12. Leiden: E. J. Brill, 1992.

Kondakov, N. P. "Les costumes orientaux à la cour byzantine." *Byzantion* 1 (1924): 7–49.
Kraemer, Joel L. *Humanism in the Renaissance of Islam: The Cultural Revival during the Buyid Age*. 2nd ed. Leiden: E. J. Brill, 1992.
Krenkow, F. "The Appearance of the Prophet in Dreams." *Journal of the Royal Asiatic Society* (1912): 77–79.
Kruger, Steven F. *Dreaming in the Middle Ages*. Cambridge Studies in Medieval Literature, no. 14. Cambridge: Cambridge University Press, 1992.
Kunitzsch, Paul. "Die arabische Herkunft von zwei Sternverzeichnissen in cod. Vat. gr. 1056." *Zeitschrift der deutschen morgenländischen Gesellschaft* 120 (1970): 281–87.
Lamoreaux, John C. "New Light on the Textual Tradition of Bar Bahlūl's *Book of Signs*." *Le muséon* 112 (1999): 227–30.
———. "The Sources of Ibn Bahlul's Chapter on Dream Divination." In *Studia patristica*, vol. 33. Louvain: Éditions Peeters, 1996. 553–57.
———. "Some Notes on the Dream Manual of al-Dārī." *Rivista degli studi orientali* 70 (1996): 47–52.
Le Strange, Guy. *Lands of the Eastern Caliphate*. Cambridge: Cambridge University Press, 1905.
Lecerf, Jean. "The Dream in Popular Culture: Arab and Islamic." In *The Dream and Human Societies*. Eds. G. E. von Grunebaum and Roger Caillois. Berkeley and Los Angeles: University of California Press, 1966. 368–70.
Lecomte, G. "Ibn Ḳutayba, Abū Muḥammad b. ᶜAbd Allāh b. Muslim al-Dīnawarī." *Encyclopedia of Islam*, 2nd ed. (1971), 3:844–47.
———. *Ibn Qutayba (mort en 276/889): L'homme, son ouvres, ses idées*. Damascus: Institut français de Damas, 1965.
Lemay, R. "L'Islam historique et les sciences occultes." *Bulletin d'études orientales* 44 (1992): 19–32.
Mahdavi, Yahya. *Bibliographie d'Ibn Sina*. Teheran: n.p., 1954.
Majlisī *Bihār* = Mollā Muḥammad-Bāqir b. Muḥammad-Taqī Majlisī. *Bihār al-anwār*. 110 vols. Teheran: Dār al-Kutub al-Islāmīyah, 1956–.
Makdisi, G., ed. and trans. "Autograph Diary of an Eleventh-Century Historian of Baghdād." *Bulletin of the School of Oriental and African Studies* 18 (1956): 9–31, 239–60; 19 (1957): 13–48, 281–303, 426–43.
Makhlūf, Muḥammad b. Muḥammad. *Shajarat al-nūr al-zakīyah fī ṭabaqāt al-Mālikīyah*. 2 vols. in 1. Beirut: Dār al-Kutub al-ᶜArabīyah, n.d.
Mango, Cyril. "Greek Culture in Palestine after the Arab Conquest." In *Scritture, libri e testi nelle aree provinciali di Bisanzio*. 2 vols. Ed. Guglielmo Cavallo et al. Spoleto: Centro Italiano di studi sull'alto medioevo, 1991. 1:149–60.
Meier, Fritz. "Eine Auferstehung Mohammeds bei Suyūṭī." *Der Islam* 62 (1985): 20–58.
Miller, Patricia Cox. *Dreams in Late Antiquity: Studies in the Imagination of a Culture*. Princeton: Princeton University Press, 1994.
Mogenet, Joseph. "L'influence de l'astronomie arabe à Byzance du IXe au XIVe siècle." In *Colloques d'histoire des sciences, I (1972) et II (1973): I. Résistance et ouverture aux découvertes et aux théories scientifiques dans le passé*. Université de Louvain, Recueil de travaux d'histoire et de philologie, 6th series, fasc. 9. Louvain: Éditions Nauwelaerts, 1976. 45–55.

———. "Une scholie inédite du Vat. gr. 1594 sur les rapports entre l'astronomie arabe et Byzance." *Osiris* 14 (1962): 198–221.

Motzki, Harald. "*Quo vadis Ḥadīṯ*-Forschung? Eine kritische Untersuchung von G. H. A. Juynboll: 'Nāfiᶜ the *Mawlā* of Ibn ᶜUmar, and His Position in Muslim *Ḥadīṯ* Literature.'" *Der Islam* 73 (1996): 40–80.

Muslim *Ṣaḥīḥ* = Abū al-Ḥusayn Muslim b. al-Ḥajjāj b. Muslim al-Qushayrī. *Ṣaḥīḥ Muslim bi-Sharḥ al-Nawawī*. 18 vols. Beirut: Dār al-Kitāb al-ᶜArabī, 1987.

Nābulsī *ᶜAbīr* = ᶜAbd al-Ghanī b. Ismāᶜīl al-Nābulsī. *Tafsīr al-aḥlām al-musammā al-ᶜAbīr fī al-taᶜbīr*. Ed. Khālid Sayyid ᶜAlī. 2nd printing. Kuwait: Maktabat Dār al-Turāth, 1991.

Nābulsī *Taᶜṭīr* = Id. *Taᶜṭīr al-anām fī taᶜbīr al-manām*. 2 vols. in 1. Beirut: al-Maktabat al-Thaqāfīyah, n.d.

Najāshī *Fihrist* = Abū ᶜAbbās Aḥmad b. ᶜAlī al-Najāshī. *Fihrist asmāᵓ muṣannifī al-shīᶜah*. Qum: Maktabat al-Dāwarī, 1397/1977.

al-Naqshabandī, Usāmah Nāṣir. "Makhṭūṭāt taᶜbīr al-ruᵓyā wa-tafsīr al-aḥlām fī Dār Ṣaddām li-l-Makhṭūṭāt." *al-Mawrid* 20.2 (1992): 138–49.

Nasāᵓī *Sunan* = Abū ᶜAbd al-Raḥmān Aḥmad b. Shuᶜayb al-Nasāᵓī. *Kitāb al-sunan al-kubrā*. 6 vols. Ed. ᶜAbd al-Ghaffār Sulaymān al-Bandārī and Sayyid Kusrawī Ḥasan. Beirut: Dār al-Kutub al-ᶜIlmīyah, 1991.

Neihoff, Maren. "A Dream Which Is Not Interpreted Is Like a Letter Which Is Not Read." *Journal of Semitic Studies* 43 (1992): 58–84.

Neugebauer, O. "Commentary on the Astronomical Treatise Par. gr. 2425." *Mémoires de l'académie royale de Belgique, Cl. des lettres* 59.4 (1969): 5–45.

Oberhelman, Steven M. *The Oneirocriticon of Achmet: A Medieval Greek and Arabic Treatise on the Interpretation of Dreams*. Lubbock: Texas Tech University Press, 1991.

———. "Two Marginal Notes from Achmet in the cod. Laurent. Plut. 87, 8." *Byzantinische Zeitschrift* 74 (1981): 326–27.

———. "Prolegomena to the Byzantine *Oneirokritika*." *Byzantion* 50 (1980): 487–503.

Pacey, Arnold. *Technology in World Civilization: A Thousand Year History*. Oxford: Blackwell, 1990.

Pack, Roger A. "Artemidoriana Graeco-Arabica." *Transactions of the American Philological Association* 106 (1976): 307–12.

———, ed. "A Treatise on Prognostications by Venancius of Moerbeke." *Archives d'histoire doctrinale et littéraire du moyen âge* 43 (1976): 311–22.

———. "On Artemidorus and His Arabic Translator." *Transactions of the American Philological Association* 98 (1967): 313–26.

———, ed. "De pronosticatione sompniorum Libellus Guillelmo de Aragonia adscriptus." *Archives d'histoire doctrinale et littéraire du moyen âge* 33 (1966): 237–93.

———, ed. *Artemidori Daldiani onirocriticon libri V*. Leipzig: Teubner, 1963.

Peirce, Charles Sanders. *Collected Papers*. Eds. Charles Hartshorne and Paul Weiss. 8 vols. Cambridge: Harvard University Press, 1931–60.

Pines, S. "The Arabic Recension of *Parva Naturalia* and the Philosophical Doctrine concerning Veridical Dreams according to *al-Risāla al-Manāmiyya* and Other Sources." *Israel Oriental Studies* 4 (1974): 104–53.

Pingree, David. *From Astral Omens to Astrology from Babylon to Bīkāner*. Serie orientale Roma, vol. 78. Rome: Istituto italiano per l'Africa e l'oriente, 1997.

———, ed. *Albumasaris de revolutionibus nativitatum.* Leipzig: Teubner, 1968.

———, and Alexander P. Kazhdan. "Astrology." *Oxford Dictionary of Byzantium* (1991), 1:215–18.

Price, S. R. F. "The Future of Dreams: From Freud to Artemidorus." *Past and Present* 113 (1986): 3–37.

Qāḍī ᶜIyāḍ *Tartīb* = al-Qāḍī ᶜIyāḍ b. Mūsā b. ᶜIyāḍ al-Sabtī. *Tartīb al-madārik wa-taqrīb al-masālik li-maᶜrifat aᶜlām madhhab Mālik.* 8 vols. Ed. Muḥammad b. Tāwīt al-Tanjī et al. 2nd printing. Rabat: Wizārat al-Awqāf wa-l-Shuʾūn al-Islāmīyah, n.d.

Rasāʾil ikhwān al-ṣafāʾ = *Rasāʾil ikhwān al-ṣafāʾ wa-khallān al-wafāʾ.* 4 vols. Beirut: Dār Ṣādir, n.d.

Riedinger, U. *Die heilige Schrift im Kampf der griechischen Kirche gegen die Astrologie von Origenes bis Johannes von Damaskos.* Innsbruck: Universitätverlag, 1956.

Ritter, Helmut. "Arabça, türkçe, farsça yazma eserlerin ilimlere göre tasnifi." *Islâm tetkikleri enstitüsü dergisi* 2 (1958): 201–8.

Riyāḍīzādeh *Asmāʾ* = ᶜAbd al-Laṭīf b. Muḥammad Riyāḍīzādeh. *Asmāʾ al-kutub al-mutammim li-kashf al-ẓunūn.* Ed. Muḥammad al-Tunjī. Egypt: Maktabat al-Khānjī, n.d.

Rochefort, Gabriel, "Une anthologie grecque du XIᵉ siècle: Le *Parisinus suppl. gr.* 690." *Scriptorium* 4 (1950): 3–17.

Rosenthal, Franz. *The Classical Heritage in Islam.* Trans. Emile and Jenny Marmorstein. 1975; London: Routledge, 1992.

———. "From Arabic Books and Manuscripts XII: The Arabic Translation of Artemidorus." *Journal of the American Oriental Society* 85 (1965): 139–44.

Ruelle, C.-E. "La clef des songes d'Achmet Abou-Mazar: Fragment inédit et bonnes variantes." *Revue des études grecques* 7 (1894): 305–12.

Ṣafadī *Wāfī* = Ṣalāḥ al-Dīn Khalīl b. Aybak al-Ṣafadī. *Kitāb al-wāfī bi-l-wafayāt.* 24 vols. to date. Leipzig: Deutsche morgenländische Gesellschaft, 1931–.

Samᶜānī *Ansāb* = Abū Saᶜd ᶜAbd al-Karīm b. Muḥammad al-Samᶜānī. *al-Ansāb.* 5 vols. Ed. ᶜAbd Allāh ᶜUmar al-Bārūrī. Beirut: Dār al-Fikr, n.d.

Sarīfīnī *Muntakhab* = Ibrāhīm b. Muḥammad al-Sarīfīnī. *Muntakhab min kitāb al-siyāq li-taʾrīkh Nīsābūr.* Fascimile edition in Richard N. Frye. *The Histories of Nishapur.* Harvard Oriental Series, vol. 45. Cambridge: Harvard University Press, 1965.

Sayyid, Fuʾād. *Fihrist al-makhṭūṭāt: Nashrah bi-l-makhṭūṭāt allatī iqtanathā al-dār min sanat 1936–1955.* 3 vols. Cairo: Dār al-Kutub, 1961–63.

Schact, Joseph. *The Origins of Muhammadan Jurisprudence.* Oxford: Clarendon Press, 1950.

Schimmel, Annemarie. *Die Träume des Kalifen: Träume und ihre Deutung in der islamischen Kultur.* Munich: C. H. Beck, 1998.

Schmitt, Elisabeth. *Lexicalische Untersuchungen zur arabischen Übersetzung von Artemidors Traumbuch.* Akademie der Wissenschaften und der Literatur, Veröffentlichungen der orientalische Kommission, Bd. 23. Wiesbaden: Franz Steiner Verlag, 1970.

Schwarz, P. "Traum und Traumdeutung nach ᶜAbdalġanī an-Nābulusī." *Zeitschrift der deutschen morgenländischen Gesellschaft* 67 (1913): 473–93.

Sezgin, Fuat. *Geschichte des arabischen Schriftums.* Bd. 1. Leiden: E. J. Brill, 1967.

———, ed. *The Book of Indications (Kitāb al-Dalāʾil) by al-Ḥasan ibn al-Bahlūl (Tenth Century* A.D.*).* Publications of the Institute for the History of Arabic-Islamic Science, C10. Frankfurt am Main: Institut für Geschichte der Arabisch-Islamischen Wissenschaften, 1985.

Shaffer, Lynda. "Southernization." *Journal of World History* 5 (1994): 1–21.

Sibṭ b. al-Jawzī *Mir'āt* = Abū al-Muẓaffar Yūsuf b. Qizughlī al-Baghdādī. *Mir'āt al-zamān fī ta'rīkh al-aʿyān: al-Ḥiqbah 345-437 hijrī.* Ed. Jinān Jalīl Muḥammad al-Hamawundī. Baghdad: al-Dār al-Waṭanīyah, 1990.

Ṣiddīque, M. Abu Bakr. *A Critical Study of Abu Mansur al-Thaʿalibi's Contribution to Arabic Literature.* Dhaka: Sultana Prokashoni, 1991.

Sjöberg, Lars Olaf, ed. *Stephanites und Ichnelates: Überlieferungsgeschichte und Text.* Acta Universitatis Upsaliensis: Studia Graeca Upsaliensia, no. 2. Stockholm: Almqvist & Wiksells, 1962.

Steinschneider, M. "Ibn Shahin und Ibn Sirin: Zur Literatur der Oneirokritik." *Zeitschrift der deutschen morgenländischen Gesellschaft* 17 (1863): 227–44.

Strohmaier, G. "Die griechischen Götter in einer christlich-arabischen Übersetzung: Zum Traumbuch des Artemidor in der Version des Ḥunain ibn Isḥāq." In *Die Araber in der alten Welt*, Bd. 5.1. Eds. F. Altheim and R. Stiehl. Berlin: de Gruyter, 1968. 127–62.

Subki *Ṭabaqāt* = Abū Naṣr ʿAbd al-Wahhāb b. ʿAlī al-Subkī. *Ṭabaqāt al-shāfiʿīyah al-kubrā.* Eds. Maḥmūd Muḥammad al-Ṭanāḥī and ʿAbd al-Fattāḥ al-Ḥilw. 11 vols. in 7. 2nd printing. Cairo: Hajar li-l-Ṭibāʿah wa-l-Nashr, 1992.

Sulamī *Ṭabaqāt* = Abū ʿAbd al-Raḥmān Muḥammad b. ʿAbd al-Raḥmān al-Sulamī. *Ṭabaqāt al-ṣūfīyah.* Ed. Nūr al-Dīn Sharībah. 2nd printing. Aleppo: Dār al-Kitāb al-Nafīs, 1986.

Ṭabarī *Jāmiʿ al-bayān* = Abū Jaʿfar Muḥammad b. Jarīr al-Ṭabarī. *Jāmiʿ al-bayān fī ta'wīl al-Qur'ān.* 12 vols. Beirut: Dār al-Kutub al-ʿIlmīyah, 1992.

Ṭabarī *Ta'rīkh* = Id. *Ta'rīkh al-umam wa-l-mulūk.* 11 vols. Ed. Muḥammad Abū al-Faḍl Ibrāhīm. n.l.: n.p., n.d.

Ṭabarsī *Dār al-salām* = Ḥusayn b. Muḥammad Taqī al-Nūrī al-Ṭabarsī. *Dār al-salām fīmā yataʿallaq bi-l-ru'yā wa-l-manām.* 4 vols. Beirut: Mu'assat al-Wafā', 1983.

Ṭāshkubrīzādeh *Miftāḥ* = Aḥmad b. Muṣṭafā al-shahīr bi-Ṭāshkubrīzādeh. *Miftāḥ al-saʿādah wa-miṣbāḥ al-siyādah fī mawḍūʿāt al-ʿulūm.* 3 vols. Ed. Kāmil Kāmil Bakrī and ʿAbd al-Wahhāb Abū al-Nūr. Cairo: Dār al-Kutub al-Ḥadīthīyah, 1968.

Thaʿālibī *Yatīmah* = Abū Manṣūr ʿAbd al-Malik b. Muḥammad al-Thaʿālibī. *Yatīmat al-dahr fī maḥāsin ahl al-ʿaṣr.* 4 vols. in 2. Ed. Muḥammad Muḥyī al-Dīn ʿAbd al-Ḥamīd. 2nd printing. Cairo: al-Maktabah al-Tijārīyah al-Kubra, 1956.

Thorndike, Lynn. *A History of Magic and Experimental Science.* 8 vols. New York: Macmillan, 1923–58.

Tiflīsī *Kāmil* = Abū al-Faḍl Ḥubaysh b. Ibrāhīm al-Tiflīsī. *Kāmil al-taʿbīr* (Persian). Ed. ʿAbd Allāh Mūsavī. Teheran: Intishārāt Fu'ād, 1367/1988.

Tihon, Anne. "L'astronomie byzantine (du Ve au XVe siècle)." *Byzantion* 51 (1981): 603–24.

Tirmidhī *Jāmiʿ* = Abū ʿĪsā Muḥammad b. ʿĪsā al-Tirmidhī. *al-Jāmiʿ al-Ṣaḥīḥ wa-huwa Sunan al-Tirmidhī.* 4 vols. Ed. Ibrāhīm ʿAṭwah ʿAwaḍ. Cairo: Maṭbaʿat Muṣṭafā al-Bābī al-Ḥalabī wa-awlādihi, 1937–62.

Trachtenberg, Joshua. *Jewish Magic and Superstition: A Study in Folk Religion.* New York: Behrman's Jewish Book House, 1939.

Ṭūsī *Fihrist* = Abū Jaʿfar Muḥammad b. al-Ḥasan b. ʿAlī al-Ṭūsī. *al-Fihrist.* Ed. Maḥmūd Rāmyār. Mashhad: Dānishgāh-i Mashhad, 1972.

Ullmann, M. "War Hunain der Übersetzer von Artemidors Traumbuch?" *Die Welt des Islams*, n.s. 13 (1971): 204–11.

ᶜUmar al-Khayyām *Taᶜbīr* = Abū al-Fatḥ ᶜUmar b. Ibrāhīm al-Khayyām. *Taᶜbīr al-manām*. Ed. ᶜAbd al-Munᶜim al-Ḥifnī. Cairo: Dār al-Rashād, 1991.

Vida, Giorgio Levi della. *Elenco dei manoscritti arabi islamici della Biblioteca Vaticana: Vaticani, Barberiniani, Borgiani, Rossiani*. Studi e Testi, no. 67. Vatican City: Biblioteca Apostolica Vaticana, 1935.

Vykoukal, F. V. *O snech a vykladech snu: Kulturni obrazek*. Prague: F. Simacek, 1898.

Watson, Andrew M. *Agricultural Innovation in the Early Islamic World: The Diffusion of Crops and Farming Techniques, 700–1100*. Cambridge Studies in Islamic Civilization. Cambridge: Cambridge University Press, 1983.

White, Lynn. *Medieval Technology and Social Change*. Oxford: Oxford University Press, 1962.

———. "Tibet, India, and Malaya as Sources of Western Medieval Technology." *The American Historical Review* 65 (1960): 515–26.

———. "Technology and Invention in the Middle Ages." *Speculum* 15 (1940): 141–59.

White, Robert J., trans. *The Interpretation of Dreams: Oneirocritica by Artemidorus*. 2nd ed. Torrance, Calif.: Original Books, 1990.

Yāqūt *Buldān*. Yāqūt b. ᶜAbd Allāh al-Ḥamawī. *Muᶜjam al-buldān*. 5 vols. Beirut: Dār Iḥyāʾ al-Turāth al-ᶜArabī, 1979.

Yāqūt *Udabāʾ* = Id. *Muᶜjam al-udabāʾ: Irshād al-arīb ilā maᶜrifat al-adīb*. 7 vols. Ed. Iḥsān ᶜAbbās. First printing. Beirut: Dār al-Gharb al-Islāmī, 1993.

al-Zarqā, Muṣṭafā Aḥmad. "Man raʾānī fa-qad raʾā al-ḥaqq fa-inna al-shayṭān lā yatamaththalu bī." *al-Durūs al-Ḥasanīyah* (1986): 121–30.

Zurqānī *Sharḥ* = Abū ᶜAbd Allāh Muḥammad b. ᶜAbd al-Bāqī al-Zurqānī. *Sharḥ ᶜalā al-mawāhib al-ladūnīyah li-l-Qastalānī*. Cairo: al-Maṭbaᶜah al-Azharīyah al-Miṣrīyah, 1325–29/1907–11.

Index